THE PHILOSOPHY OF SEX

Also by Alan Soble

THE PHILOSOPHY OF SEX

Contemporary Readings

THIRD EDITION

Edited by
ALAN SOBLE

ROWMAN & LITTLEFIELD PUBLISHERS, INC.
Lanham • Boulder • New York • Oxford

ROWMAN & LITTLEFIELD PUBLISHERS, INC.

Published in the United States of America
by Rowman & Littlefield Publishers, Inc.
4720 Boston Way, Lanham, Maryland 20706

12 Hid's Copse Road
Cummor Hill, Oxford OX2 9JJ, England

British Library Cataloguing in Publication Information Available

Library of Congress Cataloging-in-Publication Data

The philosophy of sex : contemporary readings / edited by Alan Soble. — 3rd ed.
    p. cm.
   Includes bibliographical references and index.
   ISBN 0-8476-8480-6 (cloth : alk. paper). — ISBN 0-8476-8481-4
(paper : alk. paper)
    1. Sex.   2. Sexual ethics.   I. Soble, Alan.
HQ12.P47   1997
306.7—dc21   97-12412
                                                   CIP

ISBN 0–8476–8480–6 (cloth : alk. paper)
ISBN 0–8476–8481–4 (pbk. : alk. paper)

Printed in the United States of America

∞ ™ The paper used in this publication meets the minimum requirements of
American National Standard for Information Sciences—Permanence of Paper for
Printed Library Materials, ANSI Z39.48–1984.

For Sára, again
NSzK,
Q

CONTENTS

PART 2: HOMOSEXUALITY

PART 3: ABORTION

PART 4: SADOMASOCHISM

PART 5: RAPE AND HARASSMENT

PREFACE

I have been teaching and writing about the philosophy of sex and love since 1976. That's more than twenty years: a good portion of my adult life and all my professional life. You might think that I would be sick of the subject, if not of sex itself, by now—say, by a kind of excitatory habituation. To some extent that has happened.[1] But I still experience a scholarly-sensuous frisson whenever I open the envelope in which a colleague has sent me a new piece on sexual morality for comments; whenever I page through a professional journal and find an unexpected exploration of sex; and whenever, browsing through a university press catalogue, I discover an as yet unknown scholar bringing innovative ideas and a fresh perspective to the field. This updated, third edition of *The Philosophy of Sex* contains some of the most exciting recent work in the philosophy of sex; these essays represent the kind of investigations that have sustained my interest in the field in the face of a suspicion that philosophers have been merely repeating the same old tired formulas over and over again.

Just as the second edition of *The Philosophy of Sex* was an 80 percent revision of the first edition, the third edition is an 80 percent revision of the second. Once again the core analytic essays that are central to contemporary philosophy of sex are included: Thomas Nagel's "Sexual Perversion," Robert Solomon's "Sexual Paradigms," Janice Moulton's "Sexual Behavior: Another Position," and Alan Goldman's "Plain Sex." (Robert Gray's "Sex and Sexual Perversion," which was included in the first edition but not the second, returns to this edition.) But, with the exception of H. E. Baber's provocative thoughts on rape, all the "special topics" essays in parts 2 through 6 of this volume have been newly selected. Some of the essays I have chosen to reprint are very good, even excellent; others, I think, are dead wrong. This would be an extraordinarily boring book, however, were I to assemble together only what I like, find compelling, or sympathize with ideologically. Further, such a monistic collection would not serve well the interests of students attempting to learn about the philosophy of sex or of scholars who utilize this text for research, and it would not do justice to the richness of sexual philosophy. Hence there are essays in this edition that are both critical and supportive of, for example, homosexuality, prostitution, and pornography, unlike a large number of recent collections in gender studies that are platforms for partisan views.

The section on conceptual analysis (part 1) begins with a sweet and sour essay by Greta Christina, who exhibits how the paradigmatically philosophical task of providing criteria for the identification and counting of sexual acts also arises in (some of) our sexual lives.[2] "What is sex?" is a question that is at least implicitly, when not directly, addressed in the remaining essays of part 1, although Thomas Nagel focuses on the psychological nature of human sexual interaction; Robert Solomon on the expressive functions of sexual activity; Janice Moulton on what is misleading, from a woman's perspective, with Nagel's and Solomon's accounts of sex; Alan Goldman on the lowest common denominator of all sexual activity; Robert Gray on the conceptual relationship between sexual activity and sexual pleasure; and I on the much maligned yet nearly universally practiced (among males, at least) act of masturbation—which, despite the arguments of some philosophers, is very much a sexual act.[3]

In part 2, John Finnis and Michael Levin express severe doubts about the morality, wisdom, and naturalness of homosexuality,[4] while Martha Nussbaum and John Corvino defend it. Edward Vacek's prescient paper presents an early statement of a view that has been growing in popularity and visibility, namely, that the tenets of Christianity do not entail that loving and consummated homosexual relationships are morally wrong.[5] Of course, the essays of part 1 of this volume have implications for this disagreement, as they do for all the other particular topics discussed below.

Both abortion and sexuality have been written about abundantly, but largely independently of each other. For this reason, I have reserved part 3 for two essays that examine an issue that has been, among philosophers, relatively neglected. Sidney Callahan and Ellen Willis explore the logical and social connections between the abortion controversy and contemporary sexual norms.[6] Part 4 is also concerned with a topic that has been insufficiently investigated by philosophers. Natalie Shainess opens the section by condemning fantasies of sexually motivated spankings[7]; Patrick Hopkins and Melinda Vadas argue over the compatibility of feminist theory and sadomasochistic sexuality[8]; and Jean Grimshaw insightfully studies the nature and meaning of fantasy in human sexuality, uncovering what is sensible and what is shortsighted in feminist critiques of contemporary sexuality.

In part 5, Robin Warshaw carefully presents case studies of sexually harassing behavior and shows us that analytic tangles, and hence legal and social uncertainties, plague this phenomenon. Mane Hajdin tries to clear up this perplexing territory by suggesting how a reliable demarcation criterion—one that distinguishes acceptable from unacceptable sexual advances—might be devised. H. E. Baber compares the harms caused by work in our society and the harms caused by sexual assault and reaches a surprising conclusion. And Robin West explores another fuzzy line, that between nonconsensual sex and sex that is consensual yet engaged in under pressure and is for that reason harmful.

Prostitution and pornography—which both involve, in their own way, the performing of sexual acts for compensation—are the last of the special topics, analyzed by two sets of essays in part 6. Sallie Tisdale's feisty look at pornography from a woman's perspective is enlightening[9]; Martha Nussbaum tackles the enormous task of distinguishing, both analytically and morally, the various kinds of sexual objectification that are represented in pornography (and that occur in our lives). Finally, Laurie Shrage presents a unique feminist view of prostitution, while Igor Primoratz, in part replying to Shrage, finds in prostitution—from a libertarian perspective—much less about which to complain.[10]

The University of New Orleans and its College of Liberal Arts, through the release time of a research professor appointment, provided me with the opportunity to conceive and carry out this project. Assistance in and advice about the preparation of this third edition of *The Philosophy of Sex* was provided generously by Jennifer Ruark, Robin Adler, Sue Campbell, Ed Stein, Jacob Hale, Natalie Brender, Shayma Saad, Lisa Mereaux, Dianne Charles, Jenny Brett, and the anonymous reviewers of the original manuscript. Sára was there not only during the process of completing this book, but also during all the other tasks I assumed over the last seven years. Rachel, the love of my life and now almost four years old, has made me laugh and feel a kind of joy I never anticipated experiencing.

Notes

1. This is partly why I took a break in 1994 and immersed myself in the writings of Francis Bacon. See my "In Defense of Bacon," *Philosophy of the Social Sciences* 25:2 (1995): 192–215; revision in Noretta Koertge, ed., *A House Built on Sand: Flaws in the Cultural Studies Account of Science* (Oxford University Press, forthcoming). But even this essay deals tangentially with sexual matters.

2. Christina's essay was reprinted by the magazine *Ms.* in its "Feminism and Sex" issue of November/December 1995 (pp. 60–62). But, strangely, the essay's last two paragraphs are missing from that reprint, and my inspection of that issue of *Ms.* could find no editorial warning that the essay was abridged. Those paragraphs of Christina's essay are perhaps the most provocative—and least feminist—parts of the essay: she admits to finding some sadomasochism "tremendously erotic," and she relates that when working as a nude dancer inside a peep-

show booth she had a "fabulous time" sexually with one of her quarter-laden customers.

3. "Masturbation," yet again heavily revised, is another of the essays that appears in all three editions of *The Philosophy of Sex*. One of these days I'll get it right.

4. A detailed critique of Levin's essay can be found in Timothy Murphy, "Homosexuality and Nature: Happiness and the Law at Stake," *Journal of Applied Philosophy* 4:2 (1987): 195–204.

5. See, for example, Patricia Jung and Ralph Smith, *Heterosexism: An Ethical Challenge* (Albany: State University of New York Press, 1993), which I briefly reviewed in *Ethics* 105:4 (1995): 975–76.

6. See also Roger Paden, "Abortion and Sexual Morality," and my "More on Abortion and Sexual Morality," both in my *Sex, Love, and Friendship* (Amsterdam: Editions Rodopi, 1997), 229–36 and 239–44, respectively. Although Judith Jarvis Thomson's well-known and widely reprinted essay "A Defense of Abortion" (*Philosophy and Public Affairs* 1:1 [1971]: 47–66) is commonly read as a statement about the implications of a woman's right to control what happens to and in her own body, I think it is usefully probed for its implications about the relationship between the morality of abortion and the morality of sex. For a recent discussion, see David Boonin-Vail, "A Defense of 'A Defense of Abortion': On the Responsibility Objection to Thomson's Argument," *Ethics* 107:2 (1997): 286–313.

7. Shainess's essay was printed in the now extinct journal *Medical Aspects of Human Sexuality*. Her answer to the question posed by the journal followed an answer, quite different, provided by Jay Mann, to the effect that all the man needed was reassurance that masturbation and sexual fantasies, even of flagellation, "are common components of normal human experience" ("Sadistic Fantasies," *Medical Aspects of Human Sexuality* 8:2 [1974]: 142). Similarly, Irma Kurtz assures a woman who has fantasies of being spanked that these fantasies are "common." Kurtz advises, "Climb over his knee . . . and savor your punishment" ("Agony Column," *Cosmopolitan,* January 1997, p. 34). For an at least tentative, if not an outright, approval of Kurtz's position, see Daphne Merkin, "Unlikely Obsession: Confronting a Taboo," *The New Yorker* (26 February and 4 March 1996), 98–115.

8. Hopkins continues the debate with Vadas in "Simulation and the Reproduction of Injustice: A Reply," *Hypatia* 10:2 (1995): 162–70.

9. The essay by Tisdale contained in this volume was published in *Harper's* in February 1992. Afterwards, she gave her thoughts on sex fuller treatment in *Talk Dirty to Me: An Intimate Philosophy of Sex* (New York: Doubleday, 1994). See the review by James Wolcott, "Position Papers," *The New Yorker* (21 November 1994), 115–19, and the color cartoon of her in a pornography store, *ibid.*, 115. Readers' letters of reply to her *Harper's* essay, as well as her response to them, appeared in the May 1992 issue of that magazine, pp. 4–7, 72–73, and 76–78.

10. Shrage continues the debate with Primoratz in her *Moral Dilemmas of Feminism: Prostitution, Adultery, and Abortion* (New York: Routledge, 1994); see chap. 5 and p. 207, n. 22. Some thoughts about Shrage and Primoratz can be found in my *Sexual Investigations* (New York: New York University Press, 1996), 33–34 and 125–26.

PART 1
CONCEPTUAL ANALYSIS

Chapter 1

ARE WE HAVING SEX NOW OR WHAT?

Greta Christina

When I first started having sex with other people, I used to like to count them. I wanted to keep track of how many there had been. It was a source of some kind of pride, or identity anyway, to know how many people I'd had sex with in my lifetime. So, in my mind, Len was number one, Chris was number two, that slimy awful little heavy metal barbiturate addict whose name I can't remember was number three, Alan was number four, and so on. It got to the point where, when I'd start having sex with a new person for the first time, when he first entered my body (I was only having sex with men at the time), what would flash through my head wouldn't be "Oh, baby, baby you feel so good inside me," or "What the hell am I doing with this creep," or "This is boring, I wonder what's on TV." What flashed through my head was "Seven!"

Doing this had some interesting results. I'd look for patterns in the numbers. I had a theory for a while that every fourth lover turned out to be really great in bed, and would ponder what the cosmic significance of the phenomenon might be. Sometimes I'd try to determine what kind of person I was by how many people I'd had sex with. At eighteen, I'd had sex with ten different people. Did that make me normal, repressed, a total slut, a free-spirited bohemian, or what? Not that I compared my numbers with anyone else's—I didn't. It was my own exclusive structure, a game I played in the privacy of my own head.

Then the numbers started getting a little larger, as numbers tend to do, and keeping track became more difficult. I'd remember that the last one was *seventeen* and so this one must be *eighteen,* and then I'd start having doubts about whether I'd been keeping score accurately or not. I'd lie awake at night thinking to myself, well, there was Brad, and there was that guy on my birthday, and there was David and . . . no, wait, I forgot that guy I got drunk with at the social my first week at college . . . so that's seven, eight, nine . . . and by two in the morning I'd finally have it figured out. But there was always a nagging suspicion that maybe I'd missed someone, some dreadful tacky little scumball that I was trying to forget about having invited inside my body. And as much as I maybe wanted to forget about the sleazy little scumball, I wanted more to get that number right.

It kept getting harder, though. I began to question what counted as sex and what didn't. There was that time with Gene, for instance. I was pissed off at my boyfriend, David, for cheating on me. It was a major crisis, and Gene and I were friends and he'd been trying to get at me for weeks and I hadn't exactly been discouraging him. I went to see him that night to gripe about David. He was very sympathetic of course, and he gave me a backrub, and we talked and touched and confided and hugged, and then we started kissing, and then we snuggled up a little closer, and then we started fondling each other, you know, and then all heck broke loose, and we rolled around on the bed groping and rubbing and grabbing and smooching and pushing and pressing and squeezing. He never did actually get it in. He wanted to, and I wanted to too, but I had this thing about being faithful to my boyfriend, so I kept saying, "No, you can't do that, Yes, that feels so good, No, wait that's too much, Yes, yes, don't stop, No, stop that's enough." We never even got our clothes off. Jesus Christ, though, it was some night. One of the best, really. But for a long time I didn't count it as one of the times I'd had sex. He never got inside, so it didn't count.

Later, months and years later, when I lay awake putting my list together, I'd start to wonder: Why doesn't Gene count? Does he not count because he never got inside? Or does he not count because I had to preserve my moral edge over David, my status as the patient, ever-faithful, cheated-on, martyred girlfriend, and if what I did with Gene counts then I don't get to feel wounded and superior?

Years later, I did end up fucking Gene and I felt a profound relief because, at last, he definitely had a number, and I knew for sure that he did in fact count.

Then I started having sex with women, and, boy, howdy, did *that* ever shoot holes in the system. I'd always made my list of sex partners by defining sex as penile-vaginal intercourse—you know, screwing. It's a pretty simple distinction, a straightforward binary system. Did it go in or didn't it? Yes or no? One or zero? On or off? Granted, it's a pretty arbitrary definition, but it's the customary one, with an ancient and respected tradition behind it, and when I was just screwing men, there was no compelling reason to question it.

But with women, well, first of all there's no penis, so right from the start the tracking system is defective. And then, there are so many ways women can have sex with each other, touching and licking and grinding and fingering and fisting—with dildoes or vibrators or vegetables or whatever happens to be lying around the house, or with nothing at all except human bodies. Of course, that's true for sex between women and men as well. But between women, no one method has a centuries-old tradition of being the one that counts. Even when we do fuck each other there's no dick, so you don't get that feeling of This Is What's Important, We Are Now Having Sex, objectively speaking, and all that other stuff is just foreplay or afterplay. So when I started having sex with women the binary system had to go, in favor of a more inclusive definition.

Which meant, of course, that my list of how many people I'd had sex with was completely trashed. In order to maintain it I would have had to go back and reconstruct the whole thing and include all those people I'd necked with and gone down on and dry-humped and played touchy-feely games with. Even the question of who filled the all-important Number One slot, something I'd never had any doubts about before, would have to be re-evaluated.

By this time I'd kind of lost interest in the list anyway. Reconstructing it would be more trouble than it was worth. But the crucial question remained: What counts as having sex with someone?

It was important for me to know. You have to know what qualifies as sex because when you have sex with someone your relationship changes. Right? *Right?* It's not that sex itself has to change things all that much. But knowing you've had sex, being conscious of a sexual connection, standing around making polite conversation with someone while thinking to yourself, "I've had sex with this person," that's what changes things. Or so I believed. And if having sex with a friend can confuse or change the friendship, think how bizarre things can get when you're not sure whether you've had sex with them or not.

The problem was, as I kept doing more kinds of sexual things, the line between *sex* and *not-sex* kept getting more hazy and indistinct. As I brought more into my sexual experience, things were showing up on the dividing line demanding my attention. It wasn't just that the territory I labeled *sex* was expanding. The line itself had swollen, dilated, been transformed into a vast gray region. It had become less like a border and more like a demilitarized zone.

Which is a strange place to live. Not a bad place, just strange. It's like juggling, or watchmaking, or playing the piano—anything that demands complete concentrated awareness and attention. It feels like cognitive dissonance, only pleasant. It feels like waking up from a compelling and realistic bad dream. It feels like the way you feel when you realize that everything you know is wrong, and a bloody good thing too, because it was painful and stupid and it really screwed you up.

But, for me, living in a question naturally leads to searching for an answer. I can't simply shrug, throw up my hands, and say, "Damned if I know." I have to explore the unknown frontiers, even if I don't bring back any secret treasure. So even if it's incomplete or provisional, I do want to find some sort of definition of what is and isn't sex.

I know when I'm *feeling* sexual. I'm feeling sexual if my pussy's wet, my nipples are hard, my palms are clammy, my brain is fogged, my skin is tingly and super-sensitive, my butt muscles clench, my heartbeat speeds up, I have an orgasm (that's the real giveaway), and so on. But feeling sexual with someone isn't the same as having sex with them. Good Lord, if I called it sex every time I was attracted to someone who returned the favor I'd be even more bewildered than I am now. Even *being* sexual with someone isn't the same as *having* sex with them. I've danced and flirted with too many people, given and received too many sexy, would-be-seductive backrubs, to believe otherwise.

I have friends who say, if you thought of it as sex when you were doing it, then it was. That's an interesting idea. It's certainly helped me construct a coherent sexual history without being a revisionist swine: redefining my past according to current definitions. But it really just begs the question. It's fine to say that sex is whatever I think it is; but then what do I think it *is?* What if, when I was doing it, I was *wondering* whether it counted?

Perhaps having sex with someone is the conscious, consenting, mutually acknowledged pursuit of shared sexual pleasure. Not a bad definition. If you are turning each other on and you say so and you keep doing it, then it's sex. It's broad enough to encompass a lot of sexual behavior beyond genital contact/orgasm; it's distinct enough *not* to include every instance of sexual awareness or arousal; and it contains the elements I feel are vital—acknowledgment, consent, reciprocity, and the pursuit of pleasure. But what about the situation where one person consents to sex without really enjoying it? Lots of people (myself included) have had sexual interactions that we didn't find satisfying or didn't really want and, unless they were actually forced on us against our will, I think most of us would still classify them as sex.

Maybe if *both* of you (or all of you) think of it as sex, then it's sex whether you're having fun or not. That clears up the problem of sex that's consented to but not wished-for or enjoyed. Unfortunately, it begs the question again, only worse: now you have to mesh different people's vague and inarticulate notions of what is and isn't sex and find the place where they overlap. Too messy.

How about sex as the conscious, consenting, mutually acknowledged pursuit of sexual pleasure of *at least one* of the people involved. That's better. It has all the key components, and it includes the situation where one person is doing it for a reason other than sexual pleasure—status, reassurance, money, the satisfaction and pleasure of someone they love, etc. But what if *neither* of you is enjoying it, if you're both doing it because you think the other one wants to? Ugh.

I'm having trouble here. Even the conventional standby—sex equals intercourse—has a serious flaw: it includes rape, which is something I emphatically refuse to accept. As far as I'm concerned, if there's no consent, it ain't sex. But I feel that's about the only place in this whole quagmire where I have a grip. The longer I think about the subject, the more questions I come up with. At what point in an encounter does it *become* sexual? If an interaction that begins nonsexually turns into sex, was it sex all along? What about sex with someone who's asleep? Can you have a situation where one person is having sex and the other isn't? It seems that no matter what definition I come up with, I can think of some real-life experience that calls it into question.

For instance, a couple of years ago I attended (well, hosted) an all-girl sex party. Out of the twelve other women there, there were only a few with whom I got seriously physically nasty. The rest I kissed or hugged or talked dirty with or just smiled at, or watched while they did seriously physically nasty things with each other. If we'd been alone, I'd probably say that what I'd done with most of the women there didn't count as having sex. But the experience, which was hot and sweet and silly and very, very special, had been created by all of us, and although I only really got down with a few, I felt that I'd been sexual with all of the women there. Now, when I meet one of the women from that party, I always ask myself: Have we had sex?

For instance, when I was first experimenting with sadomasochism, I got together with a really hot woman. We were negotiating about what we were going to do, what would and wouldn't be ok, and she said she wasn't sure she wanted to have sex. Now we'd been explicitly planning all kinds of fun and games—spanking, bondage, obedience—which I strongly identified as sexual activity. In her mind, though, *sex* meant direct genital contact, and she didn't necessarily want to do that with me. Playing with her turned out to be a tremendously erotic experience, arousing and stimulating and almost unbearably satisfying. But we spent the whole evening without even touching each other's genitals. And the fact that our definitions were so different made me wonder: Was it sex?

For instance, I worked for a few months as a nude dancer at a peep show. In case you've never been to a peep show, it works like this: the customer goes into a tiny, dingy black box, kind of like a phone booth, puts in quarters, and a metal plate goes up; the customer looks through a window at a little room/stage where naked women are dancing. One time, a guy came into one of the booths and started watching me and masturbating. I came over and squatted in front of him and started masturbating too, and we grinned at each other and watched each other and masturbated, and we both had a fabulous time. (I couldn't believe I was being paid to masturbate—tough job, but somebody has to do it . . . .) After he left I thought to myself: Did we just have sex? I mean, if it had been someone I knew, and if there had been no glass and no quarters, there'd be no question in my mind. Sitting two feet apart from someone, watching each other masturbate? Yup, I'd call that sex all right. But this was different, because it was a stranger, and because of the glass and the quarters. Was it sex?

I still don't have an answer.

Chapter 2

SEXUAL PERVERSION

Thomas Nagel

There is something to be learned about sex from the fact that we possess a concept of sexual perversion. I wish to examine the idea, defending it against the charge of unintelligibility and trying to say exactly what about human sexuality qualifies it to admit of perversions. Let me begin with some general conditions that the concept must meet if it is to be viable at all. These can be accepted without assuming any particular analysis.

First, if there are any sexual perversions, they will have to be sexual desires or practices that are in some sense unnatural, though the explanation of this natural/unnatural distinction is of course the main problem. Second, certain practices will be perversions if anything is, such as shoe fetishism, bestiality, and sadism; other practices, such as unadorned sexual intercourse, will not be; about still others there is controversy. Third, if there are perversions, they will be unnatural sexual *inclinations* rather than just unnatural practices adopted not from inclination but for other reasons. Thus contraception, even if it is thought to be a deliberate perversion of the sexual and reproductive functions, cannot be significantly described as a *sexual* perversion. A sexual perversion must reveal itself in conduct that expresses an unnatural *sexual* preference. And although there might be a form of fetishism focused on the employment of contraceptive devices, that is not the usual explanation for their use.

© Cambridge University Press, 1979. Reprinted, with the permission of Thomas Nagel and Cambridge University Press, from Thomas Nagel, *Mortal Questions,* pp. 39–52. This is a revised version of the essay that appeared in *Journal of Philosophy* 66:1 (1969), pp. 5–17.

The connection between sex and reproduction has no bearing on sexual perversion. The latter is a concept of psychological, not physiological, interest, and it is a concept that we do not apply to the lower animals, let alone to plants, all of which have reproductive functions that can go astray in various ways. (Think of seedless oranges.) Insofar as we are prepared to regard higher animals as perverted, it is because of their psychological, not their anatomical, similarity to humans. Furthermore, we do not regard as a perversion every deviation from the reproductive function of sex in humans: sterility, miscarriage, contraception, abortion.

Nor can the concept of sexual perversion be defined in terms of social disapprobation or custom. Consider all the societies that have frowned upon adultery and fornication. These have not been regarded as unnatural practices, but have been thought objectionable in other ways. What is regarded as unnatural admittedly varies from culture to culture, but the classification is not a pure expression of disapproval or distaste. In fact it is often regarded as a *ground* for disapproval, and that suggests that the classification has independent content.

I shall offer a psychological account of sexual perversion that depends on a theory of sexual desire and human sexual interactions. To approach this solution I shall first consider a contrary position that would justify skepticism about the existence of any sexual perversions at all, and perhaps even about the significance of the term. The skeptical argument runs as follows:

"Sexual desire is simply one of the appetites, like hunger and thirst. As such it may have various objects, some more common than others perhaps, but none in any sense 'natural'. An appetite is identified as sexual by means of the organs and erogenous zones in which its satisfaction can be to some extent localized, and the special sensory pleasures which form the core of that satisfaction. This enables us to recognize widely divergent goals, activities, and desires as sexual, since it is conceivable in principle that anything should produce sexual pleasure and that a nondeliberate, sexually charged desire for it should arise (as a result of conditioning, if nothing else). We may fail to empathize with some of these desires, and some of them, like sadism, may be objectionable on extraneous grounds, but once we have observed that they meet the criteria for being sexual, there is nothing more to be said on *that* score. Either they are sexual or they are not: sexuality does not admit of imperfection, or perversion, or any other such qualification—it is not that sort of affection."

This is probably the received radical position. It suggests that the cost of defending a psychological account may be to deny that sexual desire is an appetite. But insofar as that line of defense is plausible, it should make us suspicious of the simple picture of appetites on which the skepticism depends. Perhaps the standard appetites, like hunger, cannot be classed as pure appetites in that sense either, at least in their human versions.

Can we imagine anything that would qualify as a gastronomical perversion? Hunger and eating, like sex, serve a biological function and also play a significant role in our inner lives. Note that there is little temptation to describe as perverted an appetite for substances that are not nourishing: we should probably not consider someone's appetite *perverted* if he liked to eat paper, sand, wood, or cotton. Those are merely rather odd and very unhealthy tastes: they lack the psychological complexity that we expect of perversions. (Coprophilia, being already a sexual perversion, may be disregarded.) If on the other hand someone liked to eat cookbooks, or magazines with pictures of food in them, and preferred these to ordinary food—or if when hungry he sought satisfaction by fondling a napkin or ashtray from his favorite restaurant—then the concept of perversion might seem appropriate (it would be natural to call it gastronomical fetishism). It would be natural to describe as gastronomically perverted someone who could eat only by having food forced down his throat through a funnel, or only if the meal were a living animal. What helps is the peculiarity of the desire itself, rather than the inappropriateness of its object to the biological function that the desire serves. Even an appetite can have perversions if in addition to its biological function it has a significant psychological structure.

In the case of hunger, psychological complexity is provided by the activities that give it expression. Hunger is not merely a disturbing sensation that can be quelled by eating; it is an attitude toward edible portions of the external world, a desire to treat them in rather special ways. The method of ingestion: chewing, savoring, swallowing, appreciating the texture and smell, all are important components of the relation, as is the passivity and controllability of the food (the only animals we eat live are helpless mollusks). Our relation to food depends also on our size: we do not live upon it or burrow into it like aphids or worms. Some of these features are more central than others, but an adequate phenomenology of eating would have to treat it as a relation to the external world and a way of appropriating bits of that world, with characteristic affection. Displacements or serious restrictions of the desire to eat could then be described as perversions, if they undermined that direct relation between man and food which is the natural expression of hunger. This explains why it is easy to imagine gastronomical fetishism, voyeurism, exhibitionism, or even gastronomical sadism and masochism. Some of these perversions are fairly common.

If we can imagine perversions of an appetite like hunger, it should be possible to make sense of the concept of sexual perversion. I do not wish to imply that sexual desire is an appetite—only that being an appetite is no bar to admitting of perversions. Like hunger, sexual desire has as its characteristic object a certain relation with something in the external world; only in this case it is usually a person rather than an omelet, and the relation is considerably more complicated. This added complication allows scope for correspondingly complicated perversions.

The fact that sexual desire is a feeling about other persons may encourage a pious view of its psychological content—that it is properly the expression of some other attitude, like love, and that when it occurs by itself it is incomplete or subhuman. (The extreme Platonic version of such a view is that sexual practices are all vain attempts to express something they cannot in principle achieve: this makes them all perversions, in a sense.) But sexual desire is complicated enough without having to be linked to anything else as a condition for phenomenological analysis. Sex may serve various functions—economic, social, altruistic—but it also has its own content as a relation between persons.

The object of sexual attraction is a particular individual, who transcends the properties that make him attractive. When different persons are attracted to a single person for different reasons—eyes, hair, figure, laugh, intelligence—we nevertheless feel that the object of their desire is the same. There is even an inclination to feel that this is so if the lovers have different sexual aims, if they include both men and women, for example. Different specific attractive characteristics seem to provide enabling conditions for the operation of a single basic feeling, and the different aims all provide expressions of it. We approach the sexual attitude toward the person through the features that we find attractive, but these features are not the objects of that attitude.

This is very different from the case of an omelet. Various people may desire it for different reasons, one for its fluffiness, another for its mushrooms, another for its unique combination of aroma and visual aspect; yet we do not enshrine the transcendental omelet as the true common object of their affections. Instead we might say that several desires have accidentally converged on the same object: any omelet with the crucial characteristics would do as well. It is not similarly true that any person with the same flesh distribution and way of smoking can be substituted as object for a particular sexual desire that has been elicited by those characteristics. It may be that they recur, but it will be a new sexual attraction with a new particular object, not merely a transfer of the old desire to someone else. (This is true even in cases where the new object is unconsciously identified with a former one.)

The importance of this point will emerge when we see how complex a psychological interchange constitutes the natural development of sexual attraction. This would be incomprehensible if its object were not a particular person, but rather a person of a certain *kind*. Attraction is only the beginning, and fulfillment does not consist merely of behavior and contact expressing this attraction, but involves much more.

The best discussion of these matters that I have seen appears in part III of Sartre's *Being and Nothingness*.[1] Sartre's treatment of sexual desire and of love, hate, sadism, masochism, and further attitudes toward others, depends on a general theory of consciousness and the body which we can neither expound nor assume here. He does not discuss perversion, and this is partly because he regards sexual desire as one form of the perpetual attempt of an embodied consciousness to come to terms with the existence of others, an attempt that is as doomed to fail in this form as it is in any of the others, which include sadism and masochism (if not certain of the more impersonal deviations) as well as several nonsexual attitudes. According to Sartre, all attempts to incorporate the other into my world as another subject, i.e. to apprehend him at once as an object for me and as a subject for whom I am an object, are unstable and doomed to collapse into one or other of the two aspects. Either I reduce him entirely to an object, in which case his subjectivity escapes the possession or appropriation I can extend to that object; or I become merely an object for him, in which case I am no longer in a position to appropriate his subjectivity. Moreover, neither of these aspects is stable; each is continually in danger of giving way to the other. This has the consequence that there can be no such thing as a *successful* sexual relation, since the deep aim of sexual desire cannot in principle be accomplished. It seems likely, therefore, that the view will not permit a basic distinction between successful or complete and unsuccessful or incomplete sex, and therefore cannot admit the concept of perversion.

I do not adopt this aspect of the theory, nor many of its metaphysical underpinnings. What interests me is Sartre's picture of the attempt. He says that the type of possession that is the object of sexual desire is carried out by "a double reciprocal incarnation" and that this is accomplished, typically in the form of a caress, in the following way: "I make myself flesh in order to impel the Other to realize *for herself* and *for me* her own flesh, and my caresses cause my flesh to be born for me in so far as it is for the Other *flesh causing her to be born as flesh*" (*Being and Nothingness*, p. 391; Sartre's italics). This incarnation in question is described variously as a clogging or troubling of consciousness, which is inundated by the flesh in which it is embodied.

The view I am going to suggest, I hope in less obscure language, is related to this one, but it differs from Sartre's in allowing sexuality to achieve its goal on occasion and thus in providing the concept of perversion with a foothold.

Sexual desire involves a kind of perception, but not merely a single perception of its object, for in the paradigm case of mutual desire there is a complex system of superimposed mutual perceptions—not only perceptions of the sexual object, but perceptions of oneself. Moreover, sexual awareness of another involves considerable self-awareness to begin with—more than is involved in ordinary sensory perception. The experience is felt as an assault on oneself by the view (or touch, or whatever) of the sexual object.

Let us consider a case in which the elements can be separated. For clarity we will restrict ourselves initially to the somewhat artificial case of desire at a distance. Suppose a man and a woman, whom we may call Romeo and Juliet, are at opposite ends of a cocktail lounge, with many mirrors on the walls which permit unobserved observation, and even mutual unobserved observation. Each of them is sipping a martini and studying other people in the mirrors. At some point Romeo notices Juliet. He is moved, somehow, by the softness of her hair and the diffidence with which she sips her martini, and this arouses him sexually. Let us say that X *senses* Y whenever X regards Y with sexual desire. (Y need not be a person, and X's apprehension of Y can be visual, tactile, olfactory, etc., or purely imaginary; in the present example we shall concentrate on vision). So Romeo senses Juliet, rather than merely noticing her. At this stage he is aroused by an unaroused object, so he is more in the sexual grip of his body than she of hers.

Let us suppose, however, that Juliet now senses Romeo in another mirror on the opposite wall, though neither of them yet knows that he is seen by the other (the mirror angles provide three-quarter views). Romeo then begins to notice in Juliet the subtle signs of sexual arousal, heavy-lidded stare, dilating pupils, faint flush, etc. This of course intensifies her bodily presence, and he not only notices but senses this as well. His arousal is nevertheless still solitary. But now, cleverly calculating the line of her stare without actually looking her in the eyes, he realizes that it is directed at him through the mirror on the opposite wall. That is, he notices, and moreover senses, Juliet sensing him. This is definitely a new development, for it gives him a sense of embodiment not only through his own reactions but through the eyes and reactions of another. Moreover, it is separable from the initial sensing of Juliet; for sexual arousal might begin with a person's sensing that he is sensed and being assailed by the perception of the other person's desire rather than merely by the perception of the person.

But there is a further step. Let us suppose that Juliet, who is a little slower than Romeo, now senses that he senses her. This puts Romeo in a position to notice, and be aroused by, her arousal at being sensed by him. He senses that she senses that he senses her. This is still another level of arousal, for he becomes conscious of his sexuality through his awareness of its effect on her and of her awareness that this effect is due to him. Once she takes the same step and senses that he senses her sensing him, it becomes difficult to state, let alone imagine, further iterations, though they may be logically distinct. If both are alone, they will presumably turn to look at each other directly, and the proceedings will continue on another plane. Physical contact and intercourse are natural extensions of this complicated visual exchange, and mutual touch can involve all the complexities of awareness present in the visual case, but with a far greater range of subtlety and acuteness.

Ordinarily, of course, things happen in a less orderly fashion—sometimes in a great rush—but I believe that some version of this overlapping system of distinct sexual perceptions and interactions is the basic framework of any full-fledged sexual relation and that relations involving only part of the complex are significantly incomplete. The account is only schematic, as it must be to achieve generality. Every real sexual act will be psychologically far more specific and detailed, in ways that depend not only on the physical techniques employed and on anatomical details, but also on countless features of the participants' conceptions of themselves and of each other, which become embodied in the act. (It is a familiar enough fact, for example, that people often take their social roles and the social roles of their partners to bed with them.)

The general schema is important, however, and the proliferation of levels of mutual awareness it involves is an example of a type of complexity that typifies human interactions. Consider aggression, for example. If I am angry with someone, I want to make him feel it, either to produce self-reproach by getting him to see himself through the eyes of my anger, and to dislike what he sees—or else to produce reciprocal anger or fear, by getting him to perceive my anger as a threat or attack. What I want will depend on the details of my anger, but in either case it will involve a desire that the object of that anger be aroused. This accomplishment constitutes the fulfillment of my emotion, through domination of the object's feelings.

Another example of such reflexive mutual recognition is to be found in the phenomenon of meaning, which appears to involve an intention to produce a belief or other effect in another by bringing about his recognition of one's intention to produce that effect. (That result is due to H. P. Grice,[2] whose position I shall not attempt to reproduce in detail.) Sex has a related structure: it involves a desire that one's partner be aroused by the recognition of one's desire that he or she be aroused.

It is not easy to define the basic types of awareness and arousal of which these complexes are composed, and that remains a lacuna in this discussion. In a sense, the object of awareness is the same in one's own case as it is in one's sexual awareness of another, although the two awarenesses will not be the same, the difference being as great as that between feeling angry and experiencing the anger of another. All stages of sexual perception are varieties of identification of a person with his body. What is perceived is one's own or another's *subjection* to or *immersion* in his body, a phenomenon which has been recognized with loathing by St. Paul and St. Augustine, both of whom regarded "the law of sin which is in my members" as a grave threat to the dominion of the holy will.[3] In sexual desire and its expression the blending of involuntary response with deliberate control is extremely important. For Augustine, the revolution launched against him by his body is symbolized by erection and the other involuntary physical components of arousal. Sartre too stresses the fact that the penis is not a prehensile organ. But mere involuntariness characterizes other bodily processes as well. In sexual desire the involuntary responses are combined with submission to spontaneous impulses: not only one's pulse and secretions but one's actions are taken over by the body; ideally, deliberate control is needed only to guide the expression of those impulses. This is to some extent also true of an appetite like hunger, but the takeover there is more localized, less pervasive, less extreme. One's whole body does not become saturated with hunger as it can with desire. But the most characteristic feature of a specifically sexual immersion in the body is its ability to fit into the complex of mutual perceptions that we have described. Hunger leads to spontaneous interactions with food; sexual desire leads to spontaneous interactions with other persons, whose bodies are asserting their sovereignty in the same way, producing involuntary reactions and spontaneous impulses in *them*. These reactions are perceived, and the perception of them is perceived, and that perception is in turn perceived; at each step the domination of the person by his body is reinforced, and the sexual partner becomes more possessible by physical contact, penetration, and envelopment.

Desire is therefore not merely the perception of a pre-existing embodiment of the other, but ideally a contribution to his further embodiment which in turn enhances the original subject's sense of himself. This explains why it is important that the partner be aroused, and not merely aroused, but aroused by the awareness of one's desire. It also explains the sense in which desire has unity and possession as its object: physical possession must eventuate in creation of the sexual object in the image of one's desire, and not merely in the object's recognition of that desire, or in his or her own private arousal.

Even if this is a correct model of the adult sexual capacity, it is not plausible to describe as perverted every deviation from it. For example, if the partners in heterosexual intercourse indulge in private heterosexual fantasies, thus avoiding recognition of the real partner, that would, on this model, constitute a defective sexual relation. It is not, however, generally regarded as a perversion. Such examples suggest that a simple dichotomy between perverted and unperverted sex is too crude to organize the phenomena adequately.

Still, various familiar deviations constitute truncated or incomplete versions of the complete configuration, and may be regarded as perversions of the central impulse. If sexual desire is prevented from taking its full interpersonal form, it is likely to find a different one. The concept of perversion implies that a normal sexual development has been turned aside by distorting influences. I have little to say about this causal condition. But if perversions are in some sense unnatural, they must result from interference with the development of a capacity that is there potentially.

It is difficult to apply this condition, because environmental factors play a role in determining the precise form of anyone's sexual impulse. Early experiences in particular seem to determine the choice of a sexual object. To describe some causal influences as distorting and others as merely formative is to imply that certain general aspects of human sexuality realize a definite potential whereas many of the details in which people differ realize an indeterminate potential, so that they cannot be called more or less natural. What is included in the definite potential is therefore very important, although the distinction between definite and indeterminate potential is obscure. Obviously a creature incapable of developing the levels of interpersonal sexual awareness I have described could not be deviant in virtue of the failure to do so. (Though even a chicken might be called perverted in an extended sense if it had been conditioned to develop a fetishistic attachment to a telephone.) But if humans will tend to develop some version of reciprocal interpersonal sexual awareness unless prevented, then cases of blockage can be called unnatural or perverted.

Some familiar deviations can be described in this way. Narcissistic practices and intercourse with animals, infants, and inanimate objects seem to be stuck at some primitive version of the first stage of sexual feeling. If the object is not alive, the experience is reduced entirely to an awareness of one's own sexual embodiment. Small children and animals permit awareness of the embodiment of the other, but present obstacles to reciprocity, to the recognition by the sexual object of the subject's desire as the source of his (the object's) sexual self-awareness. Voyeurism and exhibitionism are also incomplete relations. The exhibitionist wishes to display his desire without needing to be desired in return; he may even fear the sexual attention of others. A voyeur, on the other hand, need not require any recognition by his object at all: certainly not a recognition of the voyeur's arousal.

On the other hand, if we apply our model to the various forms that may be taken by two-party heterosexual intercourse, none of them seem clearly to qualify as perversions. Hardly anyone can be found these days to inveigh against oral-genital contact, and the merits of buggery are urged by such respectable figures as D. H. Lawrence and Norman Mailer. In general, it would appear that any bodily contact between a man and a woman that gives them sexual pleasure is a possible vehicle for the system of multi-level interpersonal awareness that I have claimed is the basic psychological content of sexual interaction. Thus a liberal platitude about sex is upheld.

The really difficult cases are sadism, masochism, and homosexuality. The first two are widely regarded as perversions and the last is controversial. In all three cases the issue depends partly on causal factors: do these dispositions result only when normal development has been prevented? Even the form in which this question has been posed is circular, because of the word 'normal'. We appear to need an independent criterion for a distorting influence, and we do not have one.

It may be possible to class sadism and masochism as perversions because they fall short of interpersonal reciprocity. Sadism concentrates on the evocation of passive self-awareness in others, but the sadist's engagement is itself active and requires a retention of deliberate control which may impede awareness of himself as a bodily subject of passion in the required sense. De Sade claimed that the object of sexual desire was to evoke involuntary responses from one's partner, especially audible ones. The infliction of pain is no doubt the most efficient way to accomplish this, but it requires a certain abrogation of one's own exposed spontaneity. A masochist on the other hand imposes the same disability on his partner as the sadist imposes on himself. The masochist cannot find a satisfactory embodiment as the object of another's sexual desire, but only as the object of his control. He is passive not in relation to his partner's passion but in relation to his nonpassive agency. In addition, the subjection to one's body characteristic of pain and physical restraint is of a very different kind from that of sexual excitement: pain causes people to contract rather than dissolve. These descriptions may not be generally accurate. But to the extent that they are, sadism and masochism would be disorders of the second stage of awareness—the awareness of oneself as an object of desire.

Homosexuality cannot similarly be classed as a perversion on phenomenological grounds. Nothing rules out the full range of interpersonal perceptions between persons of the same sex. The issue then depends on whether homosexuality is produced by distorting influences that block or displace a natural tendency to heterosexual development. And the influences must be more distorting than those which lead to a taste for large breasts or fair hair or dark eyes. These also are contingencies of sexual preference in which people differ, without being perverted.

The question is whether heterosexuality is the natural expression of male and female sexual dispositions that have not been distorted. It is an unclear question, and I do not know how to approach it. There is much support for an aggressive–passive distinction between male and female sexuality. In our culture the male's arousal tends to initiate the perceptual exchange, he usually makes the sexual approach, largely controls the course of the act, and of course penetrates whereas the woman receives. When two men or two women engage in intercourse they cannot both adhere to these sexual roles. But a good deal of deviation from them occurs in heterosexual intercourse. Women can be sexually aggressive and men passive, and temporary reversals of role are not uncommon in heterosexual exchanges of reasonable length. For these reasons it seems to be doubtful that homosexuality must be a perversion, though like heterosexuality it has perverted forms.

Let me close with some remarks about the relation of perversion to good, bad, and morality. The concept of perversion can hardly fail to be evaluative in some sense, for it appears to involve the notion of an ideal or at least adequate sexuality which the perversions in some way fail to achieve. So, if the concept is viable, the judgment that a person or practice or desire is perverted will constitute a sexual evaluation, implying that better sex, or a better specimen of sex, is possible. This in itself is a very weak claim, since the evaluation might be in a dimension that is of little interest to us. (Though, if my account is correct, that will not be true.)

Whether it is a moral evaluation, however, is another question entirely—one whose answer would require more understanding of both morality and perversion than can be deployed here. Moral evaluation of acts and of persons is a rather special and very complicated matter, and by no means all our evaluations of persons and their activities are moral evaluations. We make judgments about people's beauty or health or intelligence which are evaluative without being moral. Assessments of their sexuality may be similar in that respect.

Furthermore, moral issues aside, it is not clear that unperverted sex is necessarily *preferable* to the perversions. It may be that sex which receives the highest marks for perfection *as sex* is less enjoyable than certain perversions; and if enjoyment is considered very important, that might outweigh considerations of sexual perfection in determining rational preference.

That raises the question of the relation between the evaluative content of judgments of perversion and the rather common *general* distinction between good and bad sex. The latter distinction is usually confined to sexual acts, and it would seem, within limits, to cut across the other: even someone who believed, for example, that homosexuality was a perversion could admit a distinction between better and worse homosexual sex, and might even allow that good homosexual sex could be better *sex* than not very good unperverted sex. If this is correct, it supports the position that, if judgments of perversion are viable at all, they represent only one aspect of the possible evaluation of sex, even *qua sex*. Moreover it is not the only important aspect: sexual deficiencies that evidently do not constitute perversions can be the object of great concern.

Finally, even if perverted sex is to that extent not so good as it might be, bad sex is generally better than none at all. This should not be controversial: it seems to hold for other important matters, like food, music, literature, and society. In the end, one must choose from among the

available alternatives, whether their availability depends on the environment or on one's own constitution. And the alternatives have to be fairly
grim before it becomes rational to opt for nothing.

Notes

1. *L'Etre et le Néant* (Paris: Gallimand, 1943), translated by Hazel E. Barnes
(New York: Philosophical Library, 1956).
2. 'Meaning', *Philosophical Review*, LXVI, no. 3 (July, 1957), 377–88.
3. See Romans, VII, 23; and the *Confessions*, bk VIII, pt v.

Chapter 3

SEXUAL PARADIGMS

Robert Solomon

It is a cocktail lounge, well-lit and mirrored, not a bar, martinis and not beer, two strangers—a furtive glance from him, shy recognition from her. It is 1950's American high comedy; boy arouses girl, both are led through ninety minutes of misunderstandings of identity and intention, and, finally, by the end of the popcorn, boy kisses girl with a clean-cut fade-out or panned clip of a postcard horizon. It is one of the dangers of conceptual analysis that the philosopher's choice of paradigms betrays a personal bias, but it is an exceptional danger of sexual conceptual analysis that one's choice of paradigms also betrays one's private fantasies and personal obsessions.[1] No doubt that is why, despite their extraprofessional interest in the subject, most philosophers would rather write about indirect discourse than intercourse, the philosophy of mind rather than the philosophy of body.

In Tom Nagel's pioneering effort[2] there are too many recognizable symptoms of liberal American sexual mythology. His analysis is cautious and competent, but absolutely sexless. His Romeo and Juliet exemplify at most a romanticized version of the initial phases of (hetero)-sexual attraction in a casual and innocent pickup. They "arouse" each other, but there is no indication to what end. They "incarnate each other as flesh," in Sartre's awkward but precise terminology, but Nagel gives us no clue as to why they should indulge in such a peculiar activity. Presumably a pair of dermatologists or fashion models might have a similar effect on

Reprinted, with the permission of Robert Solomon and the *Journal of Philosophy*, from *Journal of Philosophy* 71:11 (1974), pp. 336–45.

each other, but without the slightest hint of sexual intention. What makes this situation paradigmatically sexual? We may assume, as we would in a Doris Day comedy, that the object of this protracted arousal is sexual intercourse, but we are not told this. Sexuality without content. Liberal sexual mythology takes this Hollywood element of "leave it to the imagination" as its starting point and adds the equally inexplicit suggestion that whatever activities two consenting adults choose as the object of their arousal and its gratification is "their business." In a society with such secrets, pornography is bound to serve a radical end as a vulgar valve of reality. In a philosophical analysis that stops short of the very matter investigated, a bit of perverseness may be necessary just in order to refocus the question.

Sexual desire is distinguished, like all desires, by its aims and objects. What are these peculiarly sexual aims and objects? Notice that Nagel employs a fairly standard "paradigm case argument" in his analysis; he begins,

> ... certain practices will be perversions if anything is, such as shoe fetishism, bestiality, and sadism; other practices, such as unadorned sexual intercourse, will not be. (9)

So we can assume that the end of Romeo and Juliet's tryst will be intercourse—we do not know whether "adorned" or not. But what is it that makes intercourse the paradigm of sexual activity—its biological role in conception, its heterosexuality, its convenience for mutual orgasm? Would Nagel's drama still serve as a sexual paradigm if Juliet turns out to be a virgin, or if Romeo and Juliet find that they are complementarily sado-masochistic, if Romeo is in drag, if they are both knee-fetishists? Why does Nagel choose two *strangers*? Why not, as in the days of sexual moralism, a happily married couple enjoying their seventh anniversary? Or is not the essence of sex, as Sartre so brutally argues, Romeo and Juliet's mutual attempts to possess each other, with each's own enjoyment only a secondary and essentially distracting effect? Are we expected to presume the most prominent paradigm, at least since Freud, the lusty ejaculation of Romeo into the submissive, if not passive, Juliet? Suppose Juliet is in fact a prostitute, skillfully mocking the signs of innocent arousal: is this a breach of the paradigm, or might not such subsequent "unadorned" intercourse be just the model that Nagel claims to defend?

To what end does Romeo arouse Juliet? And to what end does Juliet become affected and in turn excite Romeo? In this exemplary instance, I would think that "unadorned" intercourse would be perverse, or at least distasteful, in the extreme. It would be different, however, if the paradigm were our seven-year married couple, for in such cases "adorned" intercourse might well be something of a rarity. In homosexual encounters, in the frenzy of adolescent virginal petting, in cases in which intercourse is restricted for temporary medical or political reasons, arousal may be no different, even though intercourse cannot be the end. And it is only in the crudest cases of physiological need that the desire for intercourse is the sole or even the leading component in the convoluted motivation of sexuality. A nineteen-year-old sailor back after having discussed nothing but sex on a three-month cruise may be so aroused, but that surely is not the nature of Juliet's arousal. Romeo may remind her of her father, or of her favorite philosophy professor, and he may inspire respect, or fear, or curiosity. He may simply arouse self-consciousness or embarrassment. Any of these attitudes may be dominant, but none is particularly sexual.

Sexuality has an essential bodily dimension, and this might well be described as the "incarnation" or "submersion" of a person into his body. The end of this desire is interpersonal communication; but where Sartre gives a complex theory of the nature of this communication, Nagel gives us only an empty notion of "multi-level interpersonal awareness." Presumably the mutual arousal that is the means to this awareness is enjoyable in itself. But it is important that Nagel resists the current (W.) Reichian-American fetish for the wonders of the genital orgasm, for he does not leap to the facile conclusion that the aim of sexual activity is mutual or at least personal orgasm. It is here that Nagel opens a breach with liberal sexual mythology, one that might at first appear absurd because of his total neglect of the role of the genitalia and orgasm in sexuality. But we have an overgenitalized conception of sexuality, and, if sexual satisfaction involves and even requires orgasm, it does not follow that orgasm is the goal of the convoluted sexual games we play with each other. Orgasm is the "end" of sexual activity, perhaps, but only in the sense that swallowing is the "end" of tasting a Viennese torte.

There was a time, and it was not long ago and may come soon again, when sexuality required defending. It had to be argued that we had a right to sex, not for any purpose other than our personal enjoyment. But that defense has turned stale, and sexual deprivation is no longer our problem. The "swollen bladder" model of repressed sexuality may have been convincing in sex-scared bourgeois Vienna of 1905, but not today, where the problem is not sexual deprivation but sexual dissatisfaction. The fetishism of the orgasm, now shared by women as well as men, threatens our sex lives with becoming antipersonal and mechanical, anxiety-filled athletic arenas with mutual multiple orgasm its goal. Behind much of this unhappiness and anxiety, ironically, stands the liberal defense of sexuality as enjoyment. It is one of the virtues of Nagel's essay that he begins to overcome this oppressive liberal mythology. But at the same time he relies upon it for his support and becomes trapped in it, and the result is an account which displays the emptiness we have pointed out and the final note of despair with which he ends his essay.

Liberal sexual mythology appears to stand upon a tripod of mutually supporting platitudes: (1) and foremost, that the essential aim (and even the sole aim) of sex is enjoyment; (2) that sexual activity is and ought to be essentially private activity; and (3) that any sexual activity is as valid as any other. The first platitude was once a radical proposition, a reaction to the conservative and pious belief that sexual activity was activity whose end was reproduction, the serving of God's will or natural law. Kant, for example, always good for a shocking opinion in the realm of normative ethics, suggests that sexual lust is an appetite with an end intended by nature, and that any sexual activity contrary to that end is "unnatural and revolting," by which one "makes himself an object of abomination and stands bereft of all reverence of any kind."[3] It was Sigmund Freud who destroyed this long-standing paradigm, in identifying sexuality as "discharge of tension" (physical and psychological), which he simply equated with "pleasure," regardless of the areas of the body or what activities or how many people happened to be involved. Sex was thus defined as self-serving, activity for its own sake, with pleasure as its only principle. If Freud is now accused of sexual conservatism, it is necessary to remind ourselves that he introduced the radical paradigm that is now used against him. Since Freud's classic efforts, the conception of sexuality as a means to other ends, whether procreation or pious love, has become bankrupt in terms of the currency of opinion. Even radical sexual ideology has confined its critique to the social and political *abuses* of this liberal platitude without openly rejecting it.

The second platitude is a hold-over from more conservative days, in which sexual activity, like defecation, menstruation, and the bodily reactions to illness, was considered distasteful, if not shameful and to be hidden from view. Yet this conservative platitude is as essential as the first, for the typically utilitarian argument in defense of sexuality as enjoyment is based on the idea that sex is private activity and, when confined to "consenting adults," should be left as a matter of taste. And sex is, we are reminded by liberals, a natural appetite, and therefore a matter of taste.

The platitude of privacy also bolsters the third principle, still considered a radical principle by many, that any sexual activity is as valid as any other. Again, the utilitarian argument prevails, that private and mutually consented activity between adults, no matter how distasteful it might be to others and no matter how we may think its enthusiasts to be depraved, is "their own business."

Nagel's analysis calls this tri-part ideology to his side, although he clearly attempts to go beyond it as well. The platitude of enjoyment functions only loosely in his essay, and at one point he makes it clear that sexuality need not aim at enjoyment. ("It may be that . . . perfection *as sex* is less enjoyable than certain perversions; and if enjoyment is considered very important, that might outweigh considerations of sexual perfection in determining rational preference" (19). His central notion of "arousal," however, is equivocal. On the one hand, arousal is itself not necessarily enjoyable, particularly if it fails to be accompanied with expectations of release. But on the other hand, Nagel's "arousal" plays precisely the same role in his analysis that "tension" (or "cathexis") plays in Freud, and though the arousal itself is not enjoyable, its release is, and the impression we get from Nagel, which Freud makes explicit, is that sexual activity is the intentional arousal both of self and other in order to enjoy its release. On this interpretation, Nagel's analysis is perfectly in line with post-Freudian liberal theory.

Regarding the second platitude, Nagel's analysis does not mention it, but rather it appears to be presupposed throughout that sexuality is a private affair. One might repeat that the notion of privacy is more symptomatic of his analysis itself. One cannot imagine J. L. Austin spending a dozen pages describing the intentions and inclinations involved in a public performance of making a promise or christening a ship without mentioning the performance itself. Yet Nagel spends that much space giving us the preliminaries of sexuality without ever quite breaching the private sector in which sexual activity is to be found.

The third platitude emerges only slowly in Nagel's essay. He begins by chastising an approach to that same conclusion by a radical "skeptic," who argues of sexual desires, as "appetites,"

> Either they are sexual or they are not: sexuality does not admit of imperfection, or perversion, or any other such qualification. (10)

Nagel's analysis goes beyond this "skepticism" in important ways, yet he does conclude that "any bodily contact between a man and a woman that gives them sexual *pleasure* [italics mine] is a possible vehicle for the system of multi-level interpersonal awareness that I have claimed is the basic psychological content of sexual interaction" (17). Here the first platitude is partially employed to support the third, presumably with the second implied. Notice again that Nagel has given us no indication what distinguishes "sexual pleasure" from other pleasures, whether bodily pleasures or the enjoyment of conquest or domination, seduction or submission, sleeping with the president's daughter or earning thirty dollars.

To knock down a tripod, one need kick out only one of its supporting legs. I for one would not wish to advocate, along with several recent sexual pundits, an increased display of fornication and fellatio in public places, nor would I view the return of "sexual morality" as a desirable state of affairs. Surprisingly, it is the essential enjoyment of sex that is the least palatable of the liberal myths.

No one would deny that sex is enjoyable, but it does not follow that sexuality is the activity of "pure enjoyment" and that "gratification," or "pure physical pleasure," that is, orgasm, is its end. Sex is indeed pleasurable, but, as Aristotle argued against the hedonists of his day, this enjoyment accompanies sexual activity and its ends, but is not that activity or these ends. We enjoy being sexually satisfied; we are not satisfied by our enjoyment. In fact, one might reasonably hypothesize that the performance of any activity, pleasurable or not, which is as intensely promoted and obsessively pursued as sex in America would provide tremendous gratification. [One might further speculate on the fact that recent American politics shows that "every (white, male Christian) American boy's dream of becoming President" seems to encourage the exploitation of all three sexual platitudes of enjoyment, privacy, and "anything goes." (Cf. H. Kissinger, "Power is the ultimate aphrodisiac.")]

If sexuality does not essentially aim at pleasure, does it have any purpose? Jean-Paul Sartre has given us an alternative to the liberal theory in his *Being and Nothingness*, in which he argues that our sexual relations with others, like all our various relationships with others, are to be construed as *conflicts*, modeled after Hegel's parable of master and slave. Sexual desire is not desire for pleasure, and pleasure is more likely to distract us from sexuality than to deepen our involvement. For Sartre, sexual desire is the desire to possess, to gain recognition of one's own freedom at the expense of the other. By "incarnating" and degrading him/her in flesh, one reduces him/her to an object. Sadism is but an extension of this domination over the other. Or one allows himself to be "incarnated" as a devious route to the same end, making the other his/her sexual slave. Sexual activity concentrates its attention on the least personal, most inert parts of the body—breasts, thighs, stomach, and emphasizes awkward and immobile postures and activities. On this model, degradation is the central activity of sex, to convince the other that he/she is a slave, to persuade the other of one's own power, whether it be through the skills of sexual technique or through the passive demands of being sexually served. Intercourse has no privileged position in this model, except that intercourse, particularly in these liberated times in which it has become a contest, is ideal for this competition for power and recognition. And no doubt Sartre, who, like Freud, adopts a paradigmatically male perspective, senses that intercourse is more likely to be degrading to the woman, who thus begins at a disadvantage.

Sartre's notion of sexuality, taken seriously, would be enough to keep us out of bed for a month. Surely, we must object, something has been left out of account, for example, the two-person *Mitsein* that Sartre himself suggests in the same book. It is impossible for us to delve into the complex ontology that leads Sartre into this pessimistic model, but its essential structure is precisely what we need to carry us beyond the liberal mythology. According to Sartre, sexuality is interpersonal communication with the body as its medium. Sartre's mistake, if we may be brief, is his narrow constriction of the message of that communication to mutual degradation and conflict. Nagel, who accepts Sartre's communication model but, in line with the liberal mythology, seeks to reject its pessimistic conclusions, makes a mistake in the opposite direction. He accepts the communication model, but leaves it utterly without content. What is communicated, he suggests, is arousal. But, as we have seen, arousal is too broad a notion; we must know arousal of what, for what, to what end. Nagel's notion of "arousal" and "interpersonal awareness" gives us an outline of the grammar of the communication model, but no semantics. One might add that sexual activity in which what is aroused and intended are pleasurable sensations alone is a limiting and rare case. A sensation is only pleasurable or enjoyable, not in itself, but in the context of the meaning of the activity in which it is embedded. This is as true of orgasm as it is of a hard passion-bite on the shoulder.

This view of sexuality answers some strong questions which the liberal model leaves a mystery. If sex is pure physical enjoyment, why is sexual activity between persons far more satisfying than masturbation, where, if we accept recent physiological studies, orgasm is at its highest intensity and the post-coital period is cleansed of its interpersonal hassles and arguments? On the Freudian model, sex with other people ("objects") becomes a matter of "secondary process," with masturbation primary. On the communication model, masturbation is like talking to yourself; possible, even enjoyable, but clearly secondary to sexuality in its broader interpersonal context. (It is significant that even this carnal solipsism is typically accompanied by imaginings and pictures; "No masturbation without representation," perhaps.) If sex is physical pleasure, then the fetish of the genital orgasm is no doubt justifiable, but then why in our orgasm-cluttered sex lives are we so dissatisfied? Because orgasm is not the "end" of sex but its resolution, and obsessive concentration on reaching climax effectively overwhelms or distorts whatever else is being said sexually. It is this focus on orgasm that has made Sartre's model more persuasive; for the battle over the orgasm, whether in selfish or altruistic guise ("my orgasm first" or "I'll *give* you the best ever") has become an unavoidable medium for conflict and control. "Unadorned sexual intercourse," on this model, becomes the ultimate perversion, since it is the sexual equivalent of hanging up the telephone without saying anything. Even an obscene telephone caller has a message to convey.

Sexual activity consists in speaking what we might call "body language." It has its own grammar, delineated by the body, and its own phonetics of touch and movement. Its unit of meaningfulness, the bodily equivalent of a sentence, is the *gesture*. No doubt one could add considerably to its vocabulary, and perhaps it could be possible to discuss world

politics or the mind-body problem by an appropriate set of invented gestures. But body language is essentially expressive, and its content is limited to interpersonal attitudes and feelings—shyness, domination, fear,
submissiveness and dependence, love or hatred or indifference, lack of
confidence and embarrassment, shame, jealousy, possessiveness. There
is little value in stressing the overworked point that such expressions are
"natural" expressions, as opposed to verbal expressions of the same attitudes and feelings. In our highly verbal society, it may well be that verbal
expression, whether it be poetry or clumsy blurting, feels more natural
than the use of our bodies. Yet it does seem true that some attitudes, e.g.,
tenderness and trust, domination and passivity, are best expressed sexually. Love, it seems, is not best expressed sexually, for its sexual expression is indistinguishable from the expressions of a number of other
attitudes. Possessiveness, mutual recognition, "being-with," and conflict
are expressed by body language almost essentially, virtually as its deep
structure, and here Sartre's model obtains its plausibility.

According to Nagel, "perversion" is "truncated or incomplete versions
of the complete configuration" (16). But again, his emphasis is entirely
on the form of "interpersonal awareness" rather than its content. For example, he analyzes sadism as "the concentration on the evocation of passive self-awareness in others . . . which impedes awareness of himself as a
bodily subject of passion in the required sense." But surely sadism is not
so much a breakdown in communication (any more than the domination of a conversation by one speaker, with the agreement of his listener,
is a breach of language) as an excessive expression of a particular content, namely the attitude of domination, perhaps mixed with hatred,
fear, and other negative attitudes. Similarly, masochism is not simply the
relinquishing of one's activity (an inability to speak, in a sense), for the
masochist may well be active in inviting punishment from his sadistic
partner. Masochism is excessive expression of an attitude of victimization, shame, or inferiority. Moreover, it is clear that there is not the
slightest taint of "perversion" in homosexuality, which need differ from
heterosexuality only in its mode of resolution. Fetishism and bestiality
certainly do constitute perversions, since the first is the same as, for example, talking to someone else's shoes, and the second like discussing
Spinoza with a moderately intelligent sheep.

This model also makes it evident why Nagel chose as his example a
couple of strangers; one has far more to say, for one can freely express
one's fantasies as well as the truth, to a stranger. A husband and wife of
seven years have probably been repeating the same messages for years,
and their sexual activity now is probably no more than an abbreviated ritual incantation of the lengthy conversations they had years before. One
can imagine Romeo and Juliet climbing into bed together each with a
spectacular set of expectations and fantasies, trying to overwhelm each

other with extravagant expressions and experiments. But it may be, accordingly, that they won't understand each other, or, as the weekend plods on, sex, like any extended conversation, tends to become either more truthful or more incoherent.

Qua body language, sex admits of at least two forms of perversion: one deviance of form, the other deviance in content. There are the techniques of sexuality, overly celebrated in our society, and there are the attitudes that these techniques allegedly express. Nagel and most theorists have concentrated on perversions in technique, deviations in the forms of sexual activity. But it seems to me that the more problematic perversions are the semantic deviations, of which the most serious are those involving insincerity, the bodily equivalent of the lie. Entertaining private fantasies and neglecting one's real sexual partner is thus an innocent semantic perversion, while pretended tenderness and affection that reverses itself soon after orgasm is a potentially vicious perversion. However, again joining Nagel, I would argue that perverse sex is not necessarily bad or immoral sex. Pretense is the premise of imagination as well as of falsehood, and sexual fantasies may enrich our lives far more than sexual realities alone. Perhaps it is an unfortunate comment on the poverty of contemporary life that our fantasies have become so confined, that our sexuality has been forced to serve needs which far exceed its expressive capacity. That is why the liberal mythology has been so disastrous, for it has rendered unconscious the expressive functions of sex in its stress on enjoyment and, in its platitude of privacy, has reduced sexuality to each man's/woman's private language, first spoken clumsily and barely articulately on wedding nights and in the back seats of Fords. It is thus understandable why sex is so utterly important in our lives, and why it is typically so unsatisfactory.

Notes

1. I confess, for example, that certain male biases infiltrate my own analysis. I thank Janice Moulton for pointing this out to me.

2. "Sexual Perversion," *The Journal of Philosophy* 66, no. 1 (1969), pp. 5–17. (This volume, pp. 9–20.)

3. *Metaphysics of Ethics*, trans. Semple (Edinburgh: Clark, 1971) IV, pt. I, ch. 1, sec. 7.

Chapter 4

SEXUAL BEHAVIOR:
ANOTHER POSITION

Janice Moulton

We can often distinguish behavior that is sexual from behavior that is not. Sexual intercourse may be one clear example of the former, but other sexual behaviors are not so clearly defined. Some kissing is sexual; some is not. Sometimes looking is sexual; sometimes *not* looking is sexual. Is it possible, then, to *characterize* sexual behavior?

Thomas Nagel in "Sexual Perversion"[1] and Robert Solomon in "Sexual Paradigms"[2] each offer an answer to this question. Nagel analyzes sexual desire as a "complex system of superimposed mutual perceptions" (13). He claims that sexual relations that do not fit his account are incomplete and, consequently, perversions.

Solomon claims that sexual behavior should be analyzed in terms of goals rather than feelings. He maintains that "the end of this desire is interpersonal communication" (23) and not enjoyment. According to Solomon, the sexual relations between regular partners will be inferior to novel encounters because there is less remaining to communicate sexually.

I believe that sexual behavior will not fit any single characterization; that there are at least two sorts of sexual behavior to characterize. Both Nagel and Solomon have interesting things to say about one sort of sexual behavior. However, both have assumed that a model of flirtation and

Reprinted, with the permission of Janice Moulton and the *Journal of Philosophy*, from *Journal of Philosophy* 73:16 (1976), pp. 537–46.

seduction constitutes an adequate model of sexual behavior in general. Although a characterization of flirtation and seduction can continue to apply to a relationship that is secret, forbidden, or in which there is some reason to remain unsure of one's sexual acceptability, I shall argue that most sexual behavior does not involve flirtation and seduction, and that what characterizes flirtation and seduction is not what characterizes the sexual behavior of regular partners. Nagel takes the development of what I shall call "sexual anticipation" to be characteristic of all sexual behavior and gives no account of sexual satisfaction.[3] Solomon believes that flirtation and seduction are different from regular sexual relationships. However, he too considers only characteristics of sexual anticipation in his analysis and concludes that regular sexual relationships are inferior to novel ones because they lack some of those characteristics.

Flirtation, seduction, and traditional courtship involve sexual feelings that are quite independent of physical contact. These feelings are increased by anticipation of success, winning, or conquest. Because what is anticipated is the opportunity for sexual intimacy and satisfaction, the feelings of sexual satisfaction are usually not distinguished from those of sexual anticipation. Sexual satisfaction involves sexual feelings which are increased by the other person's knowledge of one's preferences and sensitivities, the familiarity of their touch or smell or way of moving, and not by the novelty of their sexual interest.

It is easy to think that the more excitement and enthusiasm involved in the anticipation of an event, the more enjoyable and exciting the event itself is likely to be. However, anticipation and satisfaction are often divorced. Many experiences with no associated build-up of anticipation are very satisfying, and others, awaited and begun with great eagerness, produce no feelings of satisfaction at all. In sexual activity this dissociation is likely to be frequent. A strong feeling of sexual anticipation is produced by the uncertainty, challenge, or secrecy of novel sexual experiences, but the tension and excitement that increase anticipation often interfere with sexual satisfaction. The comfort and trust and experience with familiar partners may increase sexual satisfaction, but decrease the uncertainty and challenge that heighten sexual anticipation. Given the distinction between anticipation and satisfaction, there is no reason to believe that an increase of trust and love ought to increase feelings of sexual anticipation nor that sexual anticipation should be a prerequisite for any long-term sexual relationship.

For some people the processes that create sexual anticipation, the exchange of indirect signals, the awareness of the other person's sexual interest, and the accompanying sexual anticipation may be *all* that is valued in sexual behavior. Satisfaction is equated with release, the end of a good time, and is not considered a process in its own right. But although flirtation and seduction are the main objects of sexual fantasy and fiction, most people, even those whose sexual relations are frequently casual, seek to continue some sexual relationships after the flirtation and seduction are over, when the uncertainty and challenge are gone. And the motives, goals, and feelings of sexual satisfaction that characterize these continued sexual relations are not the same as the motives, goals, and feelings of sexual anticipation that characterize the novel sexual relations Nagel and Solomon have tried to analyze. Let us consider their accounts.

Nagel's account is illustrated by a tale of a Romeo and a Juliet who are sexually aroused by each other, notice each other's arousal and become further aroused by that:

> He senses that she senses that he senses her. This is still another level of arousal, for he becomes conscious of his sexuality through his awareness of its effect on her and of her awareness that this effect is due to him. Once she takes the same step and senses that he senses her sensing him, it becomes difficult to state, let alone imagine, further iterations, though they may be logically distinct. If both are alone, they will presumably turn to look at each other directly, and the proceedings will continue on another plane. Physical contact and intercourse are natural extensions of this complicated visual exchange, and mutual touch can involve all the complexities of awareness present in the visual case, but with a far greater range of subtlety and acuteness.
>
> Ordinarily, of course, things happen in a less orderly fashion—sometimes in a great rush—but I believe that some version of this overlapping system of distinct sexual perceptions and interactions is the basic framework of any full-fledged sexual relation and that relations involving only part of the complex are significantly incomplete. (14–15)

Nagel then characterizes sexual perversion as a "truncated or incomplete version" (16) of sexual *arousal,* rather than as some deviation from a standard of subsequent physical interaction.

Nagel's account applies only to the development of sexual anticipation. He says that "the proliferation of levels of mutual awareness . . . is [a type] of complexity that typifies human interactions" (15), so he might argue that his account will cover Romeo and Juliet's later relationship as well. Granted that levels of mutual awareness exist in any close human relationship. But it does not follow that the development of levels of awareness *characterize* all human relationships, particularly sexual relationships between familiar partners. In particular, the sort of awareness Nagel emphasizes—"a desire that one's partner be aroused by the recognition of one's desire that he or she be aroused" (15)—does not seem essential to regular sexual relationships. If we accept Nagel's account for sexual behavior in general, then we must classify as a perversion the behavior of an intimate and satisfying sexual relation begun without any preliminary exchange of multilevel arousals.[4]

Sexual desire can be generated by many different things—a smell, a phrase in a book, a familiar voice. The sexual interest of another person is only on occasion novel enough to be the main cause or focus of sexual arousal. A characterization of sexual behavior on other occasions should describe the development and sharing of sexual pleasure—the creation of sexual satisfaction. Nagel's contribution lies in directing our attention to the analysis of sexual behavior in terms of its perceptions and feelings. However, he characterizes only a limited sort of sexual behavior, flirtation and seduction.

Solomon characterizes sexual behavior by analogy with linguistic behavior, emphasizing that the goals are the same. He says:

> Sexual activity consists in speaking what we might call "body language." It has it own grammar, delineated by the body, and its own phonetics of touch and movement. Its unit of meaningfulness, the bodily equivalent of a sentence, is the *gesture*. . . . Body language is essentially expressive, and its content is limited to interpersonal attitudes and feelings. (27–28)

The analogy with language can be valuable for understanding sexual behavior. However, Solomon construes the goals of both activities too narrowly and hence draws the wrong conclusions.

He argues that the aim of sexual behavior is to communicate one's attitudes and feelings, to express oneself, and further, that such self-expression is made less effective by aiming at enjoyment:

> That is why the liberal mythology has been so disastrous, for it has rendered unconscious the expressive functions of sex in its stress on enjoyment. . . .
> It is thus understandable why sex is so utterly important in our lives, and why it is typically so unsatisfactory. (29)

Does stress on enjoyment hinder self-expression? Trying to do one thing, X, may interfere with trying to do another, Y, for some Xs and Ys. For example, trying to eat peanut butter or swim under water may interfere with vocal self-expression. But enjoyment is a different sort of goal. One isn't trying to do both Y and something else when aiming at Y and enjoyment, but to do one sort of thing, Y, a certain way. Far from interfering, one is more likely to be successful at a venture if one can manage to enjoy oneself during the process.

Solomon claims to refute that enjoyment is the essential aim of sexual activity, but he erroneously identifies enjoyment with orgasm:[5]

> No one would deny that sex is enjoyable, but it does not follow that sexuality is the activity of "pure enjoyment" and that "gratification," or "pure physical pleasure," that is, orgasm, is its end (26)

and consequently he shows merely that orgasm is not the only aim of sexual activity. His main argument is:

> If sex is pure physical enjoyment, why is sexual activity between persons far more satisfying than masturbation, where, if we accept recent physiological

studies, orgasm is at its highest intensity and the post-coital period is cleansed of its interpersonal hassles and arguments? (27)

One obvious answer is that, even for people who have hassles and arguments, interpersonal sexual activity is more enjoyable, even in the "pure physical" sense.[6] Solomon's argument does not show that enjoyment is not the appropriate aim of sexual activity, only that maximum-intensity orgasm is not. As those recent physiological studies pointed out, participants report interpersonal sexual activity as more enjoyable and satisfying even though their orgasms are less intense.[7] Only someone who mistakenly equated enjoyment with orgasm would find this paradoxical.

One need not claim that orgasm is always desired or desirable in sexual activity. That might be like supposing that in all conversations the participants do, or should, express their deepest thoughts. In sexual, as in linguistic, behavior, there is great variety and subtlety of purpose. But this is not to say that the desire for orgasm should be ignored. The disappointment and physical discomfort of expected but unachieved orgasm is only faintly parallel to the frustration of not being able to "get a word in edgewise" after being moved to express an important thought. It is usually rude or boorish to use language with indifference to the interests and cares of one's listeners. Sexual behavior with such indifference can be no better.

Solomon does not need these arguments to claim that enjoyment is not the only or the essential goal of sexual behavior. His comparison of sexual behavior with linguistic (or other social) behavior could have been used to do the job. The same social and moral distinctions and evaluations can be applied to both behaviors: hurting and humiliating people is bad; making people happy is good; loyalty, kindness, intelligence, and wit are valued; stupidity, clumsiness, and insincerity are not. The purpose of contact, sexual or otherwise, with other people is not just to produce or receive enjoyment—there are times of sadness, solace, and anguish that are important and meaningful to share, but not enjoyable.

Is self-expression, then, the essential goal of sexual behavior? Solomon lists a number of feelings and attitudes that can be expressed sexually:

- love, tenderness and trust, "being-with," mutual recognition

- hatred, indifference, jealousy, conflict

- shyness, fear, lack of confidence, embarrassment, shame

- domination, submissiveness, dependence, possessiveness, passivity

He claims "some attitudes, e.g., tenderness and trust, domination and passivity, are best expressed sexually" (28), and says his account

. . . makes it evident why Nagel chose as his example a couple of strangers; one has far more to say, for one can freely express one's fantasies as well as the truth, to a stranger. A husband and wife of seven years have probably been repeating the same messages for years, and their sexual activity now is probably no more than an abbreviated ritual incantation of the lengthy conversations they had years before. (28)

A glance at the list of feelings and attitudes above will show that its items are not independent. Shame, for example, may include components of embarrassment, lack of confidence, fear, and probably mutual recognition and submissiveness. To the extent that they can be conveyed by sexual body language,[8] a mere grunt or whimper would be able to express the whole range of the attitudes and feelings as well, if not better, than sexual gestures. Moreover, it is not clear that some attitudes are best expressed sexually. Tenderness and trust are often expressed between people who are not sexual partners. The tenderness and trust that may exist between an adult and a child is not best expressed sexually. Even if we take Solomon's claim to apply only to sexual partners, a joint checking account may be a better expression of trust than sexual activity. And domination, which in sado-masochistic sexual activity is expressed most elaborately with the cooperation of the partner, is an attitude much better expressed by nonsexual activities[9] such as beating an opponent, firing an employee, or mugging a passerby, where the domination is real, and does not require the cooperation of the other person. Even if some attitudes and feelings (for example, prurience, wantonness, lust) are best expressed sexually, it would be questionable whether the primary aim of sexual activity should be to express them.

The usual conversation of strangers is "small talk": cautious, shallow, and predictable because there has not been time for the participants to assess the extent and nature of common interests they share. So too with sexual behavior; first sexual encounters may be charged with novelty and anticipation, but are usually characterized by stereotypic physical interactions. If the physical interaction is seen as "body language," the analogy with linguistic behavior suggests that first encounters are likely to consist of sexual small talk.

Solomon's comparison of sexual behavior with linguistic behavior is handicapped by the limited view he has about their purposes. Language has more purposes than transmitting information. If all there were to sexual behavior was the development of the sexual anticipation prominent in flirtation and seduction, then Solomon's conclusions might be correct. The fact that people will continue sexual relations with the same partners even after the appropriate attitudes and feelings from Solomon's list have been expressed indicates that sexual behavior, like linguistic behavior, has other functions that are important. Solomon's analogy with linguistic behavior is valuable not because communication is the main goal of sexual behavior but because he directs attention to the social nature of sexual behavior. Solomon's analogy can be made to take on new importance by considering that sexual behavior not only transmits information about feelings and attitudes—something any activity can do—but also, like language, it has a *phatic* function to evoke feelings and attitudes.

Language is often used to produce a shared experience, a feeling of togetherness or unity. Duets, greetings, and many religious services use language with little information content to establish or reaffirm a relation among the participants. Long-term sexual relationships, like regular musical ensembles, may be valued more for the feelings produced than the feelings communicated. With both sexual and linguistic behavior, an interaction with a stranger might be an enjoyable novelty, but the pleasures of linguistic and sexual activity with good friends are probably much more frequent and more reliable.

Solomon's conclusion that sexually one should have more to "say" to a stranger and will find oneself "repeating the same messages for years" to old acquaintances,[10] violates the analogy. With natural language, one usually has more to say to old friends than to strangers.

Both Nagel and Solomon give incomplete accounts because they assume that a characterization of flirtation and seduction should apply to sexual behavior in general. I have argued that this is not so. Whether we analyze sexual behavior in terms of characteristic perceptions and feelings, as Nagel does, or by a comparison with other complex social behavior, as Solomon does, the characteristics of novel sexual encounters differ from those of sexual relationships between familiar and recognized partners.

What about the philosophical enterprise of characterizing sexual behavior? A characterization of something will tell what is unique about it and how to identify a standard or paradigm case of it. Criteria for a standard or paradigm case of sexual behavior unavoidably have normative implications. It is my position that normative judgments about sexual behavior should not be unrelated to the social and moral standards that apply to other social behavior. Many people, in reaction to old standards, avoid disapproving of sexual behavior that involves deceit or humiliation to another, but will condemn or ridicule sexual behavior that hurts no one yet fails to conform to a sexual standard. Both Nagel and Solomon classify sexual behavior that does not fit their characterizations as perversion, extending this strong negative judgment to behavior that is neither morally nor socially condemned (i.e., sex without multilevel awareness of arousal; sex without communication of attitudes and feelings). Yet perversion can be more accurately accounted for as whatever makes people frightened or uncomfortable by its bizarreness.[11]

Sexual behavior differs from other behavior by virtue of its unique feelings and emotions and its unique ability to create shared intimacy. These unique features of sexual behavior may influence particular normative judgments, but they do not justify applying *different* normative principles to sexual behavior.[12]

Notes

1. *The Journal of Philosophy* 66, No. 1 (1969), pp. 5–17. (In this volume, pp. 9–20. All references are to this volume.)

2. *The Journal of Philosophy* 71, No. 11 (1974), pp. 336–345. (In this volume, pp. 21–29. All references are to this volume.)

3. Satisfaction includes the good feelings of intimacy, warm friendship, the pleasure of being appreciated and of giving pleasure. 'Satisfaction' is not intended as a euphemism for orgasm, although the physical and social discomforts of the absence of orgasm often make a feeling of satisfaction impossible.

4. This was first pointed out to me by Sara Ketchum.

5. Solomon also claims that aiming at *orgasm* "overwhelms or distorts whatever else is being said sexually" (27). In this case there might be interference. However, if one is trying to express feelings and attitudes through the giving or having of an orgasm, then "aiming at self-expression" and "aiming at orgasm" will describe the same activity and there will be no interference. It should be pointed out that whatever else is being said sexually should have been said before orgasm is imminent or should be postponed because one will not do a very good job of transmitting or receiving any other communication during orgasm. Instead of an objection to aiming at orgasm, the potential interference raises an objection to aiming at self-expression during the time that orgasm is the goal.

6. Several theories of motivation in psychology (e.g., McClelland's) easily incorporate this fact: Creatures find moderate discrepancies from predicted sensation more pleasurable than sensations that are completely expected. Sensations produced by a sexual partner are not as adequately predicted as autoerotic stimulation.

7. William Masters and Virginia Johnson, *Human Sexual Response* (Boston: Little, Brown, 1966), p. 113.

8. More than gestures must be employed to communicate such feelings as love, trust, hatred, shame, dependence, and possessiveness. I doubt that jealousy or a distinction between "one's fantasies [and] the truth" (28) can be communicated by sexual body language at all.

9. In her comments on a relative of this paper at the 1976 Pacific Division APA meetings, Sara Ketchum pointed out that I have completely overlooked one sort of sexual activity in which the domination *is* real and the cooperation of the other person is not required: rape.

10. Repeated messages about one's feelings are not merely redundant; they convey new information: the continuation, renewal, or salience of those feelings.

11. See Mary Douglas, *Purity and Danger* (London: Routledge & Kegan Paul, 1966).

12. This paper has been greatly improved by the discussions and careful criticisms of G. M. Robinson and Helen Heise, the suggestions of Tim Binkley and Jay Rosenberg that it be expanded, and the comments from audiences of The Society for Women in Philosophy and the American Philosophical Association.

Chapter 5

PLAIN SEX

Alan Goldman

I

Several recent articles on sex herald its acceptance as a legitimate topic for analytic philosophers (although it has been a topic in philosophy since Plato). One might have thought conceptual analysis unnecessary in this area; despite the notorious struggles of judges and legislators to define pornography suitably, we all might be expected to know what sex is and to be able to identify at least paradigm sexual desires and activities without much difficulty. Philosophy is nevertheless of relevance here if for no other reason than that the concept of sex remains at the center of moral and social consciousness in our, and perhaps any, society. Before we can get a sensible view of the relation of sex to morality, perversion, social regulation, and marriage, we require a sensible analysis of the concept itself; one which neither understates its animal pleasure nor overstates its importance within a theory or system of value. I say "before," but the order is not quite so clear, for questions in this area, as elsewhere in moral philosophy, are both conceptual and normative at the same time. Our concept of sex will partially determine our moral view of it, but as philosophers we should formulate a concept that will accord with its proper moral status. What we require here, as elsewhere, is "reflective equilibrium," a goal not achieved by traditional

Goldman, Alan, "Plain Sex," *Philosophy and Public Affairs* 6:3 (1977), pp. 267–87. Copyright © 1977 by Princeton University Press. Reprinted by permission of Princeton University Press.

and recent analysis together with their moral implications. Because sexual activity, like other natural functions such as eating or exercising, has become imbedded in layers of cultural, moral, and superstitious superstructure, it is hard to conceive it in its simplest terms. But partially for this reason, it is only by thinking about plain sex that we can begin to achieve this conceptual equilibrium.

I shall suggest here that sex continues to be misrepresented in recent writings, at least in philosophical writings, and I shall criticize the predominant form of analysis which I term "means-end analysis." Such conceptions attribute a necessary external goal or purpose to sexual activity, whether it be reproduction, the expression of love, simple communication, or interpersonal awareness. They analyze sexual activity as a means to one of these ends, implying that sexual desire is a desire to reproduce, to love or be loved, or to communicate with others. All definitions of this type suggest false views of the relation of sex to perversion and morality by implying that sex which does not fit one of these models or fulfill one of these functions is in some way deviant or incomplete.

The alternative, simpler analysis with which I will begin is that sexual desire is desire for contact with another person's body and for the pleasure which such contact produces; sexual activity is activity which tends to fulfill such desire of the agent. Whereas Aristotle and Butler were correct in holding that pleasure is normally a byproduct rather than a goal of purposeful action, in the case of sex this is not so clear. The desire for another's body is, principally among other things, the desire for the pleasure that physical contact brings. On the other hand, it is not a desire for a particular sensation detachable from its causal context, a sensation which can be derived in other ways. This definition in terms of the general goal of sexual desire appears preferable to an attempt to more explicitly list or define specific sexual activities, for many activities such as kissing, embracing, massaging, or holding hands may or may not be sexual, depending upon the context and more specifically upon the purposes, needs, or desires into which such activities fit. The generality of the definition also represents a refusal (common in recent psychological texts) to overemphasize orgasm as the goal of sexual desire or genital sex as the only norm of sexual activity (this will be hedged slightly in the discussion of perversion below).

Central to the definition is the fact that the goal of sexual desire and activity is the physical contact itself, rather than something else which this contact might express. By contrast, what I term "means-end analyses" posit ends which I take to be extraneous to plain sex, and they view sex as a means to these ends. Their fault lies not in defining sex in terms of its general goal, but in seeing plain sex as merely a means to other separable ends. I term these "means-end analyses" for convenience, although "means-separable-end analysis," while too cumbersome, might be more fully explanatory. The desire for physical contact with another person is a minimal criterion for (normal) sexual desire, but is both necessary and sufficient to qualify normal desire as sexual. Of course, we may want to express other feelings through sexual acts in various contexts; but without the desire for the physical contact in and for itself, or when it is sought for other reasons, activities in which contact is involved are not predominantly sexual. Furthermore, the desire for physical contact in itself, without the wish to express affection or other feelings through it, is sufficient to render sexual the activity of the agent which fulfills it. Various activities with this goal alone, such as kissing and caressing in certain contexts, qualify as sexual even without the presence of genital symptoms of sexual excitement. The latter are not therefore necessary criteria for sexual activity.

This initial analysis may seem to some either over- or underinclusive. It might seem too broad in leading us to interpret physical contact as sexual desire in activities such as football and other contact sports. In these cases, however, the desire is not for contact with another body per se, it is not directed toward a particular person for that purpose, and it is not the goal of the activity—the goal is winning or exercising or knocking someone down or displaying one's prowess. If the desire is purely for contact with another specific person's body, then to interpret it as sexual does not seem an exaggeration. A slightly more difficult case is that of a baby's desire to be cuddled and our natural response in wanting to cuddle it. In the case of the baby, the desire may be simply for the physical contact, for the pleasure of the caresses. If so, we may characterize this desire, especially in keeping with Freudian theory, as sexual or protosexual. It will differ nevertheless from full-fledged sexual desire in being more amorphous, not directed outward toward another specific person's body. It may also be that what the infant unconsciously desires is not physical contact per se but signs of affection, tenderness, or security, in which case we have further reason for hesitating to characterize its wants as clearly sexual. The intent of our response to the baby is often the showing of affection, not the pure physical contact, so that our definition in terms of action which fulfills sexual desire *on the part of the agent* does not capture such actions, whatever we say of the baby. (If it is intuitive to characterize our responses as sexual as well, there is clearly no problem here for my analysis.) The same can be said of signs of affection (or in some cultures polite greeting) among men or women: these certainly need not be homosexual when the intent is only to show friendship, something extrinsic to plain sex although valuable when added to it.

Our definition of sex in terms of the desire for physical contact may appear too narrow in that a person's personality, not merely her or his body, may be sexually attractive to another, and in that looking or conversing in a certain way can be sexual in a given context without bodily contact. Nevertheless, it is not the contents of one's thoughts per se that are sexually appealing, but one's personality as embodied in certain manners of behavior. Furthermore, if a person is sexually attracted by another's personality, he or she will desire not just further conversation, but actual sexual contact. While looking at or conversing with someone can be interpreted as sexual in given contexts it is so when intended as preliminary to, and hence parasitic upon, elemental sexual interest. Voyeurism or viewing a pornographic movie qualifies as a sexual activity, but only as an imaginative substitute for the real thing (otherwise a deviation from the norm as expressed in our definition). The same is true of masturbation as a sexual activity without a partner.

That the initial definition indicates at least an ingredient of sexual desire and activity is too obvious to argue. We all know what sex is, at least in obvious cases, and do not need philosophers to tell us. My preliminary analysis is meant to serve as a contrast to what sex is not, at least not necessarily. I concentrate upon the physically manifested desire for another's body, and I take as central the immersion in the physical aspect of one's own existence and attention to the physical embodiment of the other. One may derive pleasure in a sex act from expressing certain feelings to one's partner or from awareness of the attitude of one's partner, but sexual desire is essentially desire for physical contact itself: it is a bodily desire for the body of another that dominates our mental life for more or less brief periods. Traditional writings were correct to emphasize the purely physical or animal aspect of sex; they were wrong only in condemning it. This characterization of sex as an intensely pleasurable physical activity and acute physical desire may seem to some to capture only its barest level. But it is worth distinguishing and focusing upon this least common denominator in order to avoid the false views of sexual morality and perversion which emerge from thinking that sex is essentially something else.

II

We may turn then to what sex is not, to the arguments regarding supposed conceptual connections between sex and other activities which it is necessary to conceptually distinguish. The most comprehensible attempt to build an extraneous purpose into the sex act identifies that purpose as reproduction, its primary biological function. While this may be "nature's" purpose, it certainly need not be ours (the analogy with eating, while sometimes overworked, is pertinent here). While this identification may once have had a rational basis which also grounded the identification of the value and morality of sex with that applicable to reproduction and childrearing, the development of contraception rendered the connection weak. Methods of contraception are by now so familiar and so widely used that it is not necessary to dwell upon the changes wrought by these developments in the concept of sex itself and in a rational sexual ethic dependent upon that concept. In the past, the ever present possibility of children rendered the concepts of sex and sexual morality different from those required at present. There may be good reasons, if the presence and care of both mother and father are beneficial to children, for restricting reproduction to marriage. Insofar as society has a legitimate role in protecting children's interests, it may be justified in giving marriage a legal status, although this question is complicated by the fact (among others) that children born to single mothers deserve no penalties. In any case, the point here is simply that these questions are irrelevant at the present time to those regarding the morality of sex and its potential social regulation. (Further connections with marriage will be discussed below.)

It is obvious that the desire for sex is not necessarily a desire to reproduce, that the psychological manifestation has become, if it were not always, distinct from its biological roots. There are many parallels, as previously mentioned, with other natural functions. The pleasures of eating and exercising are to a large extent independent of their roles in nourishment or health (as the junk-food industry discovered with a vengeance). Despite the obvious parallel with sex, there is still a tendency for many to think that sex acts which can be reproductive are, if not more moral or less immoral, at least more natural. These categories of morality and "naturalness," or normality, are not to be identified with each other, as will be argued below, and neither is applicable to sex by virtue of its connection to reproduction. The tendency to identify reproduction as the conceptually connected end of sex is most prevalent now in the pronouncements of the Catholic church. There the assumed analysis is clearly tied to a restrictive sexual morality according to which acts become immoral and unnatural when they are not oriented towards reproduction, a morality which has independent roots in the Christian sexual ethic as it derives from Paul. However, the means-end analysis fails to generate a consistent sexual ethic: homosexual and oral-genital sex is condemned while kissing or caressing, acts equally unlikely to lead in themselves to fertilization, even when properly characterized as sexual according to our definition, are not.

III

Before discussing further relations of means-end analyses to false or inconsistent sexual ethics and concepts of perversion, I turn to other examples of these analyses. One common position views sex as essentially an expression of love or affection between the partners. It is generally recognized that there are other types of love besides sexual, but sex itself is taken as an expression of one type, sometimes termed "romantic" love.[1] Various factors again ought to weaken this identification. First, there are other types of love besides that which it is appropriate to express sexually, and "romantic" love itself can be expressed in many other ways. I am not denying that sex can take on heightened value and meaning when it becomes a vehicle for the expression of feelings of love or tenderness, but so can many other usually mundane activities such as getting up early to make breakfast on Sunday, cleaning the house, and so on. Second, sex itself can be used to communicate many other emotions besides love, and, as I will argue below, can communicate nothing in particular and still be good sex.

On a deeper level, an internal tension is bound to result from an identification of sex, which I have described as a physical-psychological desire, with love as a long-term, deep emotional relationship between two individuals. As this type of relationship, love is permanent, at least in intent, and more or less exclusive. A normal person cannot deeply love more than a few individuals even in a lifetime. We may be suspicious that those who attempt or claim to love many love them weakly if at all. Yet, fleeting sexual desire can arise in relation to a variety of other individuals one finds sexually attractive. It may even be, as some have claimed, that sexual desire in humans naturally seeks variety, while this is obviously false of love. For this reason, monogamous sex, even if justified, almost always represents a sacrifice or the exercise of self-control on the part of the spouses, while monogamous love generally does not. There is no such thing as casual love in the sense in which I intend the term "love." It may occasionally happen that a spouse falls deeply in love with someone else (especially when sex is conceived in terms of love), but this is relatively rare in comparison to passing sexual desires for others; and while the former often indicates a weakness or fault in the marriage relation, the latter does not.

If love is indeed more exclusive in its objects than is sexual desire, this explains why those who view sex as essentially an expression of love would again tend to hold a repressive or restrictive sexual ethic. As in the case of reproduction, there may be good reasons for reserving the total commitment of deep love to the context of marriage and family—the normal personality may not withstand additional divisions of ultimate commitment and allegiance. There is no question that marriage itself is best sustained by a deep relation of love and affection; and even if love is not naturally monogamous, the benefits of family units to children provide additional reason to avoid serious commitments elsewhere which weaken family ties. It can be argued similarly that monogamous sex strengthens families by restricting and at the same time guaranteeing an outlet for sexual desire in marriage. But there is more force to the argument that recognition of a clear distinction between sex and love in society would help avoid disastrous marriages which result from adolescent confusion of the two when sexual desire is mistaken for permanent love, and would weaken damaging jealousies which arise in marriages in relation to passing sexual desires. The love and affection of a sound marriage certainly differs from the adolescent romantic variety, which is often a mere substitute for sex in the context of a repressive sexual ethic.

In fact, the restrictive sexual ethic tied to the means-end analysis in terms of love again has failed to be consistent. At least, it has not been applied consistently, but forms part of the double standard which has curtailed the freedom of women. It is predictable in light of this history that some women would now advocate using sex as another kind of means, as a political weapon or as a way to increase unjustly denied power and freedom. The inconsistency in the sexual ethic typically attached to the sex-love analysis, according to which it has generally been taken with a grain of salt when applied to men, is simply another example of the impossibility of tailoring a plausible moral theory in this area to a conception of sex which builds in conceptually extraneous factors.

I am not suggesting here that sex ought never to be connected with love or that it is not a more significant and valuable activity when it is. Nor am I denying that individuals need love as much as sex and perhaps emotionally need at least one complete relationship which encompasses both. Just as sex can express love and take on heightened significance when it does, so love is often naturally accompanied by an intermittent desire for sex. But again love is accompanied appropriately by desires for other shared activities as well. What makes the desire for sex seem more intimately connected with love is the intimacy which is seen to be a natural feature of mutual sex acts. Like love, sex is held to lay one bare psychologically as well as physically. Sex is unquestionably intimate, but beyond that the psychological toll often attached may be a function of the restrictive sexual ethic itself, rather than a legitimate apology for it. The intimacy involved in love is psychologically consuming in a generally healthy way, while the psychological tolls of sexual relations, often including embarrassment as a correlate of intimacy, are too often the result of artificial sexual ethics and taboos. The intimacy involved in both love and sex is insufficient in any case in light of previous points to render a means-end analysis in these terms appropriate.

IV

In recent articles, Thomas Nagel and Robert Solomon, who recognize that sex is not merely a means to communicate love, nevertheless retain the form of this analysis while broadening it. For Solomon, sex remains a means of communicating (he explicitly uses the metaphor of body language), although the feelings that can be communicated now include, in addition to love and tenderness, domination, dependence, anger, trust, and so on.[2] Nagel does not refer explicitly to communication, but his analysis is similar in that he views sex as a complex form of interpersonal awareness in which desire itself is consciously communicated on several different levels. In sex, according to his analysis, two people are aroused by each other, aware of the other's arousal, and further aroused by this awareness.[3] Such multileveled conscious awareness of one's own and the other's desire is taken as the norm of a sexual relation, and this model is therefore close to that which views sex as a means of interpersonal communication.

Solomon's analysis is beset by the same difficulties as those pointed out in relation to the narrower sex-love concept. Just as love can be communicated by many activities other than sex, which do not therefore become properly analyzed as essentially vehicles of communication (making breakfast, cleaning the house, and so on), the same is true of the other feelings mentioned by Solomon. Domination can be communicated through economic manipulation, trust by a joint savings account. Driving a car can be simultaneously expressing anger, pride, joy, and so on. We may, in fact, communicate or express feelings in anything we do, but this does not make everything we do into language. Driving a car is not to be defined as an automotive means of communication, although with a little ingenuity we might work out an automotive vocabulary (tailgating as an expression of aggression or impatience; beating another car away from a stoplight as expressing domination) to match the vocabulary of "body language." That one can communicate various feelings during sex acts does not make these acts merely or primarily a means of communicating.

More importantly, to analyze sex as a means of communication is to overlook the intrinsic nature and value of the act itself. Sex is not a gesture or series of gestures, in fact not necessarily a means to any other end, but a physical activity intensely pleasurable in itself. When a language is used, the symbols normally have no importance in themselves; they function merely as vehicles for what can be communicated by them. Furthermore skill in the use of language is a technical achievement that must be carefully learned; if better sex is more successful communication by means of a more skillful use of body language, then we had all better be well schooled in the vocabulary and grammar. Solomon's analysis, which uses the language metaphor, suggests the appropriateness of a sex-manual approach, the substitution of a bit of technological prowess for the natural pleasure of the unforced surrender to feeling and desire.

It may be that Solomon's position could be improved by using the analogy of music rather than that of language, as an aesthetic form of communication. Music might be thought of as a form of aesthetic communicating, in which the experience of the "phonemes" themselves is generally pleasing. And listening to music is perhaps more of a sexual experience than having someone talk to you. Yet, it seems to me that insofar as music is aesthetic and pleasing in itself, it is not best conceived as primarily a means for communicating specific feelings. Such an analysis does injustice to aesthetic experience in much the same way as the sex-communication analysis debases sexual experience itself.[4]

For Solomon, sex that is not a totally self-conscious communicative act tends toward vulgarity,[5] whereas I would have thought it the other way around. This is another illustration of the tendency of means-end analyses to condemn what appears perfectly natural or normal sex on my account. Both Solomon and Nagel use their definitions, however, not primarily to stipulate moral norms for sex, as we saw in earlier analyses, but to define norms against which to measure perversion. Once again, neither is capable of generating consistency or reflective equilibrium with our firm intuitions as to what counts as subnormal sex, the problem being that both build factors into their norms which are extraneous to an unromanticized view of normal sexual desire and activity. If perversion represents a breakdown in communication, as Solomon maintains, then any unsuccessful or misunderstood advance should count as perverted. Furthermore, sex between husband and wife married for several years, or between any partners already familiar with each other, would be, if not perverted, nevertheless subnormal or trite and dull, in that the communicative content would be minimal in lacking all novelty. In fact the pleasures of sex need not wear off with familiarity, as they would if dependent upon the communicative content of the feelings. Finally, rather than a release or relief from physical desire through a substitute imaginative outlet, masturbation would become a way of practicing or rehearsing one's technique or vocabulary on oneself, or simply a way of talking to oneself, as Solomon himself says.[6]

Nagel fares no better in the implications of his overintellectualized norm. Spontaneous and heated sex between two familiar partners may well lack the complex conscious multileveled interpersonal awareness of which he speaks without being in the least perverted. The egotistical desire that one's partner be aroused by one's own desire does not seem a primary element of the sexual urge, and during sex acts one may like one's partner to be sometimes active and aroused, sometimes more passive. Just as sex can be more significant when love is communicated, so it can sometimes be heightened by an awareness of the other's desire. But at other times this awareness of an avid desire of one's partner can be merely distracting. The conscious awareness to which Nagel refers may actually impede the immersion in the physical of which I spoke above, just as may concentration upon one's "vocabulary" or technique.

Sex is a way of relating to another, but primarily a physical rather than intellectual way. For Nagel, the ultimate in degeneration or perversion would have to be what he calls "mutual epidermal stimulation"[7] without mutual awareness of each other's state of mind. But this sounds like normal, if not ideal, sex to me (perhaps only a minimal description of it). His model certainly seems more appropriate to a sophisticated seduction scene than to the sex act itself,[8] which according to the model would often have to count as a subnormal anticlimax to the intellectual foreplay. While Nagel's account resembles Solomon's means-end analysis of sex, here the sex act itself does not even qualify as a preferred or central means to the end of interpersonal communication.

V

I have now criticized various types of analysis sharing or suggesting a common means-end form. I have suggested that analyses of this form relate to attempts to limit moral or natural sex to that which fulfills some purpose or function extraneous to basic sexual desire. The attempts to brand forms of sex outside the idealized models as immoral or perverted fail to achieve consistency with intuitions that they themselves do not directly question. The reproductive model brands oral-genital sex a deviation, but cannot account for kissing or holding hands; the communication account holds voyeurism to be perverted but cannot accommodate sex acts without much conscious thought or seductive nonphysical foreplay; the sex-love model makes most sexual desire seem degrading or base. The first and last condemn extra-marital sex on the sound but irrelevant grounds that reproduction and deep commitment are best confined to family contexts. The romanticization of sex and the confusion of sexual desire with love operate in both directions: sex outside the context of romantic love is repressed; once it is repressed, partners become more difficult to find and sex becomes romanticized further, out of proportion to its real value for the individual.

What all these analyses share in addition to a common form is accordance with and perhaps derivation from the Platonic-Christian moral tradition, according to which the animal or purely physical element of humans is the source of immorality, and plain sex in the sense I defined it is an expression of this element, hence in itself to be condemned. All the analyses examined seem to seek a distance from sexual desire itself in attempting to extend it conceptually beyond the physical. The love and communication analyses seek refinement or intellectualization of the desire; plain physical sex becomes vulgar, and too straightforward sexual encounters without an aura of respectable cerebral communicative content are to be avoided. Solomon explicitly argues that sex cannot be a "mere" appetite, his argument being that if it were, subway exhibitionism and other vulgar forms would be pleasing.[9] This fails to recognize that sexual desire can be focused or selective at the same time as being physical. Lower animals are not attracted by every other member of their species, either. Rancid food forced down one's throat is not pleasing, but that certainly fails to show that hunger is not a physical appetite. Sexual desire lets us know that we are physical beings and, indeed, animals; this is why traditional Platonic morality is so thorough in its condemnation. Means-end analyses continue to reflect this tradition, sometimes unwittingly. They show that in conceptualizing sex it is still difficult, despite years of so-called revolution in this area, to free ourselves from the lingering suspicion that plain sex as physical desire is an expression of our "lower selves," that yielding to our animal natures is subhuman or vulgar.

VI

Having criticized these analyses for the sexual ethics and concepts of perversion they imply, it remains to contrast my account along these lines. To the question of what morality might be implied by my analysis, the answer is that there are no moral implications whatever. Any analysis of sex which imputes a moral character to sex acts in themselves is wrong for that reason. There is no morality intrinsic to sex, although general moral rules apply to the treatment of others in sex acts as they apply to all human relations. We can speak of a sexual ethic as we can speak of a business ethic, without implying that business in itself is either moral or immoral or that special rules are required to judge business practices which are not derived from rules that apply elsewhere as well. Sex is not in itself a moral category, although like business it invariably places us into relations with others in which moral rules apply. It gives us opportunity to do what is otherwise recognized as wrong, to harm others, deceive them or manipulate them against their wills. Just as the fact that an act is sexual in itself never renders it wrong or adds to its wrongness if it is wrong on other grounds (sexual acts towards minors are wrong on other grounds, as will be argued below), so no wrong act is to be excused because done from a sexual motive. If a "crime of passion" is to be excused, it would have to be on grounds of temporary insanity rather than sexual context (whether insanity does constitute a legitimate excuse for certain actions is too big a topic to argue here). Sexual motives are among others which may become deranged, and the fact that they are sexual has no bearing in itself on the moral character, whether negative or exculpatory, of the actions deriving from them. Whatever might be true of war, it is certainly not the case that all's fair in love or sex.

Our first conclusion regarding morality and sex is therefore that no conduct otherwise immoral should be excused because it is sexual conduct, and nothing in sex is immoral unless condemned by rules which apply elsewhere as well. The last clause requires further clarification. Sexual conduct can be governed by particular rules relating only to sex itself. But these precepts must be implied by general moral rules when these are applied to specific sexual relations or types of conduct. The same is true of rules of fair business, ethical medicine, or courtesy in driving a car. In the latter case, particular acts on the road may be reprehensible, such as tailgating or passing on the right, which seem to bear no resemblance as actions to any outside the context of highway safety. Nevertheless their immorality derives from the fact that they place others in danger, a circumstance which, when avoidable, is to be condemned in any context. This structure of general and specifically applicable rules describes a reasonable sexual ethic as well. To take an extreme case, rape is always a sexual act and it is always immoral. A rule against rape can therefore be considered an obvious part of sexual morality which has no bearing on nonsexual conduct. But the immorality of rape derives from its being an extreme violation of a person's body, of the right not to be humiliated, and of the general moral prohibition against using other persons against their wills, not from the fact that it is a sexual act.

The application elsewhere of general moral rules to sexual conduct is further complicated by the fact that it will be relative to the particular desires and preferences of one's partner (these may be influenced by and hence in some sense include misguided beliefs about sexual morality itself). This means that there will be fewer specific rules in the area of sexual ethics than in other areas of conduct, such as driving cars, where the relativity of preference is irrelevant to the prohibition of objectively dangerous conduct. More reliance will have to be placed upon the general moral rule, which in this area holds simply that the preferences, desires, and interests of one's partner or potential partner ought to be taken into account. This rule is certainly not specifically formulated to govern sexual relations; it is a form of the central principle of morality itself. But when applied to sex, it prohibits certain actions, such as molestation of children, which cannot be categorized as violations of the rule without at the same time being classified as sexual. I believe this last case is the closest we can come to an action which is wrong *because* it is sexual, but even here its wrongness is better characterized as deriving from the detrimental effects such behavior can have on the future emotional and sexual life of the naive victims, and from the fact that such behavior therefore involves manipulation of innocent persons without regard for their interests. Hence, this case also involves violation of a general moral rule which applies elsewhere as well.

Aside from faulty conceptual analyses of sex and the influence of the Platonic moral tradition, there are two more plausible reasons for thinking that there are moral dimensions intrinsic to sex acts per se. The first is that such acts are normally intensely pleasurable. According to a hedonistic, utilitarian moral theory they therefore should be at least prima facie morally right, rather than morally neutral in themselves. To me this seems incorrect and reflects unfavorably on the ethical theory in question. The pleasure intrinsic to sex acts is a good, but not, it seems to me, a good with much positive moral significance. Certainly I can have no duty to pursue such pleasure myself, and while it may be nice to give pleasure of any form to others, there is no ethical requirement to do so, given my right over my own body. The exception relates to the context of sex acts themselves, when one partner derives pleasure from the other and ought to return the favor. This duty to reciprocate takes us out of the domain of hedonistic utilitarianism, however, and into a Kantian moral framework, the central principles of which call for such reciprocity in human relations. Since independent moral judgments regarding sexual activities constitute one area in which ethical theories are to be tested, these observations indicate here, as I believe others indicate elsewhere, the fertility of the Kantian, as opposed to the utilitarian, principle in reconstructing reasoned moral consciousness.

It may appear from this alternative Kantian viewpoint that sexual acts must be at least prima facie wrong in themselves. This is because they invariably involve at different stages the manipulation of one's partner for one's own pleasure, which might appear to be prohibited on the formulation of Kant's principle which holds that one ought not to treat another as a means to such private ends. A more realistic rendering of this formulation, however, one which recognizes its intended equivalence to the first universalizability principle, admits no such absolute prohibition. Many human relations, most economic transactions for example, involve using other individuals for personal benefit. These relations are immoral only when they are one-sided, when the benefits are not mutual, or when the transactions are not freely and rationally endorsed by all parties. The same holds true of sexual acts. The central principle governing them is the Kantian demand for reciprocity in sexual relations. In order to comply with the second formulation of the categorical imperative, one must recognize the subjectivity of one's partner (not merely by being aroused by her or his desire, as Nagel describes). Even in an act which by its nature "objectifies" the other, one recognizes a partner as a subject with demands and desires by yielding to those desires, by allowing oneself to be a sexual object as well, by giving pleasure or ensuring that the pleasures of the acts are mutual. It is this kind of reciprocity which forms the basis for morality in sex, which distinguishes right acts from wrong in this area as in others. (Of course, prior to sex acts one must gauge their effects upon potential partners and take these longer range interests into account.)

VII

I suggested earlier that in addition to generating confusion regarding the rightness or wrongness of sex acts, false conceptual analyses of the means-end form cause confusion about the value of sex to the individual. My account recognizes the satisfaction of desire and the pleasure this brings as the central psychological function of the sex act for the individual. Sex affords us a paradigm of pleasure, but not a cornerstone of value. For most of us it is not only a needed outlet for desire but also the most enjoyable form of recreation we know. Its value is nevertheless easily mistaken by being confused with that of love, when it is taken as essentially an expression of that emotion. Although intense, the pleasures of sex are brief and repetitive rather than cumulative. They give value to the specific acts which generate them, but not the lasting kind of value which enhances one's whole life. The briefness of the pleasures contributes to their intensity (or perhaps their intensity makes them necessarily brief), but it also relegates them to the periphery of most rational plans for the good life.

By contrast, love typically develops over a long term relation; while its pleasures may be less intense and physical, they are of more cumulative value. The importance of love to the individual may well be central in a rational system of value. And it has perhaps an even deeper moral significance relating to the identification with the interests of another person, which broadens one's possible relationships with others as well. Marriage is again important in preserving this relation between adults and children, which seems as important to the adults as it is to the children in broadening concerns which have a tendency to become selfish. Sexual desire, by contrast, is desire for another which is nevertheless essentially self-regarding. Sexual pleasure is certainly a good for the individual, and for many it may be necessary in order for them to function in a reasonably cheerful way. But it bears little relation to those other values just discussed, to which some analyses falsely suggest a conceptual connection.

VIII

While my initial analysis lacks moral implications in itself, as it should, it does suggest by contrast a concept of sexual perversion. Since the concept of perversion is itself a sexual concept, it will always be defined relative to some definition of normal sex; and any conception of the norm will imply a contrary notion of perverse forms. The concept suggested by my account again differs sharply from those implied by the means-end analyses examined above. Perversion does not represent a deviation from the reproductive function (or kissing would be perverted), from a loving relationship (or most sexual desire and many heterosexual acts would be perverted), or from efficiency in communicating (or unsuccessful seduction attempts would be perverted). It is a deviation from a norm, but the norm in question is merely statistical. Of course, not all sexual acts that are statistically unusual are perverted—a three-hour continuous sexual act would be unusual but not necessarily abnormal in the requisite sense. The abnormality in question must relate to the *form of the desire* itself in order to constitute sexual perversion; for example, desire, not for contact with another, but for merely looking, for harming or being harmed, for contact with items of clothing. The concept of sexual abnormality is that suggested by my definition of normal sex in terms of its typical desire. However, not all unusual desires qualify either, only those with the typical physical sexual effects upon the individual who satisfies them. These effects, such as erection in males, were not built into the original definition of sex in terms of sexual desire, for they do not always occur in activities that are properly characterized as sexual, say, kissing for the pleasure of it. But they do seem to bear a closer relation to the definition of activities as perverted. (For those who consider only genital sex sexual, we could build such symptoms into a narrower definition, then speaking of sex in a broad sense as well as "proper" sex.)

Solomon and Nagel disagree with this statistical notion of perversion. For them the concept is evaluative rather than statistical. I do not deny that the term "perverted" is often used evaluatively (and purely emotively for that matter), or that it has a negative connotation for the average speaker. I do deny that we can find a norm, other than that of statistically usual desire, against which all and only activities that properly count as sexual perversions can be contrasted. Perverted sex is simply abnormal sex, and if the norm is not to be an idealized or romanticized extraneous end or purpose, it must express the way human sexual desires usually manifest themselves. Of course not all norms in other areas of discourse need be statistical in this way. Physical health is an example of a relatively clear norm which does not seem to depend upon the numbers of healthy people. But the concept in this case achieves its clarity through the connection of physical health with other clearly desirable physical functions and characteristics, for example, living longer. In the case of sex, that which is statistically abnormal is not necessarily incapacitating in other ways, and yet these abnormal desires with sexual effects upon their subject do count as perverted to the degree to which their objects deviate from usual ones. The connotations of the concept of perversion beyond those connected with abnormality or statistical deviation derive more from the attitudes of those likely to call certain acts perverted than from specifiable features of the acts themselves. These connotations add to the concept of abnormality that of *sub*-normality, but there is no norm against which the latter can be measured intelligibly in accord with all and only acts intuitively called perverted.

The only proper evaluative norms relating to sex involve degrees of pleasure in the acts and moral norms, but neither of these scales coincides with statistical degrees of abnormality, according to which perversion is to be measured. The three parameters operate independently (this was implied for the first two when it was held above that the pleasure of sex is a good, but not necessarily a moral good). Perverted sex may be more or less enjoyable to particular individuals than normal sex, and more or less moral, depending upon the particular relations involved. Raping a sheep may be more perverted than raping a woman, but certainly not more condemnable morally.[10] It is nevertheless true that the evaluative connotations attaching to the term "perverted" derive partly from the fact that most people consider perverted sex highly immoral. Many such acts are forbidden by long standing taboos, and it is sometimes difficult to distinguish what is forbidden from what is immoral. Others, such as sadistic acts, are genuinely immoral, but again not at all because of their connection with sex or abnormality. The principles which condemn these acts would condemn them equally if they were common and nonsexual. It is not true that we properly could continue to consider acts perverted which were found to be very common practice across societies. Such acts, if harmful, might continue to be condemned properly as immoral, but it was just shown that the immorality of an act does not vary with its degree of perversion. If not harmful, common acts previously considered abnormal might continue to be called perverted for a time by the moralistic minority; but the term when applied to such cases would retain only its emotive negative connotation without consistent logical criteria for application. It would represent merely prejudiced moral judgments.

To adequately explain why there is a tendency to so deeply condemn perverted acts would require a treatise in psychology beyond the scope of this paper. Part of the reason undoubtedly relates to the tradition of repressive sexual ethics and false conceptions of sex; another part to the fact that all abnormality seems to disturb and fascinate us at the same time. The former explains why sexual perversion is more abhorrent to many than other forms of abnormality; the latter indicates why we tend to have an emotive and evaluative reaction to perversion in the first place. It may be, as has been suggested according to a Freudian line,[11] that our uneasiness derives from latent desires we are loathe to admit, but this thesis takes us into psychological issues I am not competent to judge. Whatever the psychological explanation, it suffices to point out here that the conceptual connection between perversion and genuine or consistent moral evaluation is spurious and again suggested by misleading means-end idealizations of the concept of sex.

The position I have taken in this paper against those concepts is not totally new. Something similar to it is found in Freud's view of sex, which of course was genuinely revolutionary, and in the body of writings deriving from Freud to the present time. But in his revolt against romanticized and repressive conceptions, Freud went too far—from a refusal to view sex as merely a means to a view of it as the end of all human behavior, although sometimes an elaborately disguised end. This pansexualism led to the thesis (among others) that repression was indeed an inevitable and necessary part of social regulation of any form, a strange consequence of a position that began by opposing the repressive aspects of the means-end view. Perhaps the time finally has arrived when we can achieve a reasonable middle ground in this area, at least in philosophy if not in society.

Notes

1. Even Bertrand Russell, whose writing in this area was a model of rationality, at least for its period, tends to make this identification and to condemn plain sex in the absence of love: "sex intercourse apart from love has little value, and is to be regarded primarily as experimentation with a view to love." *Marriage and Morals* (New York: Bantam, 1959), p. 87.

2. Robert Solomon, "Sex and Perversion," *Philosophy and Sex*, ed. R. Baker and F. Elliston (Buffalo: Prometheus, 1975).

3. Thomas Nagel, "Sexual Perversion," *The Journal of Philosophy* 66, No. 1 (1960), pp. 5–17. (This volume, pp. 9–20.)

4. Sex might be considered (at least partially) as communication in a very broad sense in the same way as performing ensemble music, in the sense that there is in both ideally a communion or perfectly shared experience with another. This is, however, one possible ideal view whose central feature is not necessary to sexual acts or desire per se. And in emphasizing the communication of specific feelings by means of body language, the analysis under consideration narrows the end to one clearly extrinsic to plain and even good sex.

5. Solomon, pp. 284–285.

6. *Ibid.*, p. 283. One is reminded of Woody Allen's rejoinder to praise of his technique: "I practice a lot when I'm alone."

7. Nagel, p. 15. [This passage is not in the version of Nagel's essay reprinted above.]

8. Janice Moulton made the same point in a paper at the Pacific APA meeting, March 1976. (This volume, pp. 31–38.)

9. Solomon, p. 285.

10. The example is like one from Sara Ruddick, "Better Sex," *Philosophy and Sex*, p. 96.

11. See Michael Slote, "Inapplicable Concepts and Sexual Perversion," *Philosophy and Sex*.

Chapter 6

SEX AND SEXUAL PERVERSION

Robert Gray

Sara Ruddick has suggested, what seems probable, that intrinsic to the notion of perversion is that of unnaturalness.[1] That and only that sexual activity which is unnatural is perverted. There are, of course, difficulties with the notion of naturalness itself. 'Natural' may be used synonymously with 'usual' or 'ordinary', in which case perversion would appear to be entirely culturally relative. (We should have, perhaps, to except such things as adultery, which seem to be common to virtually all human societies.) On the other hand, 'natural' may be used to describe particular activities as the outcomes of naturally occurring processes. Ignoring the circularity in this, such a definition would have as a consequence that all perversions are natural, since the fetishes of the coprophiliac are as much the outcome of his natural desires and propensities as those of the "normal" heterosexual. Even if it were argued that there has been some sort of breakdown in the control mechanisms governing the behavior of the coprophiliac, still that breakdown itself could be accounted for ultimately only by an appeal to naturally occurring events, in this case, perhaps, biological laws. There is, however, a sense of 'natural' which may allow an argument such as Ruddick's to get off the ground.

Typically, by 'unnatural' we mean not just "unusual," but something more like "contrary to nature." The question is, in what sense anything may be regarded as contrary to nature. To this, the best answer would

---

Reprinted, with the permission of Robert Gray and the *Journal of Philosophy,* from *Journal of Philosophy* 75:4 (1978), pp. 189–99.

appear to be that something is contrary to (its own) nature if it is counterproductive. What this requires, of course, is that there be some end or
function of a given kind of behavior in terms of which we may say that a
particular behavior is counterproductive or contrary to its nature as an
instance of behavior of that kind, and the question is, "How do we fix
that end or function in a noncircular way?" The way Ruddick would
seem to favor, and the only way I see if we are to avoid cultural relativism,
is in terms of evolutionary theory. If, then, we are able to show that there
is some adaptive function or end that sexual activity evolved to fulfill, we
may speak of sexual activity that departs from that function and, more
clearly, of sexual activity that, by departing from that function, is maladaptive, as counterproductive and, in that sense, contrary to nature or
unnatural. Thus, if reproduction is the adaption function of sexual activity, those forms of sexual activity which are nonreproductive and,
more clearly, those which are inimical to successful reproduction (for
example, any nonreproductive sexual obsession) would be unnatural
and perverted; they would constitute, as it were, a twisting of sexual activity away from its "natural" object or function. Put more simply, those
forms of sexual activity would be perverted which, in evolutionary terms,
are dysfunctional.

This would, in fact, seem to be Ruddick's position. On her view, the
adaptive function or, if one prefers, the natural end of sexual activity is
reproduction, and she concludes that all and only those forms of sexual
activity which may, under normal conditions, be expected to fulfill this
end are natural (24). All others are unnatural and perverted. However,
this view raises some problems.

In the first place, one might ask how sexual activities are to be identified. If, for example, the natural function of sexual activity is reproduction, an end to which coprophilia has no relation at all, would that not
by itself be ground for suggesting that the activities of the coprophiliac
are not *sexual* activities at all, and so, of course, not sexual perversions?
The problem may not be one whose solution is difficult, but for our
question it is important, for in order to elucidate the notion of sexual
perversion it would seem crucial that we be able to specify just what it is
about an activity that makes it an instance of sexual activity. The coprophiliac's activities might well be perverted, but there need be nothing
about them in virtue of which they are sexually perverted. I might, for
example, have developed some sort of penchant for eating cow dung,
doubtless disgusting, doubtless nonnutritive, almost certainly perverted,
but what has this to do with sex? Clearly, if I regard the eating of manure
simply as the only means of fulfilling my appetite for food, if in other
words, I eat because I am hungry and because it tastes good or better
than the available alternatives, or, if it tastes worse, because it leaves me
feeling less hungry, my perversion is not sexual. Sexually, I might be

entirely normal. Now the only thing I can see in this example that would constitute it as a nonsexual form of coprophilia and the only thing whose change could conceivably make it an example of coprophilia in the sexual sense, is the motive assigned. Hunger is a fairly distinct, clearly recognizable form of displeasure; as such, it gives rise, circumstances permitting, to activities that will remove or assuage it. In the same way, sexual desire (although, unlike hunger, it may be in itself pleasant or partially so) is a distinct, recognizable appetite, typically unpleasant if unfulfilled, which gives rise to activities that will remove or assuage it.

What is to be noted here is that neither hunger nor sexual desire is in itself a desire for a particular (kind of) object. In itself, each is a feeling which, all things considered, it would, at the time, be better not to have, or, better, which one would, when circumstances permit, so act as to remove. Hunger seems to be a desire for food because, typically, it is food that relieves it, and it is therefore food that the hungry person seeks. But it is entirely possible that someone should develop a food fetish for the coprolites of cattle; that is to say, it is entirely possible that, for whatever reason, someone's feeling of hunger might be relieved only by the ingestion of manure. Such a person we might well call a food pervert. But we would not call him a sexual pervert. The difference lies in his motive. His motive is hunger, not sex. On the other hand, if what he had eaten gave him sexual pleasure, his perversion, and therefore his activity, would have been sexual. Since the activities I have described here are otherwise identical (need the coprophiliac who is sexually perverted display any overt signs of sexual excitement?), I see no other way by which the one might be classed as sexual and the other not. Those activities, accordingly, are sexual which serve to relieve sexual feeling or, alternatively put, which give rise to sexual pleasure.

Of course, it might well be objected that sexual activity does not, in fact, serve so much to relieve, as to heighten sexual feeling (which, for purposes of this discussion, we may take to refer, at least initially, to a physiological state, although many emotional and cognitive states may, and typically do, come to be intimately associated with it). The objection has some force; however, I believe it may be fairly easily answered, for, in much the same way, food, which typically serves to relieve hunger, may also serve to heighten it. There is, of course, a point at which the analogy between hunger and sexual feeling breaks down, for sexual feeling is typically relieved by intensifying it. Whereas a little food may, in some cases, be very satisfying, a little bit of sex often leaves an individual feeling less satisfied than he might otherwise have been. Accordingly, I prefer to speak of sexual activity in terms of sexual pleasure. The activities by which sexual feeling is removed are experienced as (an intensification of) pleasurable sexual feeling. When they cease to be pleasurable, that is to say, when the sexual feeling has been removed, the activities lose their specifically sexual character, and, unless there is some other reason for continuing, the behavior ceases.

Sexual perversions, then, will be all and only those activities which are dysfunctional (in the sense given above) in terms of sexual pleasure, or, as Thomas Nagel expresses it, "A sexual perversion must reveal itself in conduct that expresses an unnatural *sexual* preference" (9). However, as the quotation from Nagel shows, this is not quite adequate. Perversion, as a category, applies not only to activities, but to persons, in which case the perversion must reveal itself in an unnatural sexual *preference*. There are many sorts of activities from which we might derive sexual pleasure, some of which are undoubtedly perverted, but it is not the fact that a person might derive sexual pleasure from a given activity that makes him perverted; it is, rather, that he desires or prefers to engage in such sexual activities. We may say, accordingly, that a person will be sexually perverted if his sexual desires are for, or lead him to perform, activities which, given the adaptive function(s) of sexual activity (e.g., that it ends in reproduction), are counterproductive or maladaptive.

The definitions given here have some interesting implications, which may be best seen by contrasting them with the views taken by Ruddick. Ms. Ruddick is concerned, not so much with sexual perversion, as with what she calls "better sex," of which, on her account, pleasure, naturalness (nonpervertedness), and "completeness" are the three criteria (18). As I have developed the notion of sexual activity, however, it is clear that pleasure is a criterion not so much of better sex as of sex itself. Those activities not serving to relieve sexual feeling, or from which no sexual pleasure is derived, would thus not be sexual activities at all. This at first sight seems counterintuitive, since we often speak, for example, of a person's not enjoying (in the sense of deriving pleasure from) sexual relations with his or her spouse. In this case, the difficulty lies, I think, with ordinary language. Sexual intercourse is thought to be, and is spoken of as, sexual activity, because it is that activity to which sexual desire paradigmatically leads. The unacceptability of the ordinary-language criterion is best shown, however, by the fact that, if we accept it, we are led to the unhappy conclusion that the rape victim has engaged in sexual activity, although, from her point of view, the activity may not have been sexual at all. It may make the analysis of sexual relations more difficult, but there is nothing intrinsically objectionable in the suggestion that what is, from the point of view of one of the participants, a sexual activity, may not be so from the point of view of the other. In fact, it would seem that ordinary language itself recognizes sexual pleasure as a criterion of sexual activity, at least implicitly and on some occasions. For example, ordinary persons are fond of bewailing the amount of sex and violence shown on commercial television. Just what constitutes sex in this case, however, is not clear, since neither nudity nor the portrayal of it is, in itself, a sexual activity. Were it so, the ordinary man, it seems to me, would be forced to conclude that he engages in sexual activities far more frequently than he might otherwise think, e.g., in taking a bath or changing his clothes. The only thing I can see in this example in virtue of which televised nudity might be called sexual is the fact that it is intended to, and in fact does, arouse sexual feelings. The fact that it is so intended, however, may not be crucial. To take another example, Dr. David Reuben relates that, in the early days of the garment industry, women found that the operation of treadle sewing machines could be employed as a masturbatory technique,[2] and, to the extent that they so employed it, I think it is clear that they would, in ordinary parlance, be said to be engaging in sexual activity. We must assume, however, that at some point the sexual possibilities of operating a treadle sewing machine must have been discovered, presumably, at least in some cases, by accident. Those women who made this discovery would then have found themselves engaging in sexual activity quite unintentionally. They may or may not have found this a welcome discovery, but that is quite beside the point.

If these examples are compelling, and taken in sum I think they are, we are forced to the conclusion that what makes an activity a sexual activity, even in terms of ordinary language, is just the sexual nature of the pleasure deriving from it. Accordingly, it is quite possible that any activity might become a sexual activity and, as the last example shows, that it might become a sexual activity unintentionally. And, of course, it would follow too that no activity is a sexual activity unless sexual pleasure is derived from it. And, since no activity could be sexually perverted unless it were also a sexual activity, the same thing would hold for sexual perversion.

Although pleasure would thus seem to enter the analysis of sexual activity only as a matter of degree, as one means of determining the comparative worth, in sexual terms, of any given sexual experience, the notion of completeness would not appear to enter at all. Ruddick, who seems to take the notion principally from Nagel, defines it in this way:

> A sex act is complete if each partner (1) allows himself to be "taken over" by desire, which (2) is desire not merely for the other's body but also for *his* desire, and (3) where each desire is occasioned by a response to the partner's desire (20).

Though she offers a defense of sorts for the claim that, in a complete sex act, the participant is "taken over" or "embodied" by his or her desire, Ruddick would seem to have no real argument in support of the other elements of her definition. In fact, she goes so far as to say at the end of her discussion of completeness that "incompleteness does not disqualify a sex act from being fully sexual" (23). Presumably, these other aspects

of the completeness of a sex act are just accidental components, characteristics which may or may not be present but which serve to make the
sex act "better" when they are. It should be noted, however, that when
Ruddick comes to discuss the contribution that completeness makes to
the sex act, it is not the sex act itself that is said to be improved. (This will
not hold for the condition of "embodiment.") She argues, rather, that
completeness contributes to the psychological and social well-being of
the participants (29–30).

For Nagel, on the other hand, completeness would appear to be, at
least partially, constitutive of sexual activity. Completeness, on his view,
would appear to consist in a complex interaction between the desires of
the two participants ("It is important that the partner be aroused, and
not merely aroused, but aroused by the awareness of one's desire"—16),
and he writes accordingly that

> . . . this overlapping system of distinct sexual perceptions and interactions
> is the basic framework of any full-fledged sexual relation and that relations
> involving only part of the complex are significantly incomplete. (15)

That Nagel should have attached such significance to the notion of completeness (a perversion is, for him, simply an incomplete sex act—16) is
fairly easily explained. Nagel has incorrectly assumed that "sexual desire
is a feeling about other persons." It "has its own content as a relation between persons." Accordingly, "it is only by analyzing that relation that we
can understand the conditions of sexual perversion" (12). This mistake,
as has already been pointed out, is understandable and is, furthermore,
one we commonly make. Copulation is the paradigmatic object of sexual desire; it is just such a relation between persons that sexual desire has
as its "characteristic object." But it is a mistake to go from this to the view
that sexual desire has such an object as its content (or to the view that,
in the analysis of sexual activity, the nature of sexual desire is in any way
fundamental). A given desire is sexual, not because it has a particular object, but because it arises from a particular kind of feeling. Put differently, it is the desire (or feeling) itself that is sexual, and it is in terms of
this that the activity it has as its object is perceived as a sexual activity. The
relationship is not the other way around. If it were, it would be difficult,
if not impossible, to see how many of the more exotic perversions could
be considered sexual. One might characterize an activity such as masturbation (which Nagel apparently regards as a perversion—17) as sexual on the basis of some sort of family relation with coital activity, but this
seems unlikely as a means of categorizing all sexual activities as sexual.
Even in the case of masturbation this approach would raise problems
(one could, for example, conceive a situation in which a person might
masturbate, while feeling nothing at all—perhaps by using anesthetic

ointments—for reasons having nothing to do with sexual desire or gratification—as part of a medical experiment, for instance. Would this activity in that case be sexual?), but one wonders what the family
resemblance might be in the, admittedly strange, case of coprophilia described earlier.

This, however, is not the only difficulty with Nagel's notion of completeness, although I think it is the most serious. As Janice Moulton has
argued, both Nagel and Robert Solomon (who sees the specific content
of sexual desire in terms of interpersonal communication—sexual activity is a kind of "body language")[3] have "assumed that a model of flirtation and seduction constitute an adequate model of sexual behavior in
general," whereas, as she argues, "most sexual behavior does not involve
flirtation and seduction, and . . . what characterizes flirtation and seduction is not what characterizes the sexual behavior of regular partners."[4] This itself, however, leads Moulton into difficulties. She is forced
to conclude that it is impossible to characterize sexual behavior, because
there are two kinds of it: "sexual anticipation," which includes "flirtation,
seduction, and traditional courtship," and "sexual satisfaction," which
"involves sexual feelings which are increased by the other person's
knowledge of one's preferences and sensitivities, the familiarity of their
touch or smell or way of moving, and not by the novelty of their sexual
interest" (32). "However, anticipation and satisfaction are often divorced" (32). But even this classification is too narrow, for, to the extent
that satisfaction is here defined in interpersonal terms, "the *other* person's knowledge . . . the familiarity of *their* touch," etc., masturbation and
related types of sexual activities would, again, be excluded from the possible range of sexual behaviors. However, there is, as we have seen, a
means, if not of characterizing, at least of identifying behavior as sexual,
and the ground here, sexual feeling, is independent of any particular
model of sexual activity. Note that this is not equivalent to saying that, as
Solomon puts it, "sex is pure physical enjoyment" (27). To put it in
Solomon's words again, "this enjoyment accompanies sexual activity and
its ends, but is not that activity or these ends" (26). Sexual activity may
have many ends, interpersonal communication among them, but if we
take the view that it is the end that identifies it as sexual, then we are left
squarely facing the problem that any sexual activity that does not have
that specific end is not, in fact, sexual activity or is somehow less than
fully sexual. Thus, on Solomon's communication model, masturbation
turns out to be like "talking to yourself" and therefore "clearly secondary
to sexuality in its broader interpersonal context." And " 'Unadorned sexual intercourse' . . . becomes the ultimate perversion, since it is the sexual equivalent of hanging up the telephone without saying anything"
(27). One is inclined to take the view, in fact, that, if Solomon has concentrated too narrowly on one model of sexuality, it is not that of antic-

ipation, but of satisfaction. Like most men, Solomon seems to be fully persuaded of the fundamental role of genital-genital intercourse (which is entirely satisfactory from a male point of view) in human sexuality. There is evidence, however, to show that, at least from the female point of view, it is not (this sort of) intercourse, but masturbation that is crucial.[5] This may, of course, take place in an interpersonal context, and it may be preferable when it does. All it shows is that our models must not be so constructed as to exclude it.

* * *

What the foregoing discussion will show is that the classification of a given (type of) sexual behavior as perverted is purely descriptive. Which activities are and are not perverted will depend on what we ultimately discover the natural adaptive function of sexual activity to be, and this is a question whose answer must be given by the scientist whose business it is to study such things. Of course, if reproduction were, as some think, the sole function of sexual activity, the scientist would have no further questions to ask about the matter, and all nonreproductive sexual activity might correctly be described as perverted. However, it would seem that this is not the case. "Reproduction" is, as Nagel claims, a biological concept. As such, it includes such biological functions as conception, gestation, and birth, and, if men were fruit flies, sexual behavior might have been just that behavior minimally sufficient to ensure reproduction in this limited sense. Copulation, then, might have been enough to ensure conception; conception, enough to ensure gestation; and gestation, enough to ensure birth. The fact is, however (and the world may or may not be better off for it), that men are not fruit flies, and reproduction in man includes far more than just the production of new individuals. Reproductive activity in man must be construed as the sum of all those activities minimally necessary to bring those new individuals themselves to reproductive maturity. Among other things, this would seem to include the formation and maintenance of well-organized, stable societies and the establishment and maintenance of fairly stable male-female reproductive pairs. Since the latter would seem ultimately to depend on sexual attraction and since there is substantial evidence to show that many characteristics of human sexual behavior contribute as well to the former, it would seem probable at least that maintenance of that degree (and kind) of social organization and stability requisite to the maintenance of human society is a function that human sexual behavior has evolved to fulfill, and, if this is so, it is clear that the range of nonperverted sexual activity will be much broader than it has traditionally been taken to be. It may turn out, too, that the natural adaptive functions of human sexual activity are not culturally independent. In this case, a behavior that is maladaptive in one society may not be so in another. Thus, for example, male homosexual behavior may be maladaptive in a society with a high ratio of females to males and a birth rate too low to make the society viable. In another society, however, where the sex ratios are reversed, male homosexual behavior, by reducing sexual rivalry, might be adaptive. A similar argument would serve to demonstrate the possible adaptive character of such activities as masturbation, whatever the techniques used, including "intercourse with . . . inanimate objects," which Nagel classes as a perversion. We could, perhaps, say then that variability of sexual objects is a natural characteristic, or natural adaptive function, of human sexual desire and that, where it contributes to (or, at least, does not detract from) the maintenance of the over-all social order, or to the long-term viability of society, such variability is adaptive (or, at least, not maladaptive) and nonperverted.

Of course, it may well be that, as many stalwarts claim, all and only those sexual activities traditionally approved in our society are natural (or adaptive) and nonperverted, and what the discussion so far will show is that those who agitate against the increasing sexual permissiveness of contemporary society on the ground that it is destructive of the family, presumably the bulwark of modern social institutions, are at least on the right track. However, if the view of the nature of sexual perversion taken here is correct, to uphold the claim that such practices are sexually perverted, it will be necessary to show that societies that encourage divergent sexual behaviors are, for that reason, substantially less viable than our own (since evolutionary theory regards the reproductive group rather than the individual, it should be noted, too, that a particular practice detrimental to a given group or institution may benefit the society as a whole), or that our own society, with its peculiar institutions, would be made substantially less viable, and not merely different, if it permitted or encouraged other sexual practices. In any case, the judgment whether or not a given activity is sexually perverted, to the extent that it is properly an answer to the factual question whether the behavior is or is not consonant with the natural adaptive function(s) of sexual activity, would be descriptive and nonevaluative and need not, therefore, carry any moral connotations.

This, of course, is not to say that sexual perversion is not immoral. In fact, depending on the moral view we take, there may well be ground for claiming that any and all sexual perversion is immoral. For example, one might adopt a moral view according to which the natural is the moral. This would not automatically brand sexual perversion as immoral, since it may be the case, as we have seen, that human sexual activity is naturally variable. If, however, this theory were cast in evolutionary terms, so that natural is taken to mean the naturally adaptive function of given behavior, sexual perversion would, by definition, be immoral. I am not myself inclined to such a moral view. I am, rather, inclined to take a somewhat

Hobbesian view, according to which morality is the sum of those rules minimally necessary to social cohesion. On this view, all sexual activities that are perverted by virtue of the fact that they disrupt the cohesiveness of society, assuming social cohesion is a natural function of human sexual activity, would be immoral. But it should be noted that this judgment is logically independent of the judgment that those activities are perverted. One might, therefore, make the suggestion, since 'perversion' has acquired such a strong pejorative connotation in our society, that the term be dropped from our sexual vocabulary altogether. Other clearer and less emotive terms may just as easily be substituted for it.

But, whatever the moral implications, this much seems clear. If we have correctly defined what it is for behavior to be sexually perverted and, in that sense, "contrary to nature," as any practice or activity from which sexual pleasure is derived and which, given the natural adaptive function(s) of sexual activity, is counterproductive or maladaptive, we will at least have succeeded in putting the question, "What specific activities are and are not perverted?" in terms amenable to investigation by the behavioral sciences. In such questions as these, no more really can be asked of the philosopher.

Notes

1. "On Sexual Morality," in James Rachels, ed., *Moral Problems,* 2nd ed. (New York: Harper & Row, 1975), pp. 23–24. See also Thomas Nagel, "Sexual Perversion," *The Journal of Philosophy* 66, No. 1 (1969), pp. 5–17. (This volume, pp. 9–20.)

2. *Everything You Always Wanted to Know About Sex* (New York: Bantam, 1971), pp. 201–202. (Originally: McKay, 1969.)

3. "Sexual Paradigms," *The Journal of Philosophy* 71, No. 1 (1974), pp. 336–345, p. 343. (This volume, pp. 21–29; p. 27.)

4. "Sexual Behavior: Another Position," *The Journal of Philosophy* 73, No. 16 (1976), pp. 537–546, p. 538 (This volume, pp. 31–38; p. 32.)

5. Shere Hite, *The Hite Report* (New York: Macmillan, 1976), pp. 229–252.

Chapter 7

MASTURBATION

Alan Soble

This vice, which shame and timidity find so convenient, has a particular attraction for lively imaginations. It allows them to dispose, so to speak, of the whole female sex at their will, and to make any beauty who tempts them serve their pleasure without the need of first obtaining her consent.

Rousseau, *Confessions,* Book III

[I]f your right hand causes you to sin, cut it off and throw it away. It is better for you to lose one part of your body than for your whole body to go into hell.

Jesus [according to Matthew 5: 30]

Reflecting on the special virtues, and not only the vices, of adultery, prostitution, homosexuality, bisexuality, group sex, sadomasochism, and sex with anonymous strangers is a valuable exercise. Indeed, when thinking philosophically about sexuality, it is mandatory to compare these practices with a privileged pattern of relationship in which two adult heterosexuals love each other, are committed and faithful to each other within a formal marriage, and look forward to procreation and family. Some people sincerely strive to attain this pattern; some live

This essay began its life as "Sexual Desire and Sexual Objects," a paper presented at the Pacific Division meetings of the American Philosophical Association, San Francisco, March 1978. It was first published as "Masturbation" in *Pacific Philosophical Quarterly* 61 (1980): 233–44 and reprinted, greatly revised, as "Masturbation and Sexual Philosophy" in Alan Soble, ed., *Philosophy of Sex,* 2d ed. That version was again revised to become Chapter Two of my *Sexual Investigations* (New York University Press, 1996), of which the present version is an abbreviation and modification.

it effortlessly; the sexual lives of others are more complex, even chaotic. It does not matter whether the privileged pattern is actually a widespread form of behavior or a piece of ideology that attempts to influence behavior. Regardless, the contrast between the pattern and the practices mentioned above provides the material for the conceptual and ethical thinking that is the philosophy of sex.

Masturbation, too, violates the spirit and letter of the privileged pattern: it is unpaired, nonprocreative sex in which pleasure is relished for its own sake. Masturbation mocks the categories of our sexual discourse: it is sex with someone I care about, to whose satisfaction and welfare I am devoted; it is incestuous; if I'm married, it is sex with someone who is not my spouse and hence adulterous; it is homosexual; it is often pederastic; it is sex we occasionally fall into inadvertently ("if you shake it more than twice, you're playing with it"); and, with a Rousseauvian stretch, it is the promiscuous rape of every man, woman, or beast to whom I take a fancy. No wonder, then, that we advertise our marriages and brag about our affairs, but keep our masturbatory practices and fantasies to ourselves. The sexual revolution has made living together outside matrimony acceptable; it has encouraged toleration of homosexuality; it has even breathed life into the practices of the daughters and sons of the Marquis de Sade. But to call a man a "jerk off" is still derogatory. Masturbation is the black sheep of the family of sex, scorned, as we shall see, by both the Right and the Left.

The Concept

Conceptual questions about masturbation arise when we critically examine the paradigm case: a person in a private place manually rubs the penis or clitoris and produces an orgasm. The salient features of the paradigm case are conceptually unnecessary. (1) One can openly masturbate in the crowded waiting room of a bus terminal, with erect penis displayed for all to see or with fingers conspicuously rubbing the clitoris. (2) The hands do not have to be employed, as long as the target areas are pressed against a suitably shaped object of comfortable composition—the back of a horse, a bicycle seat, a rug. (3) Orgasm need not be attained, nor need it be the goal. Sexual pleasure is the point. (4) The penis or clitoris need not receive the most, or any, attention. There are other sensitive areas one can touch and press: the anus, nipples, thighs, lips. What remains in the paradigm case does seem indispensable: (5) the person who, by pressing the sensitive areas, causally produces the pleasurable sensations is the person who experiences them; the rubber is the rubbed. Masturbation, the "solitary vice" of "self-abuse," looks logically reflexive.

But *mutual* masturbation would be impossible if masturbation were logically solitary, and we have a paradigmatic case of mutual masturbation: two persons rubbing each other between the legs. Further, if it is conceptually possible for *X* and *Y* to masturbate each other, it must be possible for *X* to masturbate *Y*, while *Y* simply receives this attention, not doing anything to *X*. "To masturbate" is both transitive and intransitive; like respect and deception, it can take the self or other as object. Reflexivity, then, might be sufficient but it is not necessary for a sexual act to be masturbatory. But explaining why mutual masturbation *is* masturbation is not easy. Saying that these activities are masturbatory just because they involve the hands and genitals is awkward; we would end up claiming that all solitary sex acts are masturbatory, even those that do not involve the manual rubbing of the genitals, while paired acts are masturbatory exactly when they do involve the manual rubbing of the genitals. On this view, *X*'s tweaking her own nipples is masturbatory, *Y*'s doing it for *X* is not masturbatory, yet *Y*'s tweaking *X*'s clitoris is masturbatory.

One way to distinguish masturbatory from nonmasturbatory acts is to contrast sexual acts that do not involve any insertion and those that do. The idea is that without the insertion of something, no mixing together of two fleshes occurs, and so the participants remain isolated. Solitary acts of self-pleasuring would be masturbatory for the reason that no insertion occurs (but what about digital anal or vaginal masturbation?); the paradigm case of mutual masturbation also need not involve insertion (but it might, of fingers into vagina); and both male-female coitus and male-male anal coitus would not be masturbatory because they do involve insertion. This view entails that *X*'s fellating *Y* is not a case of masturbation (which seems correct), it has the plausible implication that coitus between a human male and a female animal (a sheep), or a human female and a male animal (a dog), is not masturbatory (even though each activity involves only one *person* and is, in that sense, a solitary activity—unless mammals are persons), and it is consistent with the not incredible intuitions that frottage in a crowded subway car is masturbatory and that tribadism can be mutually masturbatory. But to distinguish between masturbatory and nonmasturbatory sexual activity by distinguishing between acts that do not and acts that do involve insertion is inadequate, as my examples have already hinted. Consider others. Cunnilingus might or might not involve insertion, in this case of the tongue or lips or nose; to say it is masturbatory when and only when it does not involve insertion implies that one continuous act of cunnilingus changes from masturbatory to not masturbatory and back again often in a few minutes. And what about a male who punctures a hole in a watermelon to make room for his penis, or a female who reaches for her g-spot with a zucchini inside her vagina? These acts are masturbatory yet involve insertion.

Some of these problem examples can be avoided by narrowing what counts as "insertion." Masturbation might be characterized more specifically as sexual activity not involving the insertion of a real penis into a hole of a living being. Then all lesbian sexuality is masturbatory, while many acts of male homosexuals would not be. Were we to decide that a male having intercourse with an animal is, after all, masturbating—that is, if there is no significant difference between this act and a man's rubbing his penis with a woman's panties—masturbation could be defined more specifically as sexual activity not involving the insertion of a real penis into a hole of a living human being. This refined view is literally phallocentric in characterizing sexual acts with reference to the male organ. As a result, the analysis implies a *conceptual* double standard: fellatio, oral sex done on a male, is not masturbatory, but cunnilingus, oral sex done on a female, always is. And an *evaluative* double standard looms when the usual disparagement of masturbation is added: fellatio is acceptable, real sex, cunnilingus is a fraud. This scholastic view (which is sexist but not heterosexist—its point does not depend on the sex/gender of the fellator) is similar to the claim (which is heterosexist but not necessarily sexist) that the paradigm case of natural sexual activity is male-female genital intercourse. What is conceptually emphasized in such a view— the most specific we can get—is the insertion of a real penis not into any hole of a living human being, but into a particular hole, the vagina. This suggests that masturbation be understood as any nonprocreative sexual activity, whether solitary or paired. If so, our sexual lives contain a lot more masturbation than we had thought.

There is usually a clear distinction between solitary and paired sexual activity. But suppose X is having sex with Y, and X's arousal is sustained by X's private fantasies. The act is solitary masturbation in the sense that the other person is absent from X's sexual consciousness. That which would arouse X during solitary masturbation is doing the same thing for X while X rubs his penis or clitoris on/with Y's body instead of X's hand. Even so, the difference between solitary and paired sex is not that between masturbatory and nonmasturbatory sex. But under certain descriptions of sexual activity, no difference exists between the paradigm case of mutual masturbation and two ordinary cases of nonmasturbatory sex: heterosexual genital intercourse and homosexual anal intercourse. Listen to helpful Alexander Portnoy offering his cheating father a redescription of adultery: "What after all does it consist of? You put your dick some place and moved it back and forth and stuff came out the front. So, Jake, what's the big deal?"[1] Adulterous coitus is redescribed, defined "downward," almost as if it were solitary masturbation. Portnoy's sarcasm suggests why there is no essential difference between mutual masturbation and genital or anal intercourse: *every* paired sexual act is masturbatory because the mutual rubbing of sensitive areas, the friction of skin against skin, that occurs during mutual masturbation is the same, physically, as the mutual rubbing of skin against skin that occurs during coitus. The only difference is that different parts of the body or patches of skin are involved in the rubbings; but no one patch or set of patches of skin has any ontological privilege over any other. Further, the difference between solitary and paired masturbation is only the number of people who accomplish these same rubbings.

A similar conclusion can be reached on Kantian grounds. For Kant, human sexual interaction by its nature involves a person's merely using another person for the sake of pleasure:

> [T]here is no way in which a human being can be made an Object of indulgence for another except through sexual impulse. . . . Sexual love . . . by itself . . . is nothing more than appetite. Taken by itself it is a degradation of human nature. . . . [A]s an Object of appetite for another a person becomes a thing.[2]

Kant is not asserting the physical indistinguishability of mutual masturbation and coitus. Instead, he is insisting that the intentions involved in both activities—to get pleasure for oneself through the vehicle of the other's body and compliance with one's wishes—are the same. But in portraying all sexual acts as objectifying and instrumental, Kant makes us wonder: is not celibacy required? He answers in the negative:

> The sole condition on which we are free to make use of our sexual desire depends upon the right to dispose over the person as a whole. . . . [I] obtain these rights over the whole person . . . [o]nly by giving that person the same rights over the whole of myself. This happens only in marriage. . . . In this way the two persons become a unity of will. . . . Thus sexuality leads to a union . . . and in that union alone its exercise is possible.[3]

Kant is not claiming that the marital pledge assures that even if the spouses are a means to each other's pleasure in the marriage bed, they are not treating each other only as means but also as ends, as persons to whom respect and consideration are due during sex, as well as before and after. Instead, Kant justifies marital sex by abolishing the possibility of instrumentality altogether; he literally unites two persons into one person by marriage.[4] This is to justify all marital sex by reducing or equating it to solitary masturbation, the sex of a single (even if larger or more complex) person.[5]

Kant's notion that the marital union of two people into one cleanses sexuality of its instrumentality apparently has two radical implications: that homosexual marriage would similarly cleanse same-sex sexuality[6] and that solitary masturbation is permissible. Kant resists both conclusions, asserting that masturbation and homosexuality are *crimina carnis contra naturam*:

[O]nanism . . . is abuse of the sexual faculty without any object. . . . By it man sets aside his person and degrades himself below the level of animals. . . . [I]ntercourse between *sexus homogenii* . . . too is contrary to the ends of humanity; for the end of humanity in respect of sexuality is to preserve the species.[7]

Kant concludes his denouncement of these aberrations nastily: "He," the masturbator or homosexual, "no longer deserves to be a person."

Kant has not provided a criterion for distinguishing paired masturbatory sexual activity from paired nonmasturbatory sex—quite the opposite— but Kant's thought suggests a criterion that concedes the *physical* similarity of mutual masturbation and coitus and focuses instead on a *mental* difference: sexual activity between two persons, each of whom is concerned not only with her or his own pleasure but also with the pleasure of the other person, is not masturbatory (regardless of what physical acts they engage in), while sexual activity in which a person is concerned solely with her or his own pleasure is masturbatory. Conceiving of another person merely as a means might be a mark of the immoral; here it is being regarded, in addition, as a mark of the masturbatory. This view implies that inconsiderate husbands and rapists are largely the authors of masturbatory acts. It also implies that mutual masturbation is *not* masturbatory if the touchings are meant to produce pleasure not only for the toucher but also for one's partner.

This Kantian criterion does not sufficiently distinguish between the definition and the evaluation of masturbation. What seems to be at the heart of masturbation is the effort to cause sexual pleasure for the self— full stop. It is not part of the core idea that masturbation be solitary; the attempt to produce sexual pleasure for the self can causally involve other people, animals, the whole universe. That masturbation is logically reflexive—*X* acts to produce sexual pleasure for *X*—is neither equivalent to nor entails its being solitary. Given the kind of physical creatures we are, attempting to please the self by acting on oneself is easier, even if not always successful. Our own bodies are handy. Hence we misleadingly associate masturbation entirely with one form of it, the case in which *X* touches and pleasures *X*. But the attempt to produce one's own pleasure can involve other people. Solitary and paired sexual acts are masturbatory, then, to the extent that the actor attempts to produce pleasure for the self; paired sex is not masturbatory when one person attempts to produce pleasure for another. This notion of masturbation is descriptive, not normative; it neither praises nor condemns masturbation. That the attempt to produce, and the search for, one's own sexual pleasure, either in solitary or paired acts, is selfish or, instead, merely self-interested, or even benevolent (which is possible), is not part of the core idea. Seeking to produce sexual pleasure for the self is that which marks the masturbatory, not these other motivational factors that are more directly relevant to a distinct moral evaluation of sexual acts.

Fulfilling Desire

Three contemporary philosophical accounts of sexuality, proffered by thinkers within the sexually liberal tradition, yield the conclusions that solitary masturbation is not a sexual activity at all (Alan Goldman), is perverted (Thomas Nagel), or is "empty" (Robert Solomon). These conclusions are surprising, given the sexual pedigree of these philosophers.[8] I propose to take a careful look at them.

Let's begin with Alan Goldman's definitions of "sexual desire" and "sexual activity":[9]

> [S]exual desire is desire for contact with another person's body and for the pleasure which such contact produces; sexual activity is activity which tends to fulfill such desire of the agent. (40)

On Goldman's view, sexual desire is strictly the desire for the pleasure of physical contact itself, nothing else, and so does not include a component desire for, say, love, communication, or progeny. Goldman thus takes himself to be offering a liberating analysis of sexuality that does not tether sex normatively or conceptually to love, the emotions, or procreation. But while advocating the superiority of his notion of "plain sex," Goldman forgot that masturbation needed protection from the same (usually conservative) philosophy that obliged sex to occur within a loving marriage or to be procreative in order to be morally proper. On Goldman's analysis, solitary masturbation is not a sexual activity to begin with: it does not "tend to fulfill" sexual desire, viz., the desire for contact with another person's body. Solitary masturbation is unlike mutual masturbation, which does tend to fulfill the desire for contact, since it involves the desired contact and hence is fully sexual. Goldman seems not to be troubled that on his view solitary masturbation is not a sexual act. But it's funny that masturbation is, for Goldman, not sexual, for the conservative philosophy that he rejects would reply to his account like this: by *reducing* sexuality entirely to the meaningless desire for the pleasure of physical contact, what Goldman has analyzed is merely a form of masturbation.

The vague "tends to fulfill" in Goldman's analysis of sexual activity presents problems. Goldman intended, I think, a narrow causal reading of this phrase; actually touching another person's body is a sexual act just because by the operation of a simple mechanism the act fulfills the desire for that contact and its pleasure. The qualification "tends to" functions to allow bungled kisses to count as sexual acts, even though they did not do what they were intended to do; kisses tend to fulfill desire in the sense that they normally and effectively produce pleasure, prevented from doing so only by the odd interfering event (the braces get tangled; the hurrying lips land on the chin). It also functions to allow disappointing or bad sex, that which does not bring what anticipation promised, to count as sex. In this sense of "tends to fulfill," solitary masturbation is not sex. Suppose that X desires sex with Y, but Y declines the invitation, and so X masturbates thinking about Y. Goldman's view is not that X's masturbation satisfies X's desire for contact with Y only, or at least, a little and hence is a sexual act even if inefficient. This masturbation is not a sexual act at all, despite the sexual pleasure it yields for X, unlike the not pleasurable but still sexual bungled kiss. X's masturbation cannot "tend to fulfill" X's desire for contact with Y, since it excludes that contact.

Suppose we read "tends to fulfill" in a causally broader way. Then giving money to a prostitute—the act of taking bills out of a wallet and handing them to her—might be a sexual act (even if no sexual arousal accompanies it), because doing so allows the patron to fulfill his desire for contact with her body. Handing over $100 would be a *more efficient* sexual act than handing over a ten. Even on this broader reading, solitary masturbation would not be a sexual activity; despite the causal generosity, masturbation is still precluded from fulfilling sexual desire in Goldman's sense. (For similar reasons, someone masturbating while looking at erotic photographs is not engaged in a sexual act.) Indeed, masturbation will be a *contrasexual* act, on Goldman's view, if the more a person masturbates, the less time, energy, or interest he or she has for fulfilling the desire for contact with someone's body.

Goldman does acknowledge one sense in which masturbation is a sexual activity:

> Voyeurism or viewing a pornographic movie qualifies as a sexual activity, but only as an imaginative substitute for the real thing (otherwise a deviation from the norm as expressed in our definition). The same is true of masturbation as a sexual activity without a partner. (42)

Masturbation done for its own sake, for the specific pleasure it yields, is *not* sexual; masturbation is a sexual act only when done as a substitute for the not available "real thing." But on what grounds could Goldman claim that masturbation's being an "imaginative substitute" for a sexual act makes it a sexual act? In general, being a *substitute for* a certain kind of act does not make something an occurrence of that act-kind. To eat soyburger as a beef substitute is not to eat hamburger, even if it tastes exactly like hamburger. Eating a hamburger as a substitute for the sex I want but cannot have does not make my going to Queen Burger a sexual event, not even if out of frustration I gorge myself on burgers as compensation.

On the other hand, given Goldman's analyses of sexual desire and activity, the claim that masturbation done for its own sake is not sexual makes some sense. If the masturbator desires the pleasure of physical contact, and masturbates trying (in vain) to get that pleasure, the act, by a stretch, is sexual, because it at least involves genuine sexual desire. By contrast, if the masturbator wants only to experience pleasurable clitoral or penile sensations, then the masturbator does not have sexual desire in Goldman's sense, and activity engaged in to fulfill this (on his view, nonsexual) desire is not sexual activity. But now we have a different problem: what are we to call the act of this masturbator? In what category does it belong, if not the sexual? Note that Goldman argues (41), along the same lines, that if a parent's desire to cuddle a baby is only the desire to show affection, and not the desire for the pleasure of physical contact itself, then the parent's act is not sexual. Goldman assumes that if the desire that causes or leads to the act is not sexual, neither is the act. But if so, a woman who performs fellatio on a man for the money she gets from doing so is not performing a sexual act. It does not fulfill the sexual desire "of the agent," for, like the baby-cuddling parent, she has no sexual desire to begin with. Thus the prostitute's contribution to fellatio must be called, instead, a "rent paying" or "food gathering" act, since it tends to fulfill her desires to have shelter and eat.

Completeness

Thomas Nagel's theory of sexuality was designed to distinguish, in human sexuality, between the natural and the unnatural (the perverted.)[10] Human sexuality differs from animal sexuality in the role played by a spiral phenomenon that depends on self-consciousness. Suppose (1) X looks at Y or hears Y's voice or smells Y's hair—that is, X "senses" Y—and as a result is sexually aroused. Also suppose (2) Y senses X, too, and as a result becomes aroused. X and Y are at the earliest stage of sexual interaction: the animal level of awareness, response, and arousal. But if (3) X becomes aroused further by noticing (or "sensing") that Y is aroused by looking at X, and (4) Y becomes further aroused by noticing that X is aroused by sensing Y, then X and Y have reached the first level of natural human sexuality. Higher iterations of the pattern are also psychologically characteristic of human sexuality: (5) X is aroused even further by noticing (4). On Nagel's view of human sexuality, when X senses Y at the purely animal stage of sexual interaction, X is in X's own consciousness a subject and only a subject; while Y is for X at this stage only an object of sexual attention. But when X advances to the first distinctively human level of sexuality, and notices that Y is aroused by sensing X, X becomes in X's own consciousness also an object, and so at this level X experiences

X-self as both subject and object. If *Y*, too, is progressing up the spiral, *Y*'s self-consciousness is also composed of feeling *Y*-self as subject and object. For Nagel, the awareness of oneself as *both subject and object* in a sexual interaction marks it as "complete," that is, psychologically natural.

Nagel's theory, because it is about natural sex and not the essence of the sexual, does not entail that masturbation is not sexual. However, the judgment that solitary masturbation is perverted *seems* to follow from Nagel's account. Solitary masturbation, unlike mutual masturbation, does not exhibit the completeness of natural sexuality; it lacks the combination of an awareness of the embodiment of another person and an awareness of being sensed as embodied, in turn, by that person. This is apparently why Nagel claims that "narcissistic practices"—which for him seem to include solitary masturbation—are "stuck at some primitive version of the first stage" (17) of the spiral of arousal; they are sexually perverted because they are "truncated or incomplete versions of the complete configuration" (16). There is a world of difference between narcissism in some technical sense and masturbation, so even if looking upon one's own body in a mirror with delight is a sexual perversion, a theorist of sex should not feel compelled for that reason to judge perverted the prosaic practice of solitary masturbation. Nagel claims that shoe fetishism is perverted (9); "intercourse with . . . inanimate objects" is incomplete (17). But just because shoe fetishism might be a perversion that involves masturbation, a theory of sex need not entail that shoeless masturbation is perverted.

A case can be made, however, that the nature of effective sexual fantasy allows masturbation to be complete enough to be natural. Consider someone who masturbates while looking at erotic photographs. This sexual act avoids incompleteness insofar as the person is aroused not only by sensing the model's body (the animal level) but by recognizing the model's intention to arouse or by sensing her real or feigned arousal (the human level), as much as these things are captured by the camera or read into the photograph by the masturbator. Completeness seems not to require that *X*'s arousal and pleasure as a result of *X*'s awareness of *Y*'s arousal occur at the same time as *Y*'s arousal. Nor does it require that *X* and *Y* be in the same place: *X* and *Y* can arouse and cause each other pleasure by talking over the telephone. Further, if *X* masturbates while fantasizing, *sans* photograph, about another person, *X* might be aroused by the intentions expressed or arousal experienced by the imagined partner. (Nagel does allow [14] that *X* might become aroused in response to a "purely imaginary" *Y*.) A masturbator having a powerful imagination can conjure up these details and experience heightened pleasure as a result. If the masturbator is aroused not only by sensing, in imagination, the other's body, but also aroused by noticing (having created the appropriate fantasy) that the other is aroused by sensing *X*'s body, then *X* can be conscious of *X*-self as both subject and object, which is the mark of complete sexuality.

Communication

Robert Solomon, like Nagel, wants to distinguish between animal and human sexuality.[11] On Solomon's view, human sexuality is differentiated by its being "primarily a means of communicating with other people" (*SAP*, 279). Sensual pleasure is important in sex, but it is not the main point of sexual interaction or its defining characteristic ("Sexual Paradigms," 26; *SAP*, 277–79). Sexuality is, instead, "first of all language" (*SAP*, 281). As "a means of communication, it is . . . *essentially* an activity performed with other people" (*SAP*, 279). Could such a view of sexuality be kind to solitary masturbation? Apparently not:

> If sexuality is essentially a language, it follows that masturbation, while not a perversion, is a deviation. . . . Masturbation is not "self-abuse" . . . but it is, in an important sense, self-denial. It represents an inability or a refusal to say what one wants to say. . . . Masturbation is . . . essential as an ultimate retreat, but empty and without content. Masturbation is the sexual equivalent of a Cartesian soliloquy. (*SAP*, 283)

If sexuality is communicative, solitary masturbation can *be* sexual; conversing with oneself is not impossible, even if not the paradigm case. The distinctive flaw of masturbation, for Solomon, is that communicative intent, success, or content is missing. Hence solitary masturbation is "empty," a conclusion that seems to follow naturally from the idea that sexuality is "essentially" a way persons communicate *with each other.*

But denouncing masturbation as a "refusal to say what one wants to say" slights the fact that one might not have, at any given time, something to say (without being dull); or that there might be nothing worthy of being said, and so silence is appropriate. Solomon's communication model of sexuality seems to force people to talk to each other, to have empty sex, even when there is nothing to be said. Further, even if the masturbator is merely babbling to himself, he still enjoys this harmless pastime as much as does the infant who, for the pure joy of it, makes noises having no communicative intent or meaning. Thus to call masturbation "self-denial" is wrongheaded, but at least a change from the popular criticism of masturbation as a *failure* of self-denial, a giving-in to temptation, an immersing of the self in the hedonistic excesses of self-gratification.

The simple point is that there is no warrant to conclude, within a model that likens sexuality to linguistic behavior, that solitary masturbation is inferior.[12] Solomon meant the analogy between masturbation and a "Cartesian soliloquy" to reveal the shallowness of solitary sexuality. But Descartes's philosophical soliloquies are hardly uninteresting, and I suspect many would be proud to masturbate as well as the *Meditations* does philosophy. Diaries are not often masterpieces of literature, but that does not make them "empty." Some of the most fruitful discussions one can have are with oneself, not as a substitute for dialogue with another person, or as compensation for lacking it, but to explore one's mind, to get one's thoughts straight. This is the stuff of intellectual integrity, not preparation for public utterances.

Solomon acknowledges that not only "children, lunatics, and hermits" talk to themselves; "poets and philosophers" do so as well (*SAP*, 283). This misleading concession plays upon the silly notion that philosophers and poets are a type of lunatic. Where are the bus drivers and cooks? Solomon's abuse of masturbation trades unfairly on the fact that talking to oneself has always received bad publicity—unfair because we all do it, lips moving and heads bouncing, without damning ourselves. Solomon admits, in light of the fact that philosophers speak to themselves—a counterexample to his argument that "sexuality is a language . . . and primarily communicative" and hence masturbation *must* be deviant—that "masturbation might, *in different contexts,* count as wholly different extensions of language" (*SAP,* 283; italics added). But this qualification implies that Solomon's negative judgment of masturbation is unjustified. Sometimes we want to converse with another person; sometimes we want to have that conversation sexually. In other contexts—in other moods, with other people, in different settings—we want only the pleasure of touching the other's body or of being touched and no serious messages are communicated. To turn around one of Solomon's points: sometimes pleasure is the goal of sexual activity, and even though communication might occur it is not the desired or intended result but only an unremarkable or merely curious side effect. In still other contexts, we will not want to talk with anyone at all, but spend time alone. We might want to avoid intercourse, of both types, with human beings, those hordes from whose noisy prattle we try to escape by running off to Montana—not an "ultimate retreat" but a blessed haven. For Solomon to call masturbation "empty" in the face of such obvious facts about the importance of context to human sexuality in its many forms is to confess that he did not understand his own qualification.

Men's Liberation

One of the conspicuous curiosities of the late 20th century is that telling the liberal from the conservative is no longer easy. Consider the views of John Stoltenberg, a student of the feminists Catharine MacKinnon and Andrea Dworkin. Stoltenberg rightly complains about the "cultural imperative" according to which men in our society must "fuck" in order to *be* men, and he rightly calls "baloney" the idea that "if two people don't have intercourse, they have not had real sex."[13] Stoltenberg also observes that "sometimes men have coital sex . . . not because they particularly feel like it but because they feel they *should* feel like it." This is a reasonable philosophy of men's liberation and men's feminism. But from these observations Stoltenberg fails to draw the almost obvious masturbatory conclusion. Indeed, it is jolting to behold Stoltenberg, in an argument reminiscent of religious objections to contraception (it makes women sexual objects), laying a guilt trip on men who masturbate with pornography:

> Pay your money and imagine. Pay your money and get real turned on. Pay your money and jerk off. That kind of sex helps . . . support an industry committed to making people with penises believe that people without are sluts who just want to be ravished and reviled—an industry dedicated to maintaining a sex-class system in which men believe themselves sex machines and men believe women are mindless fuck tubes. (35–36)

Given Kant's dismal view of human sexual interaction as essentially instrumental, and Stoltenberg's criticism of the social imperative that men must fuck women to be men, surely *something* can be said on behalf of solitary masturbation. The men's movement attack on oppressive cultural definitions of masculinity and feminist worries about the integrity of sexual activity between unequally empowered men and women suggest that men's masturbation is at least a partial solution to a handful of problems. A man pleasing himself by masturbating is not taking advantage of economically and socially less powerful women; he is not refurbishing the infrastructure of his fragile ego at the expense of womankind. He is, instead, flouting cultural standards of masculinity that instruct him that he must perform sexually with women in order to be a man. Yet it is fantasizing and the heightened sexual pleasure that the imagination makes possible (44)—the things I mentioned in arguing that masturbation is complete, in Nagel's sense—that Stoltenberg points to as constituents of wrongful sexual objectification. He does not merely condemn masturbating with pornography (35–36, 42–43, 49–50). Fantasy *per se* is a fault: Stoltenberg condemns men's masturbating with memories of and passing thoughts about women, even when these fantasies are not violent (41–44). According to Stoltenberg, a man's conjuring up a mental image of a woman, her body, or its various parts, is to view her as an object, as a thing.

The mental objectification involved in sexual fantasy is, for Stoltenberg, both a cause and a result of our social system of "male supremacy" (51, 53–54). Further, mental sexual objectification contributes to violence against women (54–55). Stoltenberg's reason for thinking this is flimsy. He supposes that when a man fantasizes sexually about women, he reduces them from persons to objects. Further, when a man thinks of women as things, he has given himself *carte blanche* in his behavior toward them, including violence: regarding an object "you can do anything to it you want" (55). Of course the last claim is false; there are innumerable lifeless objects to which I would never lay a hand, either because other people value them, and I value these people, or because I dearly value the objects. Therefore, reducing a woman to a thing—or, to describe it more faithfully to men's experiences than Stoltenberg: emphasizing for a while the beauty of only one aspect of a person's existence—does not mean, either logically or psychologically, that she can or will be tossed around the way a young girl slings her Barbie.

Stoltenberg vastly underestimates the nuances of men's fantasies about women; his phenomenological account of what occurs in the minds of fantasizing men—the purported reduction of persons to things—is crude. Her smile, the way she moves down the stairs, the bounce of her tush, the sexy thoughts in her own mind, her lusty yearning for me—these are mere parts of her. But fantasizing or imagining them while masturbating, or driving my car, or having coffee, need not amount to, indeed is *the opposite of,* my reducing her to plastic. These are fantasies about people, not things. My fantasy of her (having a) fantasy of me (or of my [having a] fantasy of her) is structurally too sophisticated to be called objectification. The fantasizer makes himself in his consciousness both subject and object and imagines his partner as both subject and object. Recognizing the imagined person ontologically as a person is hardly a superfluous component of men's—or women's—fantasies. That Stoltenberg overlooks the complex structure of men's fantasies about women is not surprising; the primitive idea that men vulgarly reduce women to objects in their fantasies is precisely what would occur to someone who has already objectified men, who has reduced men from full persons having intricate psychologies to robots with penises.

Conjugal Union

The conservative philosopher and legal scholar John Finnis claims, plausibly, that there are morally worthless sexual acts in which "one's body is treated as instrumental for the securing of the experiential satisfaction of the conscious self."[14] Out of context, this seems to be condemning rape, the use of one person by another for mere "experiential satisfaction." But rape is the farthest thing from Finnis's mind; he is talking not about coerced sex, but that which is fully voluntary. When is sex instrumental, and hence worthless, even though consensual? Finnis immediately mentions, creating the impression that these are his primary targets, that "in masturbating, as in being . . . sodomized," the body is just a tool of satisfaction. As a result of one's body being used, a person undergoes "disintegration": in masturbation and homosexual anal intercourse "one's choosing self [becomes] the quasi-slave of the experiencing self which is demanding gratification." We should ask—since Finnis sounds remarkably like the Kant who claims that sex by its nature is instrumental and objectifying—how acts other than sodomy and masturbation avoid this problem. Finnis's answer is that they do not; the worthlessness and disintegration attaching to sodomy attach to "all extramarital sexual gratification." The physical character of the act is not the decisive factor; the division between the wholesome and the worthless, for Finnis, is between "conjugal activity" and everything else.

The question, then, is: what is special about the conjugal bed that allows marital sex to avoid promoting disintegration? Finnis replies that worthlessness and disintegration attach to masturbation and sodomy in virtue of the fact that in these activities "one's conduct is not the actualizing and experiencing of a real common good." Marriage, on the other hand,

> with its double blessing—procreation and friendship—is a real common good . . . that can be both actualized and experienced in the orgasmic union of the reproductive organs of a man and a woman united in commitment to that good.

Maybe being married *is* conducive to the worthiness of sexual activity. Even so, what is wrong with sex between two single consenting adults who care about and enjoy pleasing each other in bed? Does not this mutual pleasuring avoid shamefulness and worthlessness? No: the friends might only be seeking pleasure for its own sake, as occurs in sodomy and masturbation. And although Finnis thinks that "pleasure is indeed a good," he qualifies that concession with "*when* it is the experienced aspect of one's participation in some intelligible good" (italics added). For Finnis's argument to work, he must claim that pleasure is a good *only when* it is an aspect of the pursuit or achievement of some other good. This is not quite what he says. Perhaps he does not say it because he fears his readers will reject such an extreme reservation about pleasure, or because he realizes it is false: the pleasure of tasting food is good in itself, regardless of whether the eating is part of the goods of securing nutrition or sharing table.

What if the friends say that they do have a common good, their friendship, the same way a married couple has the common good that is their marriage? If "their friendship is not marital . . . activation of their reproductive organs cannot be, in reality, an . . . actualization of their friendship's common good." The claim is obscure. Finnis tries to explain, and in doing so reveals the crux of his sexual philosophy:

the common good of friends who are not and cannot be married (man and
man, man and boy, woman and woman) has nothing to do with their having children by each other, and their reproductive organs cannot make
them a biological (and therefore a personal) unit.

Finnis began with the Kantian intuition that sexual activity involves
treating the body instrumentally, and he concludes with the Kantian
intuition that sex in marriage avoids disintegrity since the couple is a
(biological) "unit," or insofar as "the orgasmic union of the reproductive organs of husband and wife really unites them biologically." In order for persons to be part of a genuine union, their sexual activity must
be both marital and procreative. The psychic falling apart each person
would undergo in nonmarital sex is prevented in marital sex by their
joining into one; this bolstering of the self against a metaphysical hur-
ricane is gained by the tempestuous orgasm, of all things. At the heart
of Finnis's philosophy is a scientific absurdity, and further conversation with him becomes difficult. But the argument, even if it shows the
worthlessness of sterile homosexuality and solitary masturbation, has
no relevance for heterosexual friends, for those who are not, but could
be, married. After all, if marriage has the "double blessing" of procreation and friendship, heterosexual friendship can have the same double blessing. Does Finnis want to claim that if these friends are
committed to each other for a lifetime and plan to, or do, have children by each other, they are *married* and hence their sexual interactions are fine? That claim might be true, but Finnis does not and would
not assert it. Others in his school make it clear that marriage requires
more than an informal agreement between people to spend their lives
together indefinitely; no genuine commitment (or love, or union) exists without a formal compact, since a promise too easily fled is no
promise at all.

Transcendental Illusions

For Finnis, the self is so fragile metaphysically that sex for the sheer
pleasure of it threatens to burst it apart. For Roger Scruton, another
conservative who condemns masturbation, the ephemeral self is in
continual danger of being exposed as a fraud: "In my [sexual] desire
[for you] I am gripped by the illusion of a transcendental unity behind the opacity of [your] flesh."[15] We are not transcendental selves
but material beings; "excretion is the final 'no' to all our transcendental illusions" (151). We are redeemed only through "a metaphysical illusion residing in the heart of sexual desire" (95). Our passions
make it *appear* that we are ontologically more than we really are. Sexuality must be treated with kid gloves, then, lest we lose the socially

useful and spiritually uplifting reassurance that we humans are the pride of the universe.

The requirement that sex be approached somberly translates, for Scruton, not only into the ordinary claim that sex must be educated to be the partner of heterosexual love, but also into a number of silly judgments. While discussing the "obscenity" of masturbation, Scruton offers this example:

> Consider the woman who plays with her clitoris during the act of coition. Such a person affronts her lover with the obscene display of her body, and, in perceiving her thus, the lover perceives his own irrelevance. She becomes disgusting to him, and his desire may be extinguished. The woman's desire is satisfied at the expense of her lover's, and no real union can be achieved between them. (319)

Feminism has contested the tradition, revived by Scruton, in which the clitoris, the organ of women's masturbation and pleasure and a symbol of their autonomy, is suspicious.[16] Even if in rubbing herself during coitus, a woman asserts independence from her partner, must that be bad? One reply to Scruton, then, is that without masturbation, *her* desire might be extinguished and *his* desire satisfied at the expense of hers, and still there is no union. We could, instead, recommend to the man who "perceives his own irrelevance" that he become more involved in his partner's pleasure by helping her massage her clitoral or some other region or doing the rubbing for her; even when they are linked together coitally, he will find the arms long and the body flexible. But Scruton's claim is false (in this country) that most men would perceive a woman's masturbation during coitus as "disgusting." Her doing so can even help the couple attain the very union Scruton hopes for as the way to perpetrate our metaphysical illusion, by letting them experience and recognize the mutual pleasure, perhaps the mutual orgasm, that results.

Why does Scruton judge the woman's masturbation an "obscene display"? One part of his thinking is this. When masturbation is done in public (say, a bus station), it is obscene; it "cannot be witnessed without a sense of obscenity." Scruton then draws the astounding conclusion that *all* masturbation is obscene, even when done privately, on the grounds that "that which cannot be witnessed without obscene perception is itself obscene" (319). Scruton seems not to notice that his argument proves too much; it implies that heterosexual coitus engaged in by a loving, married couple in private is also obscene, if we assume—as I think he would—that this act "cannot be witnessed," in public, "without obscene perception." The fault lies in the major premise of Scruton's syllogism. Whether an act is obscene might turn exactly on whether it is done publicly or privately. Scruton has failed to acknowledge a difference between exposing oneself to anonymous spectators and opening oneself to the gaze of a lover.

All masturbation is obscene, for Scruton, also because it "involves a concentration on the body and its curious pleasures" (319). Obscenity is an "obsession . . . with the organs themselves and with the pleasures of sensation" (154), and even if the acts that focus on the body and its pleasures are paired, they are "masturbatory" (recall how the conservative criticized Goldman's "plain sex"). "In obscenity, attention is taken away from embodiment towards the body" (32), and there is "a 'depersonalized' perception of human sexuality, in which the body and its sexual function are uppermost in our thoughts" (138). A woman's masturbation during coitus is obscene since it leads the pair to focus too sharply on the physical; she is a depersonalized body instead of a person-in-a-body. Thus, for Scruton, this obscene masturbation cannot sustain, indeed threatens, the couple's metaphysical illusion. But if a woman's masturbation during coitus is greeted with delight by a partner, rather than with disgust, and increases the pleasure they realize and recognize in the act together, then, contrary to Scruton, either not all masturbation is obscene (the parties have not been reduced altogether to flesh) or obscenity, all things considered, is not a total sexual, normative, or metaphysical disaster.

Guilt

A common platitude says, "there is not one shred of evidence that masturbation is harmful. . . . The only harm that can result from masturbation is if the individual is plagued with feelings of guilt."[17] Thus, in reply to the oft-heard advice that we should not masturbate because doing so will make us feel anxious, depressed, or guilty, it is just as often mentioned that only because philosophy, medicine, theology, and popular opinion treat the act in a disparaging way do we run the risk of experiencing anxiety or guilt in the first place. That is to some extent true, but to repeat this rejoinder might no longer be convincing. Maybe we have gone too far in reaction against views critical of masturbation and it is time for a swing back to traditional intuitions, if not thermoelectrocautery. There are other reasons for the moral criticism of fantasy and masturbation, some of which have emerged from feminist thought, especially among those who have continued to press the question of pornography: if pornography is morally objectionable, seriously degrading to women, making heterosexual men feel guilty for masturbating with such horrible stuff might be legitimate. Maybe Rousseau was right, after all, to imply that sexual fantasy, a mental depiction, is little different from rape.

Notes

1. Philip Roth, *Portnoy's Complaint* (New York: Random House, 1969), 88.

2. Immanuel Kant, *Lectures on Ethics,* trans. Louis Infield (New York: Harper and Row, 1963), 162–71, at 163.

3. *Lectures on Ethics,* 166–67.

4. "If a fusion of one and the other truly exists, . . . the very possibility of using an *other* as a means no longer exists" (Robert Baker and Frederick Elliston, eds., *Philosophy and Sex* [Buffalo: Prometheus, 1975, 1984], 1st ed., 18; 2d ed., 26–27). Kantian fusion seems to make rape in marriage (a kind of use) logically impossible.

5. "Masturbation" is thus the answer to Barbara Herman's question, "sex would then be what?" if Kant were right that (in her words) "we become parts of a new self that has two bodies" ("Could It Be Worth Thinking About Kant on Sex and Marriage?" in Louise M. Antony and Charlotte Witt, eds., *A Mind of One's Own* [Boulder: Westview, 1993], 49–67, at 61).

6. Herman, "Could It Be Worth Thinking," 66 n. 22.

7. *Lectures on Ethics,* 170.

8. A notable contrast is Russell Vannoy's treatment of masturbation, *Sex Without Love* (Buffalo: Prometheus, 1980), 111–17.

9. "Plain Sex," *Philosophy and Public Affairs* 6 (1977): 267–87; reprinted in Alan Soble, ed., *Philosophy of Sex* (Totowa, N.J.: Rowman & Littlefield, 1980; Savage, Md., 1991), 1st ed., 119–38; 2d ed., 73–92; this volume, 39–55.

10. "Sexual Perversion," *Journal of Philosophy* 66 (1969): 5–17; reprinted in Soble, *Philosophy of Sex,* 1st ed., 76–88; 2d ed., 39–51; this volume, 9–20.

11. "Sexual Paradigms," *Journal of Philosophy* 71 (1974): 336–45; reprinted in Soble, *Philosophy of Sex,* 1st ed., 89–98; 2d ed., 53–62; this volume, 21–29; and "Sex and Perversion," Baker and Elliston, *Philosophy and Sex,* 1st ed., 268–87 (references to this essay are preceded by *SAP*).

12. See Goldman, "Plain Sex," 45–48; Hugh Wilder, "The Language of Sex and the Sex of Language," in Alan Soble, ed., *Sex, Love, and Friendship* (Amsterdam: Editions Rodopi, 1997), 23–31.

13. *Refusing to Be a Man* (Portland, Ore.: Breitenbush Books, 1989), 39.

14. John Finnis and Martha Nussbaum, "Is Homosexual Conduct Wrong? A Philosophical Exchange," *The New Republic* (15 November 1993), 12–13; this volume, 89–94.

15. *Sexual Desire: A Moral Philosophy of the Erotic* (New York: Free Press, 1986), 130.

16. See Shere Hite, *The Hite Report: A Nationwide Study on Female Sexuality* (New York: Dell, 1976).

17. James Haynes, "Masturbation," in V. Bullough and B. Bullough, eds., *Human Sexuality: An Encyclopedia* (New York: Garland, 1994), 381–85, at 384.

PART 2
HOMOSEXUALITY

Chapter 8

IS HOMOSEXUAL CONDUCT WRONG?
A PHILOSOPHICAL EXCHANGE

John Finnis and Martha C. Nussbaum

John Finnis

The underlying thought is on the following lines. In masturbating, as in being masturbated or sodomized, one's body is treated as instrumental for the securing of the experiential satisfaction of the conscious self. Thus one disintegrates oneself in two ways, (1) by treating one's body as a mere instrument of the consciously operating self, and (2) by making one's choosing self the quasi-slave of the experiencing self which is demanding gratification. The worthlessness of the gratification, and the disintegration of oneself, are both the result of the fact that, in these sorts of behavior, one's conduct is not the actualizing and experiencing of a real common good. Marriage, with its double blessing—procreation and friendship—is a real common good. Moreover, it is a common good that can be both actualized and experienced in the orgasmic union of the reproductive organs of a man and a woman united in commitment to that good. Conjugal sexual activity, and—as Plato and Aristotle and Plutarch and Kant all argue—*only* conjugal activity is free from the shamefulness of instrumentalization that is found in masturbating and in being masturbated or sodomized.

©1993, *The New Republic*. Reprinted with permission from *The New Republic*, 15 November 1993, pp. 12–13. This material was extracted from legal depositions filed in *Romer v. Evans* (the 1993 "Colorado Amendment 2" case).

At the very heart of the reflections of Plato, Xenophon, Aristotle, Musonius Rufus, and Plutarch on the homoerotic culture around them is the very deliberate and careful judgment that homosexual *conduct* (and indeed all extramarital sexual gratification) is radically incapable of participating in, or actualizing, the common good of friendship. Friends who engage in such conduct are following a natural impulse and doubtless often wish their genital conduct to be an intimate expression of their mutual affection. But they are deceiving themselves. The attempt to express affection by orgasmic nonmarital sex is the pursuit of an illusion. The orgasmic union of the reproductive organs of husband and wife really unites them biologically (and their biological reality is part of, not merely an instrument of, their *personal* reality); that orgasmic union therefore can actualize and allow them to experience their real common good—their marriage with the two goods, children and friendship, which are the parts of its wholeness as an intelligible common good. But the common good of friends who are not and cannot be married (man and man, man and boy, woman and woman) has nothing to do with their having children by each other, and their reproductive organs cannot make them a biological (and therefore a personal) unit. So their genital acts together cannot do what they may hope and imagine.

In giving their considered judgment that homosexual conduct cannot actualize the good of friendship, Plato and the many philosophers who followed him intimate an answer to the questions why it should be considered shameful to use, or allow another to use, one's body to give pleasure, and why this use of one's body differs from one's bodily participation in countless other activities (e.g., games) in which one takes and/or gets pleasure. Their response is that pleasure is indeed a good, when it is the experienced aspect of one's participation in some intelligible good, such as a task going well, or a game or a dance or a meal or a reunion. Of course, the activation of sexual organs with a view to the pleasures of orgasm is sometimes spoken of as if it were a game. But it differs from real games in that its point is not the exercise of skill; rather, this activation of reproductive organs is focused upon the body precisely as a source of pleasure for one's consciousness. So this is a "use of the body" in a strongly different sense of "use." The body now is functioning not in the way one, as a bodily person, acts to instantiate some other intelligible good, but precisely as providing a service to one's consciousness, to satisfy one's desire for satisfaction.

This disintegrity is much more obvious when masturbation is solitary. Friends are tempted to think that pleasuring each other by some forms of mutual masturbation could be an instantiation or actualization or promotion of their friendship. But that line of thought overlooks the fact that if their friendship is not marital . . . activation of their reproductive organs cannot be, in reality, an instantiation or actualization of their friendship's common good. In reality, whatever the generous hopes and dreams with which the loving partners surround their use of their genitals, *that use* cannot express more than is expressed if two strangers engage in genital activity to give each other orgasm, or a prostitute pleasures a client, or a man pleasures himself. Hence, Plato's judgment, at the decisive moment of the *Gorgias,* that there is no important distinction in essential moral worthlessness between solitary masturbation, being sodomized as a prostitute and being sodomized for the pleasure of it. . . .

Societies such as classical Athens and contemporary England (and virtually every other) draw a distinction between behavior found merely (perhaps extremely) offensive (such as eating excrement) and behavior to be repudiated as destructive of human character and relationships. Copulation of humans with animals is repudiated because it treats human sexual activity and satisfaction as something appropriately sought in a manner that, like the coupling of animals, is divorced from the expressing of an intelligible common good—and so treats human bodily life, in one of its most intense activities, as merely animal. The deliberate genital coupling of persons of the same sex is repudiated for a very similar reason. It is not simply that it is sterile and disposes the participants to an abdication of responsibility for the future of humankind. Nor is it simply that it cannot *really* actualize the mutual devotion that some homosexual persons hope to manifest and experience by it; nor merely that it harms the personalities of its participants by its disintegrative manipulation of different parts of their one personal reality. It is also that it treats human sexual capacities in a way that is deeply hostile to the self-understanding of those members of the community who are willing to commit themselves to real marriage [even one that happens to be sterile] in the understanding that its sexual joys are not mere instruments or accompaniments to, or mere compensation for, the accomplishments of marriage's responsibilities, but rather are the *actualizing and experiencing* of the intelligent commitment to share in those responsibilities. . . .

This pattern of judgment, both widespread and sound, concludes as follows. Homosexual orientation—the deliberate willingness to promote and engage in homosexual acts—is a standing denial of the intrinsic aptness of sexual intercourse to actualize and give expression to the exclusiveness and open-ended commitment of marriage as something good in itself. All who accept that homosexual acts can be a humanly appropriate use of sexual capacities must, if consistent, regard sexual capacities, organs, and acts as instruments to be put to whatever suits the purposes of the individual "self" who has them. Such an acceptance is commonly (and in my opinion rightly) judged to be an active threat to the stability of existing and future marriages; it makes nonsense, for example, of the view that adultery is per se (and not merely because it may involve deception), and in an important way, inconsistent with conjugal love. A political community that judges that the stability and educative generosity of family life is of fundamental importance to the community's present and future can rightly judge that it has a compelling interest in denying that homosexual conduct is a valid, humanly acceptable choice and form of life, and in doing whatever it properly can, as a community with uniquely wide but still subsidiary functions, to discourage such conduct.

Martha C. Nussbaum

Finnis's arguments against homosexuality set themselves in a tradition of "natural law" argumentation that derives from ancient Greek traditions. The term "law of nature" was first used by Plato in his *Gorgias*. The approach is further developed by Aristotle and, above all, by the Greek and Roman Stoics, who are usually considered to be the founders of natural law argumentation in the modern legal tradition, through their influence on Roman law. This being so, it is worth looking to see whether those traditions did in fact use "natural law" arguments to rule homosexual conduct morally or legally substandard.

Plato's dialogues contain several extremely moving celebrations of male–male love, and judge this form of love to be, on the whole, superior to male–female love because of its potential for spirituality and friendship. The *Symposium* contains a series of speeches, each expressing conventional views about this subject that Plato depicts in an appealing light. The speech by Phaedrus points to the military advantages derived by including homosexual couples in a fighting force: Because of their intense love, each will fight better, wishing to show himself in the best light before his lover. The speech of Pausanias criticizes males who seek physical pleasure alone in their homosexual relationships, and praises those who seek in sex deeper spiritual communication. Pausanias mentions that tyrants will sometimes promulgate the view that same-sex relations are shameful in order to discourage the kind of community of dedication to political liberty that such relations foster. The speech of Aristophanes holds that all human beings are divided halves of formerly whole beings, and that sexual desire is the pursuit of one's lost other half; he points out that the superior people in any society are those whose lost "other half" is of the same sex—especially the male–male pairs—since these are likely to be the strongest and most warlike and civically minded people. Finally, Socrates' speech recounts a process of religious-mystical education in which male–male love plays a central guiding role and is a primary source of insight and inspiration into the nature of the good and beautiful.

Plato's *Phaedrus* contains a closely related praise of the intellectual, political, and spiritual benefits of a life centered around male–male love. Plato says that the highest form of human life is one in which a male pursues "the love of a young man along with philosophy," and is transported by passionate desire. He describes the experience of falling in love with another male in moving terms, and defends relationships that are mutual and reciprocal over relationships that are one-sided. He depicts his pairs of lovers as spending their life together in the pursuit of intellectual and spiritual activities, combined with political participation. (Although no marriages for these lovers are mentioned, it was the view of the time that this form of life does not prevent its participants from having a wife at home, whom they saw only rarely and for procreative purposes.)

Aristotle speaks far less about sexual love than does Plato, but it is evident that he too finds in male–male relationships the potential for the highest form of friendship, a friendship based on mutual well-wishing and mutual awareness of good character and good aims. He does not find this potential in male–female relationships, since he holds that females are incapable of good character. Like Pausanias in Plato's *Symposium,* Aristotle is critical of relationships that are superficial and concerned only with bodily pleasure; but he finds in male–male relationships—including many that begin in this way—the potential for much richer developments.

The ideal city of the Greek Stoics was built around the idea of pairs of male lovers whose bonds gave the city rich sources of motivation for virtue. Although the Stoics wished their "wise man" to eliminate most passions from his life, they encouraged him to foster a type of erotic love that they defined as "the attempt to form a friendship inspired by the perceived beauty of young men in their prime." They held that this love, unlike other passions, was supportive of virtue and philosophical activity.

Furthermore, Finnis's argument . . . against homosexuality is a bad moral argument by any standard, secular or theological. First of all, it assumes that the purpose of a homosexual act is always or usually casual bodily pleasure and the instrumental use of another person for one's own gratification. But this is a false premise, easily disproved by the long historical tradition I have described and by the contemporary lives of real men and women. Finnis offers no evidence for this premise, or for the equally false idea that procreative relations cannot be selfish and manipulative. Second, having argued that a relationship is better if it seeks not casual pleasure but the creation of a community, he then assumes without argument that the only sort of community a sexual relationship can create is a "procreative community." This is, of course, plainly false. A sexual relationship may create, quite apart from the possibility of procreation, a community of love and friendship, which no religious tradition would deny to be important human goods. Indeed, in many moral traditions, including those of Plato and Aristotle, the procreative community is ranked beneath other communities created by sex, since it is thought that the procreative community will probably not be based on the best sort of friendship and the deepest spiritual concerns. That may not be true in a culture that values women more highly than ancient Greek culture did; but the possibility of love and friendship between individuals of the same sex has not been removed by these historical changes.

Chapter 9

WHY HOMOSEXUALITY IS ABNORMAL

Michael Levin

1. Introduction

This paper defends the view that homosexuality is abnormal and hence undesirable—not because it is immoral or sinful, or because it weakens society or hampers evolutionary development, but for a purely mechanical reason. It is a misuse of bodily parts. Clear empirical sense attaches to the idea of *the use* of such bodily parts as genitals, the idea that they are *for* something, and consequently to the idea of their misuse. I argue on grounds involving natural selection that misuse of bodily parts can with high probability be connected to unhappiness. I regard these matters as prolegomena to such policy issues as the rights of homosexuals, the rights of those desiring not to associate with homosexuals, and legislation concerning homosexuality, issues which I shall not discuss systematically here. However, I do in the last section draw a seemingly evident corollary from my view that homosexuality is abnormal and likely to lead to unhappiness.

I have confined myself to male homosexuality for brevity's sake, but I believe that much of what I say applies *mutatis mutandis* to lesbianism. There may well be significant differences between the two: the data of [5], for example, support the popular idea that sex *per se* is less important to women and in particular lesbians than it is to men. On the other hand, lesbians are generally denied motherhood, which seems more important to women than is fatherhood—normally denied homosexual males—to men. On this matter, [5] offers no data. Overall, it is reasonable to expect general innate gender differences to explain the major differences between male homosexuals and lesbians.

Despite the publicity currently enjoyed by the claim that one's "sexual preference" is nobody's business but one's own, the intuition that there is something unnatural about homosexuality remains vital. The erect penis fits the vagina, and fits it better than any other natural orifice; penis and vagina seem made for each other. This intuition ultimately derives from, or is another way of capturing, the idea that the penis is not *for* inserting into the anus of another man—that so using the penis is not the way it is *supposed*, even *intended*, to be used. Such intuitions may appear to rest on an outmoded teleological view of nature, but recent work in the logic of functional ascription shows how they may be explicated, and justified, in suitably naturalistic terms. Such is the burden of Section 2, the particular application to homosexuality coming in Section 3. Furthermore, when we understand the sense in which homosexual acts involve a misuse of genitalia, we will see why such misuse is bad and not to be encouraged. (The case for this constitutes the balance of Section 3.) Clearly, the general idea that homosexuality is a pathological violation of nature's intent is not shunned by scientists. Here is Gadpille:

> The view of cultural relativity seems to be without justification. Cultural judgment is collective human caprice, and whether it accepts or rejects homosexuality is irrelevant. Biological intent . . . is to differentiate male and female both physiologically and psychologically in such a manner as to insure species survival, which can be served only through heterosexual union ([10], 193).

Gadpille refers to homosexuality as "an abiological maladaptation." The novelty of the present paper is to link adaptiveness and normality via the notion of happiness.

But before turning to these issues, I want to make four preliminary remarks. The first concerns the explicitness of my language in the foregoing paragraph and the rest of this paper. Explicit mention of bodily parts and the frank description of sexual acts are necessary to keep the phenomenon under discussion in clear focus. Euphemistic vagary about "sexual orientation" or "the gay lifestyle" encourages one to slide over homosexuality without having to face or even acknowledge what it really is. Such talk encourages one to treat "sexual preference" as if it were akin to preference among flavors of ice-cream. Since unusual taste in ice-cream is neither right nor wrong, this usage suggests, why should unusual taste in sex be regarded as objectionable? Opposed to this usage is the unblinkable fact that the sexual preferences in question are such acts as mutual fellation. Is one man's taste for pistachio ice-cream really just like another man's taste for fellation? Unwillingness to call this particular spade a spade allows delicacy to award the field by default to the view that homosexuality is normal. Anyway, such delicacy is misplaced in a day when "the love that dare not speak its name" is shouting its name from the rooftops.[1]

My second, related, point concerns the length of the present paper, which has a general and a specific cause. The general cause is that advocates of an unpopular position—as mine is, at least in intellectual circles—assume the burden of proof. My view is the one that needs defending, my presuppositions the ones not widely shared. I would not have entertained so many implausible and digressive objections had not so many competent philosophers urged them on me with great seriousness. Some of these objections even generate a dialectic among themselves. For example, I have to defend my view on two sociobiological fronts—against the view that what is innate is polymorphous sexuality shaped by culture, and against the incompatible view that not only are the details of sexual behavior innate, but homosexuality is one such behavior, and hence "normal."

The third point is this. The chain of intuitions I discussed earlier has other links, links connected to the conclusion that homosexuality is bad. They go something like this: Homosexual acts involve the use of the genitals for what they aren't for, and it is a *bad* or at least *unwise* thing to use a part of your body for what it isn't for. Calling homosexual acts "unnatural" is intended to sum up this entire line of reasoning. "Unnatural" carries disapprobative connotations, and any explication of it should capture this. One can, stipulatively or by observing the ordinary usage of biologists, coin an evaluatively neutral use for "normal," or "proper function," or any cognate thereof. One might for example take the normal use of an organ to be what the organ is used for 95% of the time. But there is a normative dimension to the concept of abnormality that all such explications miss. To have anything to do with our intuitions—even if designed to demonstrate them groundless—an explication of "abnormal" must capture the analytic truth that the abnormality of a practice is a reason for avoiding it. If our ordinary concept of normality turns out to be ill-formed, so that various acts are at worst "abnormal" in some non-evaluative sense, this will simply mean that, as we ordinarily use the expression, *nothing is abnormal.* (Not that anyone really believes this— people who deny that cacophagia or necrophilia are abnormal do so only to maintain the appearance of consistency.)

Fourth, I should mention Steven Goldberg's defense of a position similar to mine ([11]). Goldberg's first approximation to a definition of abnormality runs as follows: behavior is abnormal when it is emitted in circumstances in which it is highly negatively sanctioned. This captures the insight that even if there is nothing *intrinsically* wrong with a bit of behavior, there probably must be something wrong with anyone who persists in doing it when he knows he will be punished. There may be nothing wrong with eating beef *per se*, but there must be something wrong with a Hindu who invites death by walking the streets of Calcutta eating a hamburger. The trouble with this definition is that as it stands it brands as abnormal a highly-sanctioned behavior done to make a moral point. To exclude such cases Goldberg adds a second clause: person A's doing act B is abnormal if A is caused to do B by conditions one would intuitively judge to be abnormal. This excludes high-minded sacrifices but does include homosexuality if, as Freudians believe, homosexuality results from maternal dominance and paternal indifference, conditions most people regard as abnormal. Goldberg is aware that defining "abnormal" via "abnormal cause" is circular, but he finds the circularity benign. He contends that the definition does capture a definite reality people have in mind when they label homosexuality or necrophilia abnormal, and that anyone who brings the charge of circularity must also take this circularity to prevent us from viewing necrophilia as abnormal. Goldberg assumes that no reasonable person would carry the charge of circularity that far.

Goldberg's analysis is persuasive, and the first clause should be preserved, even if the circular second clause is jettisoned. My own analysis—which I believe to be even clearer than Goldberg's as well as more formally adequate—is indeed compatible with Goldberg's. It turns out that what Goldberg has correctly analyzed is not what "abnormal" means, but the *evidence* on which ordinary judgements of abnormality are based. That something is abnormal in Goldberg's sense is good evidence that it is abnormal in the central sense I explicate below. I will have occasion to use this lemma.

2. On "Function" and Its Cognates

To bring into relief the point of the idea that homosexuality involves a misuse of bodily parts, I will begin with an uncontroversial case of misuse, a case in which the clarity of our intuitions is not obscured by the conviction that they are untrustworthy. Mr. Jones pulls all his teeth and strings them around his neck because he thinks his teeth look nice as a necklace. He takes pureéd liquids supplemented by intravenous solutions for nourishment. It is surely natural to say that Jones is misusing his teeth, that he is not using them for what they are for, that indeed the way he is using them is incompatible with what they are for. Pedants might argue that Jones's teeth are no longer part of him and hence that he is not misusing any bodily parts. To them I offer Mr. Smith, who likes to play "Old MacDonald" on his teeth. So devoted is he to this amusement, in fact, that he never uses his teeth for chewing—like Jones, he takes nourishment intravenously. Now, not only do we find it perfectly plain that Smith and Jones are misusing their teeth, we predict a dim future for them on purely physiological grounds; we expect the muscles of Jones's jaw that are used for—that *are* for—chewing to lose their tone, and we expect this to affect Jones's gums. Those parts of Jones's digestive tract that are for processing solids will also suffer from disuse. The net result will be deteriorating health and perhaps a shortened life. Nor is this all. Human beings enjoy chewing. Not only has natural selection selected in muscles for chewing and favored creatures with such muscles, it has selected in a tendency to find the use of those muscles reinforcing. Creatures who do not enjoy using such parts of their bodies as deteriorate with disuse will tend to be selected out. Jones, product of natural selection that he is, descended from creatures who at least tended to enjoy the use of such parts. Competitors who didn't simply had fewer descendants. So we expect Jones sooner or later to experience vague yearnings to chew something, just as we find people who take no exercise to experience a general listlessness. Even waiving for now my apparent reification of the evolutionary process, let me emphasize how little anyone is tempted to say "each to his own" about Jones or to regard Jones's disposition of his teeth as simply a deviation from a statistical norm. This sort of case is my paradigm when discussing homosexuality.

The main obstacle to talk of what a process or organic structure is for is that, literally understood, such talk presupposes an agent who intends that structure or process to be used in a certain way. Talk of function derives its primitive meaning from the human use of artifacts, artifacts being for what purposive agents intend them for. Indeed, there is in this primitive context a natural reason for using something for what it is for: to use it otherwise would frustrate the intention of some purposeful agent. Since it now seems clear that our bodily parts were not emplaced by purposeful agency, it is easy to dismiss talk of what they are for as "theologically" based on a faulty theory of how we came to be built as we are:

> The idea that sex was designed for propagation is a theological argument, but not a scientific one. . . . To speak of the "fit" of penis and vagina as proof of nature's intention for their exclusive union is pure theological reasoning—imposing a meaning or purpose upon a simple, natural phenomenon ([12], 63).

Barash—who elsewhere uses its cognates freely—dismisses "unnatural" as a mere term of abuse: "people with a social or political axe to grind will call what they don't like 'unnatural' and what they do, 'natural'" ([1], 237). Hume long ago put the philosopher's case against the term 'natural' with characteristic succinctness: " 'Tis founded on final Causes;

which is a consideration, that appears to me pretty uncertain & un-philosophical. For pray, what is the End of Man? Is he created for Happiness or for Virtue? For this Life or the next? For himself or for his Maker?" ([24], 134).

Until recently, philosophers of science half-countered, half-conceded such doubts by "rationally reconstructing" the locution "structure S is for function F in organism O" as—omitting inessential refinements—"S's doing F in O is necessary for the integrity or prosperity of O" (see e.g., [25], ch. 7). This, the classical analysis, suffers from two weaknesses. First, it quite severs the link stressed earlier between a structure's having a function and the inadvisability of using that structure in a way inconsistent with its function. An organism may not be interested in survival, or prosperity, or the prosperity of some genetically defined group that contains the organism. The classical analysis provides no clue as to why Jones should desist from stringing his teeth on a necklace. It must be supplemented with the premise that survival or fitness is desirable, and however strong the desire to survive may be as a *de facto* motive, there are too many cogent arguments against survival as a basic norm for this supplement to be plausible.

None of this will disturb proponents of the classical analysis, since their very aim was, in part, to remove the teleological and normative connotations of "function" as unscientific ideas. So what if the classical analysis obstructs the inference from "Jones is not using his teeth for what they are for" to "Jones is misusing his teeth"? That is one of its virtues. However, the more decisive second objection to the classical analysis is the existence of clear counter-examples—counter-examples that turn out, on reflection, to be connected to the first objection. An accidentally incurred heart lesion might be necessary for the heart's pumping blood if it is otherwise diseased; but the lesion is not *for* pumping blood. A patient's heartbeat might be the only way his doctor can diagnose a disease that would be fatal if undiagnosed; but the beat of his heart is not *for* diagnosis.[2] Such cases suggest that the classical analysis pays insufficient attention to how structures come to be in organisms and why they persist in reproductive cohorts. In light of this, a more adequate explication of "S is for F in O" runs:

  (i) S conduces to F in O,
  (ii) O's being F is necessary for the maintenance of O or O's genetic cohort, and
  (iii) (i) and (ii) are part of the causal explanation of the existence or persistence of S in O and members of O's genetic cohort (see [6], sec. 23; [18]; and esp. [38]).

In rougher and plainer English: an organ is for a given activity if the organ's performing that activity helps its host or organisms suitably related to its host, *and* if this contribution is how the organ got and stays where it is. This disqualifies the fortuitous heart lesion and the symptomatic heartbeat, which did not arise or persist by increasing (inclusive) fitness. This definition also distinguishes what something is for from what it may be *used* for on some occasion. Teeth are for chewing—we have teeth because their use in chewing favored the survival of organisms with teeth—whereas Jones is using his teeth for ornamentation.

Counter-examples to this explication have appeared in the literature, but none administer more than superficial wounds. What if *S*'s being *F* once was, but is no longer, necessary? What if, for example, implanting semen in the vagina is no longer necessary for propagation because of artificial insemination? The overall shape of my reply will become clearer only a bit later on, but, roughly speaking, if *S* is for *F* in *O* in my sense, *O* will find the use of *S* to *F* reinforcing. This is the point behind the popular observation that whatever modern society is like, humans still carry a heritage of traits evolved by lower mammals and by their tenure as hunter-gatherers. Anyway, such evolutionary lags tend to be unstable. For example, elaborate but clumsy plumage *for* mating displays would likely disappear from a population of birds whose mating was controlled by human breeders uninterested in bright feathers. After, say, 1000 generations, all surviving structures would be used for what, *per* my definition, they *are* for.

What if every time my defective heart pumps, a Martian moves my otherwise inert blood along my arteries? This puzzle belongs to a large class of philosophical puzzles. Do I see something if it causes me to have a visual sensation not by irradiating my retina but through the agency of a Martian who controls my brain from a console? Action is behavior caused by intention—but do I act if my intention provokes a Martian to move my otherwise anesthetized limbs in the direction I intended? What goes wrong in all these puzzle cases is that the causal chain is nonminimal, and what all the foregoing analyses require is a clause to the effect that the causal pathway (between intention and movement, between object and sensation, between causal power and emplacement) be minimal. The great obstacle to refining this idea is that our notions of vision, action and function evolved before anyone knew what the typical or minimal causal path was that connected objects to sensations, or intentions to behavior, or usefulness to emplacement. At most, people had some inchoate notion that *there is* a minimum causal path characteristic of paradigm cases of seeing or acting, and that seeing or acting required a causal path similar to that one. Correct causal analyses may therefore have to be supplemented by the empirical study of such paradigm cases of vision, or action, or natural selection. In an odd sense—a sense adumbrated by Putnam and Kripke, perhaps—"*A* sees *X*" may mean "*X* causes visual sensations by sending photons to *A*'s retina." Similar remarks apply to the causal analysis of action and function.

Notice that my definition refers to an organism's "genetic cohort" rather than its species. Dawkins [7] and others have argued that species-selection does not actually occur in nature. Taking the natural unit of replication, the "gene," as whatever bit of chromosome can retain its identity through enough generations to matter, a gene will most fecundly copy itself if either the organism that contains it, or organisms with a good chance of containing it—relatives of the gene's organism—reproduce prolifically. A gene is not helping itself reproduce if it instructs the body housing it to assist unrelated members of that body's species; it helps itself reproduce by instructing the body housing it to assist the organisms that might have reproducible copies of itself. So natural selection selects for "inclusive fitness": for traits that benefit an organism taken together with some group of relatives (see [36], 343). How wide the group should be is a matter of some debate, and will indeed be different for different kinds of organisms. Nor has species-selection lost all its defenders. For this reason, I am using "genetic cohort" to name whatever degree of relatedness turns out to be most appropriate for evolutionary theory.

One might well ask how my analysis of "function" can be what people meant before Darwin was ever heard of, even if people did have some inchoate notion of "minimum chain of emplacement" in mind. Doesn't "function" inherently refer to someone with a purpose—or, if not, what is simply *de facto* beneficial to organisms? No. What happened, I believe, was that before Darwin people thought that the only way S's aptness for F could cause S's existence was for someone, namely God, to notice that S is apt for F and for this reason choose to put S in O. We now know this is false; we now know of another way S's aptness for F can result in S's implantation—mutational emergence and subsequent natural selection. The core meaning of "function" was always (i)–(iii), the idea that God put organs in organisms being merely a theory about how (iii) was or had to be realized. This theory was so "obvious," however, that it appeared to be part of the meaning of "function" itself. Perhaps in concession to our ancestor's ignorance of causes, "reproductive" ought to replace "genetic" in (iii); beyond that, the present definition does capture what people meant by "function" even before Darwin was ever heard of.

Within a Darwinian setting, the function of bodily parts can be linked to normative notions in a way that imputes no extrinsic direction to evolution. The empirical sense coaxed from "S is for F in O" explains our intuition that, since their efficacy in chewing got them selected in, teeth are for masticating and Jones is preventing his teeth from doing their proper job. To begin, it is clear that "Man has teeth because teeth grind food" cannot mean that the power of teeth to grind food is literally what provided Jones or anyone else with teeth. Causal powers aren't causes, and anyway the causal powers an object would have can hardly be what brings the object into existence. Rather, the presence or persistence of S in O's cohort is better understood in more general evolutionary terms. Genetic mutation brought forth the first S in one of our ancestors. There is a mechanism, the coding of the DNA, that transmits S. Here is where S's causal powers come in. Possession of S aided its first possessor and his cohorts in the struggle for survival, and since S is transmissible, this initial possessor survived to transmit S to his descendants, who, in turn, were better fitted than their S-less competitors to reproduce and transmit S . . . We, the descendants of S's original possessors, possess S as a result of this filtration. And it is just here that a eudaimonistic normative link begins to appear.

Consider this first-approximation guess about one of the mechanisms of natural selection. Imagine for a moment that S is for F in the sense explained, and that exercise of S does not lie wholly within the province of O's autonomic nervous system. It is, loosely speaking, up to O whether to use S, or use S for F. Imagine as well two subpopulations O_1 and O_2. Members of O_1 *enjoy* using S to F, while members of O_2 do not. Since O_2's do not enjoy using S to F, they will use S to F less frequently than do O_1's. Since S favors the survival of possessors of S precisely because S conduces to F, it is the members of O_1 who are more likely to reproduce themselves and transmit, in addition to S, a desire to use S to F. It is thus likely that present-day O's will enjoy using S to F, because they are more probably descendants of the O_1 than of the O_2. Nature is interested in making its creatures like what is (inclusively) good for them. A creature that does not enjoy using its teeth for chewing uses them less than does a toothed competitor who enjoys chewing. Since the use of teeth for chewing favors the survival of an individual with teeth, and, other things being equal, traits favorable to the survival of individuals favor survival of the relevant cohort, toothed creatures who do not enjoy chewing tend to get selected out. We today are the filtrate of this process, descendants of creatures who liked to chew.

To be sure, the best evolutionary strategy might be a mix of O_1-ness and O_2-ness, so that the filtrate of evolution will be creatures with alleles for enjoying, and alleles for not enjoying, the use of S. Constant use of S might be too much of a good thing. The filtrate would be a population mixing O_1's and O_2's. We will consider in due course whether this model is applicable to homosexuality. But even in its simplified form, the present analysis does suggest that a gene for enjoying the use of S to F would at least tend to spread rapidly through O. It is hard to imagine how the enjoyment of the use of such things as human teeth could not take over, and there seems to be no current benefit associated with the absence of this enjoyment. And here—to return to the main strand of the argument—is why it is advisable to use your organs for what they are for: you will enjoy it. Jones's behavior is ill-advised not only because of the avertible objective consequences of his defanging himself, but because he will feel that something is missing. Similarly, this is why you should exercise. It is not just that muscles are for running. We have already heard the sceptic's reply to that: "So what? Suppose I don't mind being flabby? Suppose I don't give a hang about what will propagate my genetic cohort?" Rather, running is good because nature made sure people like to run. This is, of course, the prudential "good," not the moral "good"— but I disavowed at the outset the doctrine that misuse of bodily parts is *morally* bad, at least in any narrow sense. You ought to run because running was once necessary for catching food: creatures who did not enjoy running, if there ever were any, caught less food and reproduced less frequently than competitors who enjoyed running. These competitors passed on their appetites along with their muscles *to you*. This is not to say that those who suffer the affective consequences of laziness must recognize them as such, or even be able to identify them against their general background feeling-tone. They may not realize they would feel better if they exercised. They may even doubt it. They may have allowed their muscles to deteriorate beyond the point at which satisfying exercise is possible. For all that, evolution has decreed that a life involving regular exercise is on the whole more enjoyable than a life without. The same holds for every activity that is the purpose of an organ.

My loose talk of "enjoyment" can be tightened by appeal to the notion of reinforcement. Psychologists define "R is a reinforcer or reward" as: "R makes more probable the repetition of any behavior R follows." Contrary to a surprisingly wide misconception, this definition allows internal states to be rewards, even unconditioned rewards. We can say that organism O enjoys emitting behavior B without explicitly appealing to O's feeling-tone by saying that O's emission of B puts O in a rewarding internal state. In these terms, my general evolutionary hypothesis holds that nature tends to make rewarding behavior that favors cohort survival, and to make unrewarding behavior that does not. More specifically, it holds that if S is for F, using S to F will be rewarding, while using S for something incompatible with F will be unrewarding. I should add that this standard definition of "reinforcer" does not trivialize the law of effect— the law that the probability of behavior increases as it is reinforced. What saves the law, in its usual uses, is some antecedent and independent specification of what in fact is reinforcing; for more on this, see [19], sec. 2.3.

Positing an inherited tendency to find the use of S for F rewarding coheres well with the present evolutionary hypothesis. It may not be clear how so nebulous a state as enjoyment can be transmitted, but prospects for a transmission mechanism are improved by replacing talk of enjoyment with talk of an as-yet unidentified internal state that increases the probability of behavior it follows. Even if the internal state itself is nonphysical, its presence is doubtless correlated with some physical state, and it is easy to imagine DNA instructions for building a nervous system that lapses into the physical correlate of the reinforcing state when some selected behavior is emitted. It is these instructions that transmit "a tendency to enjoy" the behavior. Indeed, its genes would "tell" an organism to emit some bit of behavior by so constructing it that emission of the behavior would be followed by the reinforcing state. It becomes nearly, but not quite fatally, analytic that, if using *S* to *F* increases fitness, cohorts or strains that are reinforced by using *S* to *F* are more likely to survive, and produce offspring that produce offspring. Finally, construing enjoyment behaviorally renders more natural the idea that one may not know that one's sense of well-being is being impaired by failure to perform certain actions. It is a commonplace that an organism need not be consciously aware of what is reinforcing it, and this holds for internal and external, conditioned and unconditioned rewards. An internal state can be reinforcing even if its subject fails to discriminate it against a general affective background, or to notice its absence.

These speculations are much in the spirit of Barash's, especially if one recalls that by the fitness of an organism Barash means the relative number of copies of that organism's genotype that appear in the next generation:

> Just as we find sugar sweet, we find certain behavior to be sweet as well. This means that, at least in part because of evolution's handiwork, we are inclined to do certain things rather than others, and it should be no surprise that in general our inclinations are those that contribute to our fitness ([1], 39).[3]

Put this way, it is surprising that anyone denies that evolution can shape behavior, even "social" behavior. We are all sociobiologists. Obviously, physical structures like hearts and earlobes are selected in. But physical structures do things. The line between structure and behavior is further blurred by the heritability of time-dependent phenomena. Stainislaw Ulam reports in his autobiography that John von Neumann's two-year-old grandson, who had never seen his grandfather, had von Neumann's distinctive walk. And who can draw a fixed line between simple patterns of behavior like a characteristic gait, and complex patterns of behavior like altruism? And who will draw a sharp line between either kind of behavior, and physical structure?

3. Applications to Homosexuality

The application of this general picture to homosexuality should be obvious. There can be no reasonable doubt that one of the functions of the penis is to introduce semen into the vagina. It does this, and it has been selected in because it does this. (Sexual intercourse itself can probably be explained by the evolutionary value of bisexual reproduction. For $n > 2$, n-sexual reproduction would increase genetic variety at the cost of hardly ever occurring (see e.g., [3]). The advantages accruing to relatively motile gametes seems to account for the emergence of bisexual reproduction itself.) Nature has consequently made this use of the penis rewarding. It is clear enough that any proto-human males who found unrewarding the insertion of penis into vagina have left no descendants. In particular, proto-human males who enjoyed inserting their penises into each other's anuses have left no descendants. This is why homosexuality is abnormal, and why its abnormality counts prudentially against it. Homosexuality is likely to cause unhappiness because it leaves unfulfilled an innate and innately rewarding desire. And should the reader's environmentalism threaten to get the upper hand, let me remind him again of an unproblematic case. Lack of exercise is bad and even abnormal not only because it is unhealthy but also because one feels poorly without regular exercise. Nature made exercise rewarding because, until recently, we had to exercise to survive. Creatures who found running after game unrewarding were eliminated. Laziness leaves unreaped the rewards nature has planted in exercise, even if the lazy man cannot tell this introspectively. If this is a correct description of the place of exercise in human life, it is by the same token a correct description of the place of heterosexuality.

It hardly needs saying, but perhaps I should say it anyway, that this argument concerns tendencies and probabilities. Generalizations about human affairs being notoriously "true by and large and for the most part" only, saying that homosexuals are bound to be less happy than heterosexuals must be understood as short for "Not coincidentally, a larger proportion of homosexuals will be unhappy than a corresponding selection of the heterosexual population." There are, after all, genuinely jolly fat men. To say that laziness leads to adverse affective consequences means that, because of our evolutionary history, the odds are relatively good that a man who takes no exercise will suffer adverse affective consequences. Obviously, some people will get away with misusing their bodily parts. Thus, when evaluating the empirical evidence that bears on this account, it will be pointless to cite cases of well-adjusted homosexuals. I do not say they are non-existent; my claim is that, of biological necessity, they are rare.

My argument might seem to show at most that heterosexual behavior is (self-) reinforcing, not that homosexuality is self-extinguishing—that homosexuals go without the built-in rewards of heterosexuality, but not that homosexuality has a built-in punishment. This distinction, however, is merely verbal. They are two different ways of saying that homosexuals will find their lives less rewarding than will heterosexuals. Even if some line demarcated happiness from unhappiness absolutely, it would be irrelevant if homosexuals were all happily above the line. It is the comparison with the heterosexual life that is at issue. A lazy man might count as happy by some mythic absolute standard, but he is likely to be less happy than someone otherwise like him who exercises.

Another objection to my argument, or conjectural evolutionary scenario, is that heterosexuality might have been selected in not because it favors survival, but as a by-product of some other inclusively fit structure or behavior. A related suggestion is that what really has been selected in is some blend of dominant heterosexual and recessive homosexual genes. As for the former, it seems extraordinarily unlikely, given how long life has reproduced itself by sexual intercourse, that the apparently self-reinforcing character of heterosexuality is a by-product of some other fitness-enhancing trait. If heterosexual intercourse is not *directly* connected to propagation, what is? Biologists have no trouble determining when bird plumage is there to attract mates, and hence favors survival. It would be astounding if the same could not be said for heterosexual intercourse.

The sophisticate might complain that I am not giving "by-product" hypotheses their due. And indeed at this point sociobiological hypotheses come thick and fast. I will be discussing some others later in this paper, and making some overall observations about sociobiology and homosexuality. Here it is appropriate to examine one hypothesis of the "by-product" school, that of Hutchinson (see [16]). Fact: there can be recessive genes for a trait that inhibits the reproduction of and even kills organisms which exhibit it, but which, when co-occurring with the dominant trait-suppressing allele, give rise to an organism or phenotype more inclusively fit than a comparable organism with two of the dominant alleles. In such cases, the "bad" allele will be passed along in fit heterozygous organisms and its associated trait will occasionally surface. For example, sickle-cell anemia persists because the heterozygote Cc (non-sickle-cell C, sickle-cell c) confers resistance to malaria. Perhaps a recessive gene predisposing to homosexuality persists in this way. Organisms of genotype Hh—a dominant allele H for heterosexuality, a recessive allele h for homosexuality—might be most fit, and then of course organisms with hh genotype will surface with some regularity.

Without even considering the empirical likelihood of this elegant hypothesis, it is clearly consistent with my chief claim. For as it stands it represents sickle-cell anemia and the perpetuation of the c allele as *unfortunate by-products* of a process that selects in resistance to malaria; and, presumably, the same would go for homosexuality. For what does it mean to say that sickle-cell anemia is a by-product? Precisely this: had immunity to malaria not been associated with the Cc genotype, the "gene" for malarial immunity would have been selected in anyway; however, had the Cc genotype and hence sickle-cell anemia not been associated with malarial immunity or some other inclusive-fitness-enhancing trait, the c allele would have disappeared. Recurring to our definition of "function," the cause of the persistence of the c allele and the Cc genotype, what that genotype is for, is fending off malaria. Sickle-cell anemia is a maladaptive by-product of the Cc genotype since, had it not been associated with what is in fact the function of the Cc genotype, sickle-cell anemia would have caused the disappearance of the Cc genotype. Nothing, not even the c allele, has sickle-cell anemia as its function. The key question, of course, is whether a maladaptive by-product, so understood, is reinforcing. On the present model, it is not. For suppose sickle-cell anemia could be contracted voluntarily, and there were a gene which (a) made contracting or becoming vulnerable to it reinforcing, but (b) was not connected with malarial immunity. A strain with the tastes this gene confers would soon be selected out. Therefore, surviving humans who get sickle-cell anemia do not find it in any way reinforcing. So the "heterozygote fitness" hypothesis (and the kin-selection hypothesis: see below) predict, consistently with my view, that homosexuality is associated with unhappiness; and, conversely, wide-spread homosexual unhappiness would confirm that homosexuality is a maladaptive by-product.

An important methodological corollary of this discussion is that a trait or tendency may be "in the genes" but still be abnormal. It is normal only if it is in the genes because it itself enhances fitness, not because it is associated with something else that enhances fitness on independent grounds. Sickle-cell anemia is a malfunction of its victims' blood, which was selected in to oxygenate the muscles. A comparable story for homosexuality would involve a gene that instructed its organism to make just a little testosterone. This might have survival value by raising phenotypic verbal sensitivity, and perhaps low testosterone is the only way nature has figured out to secure this inclusively fit trait. Suppose, too, that a disposition to homosexuality was a causal consequence, a by-product, of low testosterone—but not so disadvantageous a by-product that the gene was selected out. Homosexuality would then be a necessary condition for advantageous verbal ability, but it would not follow that homosexuality was selected in because it conduced to verbal ability, or for any other reason. It would not follow that homosexuality is the least reinforcing. Unhappy homosexuals might be the price nature pays for verbal ability, homosexuality being no more a cause of verbal ability than sickle-cell anemia is a cause of malarial resistance.

Talk of what is "in the genes" inevitably provokes the observation that we should not blame homosexuals for their homosexuality if it is "in their genes." True enough. Indeed, since nobody decides what he is going to find sexually arousing, the moral appraisal of sexual object "choice" is entirely absurd. However, so saying is quite consistent with regarding homosexuality as a misfortune, and taking steps—this being within the realm of the will—to minimize its incidence, especially among children. Calling homosexuality involuntary does not place it outside the scope of evaluation. Victims of sickle-cell anemia are not blameworthy, but it is absurd to pretend that there is nothing wrong with them. Homosexual activists are partial to genetic explanations and hostile to Freudian environmentalism in part because they see a genetic cause as exempting homosexuals from blame. But surely people are equally blameless for indelible traits acquired in early childhood. And anyway, a blameless condition may still be worth trying to prevent. (Defenders of homosexuality fear Freud at another level, because his account removes homosexuality from the biological realm altogether and deprives it of whatever legitimacy adheres to what is "in the genes.")

My sociobiological scenario also finds no place for the fashionable remark that homosexuality has become fitness-enhancing in our supposedly overpopulated world. Homosexuality is said to increase our species' chances by easing the population pressure. This observation, however correct, is irrelevant. Even if homosexuality has lately come to favor species survival, this is no part of how homosexuality is created. Salvation of the human species would be at best a fortuitous by-product of behavior having other causes. It is not easy, moreover, to see how this feature of homosexuality could get it selected in. If homosexuality enhances inclusive fitness precisely because homosexuals don't reproduce, the tendency to homosexuality cannot get selected for by a filtering process when it is passed to the next generation—it doesn't get passed to the next generation at all. The same applies, of course, to any tendency to find homosexuality rewarding.

The whole matter of the survival advantage of homosexuality is in any case beside the point. Our organs have the functions and rewards they do because of the way the world was, and what favored survival, many millions of years ago. *Then,* homosexuality decreased fitness and heterosexuality increased it; an innate tendency to homosexuality would have gotten selected out if anything did. We today have the tendencies transmitted to us by those other ancestors, whether or not the race is going to pay a price for this. That 50 years ago certain self-reinforcing behavior began to threaten the race's future is quite consistent with the behavior remaining self-reinforcing. Similarly, widespread obesity and the patent enjoyment many people experience in gorging themselves just show that our appetites were shaped in conditions of food scarcity under which gorging oneself when one had the chance was good policy. Anyway, the instability created by abundance is, presumably, temporary. If the current abundance continues for 5000 generations, natural gluttons will almost certainly disappear through early heart disease and unattractiveness to the opposite sex. The ways in which the populous human herd will be trimmed is best left to speculation.

I should also note that nothing I have said shows bisexuality or sheer polymorphous sexuality to be unnatural or self-punishing. One might cite the Greeks to show that only exclusive homosexuality conflicts with our evolved reinforcement mechanism. But in point of fact bisexuality seems to be a quite rare phenomenon—and animals, who receive no cultural conditioning, seem instinctively heterosexual in the vast majority of cases. Clinicians evidently agree that it is possible for a person to be homosexual at one period of his life and heterosexual at another, but not at the same time. Some statistics in [5] confirm this. 18% of the male homosexuals interviewed had been married; while 90% reported having intercourse with their wives during the first year of marriage, 72% reported having homosexual fantasies during intercourse, and 33% reported this "often" ([5], tables 17.1–17.7). So only 4.5% of the sample had "reciprocal" heterosexual intercourse. This coheres well with table 22.4 in [5], which indicates that roughly 95% of male homosexuals in the Bell-Weinberg sample were "exclusively homosexual." But one mustn't move too quickly or dogmatically here. On the face of it, telling its host body "Put your penis in any reasonably small, moist opening" is a sufficiently adaptive gene strategy to ensconce a gene that follows it in the gene pool. A body controlled by such a gene would reproduce itself and hence the gene often enough. The flaw in the plan is that a competitor gene might evolve to tell its body: "Put your penis only in vaginas, i.e., moist openings with a certain feel and which are accompanied by such visual clues as breasts and wide hips." The second gene would reproduce itself even more often and—waiving by-products—would eventually displace the first. But our bisexual gene isn't finished. It might evolve the following strategy: "Body, insert your penis in vaginas most of the time, but insert your penis in male anuses frequently enough to keep other males, who are competing with you for females, occupied." A body with such a gene could keep a harem pregnant. A male who put other males out of commission for n hours by stimulating them to orgasm might himself seem vulnerable to exhausting himself, but he can avoid this by refraining from orgasm during homosexual acts. The fly in *this* ointment is the counterstrategy that purely heterosexual genes could evolve: "Avoid erect penises heading for your anus." If even one such gene appeared in a population of bisexuals it would reproduce itself a little more readily, since it would never waste time spiking the guns of its competitors.

By now we are lost in speculation. There is no way to disprove the existence of a hardy bisexual gene, or to prove that heterosexual countermeasures always evolved. It is *possible,* but not likely and not suggested by anything currently known, that a bisexual gene has achieved stable existence in the human gene pool. It is also quite unlikely, on equivalent analytical grounds and the virtual nonexistence of polymorphous animal sexuality in the wild, that males are primed only for an undifferentiated enjoyment of sex that is shaped by culture into heterosexuality.

Utilitarians must take the present evolutionary scenario seriously. The utilitarian attitude toward homosexuality usually runs something like this: even if homosexuality is in some sense unnatural, as a matter of brute fact homosexuals take pleasure in sexual contact with members of the same sex. As long as they don't hurt anyone else, homosexuality is as great a good as heterosexuality. But the matter cannot end here. Not even a utilitarian doctor would have words of praise for a degenerative disease that happened to foster a certain kind of pleasure (as sore muscles uniquely conduce to the pleasure of stretching them). A utilitarian doctor would presumably try just as zealously to cure diseases that feel good as less pleasant degenerative diseases. A pleasure causally connected with great distress cannot be treated as just another pleasure to be toted up on the felicific scoreboard. Utilitarians have to reckon with the inevitable consequences of pain-causing pleasure.

Similar remarks apply to the question of whether homosexuality is a "disease." A widely-quoted pronouncement of the American Psychiatric Association runs:

> Surely the time has come for psychiatry to give up the archaic practice of classifying the millions of men and women who accept or prefer homosexual object choices as being, by virtue of that fact alone, mentally ill. The fact that their alternative life-style happens to be out of favor with current cultural conventions must not be a basis in itself for a diagnosis.

Apart from some question-begging turns of phrase, this is right. One's taste for mutual anal intercourse is nothing "in itself" for one's psychiatrist to worry about, any more than a life of indolence is anything "in itself" for one's doctor to worry about. In fact, in itself there is nothing wrong with a broken arm or an occluded artery. The fact that my right ulna is now in two pieces is just a fact of nature, not a "basis for diagnosis." But this condition is a matter for medical science anyway, because it will lead to pain. Permitted to persist, my fracture will provoke increasingly punishing states. So if homosexuality is a reliable sign of present or future misery, it is beside the point that homosexuality is not "by virtue of that fact alone" a mental illness. High rates of drug addiction, divorce and illegitimacy are in themselves no basis for diagnosing social pathology. They support this diagnosis because of what else they signify about a society which exhibits them. Part of the problem here is the presence of germs in paradigm diseases, and the lack of a germ for homosexuality (or psychosis). I myself am fairly sure that a suitably general and germ-free definition of "disease" can be extruded from the general notion of "function" exhibited in Section 2, but however that may be, whether homosexuality is a disease is a largely verbal issue. If homosexuality is a self-punishing maladaptation, it hardly matters what it is called.

4. Evidence and Further Clarification

I have argued that homosexuality is "abnormal" in both a descriptive and a normative sense because—for evolutionary reasons—homosexuals are bound to be unhappy. In Kantian terms, I have explained how it is possible for homosexuality to be unnatural even if it violates no cosmic purpose or such purposes as we retrospectively impose on nature. What is the evidence for my view? For one thing, by emphasizing homosexual unhappiness, my view explains a ubiquitous fact in a simple way. The fact is the universally acknowledged unhappiness of homosexuals. Even the staunchest defenders of homosexuality admit that, as of now, homosexuals are not happy. (Writers even in the very recent past, like Lord Devlin, could not really believe that anyone could publicly advocate homosexuality as intrinsically good: see [8], 87.) A conspicuous exception to this is [5], which has been widely taken to show that homosexuals can be just as happy as heterosexuals. A look at their statistics tells a different story—an important matter I have dealt with in some detail in the appendix.

The usual environmentalist explanation for homosexuals' unhappiness is the misunderstanding, contempt and abuse that society heaps on them. But this not only leaves unexplained why society has this attitude, it sins against parsimony by explaining a nearly universal phenomenon in terms of variable circumstances that have, by coincidence, the same upshot.[4] Parsimony urges that we seek the explanation of homosexual unhappiness in the nature of homosexuality itself, as my explanation does. Having to "stay in the closet" may be a great strain, but it does not account for all the miseries that writers on homosexuality say is the homosexual's lot.

Incorporating unhappiness into the present evolutionary picture also smooths a bothersome ad-hocness in some otherwise appealing analyses of abnormality. Many writers define abnormality as compulsiveness. On this conception, homosexuality is abnormal because it is an autonomy-obstructing compulsion.[5] Such an analysis is obviously open to the question, What if an autonomous homosexual comes along? To that, writers like van den Haag point out that homosexuality is, in fact, highly correlated with compulsiveness. The trouble here is that the definition in question sheds no light on why abnormal, compulsive traits are such. The present account not only provides a criterion for abnormality, it encapsulates an explanation of *why* behavior abnormal by its lights is indeed compulsive and bound to lead to unhappiness.

One crucial test of my account is its prediction that homosexuals will continue to be unhappy even if people altogether abandon their "prejudice" against homosexuality. This prediction, that homosexuality being unnatural homosexuals will still find their behavior self-punishing, coheres with available evidence. It is consistent with the failure of other oppressed groups, such as American Negroes and European Jews, to become warped in the direction of "cruising," sado-masochism and other practices common in homosexual life (see [23]). It is consistent as well with the admission by even so sympathetic an observer of homosexuality as Rechy ([28]) that the immediate cause of homosexual unhappiness is a taste for promiscuity, anonymous encounters, and humiliation. It is hard to see how such tastes are related to the dim view society takes of them. Such a relation would be plausible only if homosexuals courted multiple anonymous encounters *faute de mieux*, longing all the while to settle down to some sort of domesticity. But, again, Europeans abhorred Jews for centuries, but this did not create in Jews a special weakness for anonymous, promiscuous sex. Whatever drives a man away from women, to be fellated by as many different men as possible, seems independent of what society thinks of such behavior. It is this behavior that occasions misery, and we may expect the misery of homosexuals to continue.

In a 1974 study, Weinberg and Williams ([34]) found no difference in the distress experienced by homosexuals in Denmark and the Netherlands, and in the U.S., where they found public tolerance of homosexuality to be lower. This would confirm rather strikingly that homosexual unhappiness is endogenous, unless one says that Weinberg and Williams's indices for public tolerance and distress—chiefly homosexuals' self-reports of "unhappiness" and "lack of faith in others"—are unreliable. Such complaints, however, push the social causation theory toward untestability. Weinberg and Williams themselves cleave to the hypothesis that homosexual unhappiness is entirely a reaction to society's attitudes, and suggest that a condition of homosexual happiness is positive endorsement by the surrounding society.[6] It is hard to imagine a more flagrantly *ad hoc* hypothesis. Neither a Catholic living among Protestants nor a copywriter working on the great American novel in his off hours asks more of society than tolerance in order to be happy in his pursuits.

It is interesting to reflect on a natural experiment that has gotten under way in the decade since the Weinberg-Williams study. A remarkable change in public opinion, if not private sentiment, has occurred in America. For whatever reason—the prodding of homosexual activists, the desire not to seem like a fuddy-duddy—various organs of opinion are now hard at work providing a "positive image" for homosexuals. Judges allow homosexuals to adopt their lovers. The Unitarian Church now performs homosexual marriages. Hollywood produces highly sanitized movies like *Making Love* and *Personal Best* about homosexuality. Macmillan strongly urges its authors to show little boys using cosmetics. Homosexuals no longer fear revealing themselves, as is shown by the prevalence of the "clone look." Certain products run advertising obviously directed at the homosexual market. On the societal reaction theory, there ought to be an enormous rise in homosexual happiness. I know of no systematic study to determine if this is so, but anecdotal evidence suggests it may not be. The homosexual press has been just as strident in denouncing pro-homosexual movies as in denouncing Doris Day movies. Especially virulent venereal diseases have very recently appeared in homosexual communities, evidently spread in epidemic proportions by unabating homosexual promiscuity. One selling point for a presumably serious "gay rights" rally in Washington, D.C., was an "all-night disco train" from New York to Washington. What is perhaps most salient is that, even if the changed public mood results in decreased homosexual unhappiness, the question remains of why homosexuals in the recent past, who suffered greatly for being homosexuals, persisted in being homosexuals.

But does not my position also predict—contrary to fact—that any sexual activity not aimed at procreation or at least sexual intercourse leads to unhappiness? First, I am not sure this conclusion is contrary to the facts properly understood. It is universally recognized that, for humans and the higher animals, sex is more than the insertion of the penis into the vagina. Foreplay is necessary to prepare the female and, to a lesser extent, the male. Ethologists have studied the elaborate mating rituals of even relatively simple animals. Sexual intercourse must therefore be understood to include the kisses and caresses that necessarily precede copulation, behaviors that nature has made rewarding. What my view does predict is that exclusive preoccupation with behaviors normally preparatory for intercourse is highly correlated with unhappiness. And, so far as I know, psychologists do agree that such preoccupation or "fixation" with, e.g., cunnilingus, is associated with personality traits independently recognized as disorders. In this sense, sexual intercourse really is virtually necessary for well-being. Only if one is antecedently convinced that "nothing is more natural than anything else" will one confound foreplay as a prelude to intercourse with "foreplay" that leads nowhere at all. One might speculate on the evolutionary advantages of foreplay, at least for humans: by increasing the intensity and complexity of the pleasures of intercourse, it binds the partners more firmly and makes them more fit for child-rearing. In fact, such analyses of sexual perversion as Nagel's ([27]), which correctly focus on the interruption of mutuality as central to perversion, go wrong by ignoring the evolutionary role and built-in rewards of mutuality. They fail to explain why the interruption of mutuality is disturbing.

It should also be clear that my argument permits gradations in abnormality. Behavior is the more abnormal, and the less likely to be rewarding, the more its emission tends to extinguish a genetic cohort that practices it. The less likely a behavior is to get selected out, the less abnormal it is. Those of our ancestors who found certain aspects of foreplay reinforcing might have managed to reproduce themselves sufficiently to implant this strain in us. There might be an equilibrium between intercourse and such not directly reproductive behavior. It is not required that any behavior not directly linked to heterosexual intercourse lead to maximum dissatisfaction. But the existence of these gradations provides no entering wedge for homosexuality. As no behavior is more likely to get selected out than rewarding homosexuality—except perhaps an innate tendency to suicide at the onset of puberty—it is extremely unlikely that homosexuality can now be unconditionally reinforcing in humans to any extent.

Nor does my position predict, again contrary to fact, that celibate priests will be unhappy. My view is compatible with the existence of happy celibates who deny themselves as part of a higher calling which yields compensating satisfactions. Indeed, the very fact that one needs to explain how the priesthood can compensate for the lack of family means that people do regard heterosexual mating as the natural or "inertial" state of human relations. The comparison between priests and homosexuals is in any case inapt. Priests do not simply give up sexual activity without ill-effect; they give it up for a reason. Homosexuals have hardly given up the use of their sexual organs, for a higher calling or anything else. Homosexuals continue to use them, but, unlike priests, they use them for what they are not for.

I have encountered the thought that by my lights female heterosexuality must be abnormal, since according to feminism women have been unhappy down the ages. The datum is questionable, to say the least. Feminists have offered no documentation whatever for this extravagant claim; their evidence is usually the unhappiness of the feminist in question and her circle of friends. Such attempts to prove female discontent in past centuries as [14] are transparently anachronistic projections of contemporary feminist discontent onto inappropriate historical objects. An objection from a similar source runs that my argument, suitably extended, implies the naturalness and hence rewardingness of traditional monogamous marriage. Once again, instead of seeing this as a *reductio,* I am inclined to take the supposed absurdity as a truth that nicely fits my theory. It is not a theoretical contention but an observable fact that women enjoy motherhood, that failure to bear and care for children breeds unhappiness in women, and that the role of "primary caretaker" is much more important for women than men. However, there is no need to be dogmatic. This conception of the family is in extreme disrepute in contemporary America. Many women work and many marriages last less than a decade. Here we have another natural experiment about what people find reinforcing. My view predicts that women will on the whole become unhappier if current trends continue. Let us see.[7]

Not directly bearing on the issue of happiness, but still empirically pertinent, is animal homosexuality. I mentioned earlier that the overwhelmingly heterosexual tendencies of animals in all but such artificial and genetically irrelevant environs as zoos cast doubt on sheer polymorphous sexuality as a sufficiently adaptive strategy. By the same token, it renders implausible the claim in [22] that human beings are born with only a general sex drive, and that the objects of the sex drive are *entirely* learned. If this were so, who teaches male tigers to mate with female tigers? Who teaches male primates to mate with female primates? In any case, the only evidence Masters and Johnson cite is the entirely unsurprising physiological similarity between heterosexual and homosexual response. Plainly, the inability of the penile nerve endings to tell what is rubbing them has nothing to do with the innateness of the sexual object. The inability of a robin to tell twigs from clever plastic look-alikes is consistent with an innate nest-building instinct.

The work of Beach ([2]) is occasionally cited (e.g., in [37]) to document the existence of animal homosexuality and to support the contention that homosexuality has some adaptive purpose, but Beach in fact notes certain important disanalogies between mammalian homosexual behavior in the wild and human homosexuality. Citing a principle of "stimulus-response complementarity," he remarks that a male chimpanzee will mount another male if the latter emits such characteristically female behavior as display of nether parts. Male homosexual humans, on the other hand, are attracted to maleness. More significantly, the male chimpanzee's mounting is unaccompanied by erection, thrusting or, presumably, intromission. Beach suggests that this display-mounting sequence may be multipurpose in nature, signalling submission and dominance when it occurs between males. In the same vein, Barash ([1], 60) cites male-male rape in *Xylocanis maculipennis,* but here the rapist's sperm is deposited in the rape victim's storage organs. This is a smart evolutionary move reminiscent of the gun-spiking strategy mentioned in an earlier section, but it is not comparable in its effects to homosexuality in humans.

5. Sociobiology Again

The end of Section 4 brought us back to the work of sociobiologists on homosexuality. Several sociobiological hypotheses are currently under discussion about the possible function of a "gene for homosexuality," and how this function might have lodged such a gene in the human gene pool. We looked in an earlier section at Hutchinson's "by-product" hypothesis and will return to it. In this section I want to make a general point about current sociobiological speculation and homosexuality, and it will be helpful to examine briefly another hypothesis: "kin selection." This hypothesis stresses that a gene is fit if it copies itself in the next generation, even if not through the organism that houses it. We all recognize the adaptive advantages in a mother's self-sacrifice for her brood; the same holds for a brother's regard for his siblings. So, the hypothesis goes, homosexuality's reproductive costs may be more than balanced by the aid a homosexual gives his close genetic cohort. Homosexuality in one offspring might mean more fecund siblings who have a good chance of carrying the "homosexual gene" (see [36], [37]). Testing this hypothesis would obviously be very difficult, requiring complete data on the relative fecundity of humans with homosexual siblings, nephews, etc., and a detailed and plausible mechanism to explain how an individual's homosexuality contributes to his cohort's fecundity. (Such demographic data would also be pertinent to the Freudian theory, which stresses the overbearing love of the homosexual's mother. A prediction of this theory would seem to be that homosexuality is higher among only children, and decreases as the number of siblings and birth-order increases.) No sociobiologist claims to have such data, and I know of no conjectures about the mechanism. The data of the last section and the appendix suggests that no such mechanism exists because homosexuality serves no inclusively adaptive function.

Where that leaves us is in the following position. Most of the sociobiological speculation about homosexuality known to me—particularly the influential writings of Wilson—simply *assumes* that homosexuality serves a function which accounts for its retention in the human population. Sociobiologists thus see their theoretical task as discovering what this function is. So far as I can tell, they rest this assumption on a single datum: Kinsey's finding that over 10% of the U.S. male population reported itself to be homosexual, by a reasonably strict criterion of homosexuality. Thus Wilson reasons (see [37], 143): given its sheer prevalence, homosexuality must be serving some fitness-enhancing purpose. My central point, in reply, is that there is not a single reason beyond this to think that homosexuality increases fitness or serves any purpose at all. The sociobiological models I've mentioned come into play only if we *already know* that homosexuality enhances fitness. Kinsey aside, we have no reason to think this, so the sociobiological hypotheses—kin-selection, parental manipulation and superior heterozygote fitness—currently stand as explanations in search of something to explain.

Still, there are the Kinsey data and certain twin studies which suggest some genetic component to homosexuality.[8] What the latter would mean is, precisely, that there can be two males brought up in the same environment such that one becomes a homosexual and the other does not. However, as I noted in an earlier section, a giant chasm separates the existence of a genetic contribution to homosexuality and the existence of a function that homosexuality serves. The point bears amplifying, in terms of the homely example of broken bones. While on the face of it a broken arm seems purely an accident and one wholly caused by environment, at any time a significant proportion of the human race will have broken bones. This might prompt sociologists to think there is a fitness-enhancing gene for broken-bonedness. And in a sense they would be right. People's bones break because, in part, their genes have told the rest of them to hang their muscles on an armature of calcium. Had our genes told the rest of us to make our skeletons out of chrome steel, banging into walls would not break arms. A broken arm is really the result of an environmental cause triggering a genetically determined predisposition.

There is something of truth and something of parody in this account of broken bones. A calcium-based skeleton is adaptively advantageous because calcium is light. But calcium's lightness is inseparable from its softness. The frangibility of bones is genetically coded, but only as a by-product of an otherwise adaptive process. And it is relatively easy to contrive mechanisms that yield a predisposition to homosexuality in males as a by-product. Low fetal testosterone might be good for organisms. Evolution might never have had to select in genotypes which insure enough testosterone for heterosexuality come what family life may. But this would not mean that homosexuality is for anything or that the gene is for homosexuality, any more than broken arms are for anything. So even a strong form of the kin-selection hypothesis would not mean anything more than a genetic predisposition to homosexuality; the trait thus disposed need be no more adaptive or reinforcing than the breakability of bones.[9]

6. On Policy Issues

Homosexuality is intrinsically bad only in a prudential sense. It makes for unhappiness. However, this does not exempt homosexuality from the larger categories of ethics—rights, duties, liabilities. Deontic categories apply to acts which increase or decrease happiness or expose the helpless to the risk of unhappiness.

If homosexuality is unnatural, legislation which raises the odds that a given child will become homosexual raises the odds that he will be unhappy. The only gap in the syllogism is whether legislation which legitimates, endorses or protects homosexuality does increase the chances that a child will become homosexual. If so, such legislation is *prima facie* objectionable. The question is not whether homosexual elementary school teachers will molest their charges. Pro-homosexual legislation might increase the incidence of homosexuality in subtler ways. If it does, and if the protection of children is a fundamental obligation of society, legislation which legitimates homosexuality is a dereliction of duty. I am reluctant to deploy the language of "children's rights," which usually serves as one more excuse to interfere with the prerogatives of parents. But we do have obligations to our children, and one of them is to protect them from harm. If, as some have suggested, children have a right to protection from a religious education, they surely have a right to protection from homosexuality. So protecting them limits somebody else's freedom, but we are often willing to protect quite obscure children's rights at the expense of the freedom of others. There is a movement to ban TV commercials for sugar-coated cereals, to protect children from the relatively trivial harm of tooth decay. Such a ban would restrict the freedom of advertisers, and restrict it even though the last clear chance of avoiding the harm, and thus the responsibility, lies with the parents who control the TV set. I cannot see how one can consistently support such legislation and also urge homosexual rights, which risk much graver damage to children in exchange for increased freedom for homosexuals. (If homosexual behavior is largely compulsive, it is falsifying the issue to present it as balancing risks to children against the freedom of homosexuals.) The right of a homosexual to work for the Fire Department is not a negligible good. Neither is fostering a legal atmosphere in which as many people as possible grow up heterosexual.

It is commonly asserted that legislation granting homosexuals the privilege or right to be firemen endorses not homosexuality, but an expanded conception of human liberation. It is conjectural how sincerely this can be said in a legal order that forbids employers to hire whom they please and demands hours of paperwork for an interstate shipment of hamburger. But in any case legislation "legalizing homosexuality" cannot be neutral because passing it would have an inexpungeable speech-act dimension. Society cannot grant unaccustomed rights and privileges to homosexuals while remaining neutral about the value of homosexuality. Working from the assumption that society rests on the family and its consequences, the Judaeo-Christian tradition has deemed homosexuality a sin and withheld many privileges from homosexuals. Whether or not such denial was right, for our society to grant these privileges to homosexuals *now* would amount to declaring that it has rethought the matter and decided that homosexuality is not as bad as it had previously supposed. And unless such rethinking is a direct response to new empirical findings about homosexuality, it can only be a revaluing. Someone who suddenly accepts a policy he has previously opposed is open to the same interpretation: he has come to think better of the policy. And if he embraces the policy while knowing that this interpretation will be put on his behavior, and if he knows that others know that he knows they will so interpret it, he is acquiescing in this interpretation. He can be held to have intended, meant, this interpretation.[10] A society that grants privileges to homosexuals while recognizing that, in the light of generally known history, this act can be interpreted as a positive re-evaluation of homosexuality, is signalling that it now thinks homosexuality is all right. Many commentators in the popular press have observed that homosexuals, unlike members of racial minorities, can always "stay in the closet" when applying for jobs. What homosexual rights activists really want, therefore, is not access to jobs but legitimation of their homosexuality. Since this is known, giving them what they want will be seen as conceding their claim to legitimacy. And since legislators know their actions will support this interpretation, and know that their constituencies know they know this, the Gricean effect or symbolic meaning of passing anti-discrimination ordinances is to declare homosexuality legitimate (see [35]).

Legislation permitting frisbees in the park does not imply approval of frisbees for the simple reason that frisbees are new; there is no tradition of banning them from parks. The legislature's action in permitting frisbees is not interpretable, known to be interpretable, and so on, as the reversal of long-standing disapproval. It is because these Gricean conditions are met in the case of abortion that legislation—or rather judicial fiat—permitting abortions and mandating their public funding is widely interpreted as tacit approval. Up to now, society has deemed homosexuality so harmful that restricting it outweighs putative homosexual rights. If society reverses itself, it will in effect be deciding that homosexuality is not as bad as it once thought.

Appendix

The best case for inevitable homosexual unhappiness comes from [5], a study which received much attention when it appeared. As their subtitle suggests, Bell and Weinberg claim to have shown that there is no such thing as homosexuality *per se*; there are different types of homosexuals, some of whom can be as well-adjusted, on the average, as heterosexuals. Bell and Weinberg admit that demonstrating this was the aim of their study: "We are pleased at the extent to which the aims of our investigation of homosexual men and women have been realized. The tables . . . clearly show that homosexuals are a remarkably diverse group" (217). They always refer to commonly held beliefs about homosexuals as "myths" (15) and "stereotypes" (73), and blame society's "homoerotophobia" (188) on the preoccupation of Jews with survival and the Christian Church with sin (149, 195). Working on the principle that a position is seriously weakened if the evidence marshalled by its friends disconfirms it, let us look at the Bell-Weinberg data.

Bell and Weinberg studied 686 San Francisco Bay area male homosexuals (and 293 lesbians, whom I ignore as in the body of the paper). One might question their methods: apart from the nonrandomness of their sample (22), the authors are oddly credulous about their informants' reports. They determined the level of their informants' health, and that of the informants in their heterosexual control group, by simply asking them how their health was (484). Not surprisingly, 87% of the white homosexuals and 91% of the black homosexuals reported that they were in good to excellent health, about the same as for the heterosexuals. But this accords ill with their table 19.2, which shows that 58% of all homosexuals spend 3 or more nights a week out. Common sense agrees with Satchel Paige that the social whirl isn't restful, but in any case the authors use none of the standard objective measures of health—visits to the doctor, use of medication, drugs, average amount of sleep, and the like. This, incidental though it is, warrants scepticism about self-report methodology in a matter like homosexuality.

Of the 206 pages of tables, 3 entries are particularly noteworthy as measures of homosexual unhappiness. The first (337, 339) is that 27% of all homosexuals experience either some or a great deal of regret about being homosexual. Taken with the 24% who experience "very little" regret, this prompts one to ask if only 49% of a random sample of heterosexuals would report no regrets about their heterosexuality. Would 27% of heterosexuals agree or agree strongly that their condition is an emotional disorder? (Cf. 339; the control group disappears at this juncture.) More strikingly, homosexuals are more than 6 times as likely as heterosexuals to attempt suicide—a criterion of unhappiness independent of the subject's report. The authors try to explain this statistic with an aside to the effect that the suicide rate in San Francisco is very high (211–12), a testimony to their faith in the explanatory power of nonprojectible predicates. (Perhaps not all philosophers would find their explanation defective. When I asked a well-known social philosopher critical of capital punishment why the murder rate had gone up in states where capital punishment had been abandoned, he said "the crime rate is going up everywhere.") In any case, the heterosexual sample was drawn from the same population, and homosexuals constitute a significant portion of San Francisco's population, so the San Francisco suicide rate is high, in part, because so many homosexuals commit suicide.

Perhaps the most striking trait revealed—or stereotype confirmed—

is the extreme impersonality and frequency of homosexual contacts. Roughly speaking, 75% of the respondents reported having had more than 100 sexual partners, and 43% reported having had 500 or more (308). These numbers are not easy to believe. Even taken *cum grano*, they should be compared to the reader's own experience of sex as he tries to imagine what it would be like to move so promiscuously among anonymous encounters—79% of the respondents reported that more than half their partners were strangers. Surely having these many partners is a criterion for maladjustment and compulsivity, a chronic inability to find anyone satisfactory. A harder datum than these numbers is the report that 56% of the respondents usually spend several hours or less with a partner (305); in fact, the authors distinguish "several hours" from "all night." Only 2% usually spend as much as a weekend with a partner successfully "cruised." (I interpret this statistic to make it consistent with the amount of "close-coupledness" reported: see below.) Incidentally, the authors say that "the largest numbers of our respondents spent all night with their partners" (77), but this is misleading. 41% of the respondents usually spent all night, and this is the modal number; but, as noted, *most* homosexuals spend considerably less than a whole night with a partner.

What Bell and Weinberg want to emphasize, however, is that their sample tended to cluster around five "types" of homosexual, one of which—the "close-coupled"—seemed on the whole to be as well-adjusted as heterosexuals. The finding was duplicated for lesbians. Close-coupled homosexuals are those involved in a sort of marriage, living monogamously with a partner of the same sex, not cruising, not experiencing any extraordinary amount of "tension" or regret about homosexuality, and displaying much "joy and exuberance in their particular life-style" (231). This, the authors contend, shows that homosexuality "is not necessarily related to pathology" (ibid.).

The existence of close-coupled homosexuals by no means implies that homosexuality is not pathological. As I have noted, there are almost no significant exceptionless generalizations in human affairs. My evolutionary hypothesis implies only that homosexuals are more likely to be unhappy than their heterosexual counterparts. The pertinent questions are, how many "close-coupled" homosexuals are there, and how many homosexuals exhibit "stereotypic" personality disorders? In point of fact, [5] assigns only 67 homosexuals to the "close-coupled" category, less than 10% of the sample. By contrast, 12% fell into the "dysfunctional" category, tormented souls who regret their homosexuality, cruise frequently, and have many sexual partners. An additional 16% were "Asexuals," homosexuals who tend to live alone without lovers or friends, and whose suicide rate is the highest among homosexuals. On the evidence presented, sociopathic homosexuals outnumber well-adjusted ones 2.8 to 1. If one adds to these at least some of the "functionals"—"men and women [who] seem to organize their lives around their sexual experience" (223)—deeply troubled homosexuals outnumber happy ones by at least 3 to 1.

The authors mislead the reader when they say that close-coupled homosexuals are on the average as happy and well-adjusted as heterosexuals. For this is to compare the best-adjusted homosexual subtype with the homogeneous heterosexual control group, and that is special pleading. It would be more appropriate to compare close-coupled homosexuals to happily married men, something Bell and Weinberg admit in passing but for which they offer no statistics. Since a random sample of heterosexuals will include a number of lonely, twisted individuals, the adjustment level of happily "coupled" heterosexuals must be considerably higher than that of the best-adjusted homosexuals. So viewed, monogamous homosexual coupling looks like a vain attempt at marriage—and homosexual cruising looks perhaps like a realization, of sorts, of adolescent male fantasy. "Dysfunctionals and Asexuals have a difficult time of it, but there are certainly equivalent groups among heterosexuals" (231). Certainly. But do such groups make up 28% of all heterosexuals and 41% of all classifiable heterosexuals, as the Dysfunctionals and Asexuals jointly comprise 41% of all classifiable homosexuals in the Bell-Weinberg sample (346, table 13.5)? Moreover, the authors go only so far as to say that close-coupled men "did less cruising" than the homosexual average (132; also see table 13.7, p. 349), leaving the impression that even close-coupled men do sometimes cruise. No quantitative comparisons are offered between such cruising and extra-marital straying for heterosexual males. Table 22.4 shows that 1% of the coupleds cruise at least once a week, but there are no statistics on how many have cruised in, say, the preceding year. Incomplete though it is, this figure should be contrasted with the heterosexual case. It seems unlikely that 1% of the married male readership of this paper had anonymous sexual encounters last week.

Bell and Weinberg's peroration is a textbook example of circular reasoning:

> It would appear that homosexual adults who have come to terms with their homosexuality, who do not regret their sexual orientation, and who can function effectively sexually and socially, are no more distressed psychologically than are heterosexual men and women (216).

Obviously, anyone who can "function effectively sexually and socially" will not be especially "distressed psychologically." But even going by the Bell-Weinberg sample drawn from volunteers from the "good scene" (27) of the Bay area, the chances that a homosexual will fall into this category are rather low.

Notes

Arthur Caplan, R. M. Hare, Michael Slote, Ed Erwin, Steven Goldberg, Ed Sagarin, Charles Winnick, Robert Gray, Thomas Nagel, David Benfield, Michael Green and my wife Margarita all commented helpfully on earlier drafts of this paper, one of which was read to the New York chapter of the Society of Philosophy and Public Policy. My definition of naturalness agrees to some extent with Gray's in [13], and I have benefitted from seeing an unpublished paper by Michael Ruse.

1. "Sexual preference" typifies the obfuscatory language in which the homosexuality debate is often couched. "Preference" suggests that sexual tastes are voluntarily chosen, whereas it is a commonplace that one cannot decide what to find sexually stimulating. True, we talk of "preferences" among flavors of ice-cream even though one cannot choose what flavor of ice-cream to like; such talk is probably a carryover from the voluntariness of *ordering* ice-cream. "Sexual preference" does not even sustain this analogy, however, since sex is a forced choice for everyone except avowed celibates, and especially for the relatively large number of homosexuals who cruise regularly (see appendix).

2. Nagel attempts to meet these counterexamples in [26], in effect by accepting such consequences of the classical analysis as that the beat of the heart is sometimes for diagnosis. The only reply to this sort of defense is that this is *not* what people mean. Met with such a reply, many philosophers feel impelled to say, "Well, it ought to be what you mean." This invitation to change the subject is attractive or relevant only if we haven't meant anything the first time around. If a coherent thought can be found behind our initial words which maximizes coherence with all hypothetical usages, it is *that thought* we were expressing and whose articulation was the aim of the analytic exercise.

3. If we replace "species" by "genetic cohort," Sayre has summed up my general point nicely: "In biological systems, reinforcers [conceived as inner states] generally are associated with behavior beneficial to the species, and usually (not always) beneficial to the organism itself. The mechanisms of natural selection assure that most members of a viable group are reinforced by what is good for the species..."([31], 125).

4. A number of authors trace the present culture's taboo against "homophilia" (Wilson's term) to the Old Testament proscription against nonreproductive practices, and summarily dismiss it as "simplistic" and "archaic" nonsense (see [37], 142–43; also the appendix). While I have no sympathy for theological teleology, it should be recalled that the ban on homosexuality in Leviticus is one of just three rules set down as absolutely binding. Another one prohibits the shedding of innocent blood. This prohibition against using convenient victims for ulterior purposes is the basis for Western law and morality, and I trust Wilson does not find it simplistic or archaic.

5. Summarizing a wide body of work on this subject, Sagarin writes: "Sick is, of course, a stigmatizing categorization when applied to mental and emotional disorders, but this does not mean that it is scientifically invalid. The misuse of a concept for political purposes is not an argument against its validity. Is homosexuality a sickness, or a behavioral symptom of a sickness? There seems to be a great deal of evidence in favor of the latter formulation. . . . [T]he evidence is

strong that homosexuality arises in most instances from faulty childhood development, is often accompanied by poor sex-role identification, and is overwhelmingly concomitant with compulsivity, inability to relate to others, poor self-image, low feeling of self-worth, and a great deal of what Bergler called 'injustice collecting'" ([29], 10).

6. This is the impression they leave, although it is hard to find them asserting it. Thus their reviewer: "the authors . . . start the book with asserting as their creed and point of departure the 'societal reaction theory', [and] try to minimize the issue by a modification, namely that tolerance is probably not enough, that is to say, it is not the same as full acceptance" ([4], 339–40; most of this review appears in [30]). Perhaps Weinberg and Williams are so inexplicit because, starting from wholly environmentalist premises, they regard the insufficiency of tolerance as the conclusion to be drawn from their data rather than as just one hypothesis to explain them.

7. Feminists are understandably hostile to sociobiology, which offers a plausible theoretical underpinning for the observable differences between the sexes. Such being the temper of the times, sociobiologists themselves get awfully cold feet when facing off against feminists. Barash hems and haws when considering if sociobiology is "sexist," a word which conveys no clear sense to him or anyone else—but which has evidently acquired powers of intimidation (see my [20]). After documenting the innateness of numerous psychophysiological gender differences, Wilson recommends a system of quotas and indoctrination for eliminating all consequences of sexual differentiation as preferable to a society of free individuals in which sexual differences would naturally manifest themselves. One would like to see a Wilsonian army take on a traditional one, like the Soviet Union's. Michael Ruse, a philosophical commentator, has even written a book with the astounding title *Is Science Sexist?*, as if the truth about men and women might be ideologically suspect. Sociobiologists tend to be braver taking on socialism, which demands an indifference to the claims of one's family that no gene which hoped to reproduce itself could permit. A sound point, but one would have thought socialism's absurdity required less arcane demonstration. Anyway, Wilson seems not to recognize that his egalitarian utopia would require far more interference with natural impulses than the most authoritarian socialism.

8. Bell and Weinberg created a stir when they published further results of their interviews with the sample in [5], which seemed to show that the families of homosexuals were no different than the families of heterosexuals, in particular that there was no preponderance of weak fathers. Such evidence gathered from self-reports is extremely thin. The subject has no special perspective on whether his father was distant, as he might have a special perspective on how he feels about the current President. Moreover, most people still think there is something "wrong" with a household in which the mother dominates, and are not likely to agree to having been brought up in one.

9. The last two paragraphs play on the fact that, in a suitably broad sense, there is a gene "for" almost everything people do. The reader should not be misled by these animadversions against current sociobiological accounts of homosexuality into thinking me generally unsympathetic to sociobiology. To the contrary, I welcome its insistence that not everything human is produced by "socialization." While some critics of sociology fob off this insistence with the

remark that "everybody knows that nature makes some contribution and nurture makes some contribution," such critics inevitably go on to ignore nature completely in every concrete case. If there is anything wrong with the general sociobiological hypothesis that interpersonal behavior is shaped by evolution, it is its obviousness. Obviousness being relative to speech community, however, this truism is regarded as revolutionary in many circles. And while some sociobiologists have been insensitive to the "is-ought gap," their work suggests important empirical limits to ethical ideals like socialism that presuppose infinite human plasticity (see n7 above). Such dismissals of sociobiology as [9] do nothing for the reputation of philosophers.

10. For this general conception of the meaning of a speech-act, see [15], [21], and [32]. For a cognate application to political philosophy, see [33].

References

[1] Barash, D. *The Whispering Within*. New York: Harper & Row, 1979.

[2] Beach, F. "Cross-Species Comparisons and the Human Heritage." *Archives of Sexual Behavior* 5 (1976): 469–85.

[3] Beadle, G. and M. *The Language of Life*. New York: Anchor, 1967.

[4] Beigl, H. Review of [34]. *Journal of Sex Research* 10: 339–40.

[5] Bell, A. and M. Weinberg. *Homosexualities*. New York: Simon and Schuster, 1978.

[6] Bennett, J. *Linguistic Behavior*. Cambridge: Cambridge University Press, 1976.

[7] Dawkins, R. *The Selfish Gene*. Oxford: Oxford University Press, 1976.

[8] Devlin, P. *The Enforcement of Morals*. Oxford: Oxford University Press, 1965.

[9] Dworkin, G. Review of [36]. *Philosophical Review* 88: 660–63.

[10] Gadpille, W. "Research into the Physiology of Maleness and Femaleness: Its Contribution to the Etiology and Psychodynamics of Homosexuality." *Archives of General Psychiatry* (1972): 193–206.

[11] Goldberg, S. "What Is 'Normal'? Logical Aspects of the Question of Homosexual Behavior." *Psychiatry* 38 (1975): 227–83.

[12] Gould, R. "What We Don't Know about Homosexuality." *New York Times Magazine,* Feb. 24, 1974.

[13] Gray, R. "Sex and Sexual Perversion." *Journal of Philosophy* 74 (1978): 189–99. [This volume, pp. 57–66.]

[14] Greer, G. *The Obstacle Race*. New York: Farrar, Straus & Giroux, 1979.

[15] Grice, H. "Utterer's Meaning, Sentence-Meaning, and Word-Meaning." *Foundations of Language* 4 (1968): 1–18.

[16] Hutchinson, G. "A Speculative Consideration of Certain Possible Forms of Sexual Selection in Man." *American Naturalist* 93 (1959): 81–91.

[17] Karlen, A. *Sexuality and Homosexuality: A New View*. New York: Norton, 1967.

[18] Levin, M. "On the Ascription of Functions to Objects." *Philosophy of the Social Sciences* 6 (1976): 227–34.

[19] Levin, M. *Metaphysics and the Mind-Body Problem.* Oxford: Oxford University Press, 1979.

[20] Levin, M. " 'Sexism' Is Meaningless." *St. John's Review* XXXIII (1981): 35–40.

[21] Lewis, D. *Convention.* Cambridge, MA: Harvard University Press, 1970.

[22] Masters, W. and V. Johnson. *Homosexuality in Perspective.* Boston, MA: Little, Brown and Company, 1979.

[23] McCracken, S. "Replies to Correspondents." *Commentary,* April 1979.

[24] Mossner, E. *The Life of David Hume,* 1st. ed. New York: Nelson & Sons, 1954.

[25] Nagel, E. *The Structure of Science.* New York: Harcourt & Brace, 1961.

[26] Nagel, E. "Teleology Revisited." *Journal of Philosophy* 74 (1977): 261–301.

[27] Nagel, T. "Sexual Perversion." *Journal of Philosophy* 66 (1969): 5–17. [This volume, pp. 9–20.]

[28] Rechy, J. *The Sexual Outlaw.* New York: Grove Press, 1977.

[29] Sagarin, E. "The Good Guys, the Bad Guys, and the Gay Guys." *Contemporary Sociology* (1973): 3–13.

[30] Sagarin, E. and R. Kelley. "The Labelling of Deviance," in W. Grove, ed., *The Labelling of Deviance.* New York: Wiley & Sons, 1975.

[31] Sayre, K. *Cybernetics and the Philosophy of Mind.* Atlantic Highlands, NJ: Humanities Press, 1976.

[32] Schiffer, S. *Meaning.* Oxford: Oxford University Press, 1972.

[33] Singer, P. *Democracy and Disobedience.* Oxford: Oxford University Press, 1968.

[34] Weinberg, M. and C. Williams. *Male Homosexuals: Their Problems and Adaptations.* Oxford: Oxford University Press, 1974.

[35] Will, G. "How Far Out of the Closet?" *Newsweek,* 30 May 1977, p. 92.

[36] Wilson, E. *Sociobiology: The New Synthesis.* Cambridge, MA: Harvard University Press, 1975.

[37] Wilson, E. *On Human Nature.* Cambridge, MA: Harvard University Press, 1978.

[38] Wright, L. "Functions." *Philosophical Review* 82 (1973): 139–68.

Chapter 10

A CHRISTIAN HOMOSEXUALITY?

Edward Vacek

The contemporary debates over homosexuality are heated up like a blast furnace. Ever since 1969 when homosexuals began to assert gay pride, the solid iron ore of traditional sexual preferences has turned into a churning, molten mass. The first, faltering moves "out of the closet" have prompted "Save Our Children" campaigns and Protestant ordinations of homosexuals. Unfortunately, like a blast furnace, the issue has generated for most people immense heat and little light.

One of the first steps toward the light is a confession of some basic ignorance. The central unknown is why some people (somewhere between 5 and 10 percent of the population) are exclusively homosexual. Some evidence suggests that homosexuality is biologically based. There is greater evidence that it results from early childhood experiences, though no one is sure what factor or factors lead to it. There is some scant evidence that it can be learned in adolescence, either when one is frustrated at heterosexual activity or is initiated into homosexual activity by someone more experienced. The best answer at present is that we do not know why people are homosexual.

Recently I asked thirty-five of my students whether they thought that being a homosexual was more like having a withered arm or like being left-handed. The point of this comparison should be clear. Most of us think that there is something biologically askew with having a deformed arm; but few of us think that left-handers have something wrong with

Reprinted with permission from *Commonweal* (5 December 1980), pp. 681–84.

their biological make-up. The world would not be greatly altered if the majority of people were left-handed. The world, however, would be a worse place if the vast majority had withered arms.

Much to my surprise, all but two of my students thought homosexuality was like being left-handed. These students are training to be future ministers, and I was consoled at the compassion and understanding they will probably show to homosexuals they will meet. And yet, I still had to ask myself, Are they correct?

Homosexual *orientation* must be distinguished from homosexual *activity*. Those who are homosexual may remain single or celibate; and they can, at least physically, engage in heterosexual acts. Many, in fact, are married. The orientation is not externally visible. It is experienced internally as an enduring, romantic, and sexual attraction to members of the same sex.

Sexual orientation is not a habit like smoking. Hence one is not morally responsible for having the orientation. One is responsible for what one does with this orientation, just as heterosexuals are responsible for how they express their own orientation.

Few people are totally homosexual or heterosexual. Children, adolescents, and even some heterosexual adults quite commonly go through homosexual phases. Good counselors usually encourage them not to make too much of a passing dalliance. Similarly, some homosexuals occasionally experience heterosexual attraction. So we are speaking of a dominant or prevailing pattern of attraction toward one sex or the other.

How do homosexuals experience themselves and their activity? Put simply, some are quite happy with their condition, some confused, and some quite unhappy. To those who are at peace with their homosexuality it seems an affront to demand that they change themselves. They ask heterosexuals to imagine wanting to extinguish one of the great sources of *their* identity, namely, the heterosexual feelings that form so much of the way a heterosexual relates to the world.

To those who are confused, gay alliances recommend that they accent the heterosexual aspect of themselves as long as they can, if only as a way of avoiding societal defamation.

Those who are unhappy with their orientation are often encouraged to change. The problem is, most will be unable to do so. The change is "morally impossible" because many homosexuals do not have the time or money to enter a therapy where there are no "sure-fire cures." The *most* optimistic of therapists report only a 60 percent "cure rate," and this cure is reached only by those homosexuals most strongly motivated to change.

Conversions in orientation due to special graces may occur, but many claims of these graced reorientations have been shown to be misleading or false. Frequently the change is from active homosexuality to a dormant, celibate homosexuality. In other cases, the "conversion" is only short-lived. In the words of a recent Vatican Declaration, many are "incurable."

It should be clear in what follows that no one recommends the kind of activity that would be condemned if it were performed in a heterosexual context. No argument for homosexual relations should be construed as an argument for promiscuity, prostitution, mate swapping, infidelity, and the like. Homosexuals must exhibit the same personalist virtues as heterosexuals. The major question is whether they should be bound to act as heterosexuals.

Now to the question, Is a homosexual orientation and consequent homosexual activity merely a different life-style, or is there something inherently wrong with it? There are at least three ways to get at an answer to this question: Scripture; authority; and human reason. Roman Catholics have traditionally tried to bring all three to bear on perplexing moral issues.

Scripture does not offer much comfort to those who engage in homosexual acts. Although homosexuality holds a very minor place in Scripture and is not mentioned by Jesus or the prophets, some terribly severe judgments are made against it. Leviticus (18:22; 20:13) tells us that active homosexuals should be put to death, a practice renewed in the form of burning at the stake during the late Middle Ages. Paul tells us that they belong to the class of idolators (Rom. 1:18–32), and that they shall never enter the kingdom of heaven (1 Cor. 6:9–10). It is hard to imagine penalties worse than loss of physical and eternal life.

The basis for these judgments is set out in the early chapters of Genesis. In order to image himself, God made both man and woman. Together, the two sexes mirror God. In order to overcome Adam's loneliness, God created a woman, not another man.

There are two approaches to the Scriptures that Roman Catholics should not take. The first is a fundamentalist attitude that protests, I take everything in the bible "just as it is written." The Catholic tradition has always seen the need for an on-going interpretation and reinterpretation of the Scriptures. That process began in the Scriptures themselves; and it continues today. The promise of the on-going presence of the Spirit is at the same time a command to interpret the Scriptures. The second erroneous approach is to ignore the Scriptures, a tack that is also not acceptable for it would deprive us of the originating inspiration of our historical faith.

A third approach is to evaluate the scriptural texts even as they judge us. We often discover upon study that they mean something other than what we have always assumed. For example, many scholars think that the sin of Sodom was not primarily homosexuality, but inhospitality, gang rape, and even attempted sexual congress with angels. Some scholars argue that what Scripture really condemns is the promiscuity that so much homosexuality involved. Still other scholars note that the sacred authors were unaware that some people are homosexual in orientation. That is, the scriptural condemnations assume a conscious choice by a heterosexual to exchange a heterosexual partner for a homosexual one. We can make no such assumption today.

Another facet of this third approach is to note the possible cultural relativity of the scriptural judgments. The Scriptures legislate on a whole range of sexual behaviors that we do not consider to be sinful. For a son to see his father naked was tantamount to a crime. For husband and wife to have sexual intercourse during the seven days of her menstrual period meant punishment. Polygamy was permitted, even required. Celibacy was abnormal; bishops were to have only one wife, and so on.

However one interprets these texts, it seems safe to say that our sexual ethic is at least partially different from the one (or, rather, the several) proposed in Scripture. The question returns, Are homosexual acts wrong? Has the evolution of culture meant only that people should not be put to death for such acts, just as we no longer stone people caught in adultery? We still judge adultery to be wrong, though we have changed the punishment. Or does it mean that we "enlightened" moderns now see that at least certain cases of homosexual acts are as sinless as the touching of menstrual fluids, an act that once made a person ritually unclean?

In sum, when reading Scripture we see that some typically cited texts do not treat of homosexuality; others do, and do so in a very direct fashion. But are these texts literally valid for us, or are they culturally bound?

Church tradition and ecclesiastical authority have continuously rejected homosexual activity. The first objection raised against homosexual activity was that it was "against nature." This unnaturalness frequently meant that men were acting like women. Women have rather regularly been seen, even by such luminaries as Thomas Aquinas, as naturally inferior to men. Therefore part of the degradation involved in homosexuality was seen to be not so much a degradation of human nature, but a degradation of a man to the level of a woman. Therefore, too, lesbianism has seldom been proscribed in our scripture or our tradition. Male homosexuality, on the other hand, was commonly thought to be a more serious sin than rape, prostitution, or fornication, all of which are "natural."

Homosexuality was also judged sinful because it is not open to procreation. The early Christian tradition showed an uneasiness with sexual passion, and procreation was in many cases thought to be the sole justification for marriage and sexual relations. Hence homosexuality was roundly condemned for being sterile. Only in the late nineteenth century did "expression of interpersonal love" come to be recognized in church teaching as a reason for sexual intercourse.

Within the past five years, church authorities have again taken strong stands against homosexual activity. Yet, at the same time, they have spoken clearly on the human rights of those who have a homosexual orientation. Their message would seem to be that it is all right to be a homosexual, as long as one does not express this orientation genitally.

As with scriptural passages, one can take a fundamentalist attitude or a "who-cares!" attitude toward church tradition and authority on the issue of homosexuality. Neither of these is acceptable. The latter position is untenable for a person who wants to be a member of the church. The former position fails to reckon with some of the dubious reasons given for opposition to homosexuality. Bad reasons, of course, do not invalidate a conclusion; but neither do they make it right. There are a number of significant questions about the church's past attitude toward sexuality that make one wonder whether it too has been culture-bound and ought to be transcended.

My own approach tries to discover the relevant biological, psychological, rational, and religious values. It then tries to weigh these values and make a judgment within an ethics of proportionality. In examining homosexuality, I find myself confronted by Jesus's demand (Lk. 12:57) "Why can you not judge for yourselves what is the right course?" Stated briefly, my judgment is this. Homosexual actions are biologically deficient, but they may be psychologically healthy, the best available exercise of one's interpersonal freedom, and may even be a form of authentic Christian spirituality. Let us look at each of these four levels of human existence.

Homosexual couples cannot do, biologically, what heterosexual couples can do, namely, bear children. The significance of that fact should be neither overestimated nor underestimated. I want to argue that to the extent that any sexual activity is closed to children, to that extent it is deficient. It represents a failure to carry out one of the most basic and fulfilling tasks of the human race, namely, to propagate the race.

Homosexual activity also contravenes the complementary aptness of the male and female sexual systems for one another. Again this biological deficiency should be neither overestimated nor ignored. Thus the human race has discouraged homosexuality because stable heterosexual unions are so utterly vital to its survival interests and because of its sense of biological fittingness. We must not ignore these factors.

Secondly, homosexual relations may be psychologically healthy. Various psychological tests show that—apart from the one characteristic of "adequate heterosexual development"—homosexuals are about as healthy as anyone else. Homosexuals take encouragement from such tests because one would expect that, since they have suffered intense discrimination, they would score significantly lower than their heterosexual counterparts. They do not.

Thirdly, persons who are homosexuals are able to function and grow at least as well as heterosexuals. They are able to be creative, put in a hard day's work, act as citizens, help their neighbor, much like heterosexuals. Somewhat surprisingly, they "make love" more humanely, largely because they are better able empathetically to feel what their partner is feeling. With regard to human psyche and mind, human persons are so richly complex that they can often compensate (which need not mean overcompensate) for whatever deficiencies they have on the biological, psychological, or mental levels. We all know, for example, people who have lost a leg and are still great workers and extraordinary human beings. Homosexual activity, however deficient, does not keep homosexuals from human greatness.

Finally, homosexuals can develop a form of authentic Christian spirituality. Their spirituality is, of course, basically like that of heterosexuals. They believe and enact in their lives the Incarnation, Cross, and Resurrection. They live or try to live, consciously dependent on the power of the Spirit. But just as grace, mind, and psyche penetrate their sexual orientation, so also this orientation affects their psyche, mind, and spirit. Whatever is distinctive about their human existence due to their homosexual orientation offers a new possibility for life in the spirit, a possibility that heterosexuals do not have. A number of articles and books have been written to explore this possibility.

"The harvest of the Spirit," Paul tells us (Gal. 5:22–23), is "love, joy, peace, patience, kindness, goodness, fidelity, gentleness, and self-control." Some homosexuals exhibit these qualities as strikingly as any heterosexual. To be sure, we human beings are so complex that we can manifest all these virtues and still be sinful in some aspect of our lives. But abundant evidence of these virtues in many active homosexuals leads one to presume that they are Spirit-filled.

Now, to apply an ethic of proportionality. The God we serve and cooperate with wants to conserve and enhance creation, bringing all things to their greatest possible fullness. A sexual act that helps to continue the human race is good. But the homosexual act is not open to generation, and so to that extent it is deficient. On the other hand, engaging in heterosexual activity can alienate genuinely homosexual persons from themselves at the level of their psyche, mind, and spirit. What they gain at the level of propagation, they lose in authenticity at the other levels of their being. Thus, the disproportionate evil of insisting that homosexual persons, if they are going to have sexual relations at all, must have them with persons of the opposite sex, must be assessed.

Should the significant numbers who are homosexual remain permanently single or celibate? Is this a cross they are given by God, to be carried all their adult life? As a personal vocation from God, it might well be that they are called to genital non-activity. The desire never to act contrary to certain explicit statements of our Scriptures and tradition may itself constitute such a vocation for some.

Apart from this personal vocation, it seems a violation of humanness automatically to deprive homosexuals of the values that Christians have found in sexuality. Such values include pleasure, romantic feelings, companionship, mutual support, sexual outlet, ecstasy, intimacy, and interpersonal communication. It seems to compound "unnaturalness" to insist that persons not heterosexually inclined must simply, without further consideration, be sexually inactive. One biological deficiency then turns all too easily into biological, psychological, rational, and spiritual alienation. A homosexual orientation would become synonymous with fate. It is not clear to me that every Christian homosexual is fated to such restrictions on his or her human expressiveness. Put perhaps too simply, if there are positive values in a committed, loving sexual relation, then very strong reasons have to be given why anyone including homosexuals should be denied those positive values. The biological deficiencies do not seem in themselves serious enough in our time to justify that denial.

The unknown and the unsuspected usually cause us to be uncomfortable. This is especially so when it deals with our sexual identity. Every one of us spends decades if not a lifetime trying to accept and become comfortable with those "deep dark urges," as they have been called, that pop up to disturb our equilibrium at the most unexpected times. This uncertainty has generated an intense hostility towards homosexuals, far out of proportion to whatever "sin" there may be in homosexual activity and far from the loving response one would expect from Spirit-filled Christians.

The American bishops have made it very clear that all persons deserve great respect, whatever their sexual orientation. No one, merely because of his or her sexual orientation, should be denied housing, jobs, or public office. Since homosexual children generally are reared in heterosexual families, and since, in the studies made thus far, children reared in homosexual environments are as likely to be heterosexual as any other, there seems to be no solid foundation for discrimination.

Finally, since homosexual persons are presently highly discriminated against, they should be especially favored by all Christians. A recent book title asks, "Is the homosexual my neighbor?" Christians who are deeply alive to the parable of the Good Samaritan can only answer yes to that question. Even if someday it becomes crystal clear that homosexual persons should not "make love" to one another, it will always be Christianly clear that we should love our homosexual sisters and brothers.

Chapter 11

HOMOSEXUALITY: THE NATURE AND HARM ARGUMENTS

John Corvino

Tommy and Jim are a homosexual couple I know. Tommy is an accountant; Jim is a botany professor. They are in their early forties and have been together fourteen years, the last five of which they've lived in a Victorian house that they've lovingly restored. Though their relationship has had its challenges, each has made sacrifices for the sake of the other's happiness and the relationship's long-term success.

I assume that Tommy and Jim have sex with each other (although I've never bothered to ask). Furthermore, I suspect that they probably *should* have sex with each other. For one thing, sex is pleasurable. But it is also much more than that: a sexual relationship can unite two people in a way that virtually nothing else can. It can be an avenue of growth, communication, and lasting interpersonal fulfillment. These are reasons most heterosexual couples have sex even if they don't want children, don't want children yet, or don't want additional children. And if these reasons are good enough for most heterosexual couples, then they should be good enough for Tommy and Jim.

Of course, having a reason to do something does not preclude there being an even better reason for not doing it. Tommy might have a good

---

This article is an abbreviated version of "Why Shouldn't Tommy and Jim Have Sex? A Defense of Homosexuality," which appears in John Corvino, ed., *Same Sex: Debating the Ethics, Science, and Culture of Homosexuality* (Rowman & Littlefield, 1997). The longer version includes a section on biblical arguments against homosexuality.

reason for drinking orange juice (it's tasty and nutritious) but an even better reason for not doing so (he's allergic). The point is that one would need a pretty good reason for denying a sexual relationship to Tommy and Jim, given the intense benefits widely associated with such relationships. The question I shall consider in this paper is thus quite simple: Why shouldn't Tommy and Jim have sex?[1]

I. Homosexuality Is Unnatural

Many contend that homosexual sex is "unnatural." But what does that mean? Many things that people value—clothing, houses, medicine, and government, for example—are unnatural in some sense. On the other hand, many things that people detest—disease, suffering, and death, for example—are natural in some sense (after all, they occur "in nature"). If the unnaturalness charge is to be more than empty rhetorical flourish, those who levy it must specify what they mean. Borrowing from Burton Leiser, I will examine several possibilities.[2]

(1) *What is unusual or abnormal is unnatural.* One meaning of "unnatural" refers to that which deviates from the norm, that is, from what most people do. Obviously, most people engage in heterosexual relationships. But does it follow that it is wrong to engage in homosexual relationships? Relatively few people read Sanskrit, pilot ships, play the mandolin, breed goats, or write with both hands, yet none of these activities is immoral simply because it is unusual. As the Ramsey Colloquium, a group of Jewish and Christian scholars who oppose homosexuality, write, "The statistical frequency of an act does not determine its moral status."[3] So while homosexuality might be "unnatural" in the sense of being unusual, that fact is morally irrelevant.

(2) *What is not practiced by other animals is unnatural.* Some people argue, "Even animals know better than to behave homosexually; homosexuality must be wrong." This argument is doubly flawed. First, it rests on a false premise. Numerous studies—including Anne Perkins's study of "gay" sheep and George and Molly Hunt's study of "lesbian" seagulls—have shown that some animals do form homosexual pair-bonds.[4] Second, even if that premise were true, it would not prove that homosexuality is immoral. After all, animals don't cook their food, brush their teeth, attend college, or drive cars; human beings do all these things without moral censure. Indeed, the idea that animals could provide us with our standards, especially our sexual standards, is simply amusing.

(3) *What does not proceed from innate desires is unnatural.* Recent studies suggesting a biological basis for homosexuality have resulted in two popular positions. One side says, "Homosexual people are born that way;

therefore it's natural (and thus good) for them to form homosexual relationships." The other side retorts, "No, homosexuality is a lifestyle choice, therefore it's unnatural (and thus wrong)." Both sides seem to assume a connection between the cause or origin of homosexual orientation, on the one hand, and the moral value of homosexual activity, on the other. And insofar as they share that assumption, both sides are wrong.

Consider first the pro-homosexual side: "They are born that way; therefore it's natural and good." This inference assumes that all innate desires are good ones (that is, that they should be acted upon). But that assumption is clearly false. Research suggests that some people are born with a predisposition towards violence, but such people have no more right to strangle their neighbors than anyone else. So while some people may be born with homosexual tendencies, it doesn't follow that they ought to act on them.

Nor does it follow that they ought *not* to act on them, even if the tendencies are not innate. I probably do not have any innate tendency to write with my left hand (since I, like everyone else in my family, have always been right-handed), but it doesn't follow that it would be immoral for me to do so. So simply asserting that homosexuality is a "lifestyle choice" will not show that it is an immoral lifestyle choice.

Do people "choose" to be homosexual? People certainly don't seem to choose their sexual *feelings*, at least not in any direct or obvious way. (Do you? Think about it.) Rather, they find certain people attractive and certain activities arousing, whether they "decide" to or not. Indeed, most people at some point in their lives wish that they could control their feelings more (for example, in situations of unrequited love) and find it frustrating that they cannot. What they *can* control to a considerable degree is how and when they act upon those feelings. In that sense, both homosexuality and heterosexuality involve "lifestyle choices." But in either case, determining the cause or origin of the feelings will not determine whether it is moral to act upon them.

(4) *What violates an organ's principal purpose is unnatural.* Perhaps when people claim that homosexual sex is unnatural they mean that it cannot result in procreation. The idea behind the argument is that human organs have various "natural" purposes: eyes are for seeing, ears are for hearing, genitals are for procreating. According to this argument, it is immoral to use an organ in a way that violates its particular purpose.

Many of our organs, however, have multiple purposes. Tommy can use his mouth for talking, eating, breathing, licking stamps, chewing gum, kissing women, or kissing Jim, and it seems rather arbitrary to claim that all but the last use are "natural."[5] (And if we say that some of the other uses are "unnatural, but not immoral," we have failed to specify a morally relevant sense of the term "natural.")

Just because people can and do use their sexual organs to procreate, it does not follow that they should not use them for other purposes. Sexual organs seem very well suited for expressing love, for giving and receiving pleasure, and for celebrating, replenishing, and enhancing a relationship, even when procreation is not a factor. Unless opponents of homosexuality are prepared to condemn heterosexual couples who use contraception or individuals who masturbate, they must abandon this version of the unnaturalness argument. Indeed, even the Roman Catholic Church, which forbids contraception and masturbation, approves of sex for sterile couples and of sex during pregnancy, neither of which can lead to procreation. The Church concedes here that intimacy and pleasure are morally legitimate purposes for sex, even in cases where procreation is impossible. But since homosexual sex can achieve these purposes as well, it is inconsistent for the Church to condemn it on the grounds that it is not procreative.

One might object that sterile heterosexual couples do not *intentionally* turn away from procreation, whereas homosexual couples do. But this distinction doesn't hold. It is no more possible for Tommy to procreate with a woman whose uterus has been removed than it is for him to procreate with Jim. By having sex with either one, he is intentionally engaging in a nonprocreative sexual act.

Yet one might press the objection further: Tommy and the woman *could* produce children if the woman were fertile. Whereas homosexual relationships are essentially infertile, heterosexual relationships are only incidentally so. But what does that prove? Granted, it might require less of a miracle for a woman without a uterus to become pregnant than for Jim to become pregnant, but it would require a miracle nonetheless. Thus it seems that the real difference here is not that one couple is fertile and the other not, nor that one couple "could" be fertile (with the help of a miracle) and the other not, but rather that one couple is male–female and the other male–male. In other words, sex between Tommy and Jim is wrong because it's male–male—that is, because it's homosexual. But that, of course, is no argument at all.[6]

(5) *What is disgusting or offensive is unnatural.* It often seems that when people call homosexuality "unnatural" they really just mean that it's disgusting. But plenty of morally neutral activities—handling snakes, eating snails, performing autopsies, cleaning toilets, and so on—disgust people. Indeed, for centuries most people found interracial relationships disgusting, yet that feeling, which has by no means disappeared, hardly proves that such relationships are wrong. In sum, the charge that homosexuality is unnatural, at least in its most common forms, is longer on rhetorical flourish than on philosophical cogency.

II. Homosexuality Is Harmful

One might argue, instead, that homosexuality is harmful. The Ramsey Colloquium, for instance, argues that homosexuality leads to the breakdown of the family and, ultimately, of human society, and points to the "alarming rates of sexual promiscuity, depression, and suicide and the ominous presence of AIDS within the homosexual subculture."[7] Thomas Schmidt marshals copious statistics to show that homosexual activity undermines physical and psychological health.[8] Such charges, if correct, would seem to provide strong evidence against homosexuality. But are the charges correct? And do they prove what they purport to prove?

One obvious (and obviously problematic) way to answer the first question is to ask people like Tommy and Jim. It would appear that no one is in a better position to judge the homosexual "lifestyle" than those who live it. Yet it is unlikely that critics would trust their testimony. Indeed, the more that homosexual people try to explain their lives, the more critics accuse them of deceitfully promoting an agenda. (It's like trying to prove that you're not crazy. The more you object, the more people think, "That's exactly what a crazy person would say.")

One might instead turn to statistics. An obvious problem with this tack is that both sides of the debate bring forth extensive statistics and "expert" testimony, leaving the average observer confused. There is a more subtle problem as well. Because of widespread antigay sentiment, many homosexual people will not acknowledge their feelings to themselves, much less to researchers.[9] I have known a number of gay men who did not "come out" until their 40s and 50s, and no amount of professional competence on the part of interviewers would have been likely to open their closets sooner. Such problems compound the usual difficulties of finding representative population samples for statistical study.

Yet even if the statistical claims of gay-rights opponents were true, would they prove what they purport to prove? I think not, for the following reasons. First, as any good statistician realizes, correlation does not equal cause. Even if homosexual people were more likely to commit suicide, be promiscuous, or contract AIDS than the general population, it would not follow that their homosexuality causes them to do these things. An alternative and very plausible explanation is that these phenomena, like the disproportionately high crime rates among blacks, are at least partly a function of society's treatment of the group in question. Suppose you were told from a very early age that the romantic feelings that you experienced were sick, unnatural, and disgusting. Suppose further that expressing these feelings put you at risk of social ostracism or, worse yet, physical violence. Is it not plausible that you would, for instance, be more inclined to depression than you would be without such obstacles? And that such depression could, in its extreme forms, lead to suicide or other self-destructive behaviors? (It is indeed remarkable that in the face of such obstacles couples like Tommy and Jim continue to flourish.)

A similar explanation can be given for the alleged promiscuity of homosexuals.[10] The denial of legal marriage, the pressure to remain in the closet, and the overt hostility toward homosexual relationships are all more conducive to transient, clandestine encounters than they are to long-term unions. As a result, that which is challenging enough for heterosexual couples—settling down and building a life together—becomes far more challenging for homosexual couples.

Indeed, there is an interesting tension in the critics' position here. Opponents of homosexuality commonly claim that "marriage and the family . . . are fragile institutions in need of careful and continuing support." [11]And they point to the increasing prevalence of divorce and premarital sex among heterosexuals as evidence that such support is declining. Yet they refuse to concede that the complete absence of similar support for homosexual relationships might explain many of the alleged problems of homosexuals. The critics can't have it both ways: If heterosexual marriages are in trouble despite the various social, economic, and legal incentives for keeping them together, society should be little surprised that homosexual relationships—which not only lack such supports but face overt attack—are difficult to maintain.

One might object that if social ostracism were the main cause of homosexual people's problems, then homosexual people in more "tolerant" cities like New York and San Francisco should exhibit fewer such problems than their small-town counterparts; yet statistics do not seem to bear this out. This objection underestimates the extent of antigay sentiment in our society. By the time many gay and lesbian people move to urban centers, much damage has already been done to their psyches. Moreover, the visibility of homosexuality in urban centers makes homosexual people there more vulnerable to attack (and thus more likely to exhibit certain difficulties). Finally, note that urbanites *in general* (not just homosexual urbanites) tend to exhibit higher rates of promiscuity, depression, and sexually transmitted disease than the rest of the population.

But what about AIDS? Opponents of homosexuality sometimes claim that even if homosexual sex is not, strictly speaking, immoral, it is still a bad idea, since it puts people at risk for AIDS and other sexually transmitted diseases. But that claim is misleading. Note that it is infinitely more risky for Tommy to have sex with a woman who is HIV-positive than with Jim, who is HIV-negative. The reason is simple: it's not homosexuality that's harmful, it's the virus, and the virus may be carried by both heterosexual and homosexual people.

Now it may be the case that in a given population a homosexual male is statistically more likely to carry the virus than a heterosexual female, and thus, from a purely statistical standpoint, male homosexual sex is more risky than heterosexual sex (in cases where the partner's HIV status is unknown). But surely opponents of homosexuality need something stronger than this statistical claim. For if it is wrong for men to have sex with men because their doing so puts them at a higher AIDS risk than heterosexual sex, then it is also wrong for women to have sex with men because their doing so puts them at a higher AIDS risk than homosexual sex (lesbians as a group have the lowest incidence of AIDS). Purely from the standpoint of AIDS risk, women ought to prefer lesbian sex.

If this response seems silly, it is because there is obviously more to choosing a romantic or sexual partner than determining AIDS risk. And a major part of the decision, one that opponents of homosexuality consistently overlook, is considering whether one can have a mutually fulfilling relationship with the partner. For many people like Tommy and Jim, such fulfillment, which most heterosexuals recognize to be an important component of human flourishing, is only possible with members of the same sex.

Of course, the foregoing argument hinges on the claim that homosexual sex can only cause harm indirectly. Some would object that there are certain activities (anal sex, for instance) that for anatomical reasons are intrinsically harmful. But an argument against anal intercourse is by no means tantamount to an argument against homosexuality: neither all nor only homosexuals engage in anal sex. There are plenty of other things for both gay men and lesbians to do in bed. Indeed, for women, it appears that the most common forms of homosexual activity may be *less* risky than penile–vaginal intercourse, since the latter has been linked to cervical cancer.[12]

In sum, there is nothing *inherently* risky about sex between persons of the same gender. It is only risky under certain conditions: for instance, if they exchange diseased bodily fluids or if they engage in certain "rough" forms of sex that could cause tearing of delicate tissue. Heterosexual sex is equally risky under such conditions. Thus, even if statistical claims like those of Schmidt and the Ramsey Colloquium were true, they would not prove that homosexuality is immoral. At best they would prove that homosexual people, like everyone else, ought to take great care when deciding to become sexually active.

Of course, there's more to a flourishing life than avoiding harm. One might argue that even if Tommy and Jim are not harming each other by their relationship, they are still failing to achieve the higher level of fulfillment possible in a heterosexual relationship, which is rooted in the complementarity of male and female. But this argument just ignores the facts. Tommy and Jim are homosexual *precisely because* they find relationships with men (and in particular, with each other) more fulfilling than relationships with women. Even evangelicals (who have long advocated "faith healing" for homosexuals) are beginning to acknowledge that the choice for most homosexual people is not between homosexual relationships and heterosexual relationships, but rather between homosexual relationships and celibacy.[13] What the critics need to show, therefore, is that no matter how loving, committed, mutual, generous, and fulfilling the relationship may be, Tommy and Jim would flourish more if they were celibate. This is a formidable (indeed, probably impossible) task.

Thus far I have focused on the allegation that homosexuality harms those who engage in it. But what about the allegation that homosexuality harms other, nonconsenting parties? Here I will briefly consider two claims: that homosexuality threatens children and that it threatens society.

Those who argue that homosexuality threatens children may mean one of two things. First, they may mean that homosexual people are child molesters. Statistically, the vast majority of reported cases of child sexual abuse involve young girls and their fathers, stepfathers, or other familiar (and presumably heterosexual) adult males.[14] But opponents of homosexuality argue that when one adjusts for relative percentage in the population, homosexual males appear more likely than heterosexual males to be child molesters. As I argued above, the problems with obtaining reliable statistics on homosexuality render such calculations difficult. Fortunately, they are also unnecessary.

Child abuse is a terrible thing. But when a heterosexual male molests a child (or rapes a woman, or commits assault), the act does not reflect upon all heterosexuals. Similarly, when a homosexual male molests a child, there is no reason why that act should reflect upon all homosexuals. Sex with adults of the same sex is one thing; sex with *children* of the same sex is quite another. Conflating the two not only slanders innocent people, it also misdirects resources intended to protect children. Furthermore, many men convicted of molesting young boys are sexually attracted to adult women and report no attraction to adult men.[15] To call such men "homosexual" or even "bisexual" is probably to stretch such terms too far.[16]

Alternatively, those who charge that homosexuality threatens children might mean that the increasing visibility of homosexual relationships makes children more likely to become homosexual. The argument for this view is patently circular. One cannot prove that doing X is bad by arguing that it causes people to do X, which is bad. One must first establish independently that X is bad. That said, there is not a shred of evidence to demonstrate that exposure to homosexuality leads children to become homosexual.

But doesn't homosexuality threaten society? A Roman Catholic priest once put the argument to me as follows: "Of course homosexuality is bad for society. If everyone were homosexual, there would be no society."

Perhaps it is true that if everyone were homosexual, there would be no society. But if everyone were a celibate priest, society would collapse just as surely, and my priest-friend didn't seem to think that he was doing anything wrong simply by failing to procreate. Jeremy Bentham made the point somewhat more acerbically roughly two hundred years ago: "If then merely out of regard to population it were right that [homosexuals] should be burnt alive, monks ought to be roasted alive by a slow fire."[17]

From the fact that the continuation of society requires procreation, it does not follow that *everyone* must procreate. Moreover, even if such an obligation existed, it would not preclude homosexuality. At best it would preclude *exclusive* homosexuality: Homosexual people who occasionally have heterosexual sex can procreate just fine. And given artificial insemination, even those who are exclusively homosexual can procreate. In short, the priest's claim—if everyone were homosexual, there would be no society—is false, and even if it were true, it would not establish that homosexuality is immoral.

The Ramsey Colloquium commits a similar fallacy.[18] Noting (correctly) that heterosexual marriage promotes the continuation of human life, they then infer that homosexuality is immoral because it fails to accomplish the same.[19] But from the fact that procreation is good it does not follow that childlessness is bad, a point that the members of the Colloquium, several of whom are Roman Catholic priests, should readily concede.

I have argued that Tommy and Jim's sexual relationship harms neither them nor society. On the contrary, it benefits both. It benefits them because it makes them happier, not merely in a short-term, hedonistic sense, but in a long-term, "big picture" sort of way. And in turn it benefits society, since it makes Tommy and Jim more stable, more productive, and more generous than they would otherwise be. In short, their relationship, including its sexual component, provides the same kinds of benefits that infertile heterosexual relationships provide (and perhaps other benefits as well). Nor should we fear that accepting their relationship and others like it will cause people to flee in droves from the institution of heterosexual marriage. After all, as Thomas Williams points out, the usual response to a gay person is not "How come he gets to be gay and I don't?"[20]

III. Conclusion

As a last resort, opponents of homosexuality typically change the subject: "But what about incest, polygamy, and bestiality? If we accept Tommy and Jim's sexual relationship, why shouldn't we accept those as well?" Opponents of interracial marriage used a similar slippery-slope argument thirty years ago when the Supreme Court struck down antimiscegenation laws.[21] It was a bad argument then and it is a bad argument now.

Just because there are no good reasons to oppose interracial or homosexual relationships, it does not follow that there are no good reasons to oppose incestuous, polygamous, or bestial relationships. One might argue, for instance, that incestuous relationships threaten delicate familial bonds, that polygamous relationships result in unhealthy jealousies (and sexism), or that bestial relationships (do I need to say it?) aren't really "relationships" at all, at least not in the sense we've been discussing. Perhaps even better arguments could be offered (given much more space than I have here). The point is that there is no logical connection between homosexuality, on the one hand, and incest, polygamy, and bestiality, on the other.

Why, then, do critics continue to push this objection? Perhaps it's because accepting homosexuality requires them to give up one of their favorite arguments: "It's wrong because we've always been taught that it's wrong." This argument—call it the argument from tradition—has an obvious appeal: People reasonably favor "tried and true" ideas over unfamiliar ones, and they recognize the foolishness of trying to invent morality from scratch. But the argument from tradition is also a dangerous argument, as any honest look at history will reveal.

To recognize Tommy and Jim's relationship as good is to admit that our moral traditions are imperfect. Condemning people out of habit is easy. Overcoming deep-seated prejudice takes courage.[22]

Notes

1. Although my central example in the paper is a gay male couple, much of what I say will apply *mutatis mutandis* to lesbians as well, since many of the same arguments are used against them. This is not to say that gay male sexuality and lesbian sexuality are largely similar or that discussions of the former will cover all that needs to be said about the latter. Furthermore, the fact that I focus on a long-term couple should not be taken to imply any judgment about homosexual activity outside of such unions. If the argument of this paper is successful, then the evaluation of homosexual activity outside of committed unions should be largely (if not entirely) similar to the evaluation of heterosexual activity outside of committed unions.

2. Burton M. Leiser, *Liberty, Justice, and Morals: Contemporary Value Conflicts* (New York: Macmillan, 1986), pp. 51–57.

3. The Ramsey Colloquium, "The Homosexual Movement," *First Things*, March 1994, pp. 15–20.

4. For an overview of some of these studies, see Simon LeVay's *Queer Science* (Cambridge, Mass.: M.I.T. Press, 1996), chap. 10.

5. I have borrowed some items in this list from Richard Mohr's pioneering work *Gays/Justice* (New York: Columbia University Press, 1988), p. 36.

6. For a fuller explication of this type of natural law argument, see John Finnis, "Law, Morality, and 'Sexual Orientation,'" *Notre Dame Law Review* 69:5

(1994): 1049–76; revised, shortened, and reprinted in John Corvino, ed., *Same Sex: Debating the Ethics, Science, and Culture of Homosexuality* (Lanham, Md.: Rowman & Littlefield, 1997). For a cogent and well-developed response, see Andrew Koppelman, "A Reply to the New Natural Lawyers," in the same volume.

7. The Ramsey Colloquium, p. 19.

8. Thomas Schmidt, *Straight and Narrow? Compassion and Clarity in the Homosexuality Debate* (Downer's Grove, Ill.: InterVarsity Press, 1995), chap. 6, "The Price of Love."

9. Both the American Psychological Association and the American Public Health Association have conceded this point. "Reliable data on the incidence of homosexual orientation are difficult to obtain due to the criminal penalties and social stigma attached to homosexual behavior and the consequent difficulty of obtaining representative samples of people to study." See *Amici Curiae* brief in *Bowers v. Hardwick*, Supreme Court No. 85–140 (October Term 1985).

10. It is worth noting that allegations of promiscuity are probably exaggerated. Note that the study most commonly cited to prove homosexual male promiscuity, the Bell and Weinberg study, took place in 1978, in an urban center (San Francisco), at the height of the sexual revolution—hardly a broad sample. (See Alan P. Bell and Martin S. Weinberg, *Homosexualities* [New York: Simon and Schuster, 1978].) The far more recent and extensive University of Chicago study agreed that homosexual and bisexual people "have higher average numbers of partners than the rest of the sexually active people in the study," but concluded that the differences in the mean number of partners "do not appear very large" (Edward O. Laumann, et al., *The Social Organization of Sexuality: Sexual Practices in the United States* [Chicago: University of Chicago Press, 1994], pp. 314, 316). I am grateful to Andrew Koppelman for drawing my attention to the Chicago study.

11. The Ramsey Colloquium, p. 19.

12. See S. R. Johnson, E. M. Smith, and S. M. Guenther, "Comparison of Gynecological Health Care Problems Between Lesbian and Bisexual Women," *Journal of Reproductive Medicine* 32 (1987): 805–11.

13. See for example Stanton L. Jones, "The Loving Opposition," *Christianity Today* 37:8 (July 19, 1993).

14. See Danya Glaser and Stephen Frosh, *Child Sexual Abuse*, 2nd ed. (Houndmills, Eng.: Macmillan, 1993), pp. 13–17, and Kathleen Coulbourn Faller, *Understanding Child Sexual Maltreatment* (Newbury Park, Calif.: Sage, 1990), pp. 16–20.

15. See Frank G. Bolton, Jr., Larry A. Morris, and Ann E. MacEachron, *Males at Risk: The Other Side of Child Sexual Abuse* (Newbury Park, Calif.: Sage, 1989), p. 61.

16. Part of the problem here arises from the grossly simplistic categorization of people into two or, at best, three sexual orientations: heterosexual, homosexual, and bisexual. Clearly, there is great variety within (and beyond) these categories. See Frederick Suppe, "Explaining Homosexuality: Philosophical Issues, and Who Cares Anyhow?" in Timothy F. Murphy, ed., *Gay Ethics: Controversies in Outing, Civil Rights, and Sexual Science* (New York: Haworth Press, 1994), especially pp. 234–38.

17. "An Essay on 'Paederasty,'" in Robert Baker and Frederick Elliston, eds., *The Philosophy of Sex* (Buffalo, N.Y.: Prometheus, 1984), pp. 360–61. Bentham uses the word "paederast" where we would use the term "homosexual"; the latter term was not coined until 1869, and the term "heterosexual" was coined a few

years after that. Today, "pederasty" refers to sex between men and boys, a different phenomenon from the one Bentham was addressing.

18. The Ramsey Colloquium, pp. 17–18.

19. The argument is a classic example of the fallacy of denying the antecedent: If X promotes procreation, then X is good; X does not promote procreation; therefore, X is not good. Compare: If X is president, then X lives in the White House; Chelsea Clinton is not president, therefore Chelsea Clinton does not live in the White House.

20. Actually, Williams makes the point with regard to celibacy, while making an analogy between celibacy and homosexuality. See Thomas Williams, "A Reply to the Ramsey Colloquium," in *Same Sex.*

21. *Loving v. Virginia,* 1967.

22. This paper grew out of a lecture, "What's (Morally) Wrong with Homosexuality?" which I first delivered at the University of Texas in 1992 and have since delivered at numerous other universities around the country. I am grateful to countless audience members, students, colleagues, and friends for helpful dialogue over the years. I would especially like to thank the following individuals for detailed comments on recent drafts of the paper: Edwin B. Allaire, Daniel Bonevac, David Bradshaw, David Cleaves, Mary Beth Mader, Richard D. Mohr, Jonathan Rauch, Robert Schuessler, Alan Soble, James P. Sterba, and Thomas Williams. I dedicate this paper to my partner, Carlos Casillas.

PART 3
ABORTION

Chapter 12

ABORTION AND THE SEXUAL AGENDA: A CASE FOR PROLIFE FEMINISM

Sidney Callahan

The abortion debate continues. In the latest and perhaps most crucial development, prolife feminists are contesting prochoice feminist claims that abortion rights are prerequisites for women's full development and social equality. The outcome of this debate may be decisive for the culture as a whole. Prolife feminists, like myself, argue on good feminist principles that women can never achieve the fulfillment of feminist goals in a society permissive toward abortion.

These new arguments over abortion take place within liberal political circles. This round of intense intra-feminist conflict has spiraled beyond earlier right-versus-left abortion debates, which focused on "tragic choices," medical judgments, and legal compromises. Feminist theorists of the prochoice position now put forth the demand for unrestricted abortion rights as a *moral imperative* and insist upon women's right to complete reproductive freedom. They morally justify the present situation and current abortion practices. Thus it is all the more important that prolife feminists articulate their different feminist perspective.

These opposing arguments can best be seen when presented in turn. Perhaps the most highly developed feminist arguments for the morality and legality of abortion can be found in Beverly Wildung Harrison's *Our Right to Choose* (Beacon Press, 1983) and Rosalind Pollack Petchesky's *Abortion and Woman's Choice* (Longman, 1984). Obviously it is difficult to

---

Reprinted with permission from *Commonweal* (25 April 1986), pp. 232–38.

do justice to these complex arguments, which draw on diverse strands of philosophy and social theory and are often interwoven in prochoice feminists' own version of a "seamless garment." Yet the fundamental feminist case for the morality of abortion, encompassing the views of Harrison and Petchesky, can be analyzed in terms of four central moral claims: (1) the moral right to control one's own body; (2) the moral necessity of autonomy and choice in personal responsibility; (3) the moral claim for the contingent value of fetal life; (4) the moral right of women to true social equality.

1. The moral right to control one's own body. Prochoice feminism argues that a woman choosing an abortion is exercising a basic right of bodily integrity granted in our common law tradition. If she does not choose to be physically involved in the demands of a pregnancy and birth, she should not be compelled to be so against her will. Just because it is *her* body which is involved, a woman should have the right to terminate any pregnancy, which at this point in medical history is tantamount to terminating fetal life. No one can be forced to donate an organ or submit to other invasive physical procedures for however good a cause. Thus no woman should be subjected to "compulsory pregnancy." And it should be noted that in pregnancy much more than a passive biological process is at stake.

From one perspective, the fetus is, as Petchesky says, a "biological parasite" taking resources from the woman's body. During pregnancy, a woman's whole life and energies will be actively involved in the nine-month process. Gestation and childbirth involve physical and psychological risks. After childbirth a woman will either be a mother who must undertake a twenty-year responsibility for child rearing, or face giving up her child for adoption or institutionalization. Since hers is the body, hers the risk, hers the burden, it is only just that she alone should be free to decide on pregnancy or abortion.

This moral claim to abortion, according to the prochoice feminists, is especially valid in an individualistic society in which women cannot count on medical care or social support in pregnancy, childbirth, or child rearing. A moral abortion decision is never made in a social vacuum, but in the real life society which exists here and now.

2. The moral necessity of autonomy and choice in personal responsibility. Beyond the claim for individual *bodily* integrity, the prochoice feminists claim that to be a full adult *morally*, a woman must be able to make responsible life commitments. To plan, choose, and exercise personal responsibility, one must have control of reproduction. A woman must be able to make yes-or-no decisions about a specific pregnancy, according to her present situation, resources, prior commitments, and life plan. Only with such reproductive freedom can a woman have the moral autonomy necessary to make mature commitments, in the area of family, work, or education.

Contraception provides a measure of personal control, but contraceptive failure or other chance events can too easily result in involuntary pregnancy. Only free access to abortion can provide the necessary guarantee. The chance biological process of an involuntary pregnancy should not be allowed to override all the other personal commitments and responsibilities a woman has: to others, to family, to work, to education, to her future development, health, or well-being. Without reproductive freedom, women's personal moral agency and human consciousness are subjected to biology and chance.

3. The moral claim for the contingent value of fetal life. Prochoice feminist exponents like Harrison and Petchesky claim that the value of fetal life is contingent upon the woman's free consent and subjective acceptance. The fetus must be invested with maternal valuing in order to become human. This process of "humanization" through personal consciousness and "sociality" can only be bestowed by the woman in whose body and psychosocial system a new life must mature. The meaning and value of fetal life are constructed by the woman; without this personal conferral there only exists a biological, physiological process. Thus fetal interests or fetal rights can never outweigh the woman's prior interest and rights. If a woman does not consent to invest her pregnancy with meaning or value, then the merely biological process can be freely terminated. Prior to her own free choice and conscious investment, a woman cannot be described as a "mother" nor can a "child" be said to exist.

Moreover, in cases of voluntary pregnancy, a woman can withdraw consent if fetal genetic defects or some other problem emerges at any time before birth. Late abortion should thus be granted without legal restrictions. Even the minimal qualifications and limitations on women embedded in *Roe v. Wade* are unacceptable—repressive remnants of patriarchal unwillingness to give power to women.

4. The moral right of women to full social equality. Women have a moral right to full social equality. They should not be restricted or subordinated because of their sex. But this morally required equality cannot be realized without abortion's certain control of reproduction. Female social equality depends upon being able to compete and participate as freely as males can in the structures of educational and economic life. If a woman cannot control when and how she will be pregnant or rear children, she is at a distinct disadvantage, especially in our male-dominated world.

Psychological equality and well-being is also at stake. Women must enjoy the basic right of a person to the free exercise of heterosexual intercourse and full sexual expression, separated from procreation. No less than males, women should be able to be sexually active without the constantly inhibiting fear of pregnancy. Abortion is necessary for women's sexual fulfillment and the growth of uninhibited feminine self-confidence and ownership of their sexual powers.

But true sexual and reproductive freedom means freedom to procreate as well as to inhibit fertility. Prochoice feminists are also worried that women's freedom to reproduce will be curtailed through the abuse of sterilization and needless hysterectomies. Besides the punitive tendencies of a male-dominated health-care system, especially in response to repeated abortions or welfare pregnancies, there are other economic and social pressures inhibiting reproduction. Genuine reproductive freedom implies that day care, medical care, and financial support would be provided mothers, while fathers would take their full share in the burdens and delights of raising children.

Many prochoice feminists identify feminist ideals with communitarian, ecologically sensitive approaches to reshaping society. Following theorists like Sara Ruddick and Carol Gilligan, they link abortion rights with the growth of "maternal thinking" in our heretofore patriarchal society. Maternal thinking is loosely defined as a responsible commitment to the loving nurture of specific human beings as they actually exist in socially embedded interpersonal contexts. It is a moral perspective very different from the abstract, competitive, isolated, and principled rigidity so characteristic of patriarchy.

How does a prolife feminist respond to these arguments? Prolife feminists grant the good intentions of their prochoice counterparts but protest that the prochoice position is flawed, morally inadequate, and inconsistent with feminism's basic demands for justice. Prolife feminists champion a more encompassing moral ideal. They recognize the claims of fetal life and offer a different perspective on what is good for women. The feminist vision is expanded and refocused.

1. *From the moral right to control one's own body to a more inclusive ideal of justice.* The moral right to control one's own body does apply to cases of organ transplants, mastectomies, contraception, and sterilization; but it is not a conceptualization adequate for abortion. The abortion dilemma is caused by the fact that 266 days following a conception in one body, another body will emerge. One's own body no longer exists as a single unit but is engendering another organism's life. This dynamic passage from conception to birth is genetically ordered and universally found in the human species. Pregnancy is not like the growth of cancer or infestation by a biological parasite; it is the way every human being enters the world. Strained philosophical analogies fail to apply: having a baby is not like rescuing a drowning person, being hooked up to a famous violinist's artificial life-support system, donating organs for transplant—or anything else.

As embryology and fetology advance, it becomes clear that human development is a continuum. Just as astronomers are studying the first three minutes in the genesis of the universe, so the first moments, days, and weeks at the beginning of human life are the subject of increasing scientific attention. While neonatology pushes the definition of viability ever earlier, ultrasound and fetology expand the concept of the patient *in utero*. Within such a continuous growth process, it is hard to defend logically any demarcation point after conception as the point at which an immature form of human life is so different from the day before or the day after, that it can be morally or legally discounted as a nonperson. Even the moment of birth can hardly differentiate a nine-month fetus from a newborn. It is not surprising that those who countenance late abortions are logically led to endorse selective infanticide.

The same legal tradition which in our society guarantees the right to control one's own body firmly recognizes the wrongfulness of harming other bodies, however immature, dependent, different looking, or powerless. The handicapped, the retarded, and newborns are legally protected from deliberate harm. Prolife feminists reject the suppositions that would except the unborn from this protection.

After all, debates similar to those about the fetus were once conducted about feminine personhood. Just as women, or blacks, were considered too different, too underdeveloped, too "biological," to have souls or to possess legal rights, so the fetus is now seen as "merely" biological life, subsidiary to a person. A woman was once viewed as incorporated into the "one flesh" of her husband's person; she too was a form of bodily property. In all patriarchal unjust systems, lesser orders of human life are granted rights only when wanted, chosen, or invested with value by the powerful.

Fortunately, in the course of civilization there has been a gradual realization that justice demands the powerless and dependent be protected against the uses of power wielded unilaterally. No human can be treated as a means to an end without consent. The fetus is an immature, dependent form of human life which only needs time and protection to develop. Surely, immaturity and dependence are not crimes.

In an effort to think about the essential requirements of a just society, philosophers like John Rawls recommend imagining yourself in an "original position," in which your position in the society to be created is hidden by a "veil of ignorance." You will have to weigh the possibility that any inequalities inherent in that society's practices may rebound upon you in the worst, as well as in the best, conceivable way. This thought experiment helps ensure justice for all.

Beverly Harrison argues that in such an envisioning of society everyone would institute abortion rights in order to guarantee that if one turned out to be a woman one would have reproductive freedom. But surely in the original position and behind the "veil of ignorance," you would have to contemplate the possibility of being the particular fetus to be aborted. Since everyone has passed through the fetal stage of development, it is false to refuse to imagine oneself in this state when thinking about a potential world in which justice would govern. Would it be just that an embryonic life—in half the cases, of course, a female life—be sacrificed to the right of a woman's control over her own body? A woman may be pregnant without consent and experience a great many penalties, but a fetus killed without consent pays the ultimate penalty.

It does not matter (*The Silent Scream* notwithstanding) whether the fetus being killed is fully conscious or feels pain. We do not sanction killing the innocent if it can be done painlessly or without the victim's awareness. Consciousness becomes important to the abortion debate because it is used as a criterion for the "personhood" so often seen as the prerequisite for legal protection. Yet certain philosophers set the standard of personhood so high that half the human race could not meet the criteria during most of their waking hours (let alone their sleeping ones). Sentience, self-consciousness, rational decision-making, social participation? Surely no infant, or child under two, could qualify. Either our idea of person must be expanded or another criterion, such as human life itself, be employed to protect the weak in a just society. Prolife feminists who defend the fetus empathetically identify with an immature state of growth passed through by themselves, their children, and everyone now alive.

It also seems a travesty of just procedures that a pregnant woman now, in effect, acts as sole judge of her own case, under the most stressful conditions. Yes, one can acknowledge that the pregnant woman will be subject to the potential burdens arising from a pregnancy, but it has never been thought right to have an interested party, especially the more powerful party, decide his or her own case when there may be a conflict of interest. If one considers the matter as a case of a powerful versus a powerless, silenced claimant, the prochoice feminist argument can rightly be inverted: since hers is the body, hers the risk, and hers the greater burden, then how in fairness can a woman be the sole judge of the fetal right to life?

Human ambivalence, a bias toward self-interest, and emotional stress have always been recognized as endangering judgment. Freud declared that love and hate are so entwined that if instant thoughts could kill, we would all be dead in the bosom of our families. In the case of a woman's involuntary pregnancy, a complex, long-term solution requiring effort and energy has to compete with the immediate solution offered by a morning's visit to an abortion clinic. On the simple, perceptual plane, with imagination and thinking curtailed, the speed, ease, and privacy of abortion, combined with the small size of the embryo, tend to make early abortions seem less morally serious—even though speed, size, technical ease, and the private nature of an act have no moral standing.

As the most recent immigrants from nonpersonhood, feminists have traditionally fought for justice for themselves and the world. Women rally to feminism as a new and better way to live. Rejecting male aggression and destruction, feminists seek alternative, peaceful, ecologically sensitive means to resolve conflicts while respecting human potentiality. It is a chilling inconsistency to see prochoice feminists demanding continued access to assembly-line, technological methods of fetal killing—the vacuum aspirator, prostaglandins, and dilation and evacuation. It is a betrayal of feminism, which has built the struggle for justice on the bedrock of women's empathy. After all, "maternal thinking" receives its name from a mother's unconditional acceptance and nurture of dependent, immature life. It is difficult to develop concern for women, children, the poor and the dispossessed—and to care about peace—and at the same time ignore fetal life.

2. *From the necessity of autonomy and choice in personal responsibility to an expanded sense of responsibility.* A distorted idea of morality over-emphasizes individual autonomy and active choice. Morality has often been viewed too exclusively as a matter of human agency and decisive action. In moral behavior persons must explicitly choose and aggressively exert their wills to intervene in the natural and social environments. The human will dominates the body, overcomes the given, breaks out of the material limits of nature. Thus if one does not choose to be pregnant or cannot rear a child, who must be given up for adoption, then better to abort the pregnancy. Willing, planning, choosing one's moral commitments through the contracting of one's individual resources becomes the premier model of moral responsibility.

But morality also consists of the good and worthy acceptance of the unexpected events that life presents. Responsiveness and response-ability to things unchosen are also instances of the highest human moral capacity. Morality is not confined to contracted agreements of isolated individuals. Yes, one is obligated by explicit contracts freely initiated, but human beings are also obligated by implicit compacts and involuntary relationships in which persons simply find themselves. To be embedded in a family, a neighborhood, a social system, brings moral obligations which were never entered into with informed consent.

Parent–child relationships are one instance of implicit moral obligations arising by virtue of our being part of the interdependent human community. A woman, involuntarily pregnant, has a moral obligation to the now-existing dependent fetus whether she explicitly consented to its existence or not. No prolife feminist would dispute the forceful observations of prochoice feminists about the extreme difficulties that bearing an unwanted child in our society can entail. But the stronger force of the fetal claim presses a woman to accept these burdens; the fetus possesses rights arising from its extreme need and the interdependency and unity of humankind. The woman's moral obligation arises both from her status as a human being embedded in the interdependent human community and her unique lifegiving female reproductive power. To

follow the prochoice feminist ideology of insistent individualistic autonomy and control is to betray a fundamental basis of the moral life.

*3. From the moral claim of the contingent value of fetal life to the moral claim
for the intrinsic value of human life.* The feminist prochoice position which
claims that the value of the fetus is contingent upon the pregnant
woman's bestowal—or willed, conscious "construction"—of human-
hood is seriously flawed. The inadequacies of this position flow from the
erroneous premises (1) that human value and rights can be granted by
individual will; (2) that the individual woman's consciousness can exist
and operate in an *a priori* isolated fashion; and (3) that "mere" biological, genetic human life has little meaning. Prolife feminism takes a very
different stance toward life and nature.

Human life from the beginning to the end of development *has* intrinsic value, which does not depend on meeting the selective criteria or
tests set up by powerful others. A fundamental humanist assumption is
at stake here. Either we are going to value embodied human life and humanity as a good thing, or take some variant of the nihilist position that
assumes human life is just one more random occurrence in the universe
such that each instance of human life must explicitly be justified to prove
itself worthy to continue. When faced with a new life, or an involuntary
pregnancy, there is a world of difference in whether one first asks, "Why
continue?" or "Why not?" Where is the burden of proof going to rest?
The concept of "compulsory pregnancy" is as distorted as labeling life
"compulsory aging."

In a sound moral tradition, human rights arise from human needs,
and it is the very nature of a right, or valid claim upon another, that it
cannot be denied, conditionally delayed, or rescinded by more powerful
others at their behest. It seems fallacious to hold that in the case of the
fetus it is the pregnant woman alone who gives or removes its right to life
and human status solely through her subjective conscious investment or
"humanization." Surely no pregnant woman (or any other individual
member of the species) has created her own human nature by an indi-
vidually willed act of consciousness, nor for that matter been able to
guarantee her own human rights. An individual woman and the unique
individual embryonic life within her can only exist because of their participation in the genetic inheritance of the human species as a whole. Biological life should never be discounted. Membership in the species, or
collective human family, is the basis for human solidarity, equality, and
natural human rights.

*4. The moral right of women to full social equality from a prolife feminist per-
spective.* Prolife feminists and prochoice feminists are totally agreed on
the moral right of women to the full social equality so far denied them.
The disagreement between them concerns the definition of the desired
goal and the best means to get there. Permissive abortion laws do not

bring women reproductive freedom, social equality, sexual fulfillment, or full personal development.

Pragmatic failures of a prochoice feminist position combined with a lack of moral vision are, in fact, causing disaffection among young women. Middle-aged prochoice feminists blamed the "big chill" on the general conservative backlash. But they should look rather to their own elitist acceptance of male models of sex and to the sad picture they present of women's lives. Pitting women against their own offspring is not only morally offensive, it is psychologically and politically destructive. Women will never climb to equality and social empowerment over mounds of dead fetuses, numbering now in the millions. As long as most women choose to bear children, they stand to gain from the same constellation of attitudes and institutions that will also protect the fetus in the woman's womb—and they stand to lose from the cultural assumptions that support permissive abortion. Despite temporary conflicts of interest, feminine and fetal liberation are ultimately one and the same cause.

Women's rights and liberation are pragmatically linked to fetal rights because to obtain true equality, women need (1) more social support and changes in the structure of society, and (2) increased self-confidence, self-expectations, and self-esteem. Society in general, and men in particular, have to provide women more support in rearing the next generation, or our devastating feminization of poverty will continue. But if a woman claims the right to decide by herself whether the fetus becomes a child or not, what does this do to paternal and communal responsibility? Why should men share responsibility for child support or child rearing if they cannot share in what is asserted to be the woman's sole decision? Furthermore, if explicit intentions and consciously accepted contracts are necessary for moral obligations, why should men be held responsible for what *they* do not voluntarily choose to happen? By prochoice reasoning, a man who does not want to have a child, or whose contraceptive fails, can be exempted from the responsibilities of fatherhood and child support. Traditionally, many men have been laggards in assuming parental responsibility and support for their children; ironically, ready abortion, often advocated as a response to male dereliction, legitimizes male irresponsibility and paves the way for even more male detachment and lack of commitment.

For that matter, why should the state provide a system of day care or child support, or require workplaces to accommodate women's maternity and the needs of child rearing? Permissive abortion, granted in the name of women's privacy and reproductive freedom, ratifies the view that pregnancies and children are a woman's private individual responsibility. More and more frequently, we hear some version of this old rationalization: if she refuses to get rid of it, it's her problem. A child becomes a product of the individual woman's freely chosen investment, a form of private property resulting from her own cost-benefit calculation. The larger community is relieved of moral responsibility.

With legal abortion freely available, a clear cultural message is given: conception and pregnancy are no longer serious moral matters. With abortion as an acceptable alternative, contraception is not as responsibly used; women take risks, often at the urging of male sexual partners. Repeat abortions increase, with all their psychological and medical repercussions. With more abortion there is more abortion. Behavior shapes thought as well as the other way round. One tends to justify morally what one has done; what becomes commonplace and institutionalized seems harmless. Habituation is a powerful psychological force. Psychologically it is also true that whatever is avoided becomes more threatening; in phobias it is the retreat from anxiety-producing events which reinforces future avoidance. Women begin to see themselves as too weak to cope with involuntary pregnancies. Finally, through the potency of social pressure and the force of inertia, it becomes more and more difficult, in fact almost unthinkable, *not* to use abortion to solve problem pregnancies. Abortion becomes no longer a choice but a "necessity."

But "necessity," beyond the organic failure and death of the body, is a dynamic social construction open to interpretation. The thrust of present feminist prochoice arguments can only increase the justifiable indications for "necessary" abortion; every unwanted fetal handicap becomes more and more unacceptable. Repeatedly assured that in the name of reproductive freedom, women have a right to specify which pregnancies and which children they will accept, women justify sex selection, and abort unwanted females. Female infanticide, after all, is probably as old a custom as the human species possesses. Indeed, all kinds of selection of the fit and the favored for the good of the family and the tribe have always existed. Selective extinction is no new program.

There are far better goals for feminists to pursue. Prolife feminists seek to expand and deepen the more communitarian, maternal elements of feminism—and move society from its male-dominated course. First and foremost, women have to insist upon a different, woman-centered approach to sex and reproduction. While Margaret Mead stressed the "womb envy" of males in other societies, it has been more or less repressed in our own. In our male-dominated world, what men don't do, doesn't count. Pregnancy, childbirth, and nursing have been characterized as passive, debilitating, animallike. The disease model of pregnancy and birth has been entrenched. This female disease or impairment, with its attendant "female troubles," naturally handicaps women in the "real" world of hunting, war, and the corporate fast track. Many prochoice feminists, deliberately childless, adopt the male perspective when they cite the "basic injustice that women have to bear the babies," instead of seeing the injustice in the fact that men cannot. Women's biologically unique capacity and privilege has been denied, despised, and suppressed under male domination; unfortunately, many women have fallen for the phallic fallacy.

Childbirth often appears in prochoice literature as a painful, traumatic, life-threatening experience. Yet giving birth is accurately seen as an arduous but normal exercise of life-giving power, a violent and ecstatic peak experience, which men can never know. Ironically, some prochoice men and women think and talk of pregnancy and childbirth with the same repugnance that ancient ascetics displayed toward orgasms and sexual intercourse. The similarity may not be accidental. The obstetrician Niles Newton, herself a mother, has written of the extended threefold sexuality of women, who can experience orgasm, birth, and nursing as passionate pleasure-giving experiences. All of these are involuntary processes of the female body. Only orgasm, which males share, has been glorified as an involuntary function that is nature's great gift; the involuntary feminine processes of childbirth and nursing have been seen as bondage to biology.

Fully accepting our bodies as ourselves, what should women want? I think women will only flourish when there is a feminization of sexuality, very different from the current cultural trend toward masculinizing female sexuality. Women can never have the self-confidence and self-esteem they need to achieve feminist goals in society until a more holistic, feminine model of sexuality becomes the dominant cultural ethos. To say this affirms the view that men and women differ in the domain of sexual functioning, although they are more alike than different in other personality characteristics and competencies. For those of us committed to achieving sexual equality in the culture, it may be hard to accept the fact that sexual differences make it imperative to talk of distinct male and female models of sexuality. But if one wants to change sexual roles, one has to recognize preexisting conditions. A great deal of evidence is accumulating which points to biological pressures for different male and female sexual functioning.

Males always and everywhere have been more physically aggressive and more likely to fuse sexuality with aggression and dominance. Females may be more variable in their sexuality, but since Masters and Johnson, we know that women have a greater capacity than men for repeated orgasm and a more tenuous path to arousal and orgasmic release. Most obviously, women also have a far greater sociobiological investment in the act of human reproduction. On the whole, women as compared to men possess a sexuality which is more complex, more intense, more extended in time, involving higher investment, risks, and psychosocial involvement.

* * *

Considering the differences in sexual functioning, it is not surprising that men and women in the same culture have often constructed different sexual ideals. In Western culture, since the nineteenth century at least, most women have espoused a version of sexual functioning in which sex acts are embedded within deep emotional bonds and secure long-term commitments. Within these committed "pair bonds" males assume parental obligations. In the idealized Victorian version of the Christian sexual ethic, culturally endorsed and maintained by women, the double standard was not countenanced. Men and women did not need to marry to be whole persons, but if they did engage in sexual functioning, they were to be equally chaste, faithful, responsible, loving, and parentally concerned. Many of the most influential women in the nineteenth-century women's movement preached and lived this sexual ethic, often by the side of exemplary feminist men. While the ideal has never been universally obtained, a culturally dominant demand for monogamy, self-control, and emotionally bonded and committed sex works well for women in every stage of their sexual life cycles. When love, chastity, fidelity, and commitment for better or worse are the ascendant cultural prerequisites for sexual functioning, young girls and women expect protection from rape and seduction, adult women justifiably demand male support in child rearing, and older women are more protected from abandonment as their biological attractions wane.

Of course, these feminine sexual ideals always coexisted in competition with another view. A more male-oriented model of erotic or amative sexuality endorses sexual permissiveness without long-term commitment or reproductive focus. Erotic sexuality emphasizes pleasure, play, passion, individual self-expression, and romantic games of courtship and conquest. It is assumed that a variety of partners and sexual experiences are necessary to stimulate romantic passion. This erotic model of the sexual life has often worked satisfactorily for men, both heterosexual and gay, and for certain cultural elites. But for the average woman, it is quite destructive. Women can only play the erotic game successfully when, like the "*Cosmopolitan* woman," they are young, physically attractive, economically powerful, and fulfilled enough in a career to be willing to sacrifice family life. Abortion is also required. As our society increasingly endorses this male-oriented, permissive view of sexuality, it is all too ready to give women abortion on demand. Abortion helps a woman's body be more like a man's. It has been observed that *Roe v. Wade* removed the last defense women possessed against male sexual demands.

Unfortunately, the modern feminist movement made a mistaken move at a critical juncture. Rightly rebelling against patriarchy, unequal education, restricted work opportunities, and women's downtrodden political status, feminists also rejected the nineteenth-century feminine sexual ethic. Amative, erotic, permissive sexuality (along with abortion rights) became symbolically identified with other struggles for social equality in education, work, and politics. This feminist mistake also turned off many potential recruits among women who could not deny the positive dimensions of their own traditional feminine roles, nor their allegiance to the older feminine sexual ethic of love and fidelity.

An ironic situation then arose in which many prochoice feminists preach their own double standard. In the world of work and career, women are urged to grow up, to display mature self-discipline and self-control; they are told to persevere in long-term commitments, to cope with unexpected obstacles by learning to tough out the inevitable sufferings and setbacks entailed in life and work. But this mature ethic of commitment and self-discipline, recommended as the only way to progress in the world of work and personal achievement, is discounted in the domain of sexuality.

In prochoice feminism, a permissive, erotic view of sexuality is assumed to be the only option. Sexual intercourse with a variety of partners is seen as "inevitable" from a young age and as a positive growth experience to be managed by access to contraception and abortion. Unfortunately, the pervasive cultural conviction that adolescents, or their elders, cannot exercise sexual self-control undermines the responsible use of contraception. When a pregnancy occurs, the first abortion is viewed in some prochoice circles as a *rite de passage*. Responsibly choosing an abortion supposedly ensures that a young woman will take charge of her own life, make her own decisions, and carefully practice contraception. But the social dynamics of a permissive, erotic model of sexuality, coupled with permissive laws, work toward repeat abortions. Instead of being empowered by their abortion choices, young women having abortions are confronting the debilitating reality of *not* bringing a baby into the world; *not* being able to count on a committed male partner; *not* accounting oneself strong enough, or the master of enough resources, to avoid killing the fetus. Young women are hardly going to develop the self-esteem, self-discipline, and self-confidence necessary to confront a male-dominated society through abortion.

The male-oriented sexual orientation has been harmful to women and children. It has helped bring us epidemics of venereal disease, infertility, pornography, sexual abuse, adolescent pregnancy, divorce, displaced older women, and abortion. Will these signals of something amiss stimulate prochoice feminists to rethink what kind of sex ideal really serves women's best interests? While the erotic model cannot encompass commitment, the committed model can—happily—encompass and encourage romance, passion, and playfulness. In fact, within the security of long-term commitments, women may be more likely to experience sexual pleasure and fulfillment.

* * *

The prolife feminist position is not a return to the old feminine mystique. That espousal of "the eternal feminine" erred by viewing sexuality as so sacred that it cannot be humanly shaped at all. Woman's *whole* nature was supposed to be opposite to man's, necessitating complementary and radically different social roles. Followed to its logical conclusion, such a view presumes that reproductive and sexual experience is necessary for human fulfillment. But as the early feminists insisted, no woman has to marry or engage in sexual intercourse to be fulfilled, nor does a woman have to give birth and raise children to be complete, nor must she stay home and function as an earth mother. But female sexuality does need to be deeply respected as a unique potential and trust. Since most contraceptives and sterilization procedures really do involve only the woman's body rather than destroying new life, they can be an acceptable and responsible moral option.

With sterilization available to accelerate the inevitable natural ending of fertility and childbearing, a woman confronts only a limited number of years in which she exercises her reproductive trust and may have to respond to an unplanned pregnancy. Responsible use of contraception can lower the probabilities even more. Yet abortion is not decreasing. The reason is the current permissive attitude embodied in the law, not the "hard cases" which constitute 3 percent of today's abortions. Since attitudes, the law, and behavior interact, prolife feminists conclude that unless there is an enforced limitation of abortion, which currently confirms the sexual and social status quo, alternatives will never be developed. For women to get what they need in order to combine childbearing, education, and careers, society has to recognize that female bodies come with wombs. Women and their reproductive power, and the children women have, must be supported in new ways. Another and different round of feminist consciousness raising is needed in which all of women's potential is accorded respect. This time, instead of humbly buying entrée by conforming to male lifestyles, women will demand that society accommodate itself to them.

New feminist efforts to rethink the meaning of sexuality, femininity, and reproduction are all the more vital as new techniques for artificial reproduction, surrogate motherhood, and the like present a whole new set of dilemmas. In the long run, the very long run, the abortion debate may be merely the opening round in a series of far-reaching struggles over the role of human sexuality and the ethics of reproduction. Significant changes in the culture, both positive and negative in outcome, may begin as local storms of controversy. We may be at one of those vaguely realized thresholds when we had best come to full attention. What kind of people are we going to be? Prolife feminists pursue a vision for their sisters, daughters, and granddaughters. Will their great-granddaughters be grateful?

Chapter 13

ABORTION: IS A WOMAN A PERSON?

Ellen Willis

If propaganda is as central to politics as I think, the opponents of legal abortion have been winning a psychological victory as important as their tangible gains. Two years ago, abortion was almost always discussed in feminist terms—as a political issue affecting the condition of women. Since then, the grounds of the debate have shifted drastically; more and more, the right-to-life movement has succeeded in getting the public and the media to see abortion as an abstract moral issue having solely to do with the rights of fetuses. Though every poll shows that most Americans favor legal abortion, it is evident that many are confused and disarmed, if not convinced, by the antiabortionists' absolutist fervor. No one likes to be accused of advocating murder. Yet the "pro-life" position is based on a crucial fallacy—that the question of fetal rights can be isolated from the question of women's rights.

Recently, Garry Wills wrote a piece suggesting that liberals who defended the snail-darter's right to life and opposed the killing in Vietnam should condemn abortion as murder. I found this notion breathtaking in its illogic. Environmentalists were protesting not the "murder" of individual snail-darters but the practice of wiping out entire species of organisms to gain a short-term economic benefit; most people who

---

Ellen Willis, "Abortion: Is a Woman a Person?" from *Beginning to See the Light*, © 1992 by Wesleyan University Press. Reprinted by permission of University Press of New England. This essay began as two columns written for *The Village Voice* (March and April 1979); they were first combined as "Abortion: Is a Woman a Person?" in *Beginning to See the Light* (New York: Knopf, 1981), pp. 205–11.

opposed our involvement in Vietnam did so because they believed the United States was waging an aggressive, unjust, and/or futile war. There was no inconsistency in holding such positions and defending abortion on the grounds that women's welfare should take precedence over fetal life. To claim that three very different issues, each with its own complicated social and political context, all came down to a simple matter of preserving life was to say that all killing was alike and equally indefensible regardless of circumstance. (Why, I wondered, had Wills left out the destruction of hapless bacteria by penicillin?) But aside from the general mushiness of the argument, I was struck by one peculiar fact: Wills had written an entire article about abortion without mentioning women, feminism, sex, or pregnancy.

Since the feminist argument for abortion rights still carries a good deal of moral and political weight, part of the antiabortionists' strategy has been to make an end run around it. Although the mainstream of the right-to-life movement is openly opposed to women's liberation, it has chosen to make its stand on the abstract "pro-life" argument. That emphasis has been reinforced by the movement's tiny left wing, which opposes abortion on pacifist grounds and includes women who call themselves "feminists for life." A minority among pacifists as well as right-to-lifers, this group nevertheless serves the crucial function of making opposition to abortion respectable among liberals, leftists, and moderates disinclined to sympathize with a right-wing crusade. Unlike most right-to-lifers, who are vulnerable to charges that their reverence for life does not apply to convicted criminals or Vietnamese peasants, antiabortion leftists are in a position to appeal to social conscience—to make analogies, however facile, between abortion and napalm. They disclaim any opposition to women's rights, insisting rather that the end cannot justify the means—murder is murder.

Well, isn't there a genuine moral issue here? If abortion *is* murder, how can a woman have the right to it? Feminists are often accused of evading this question, but in fact an evasion is built into the question itself. Most people understand "Is abortion murder?" to mean "Is the fetus a person?" But fetal personhood is ultimately as inarguable as the existence of God; either you believe in it or you don't. Putting the debate on this plane inevitably leads to the nonconclusion that it is a matter of one person's conscience against another's. From there, the discussion generally moves on to broader issues: whether laws defining the fetus as a person violate the separation of church and state; or conversely, whether people who believe an act is murder have not only the right but the obligation to prevent it. Unfortunately, amid all this lofty philosophizing, the concrete, human reality of the pregnant woman's dilemma gets lost, and with it an essential ingredient of the moral question.

Murder, as commonly defined, is killing that is unjustified, willful, and malicious. Most people would agree, for example, that killing in defense of one's life or safety is not murder. And most would accept a concept of self-defense that includes the right to fight a defensive war or revolution in behalf of one's independence or freedom from oppression. Even pacifists make moral distinctions between defensive violence, however deplorable, and murder; no thoughtful pacifist would equate Hitler's murder of the Jews with the Warsaw Ghetto rebels' killing of Nazi troops. The point is that it's impossible to judge whether an act is murder simply by looking at the act, without considering its context. Which is to say that it makes no sense to discuss whether abortion is murder without considering why women have abortions and what it means to force women to bear children they don't want.

We live in a society that defines child rearing as the mother's job; a society in which most women are denied access to work that pays enough to support a family, child-care facilities they can afford, or any relief from the constant, daily burdens of motherhood; a society that forces mothers into dependence on marriage or welfare and often into permanent poverty; a society that is actively hostile to women's ambitions for a better life. Under these conditions the unwillingly pregnant woman faces a terrifying loss of control over her fate. Even if she chooses to give up the baby, unwanted pregnancy is in itself a serious trauma. There is no way a pregnant woman can passively let the fetus live; she must create and nurture it with her own body, in a symbiosis that is often difficult, sometimes dangerous, always uniquely intimate. However gratifying pregnancy may be to a woman who desires it, for the unwilling it is literally an invasion—the closest analogy is to the difference between lovemaking and rape. Nor is there such a thing as foolproof contraception. Clearly, abortion is by normal standards an act of self-defense.

Whenever I make this case to a right-to-lifer, the exchange that follows is always substantially the same:

RTL: If a woman chooses to have sex, she should be willing to take the consequences. We must all be responsible for our actions.

EW: Men have sex, without having to "take the consequences."

RTL: You can't help that—it's biology.

EW: You don't think a woman has as much right as a man to enjoy sex? Without living in fear that one slip will transform her life?

RTL: She has no right to selfish pleasure at the expense of the unborn.

It would seem, then, that the nitty-gritty issue in the abortion debate is not life but sex. If the fetus is sacrosanct, it follows that women must be continually vulnerable to the invasion of their bodies and loss of their freedom and independence—unless they are willing to resort to the only perfectly reliable contraceptive, abstinence. This is precisely the "solution" right-to-lifers suggest, usually with a touch of glee; as Representative Elwood Rudd once put it, "If a woman has a right to control her own body, let her exercise control before she gets pregnant." A common ploy is to compare fucking to overeating or overdrinking, the idea being that pregnancy is a just punishment, like obesity or cirrhosis.

In 1979 it is depressing to have to insist that sex is not an unnecessary, morally dubious self-indulgence but a basic human need, no less for women than for men. Of course, for heterosexual women giving up sex also means doing without the love and companionship of a mate. (Presumably, married women who have had all the children they want are supposed to divorce their husbands or convince them that celibacy is the only moral alternative.) "Freedom" bought at such a cost is hardly freedom at all and certainly not equality—no one tells men that if they aspire to some measure of control over their lives, they are welcome to neuter themselves and become social isolates. The don't-have-sex argument is really another version of the familiar antifeminist dictum that autonomy and femaleness—that is, female sexuality—are incompatible; if you choose the first, you lose the second. But to pose this choice is not only inhumane; it is as deeply disingenuous as "Let them eat cake." No one, least of all the antiabortion movement, expects or wants significant numbers of women to give up sex and marriage. Nor are most right-to-lifers willing to allow abortion for rape victims. When all the cant about "responsibility" is stripped away, what the right-to-life position comes down to is, if the effect of prohibiting abortion is to keep women slaves to their biology, so be it.

In their zeal to preserve fetal life at all costs, antiabortionists are ready to grant fetuses more legal protection than people. If a man attacks me and I kill him, I can plead self-defense without having to prove that I was in danger of being killed rather than injured, raped, or kidnapped. But in the annual congressional battle over what if any exceptions to make to the Medicaid abortion ban, the House of Representatives has bitterly opposed the funding of abortions for any reason but to save the pregnant woman's life. Some right-to-lifers argue that even the danger of death does not justify abortion; others have suggested "safeguards" like requiring two or more doctors to certify that the woman's life is at least 50 percent threatened. Antiabortionists are forever worrying that any exception to a total ban on abortion will be used as a "loophole": better that any number of women should ruin their health or even die than that one woman should get away with not having a child "merely" because she doesn't want one. Clearly this mentality does not reflect equal concern for all life. Rather, antiabortionists value the lives of fetuses above the lives and welfare of women, because at bottom they do not concede women the right to an active human existence that transcends

their reproductive function. Years ago, in an interview with Paul Krassner in *The Realist,* Ken Kesey declared himself against abortion. When
Krassner asked if his objection applied to victims of rape, Kesey
replied—I may not be remembering the exact words, but I will never forget the substance—"Just because another man planted the seed, that's
no reason to destroy the crop."[1] To this day I have not heard a more eloquent or chilling metaphor for the essential premise of the right-to-life
movement: that a woman's excuse for being is her womb. It is an outrageous irony that antiabortionists are managing to pass off this profoundly immoral idea as a noble moral cause.

The conservatives who dominate the right-to-life movement have no
real problem with the antifeminism inherent in their stand; their evasion
of the issue is a matter of public relations. But the politics of antiabortion
leftists are a study in self-contradiction: in attacking what they see as the
violence of abortion, they condone and encourage violence against
women. Forced childbearing does violence to a woman's body and spirit,
and it contributes to other kinds of violence: deaths from illegal abortion;
the systematic oppression of mothers and women in general; the poverty,
neglect, and battering of unwanted children; sterilization abuse.

Radicals supposedly believe in attacking a problem at its roots. Yet surely
it is obvious that restrictive laws do not keep women from seeking abortions; they just create an illicit, dangerous industry. The only way to drastically reduce the number of abortions is to invent safer, more reliable
contraceptives, ensure universal access to all birth control methods, eliminate sexual ignorance and guilt, and change the social and economic
conditions that make motherhood a trap. Anyone who is truly committed
to fostering life should be fighting for women's liberation instead of harassing and disrupting abortion clinics (hardly a nonviolent tactic, since it
threatens the safety of patients). The "feminists for life" do talk a lot about
ending the oppression that drives so many women to abortion; in practice,
however, they are devoting all their energy to increasing it.

Despite its numerical insignificance, the antiabortion left epitomizes
the hypocrisy of the right-to-life crusade. Its need to wrap misogyny in the
rhetoric of social conscience and even feminism is actually a perverse tribute to the women's movement; it is no longer acceptable to declare openly
that women deserve to suffer for the sin of Eve. I suppose that's progress—
not that it does the victims of the Hyde Amendment much good.

Note

1. A reader later sent me a copy of the Kesey interview. The correct quotation
is "You don't plow under the corn because the seed was planted with a neighbor's shovel."

PART 4

SADOMASOCHISM

Chapter 14

SADISTIC FANTASIES

Natalie Shainess

Q.: *A patient, supposedly happily married, good sex life, and father of three children, continues to masturbate with sadistic fantasies of flagellation of females. Patient is in his thirties and completely represses this with his wife, she having no knowledge of this portion of his life. What can I do to help him overcome his fantasy? It was with great reluctance that he sought help.*

A.: If ever there was a "loaded question" this is it, because the premises underlying it are rather simple in relation to the complexities of the issues. First, let me answer, before I clarify. I do not believe he can, in fact, be helped to overcome this fantasy—at least under his present life circumstances. Observe that he sought help only with great reluctance. This suggests that he feels the status quo is the best solution possible for him. Since his wife does not know and he did not want help, one wonders who indeed it was who urged him to seek help.

A man who needs sadistic fantasies of beating females in order to enjoy sex in any sense—and note his enjoyment is in masturbation, certainly a less preferred outlet than intercourse to most (reasonably healthy) men—cannot be happily married or have a "good" sex life. Why? Because he hates women, and undoubtedly his wife most of all. Why is he married? Among many possible complex reasons is the fact that men as well as women sometimes choose marriage as a social "solution" to the problem of how to live their lives, whether really desiring it or not.

Reprinted, with the permission of Natalie Shainess, from *Medical Aspects of Human Sexuality* 8:2 (1974), pp. 144, 148.

Since he has three children, we can work on the assumption that he has had intercourse with his wife at least three times—although it is possible they are not his (possible, not probable). It is not clear to me what he *represses* in relation to his wife. His fantasies? No he doesn't, although he may not or has not told her about them. Of what portion of his life has he not told her? About masturbation? Or about being a homosexual—which is one good possibility here.

Anyone having fantasies like these must be a very difficult marriage partner in the nonsexual area as well as a tormenting and frustrating person to live with.

So what is to be done? Perhaps he must be left with his fantasy? After all, he did not want change. To overcome it would in all likelihood require a different life style, but he wants the one he has! If I were to guess who really needs and possibly wants help, I would suggest that efforts be expended on the wife!

Chapter 15

ETHICS, FANTASY AND SELF-TRANSFORMATION

Jean Grimshaw

In this paper I want to discuss an issue (usually perceived as an ethical one) which has generated a great deal of feminist discussion and some profound disagreement. The issue arises as follows. One of the most important targets of feminist action and critique has been male sexual violence and control of women, as expressed in rape and other forms of violent or aggressive sexual acts, and as represented in much pornography. Pornography itself has been the subject of major and sometimes bitter disagreements among feminists, especially around the issue of censorship. But it is not that with which I am concerned here. The issue which I want to discuss involves the question of sexual desire and fantasy, and their apparent potential incompatibility with political and ethical principles. This is by no means, of course, an issue of exclusively feminist concern; but I shall focus on some recent feminist argument, since it is that with which I am most familiar.

There is a great deal of evidence that women's sexual fantasies often involve various forms and elements of domination, submission, humiliation; even rape itself. Women can find pornographic literature such as *The Story of O* erotic; this famous pornographic novel involves the ritual rape and repeated beating and humiliation of the heroine, who is reduced to being nothing but a total sexual slave of her masters. Less obvious but more widespread ways in which women can find pleasure in scenarios involving violence and humiliation can be found in many genres of romantic mass market fiction. These may rarely involve an actual rape, at least between the pages of the book, but they routinely involve the mistreatment, humiliation and near-brutality of the hero towards the heroine, until the last pages when it is revealed that he really loves her. Ann Barr Snitow (1979) has argued that mass market romance may be seen as a kind of pornography for women.[1]

But it is also clear that such fantasies can exist in women who have a strong commitment to sexual equality, who abhor male violence or sexual domination of women. And the question of what our response should be to this fact has generated some profound disagreements. There is a range of views on the question. I shall outline some of them, and then go on to consider what seem to me to be some of the philosophical and ethical issues involved.

There are two responses to the existence of these sexual fantasies in women which seem to me to represent two ends of the spectrum. At the first end is the kind of view which suggests that the person who has the fantasies should just learn to live with them and accept them. They are harmless; there is no necessary connection at all between fantasy and real life. Any attempt to make those who have such fantasies uneasy or guilty about them is divisive and coercive. In addition, the supposition that fantasy or desire could ever be made to toe a politically 'correct' line is pointless, since fantasies can never be controlled in this way. Furthermore, even if acted upon in controlled ways (such as in various sado-masochistic sexual practices), they do not in any sense necessarily compromise political principles, or make women less likely to wish to condemn rape and real-life sexual violence. In addition, it is a good thing that sexual desire and fantasy is freed as much as possible from structures of guilt, fear, shame and psychic distress.

At the other end of the spectrum is a radically different view. A fairly extreme statement of this view can be found in a book by Sheila Jeffreys, *Anti-Climax* (1990).[2] The book offers a powerful indictment of the ways in which both much twentieth century literature about sexuality and the so-called 'sexual revolution' and increased sexual 'permissiveness' of the decades since the 1960s have been premised on sexist views of women and phallocentric views of sexuality. But Jeffreys' view of sexuality and of sexual fantasy is nevertheless one that I find troubling and problematic for many reasons. Jeffreys argues that far from heterosexual intercourse being something that all women 'naturally' like or enjoy, it is something into which many of them are pressured by the power of ideology and social sanctions. She does indeed show how concepts such as those of 'inhibition', 'frigidity' and 'repression' have been used in large numbers of books about sexuality to disallow any kind of response from women that was unhappy with a model of sexuality totally dominated by intercourse and male pleasure. But her own view of women's sexuality runs something like this. Women's sexuality as currently constructed, including many of their sexual fantasies, is almost wholly adapted to, or colonized by, male needs and desires. Even many ideas of a more 'autonomous' and active female sexuality are, she argues, constructed on models of male sexuality—as continuously capable of sex and always desiring it, for example, or as capable of separating sex from loving emotion and making use of all sexual opportunities.

But male sexuality—and heterosexuality itself—is a ruling class sexuality, constructed around the domination and subordination of women. Heterosexual desire is eroticised power difference; men's desire for women is based on eroticising the powerlessness, 'otherness' and subordination of women. And women's desire for men is based on the same structures; they too have been conditioned to think that inequality and subordination are sexy. Women's sexual response to men has been based partly on the material need to cope with male power and their own frequent dependence; but they have also learned the 'deep structures' of their own eroticism in a male dominated society. The reason why women have such things as sadomasochistic fantasies is that they are born into, and conditioned by, a system of subordination, which has a 'negative' effect on their sexual feelings and responses.

Jeffreys argues that we need to move away from the assumption that all forms of sexual arousal or fantasy should be seen simply as 'pleasurable'; we need to be able to describe sexual responses in a way that firmly sees some of them as negative and as destructive. And women need to 'unlearn' their sexual and emotional responses; to develop sexual responses and fantasies that are not premised on subordination and inequality. We need to democratize desire; to learn to eroticise sameness, equality and mutuality. Women need to monitor and try to change the responses of their bodies to those things which indicate their own oppression. Thus, writes Jeffreys (1990, 305):

> If we listen to our feelings about sex sensitively instead of riding roughshod over them through guilt or anxiety about being prudes, we can work out what is positive and what is negative. The negative feelings are about eroticized subordination or heterosexual desire.

We should therefore try to shut down those responses which are about subordination, rather than 'pleasure'. Jeffreys suggests that we should forget about 'surrendering' or 'letting go', about 'submissiveness' and 'giving in'—all those words which, according to her, carry connotations of passivity, dependence and subordination. Instead, we should learn to eroticise the meeting of 'equals'.

Jeffreys admits to not knowing what desire or fantasy might look like
in a world in which it was not premised on 'subordination'; but she also
thinks that it is a moral task for women (with no shirkers allowed) to try
to change their sexual feelings and fantasies. Nor, she implicitly suggests, is this as difficult to do as one might think; association with other
women in a feminist environment might do the trick. But if we cannot
do it, then perhaps it is so much the worse for sex. Sexual desire and fantasy as we know them are incompatible with freedom; if forced to choose
between freedom and sex then we should choose freedom. We should
of course also change our sexual behaviour and practices; but the 'inner'
is as important as the 'outer'. Jeffreys sees the persistence of certain sorts
of fantasy, I think, as one of the strongest marks of the colonization of
women's sexual life and imagination. Without eradicating what she sees
as the negative forms of this imagination, there can be no freedom for
women. Women need to try to shut down those responses which in any
way eroticise their subordination.

However, not at all those who argue that women might try to change
their desires and their fantasies believe, like Jeffreys seems to do, in sexual voluntarism: any woman can change her desires and fantasies if she
tries hard enough. In an article, 'Feminine Masochism and the Politics
of Personal Transformation' (1990),[3] Sandra Bartky considers the issues
in a much more complex kind of way. She presents us with the case of an
imaginary protagonist, P, who is prone to various desires and fantasies of
a sadomasochistic nature, yet is also an active and committed feminist
and a believer in sexual equality. P, as Bartky presents her, feels shame
and anxiety at the persistence of these fantasies, which do not seem to
be in line with her politics. There are two possible courses of action,
Bartky suggests, which P might think of adopting: she could try to get rid
of her shame, or she could try to change her desires.

Bartky argues that whilst P should not be *made* to feel shame by others,
she is nevertheless entitled to her shame. Those sexual liberals who argue that anything goes in the matter of sexual desire and fantasy (provided, of course, that they are not acted on in such a way as to harm
others) have simply failed to respond to radical critiques of female subordination. They do not recognize how deeply the female psyche and
imagination has been colonized, or the extent to which sadomasochistic
fantasies may both be an expression of a woman-hating culture and dis-
tressing to those who have them. Bartky concludes that it is a good and
sensible project for P to try to change her desires, *if* she can. But there is
the rub. Bartky argues that sexual voluntarism—the idea that people can,
with sufficient will-power, simply change their fantasies—is inadequate
on many grounds. First, it fails to recognise the ways in which many fantasies may be extremely deep-rooted in the psyche; they may, for example, be mechanisms for psychic survival or well-being whose nature and

motivation is highly obscure. Second (but related), Bartky argues, correctly I think, that the view of the sexual voluntarists is often based on a wholly inadequate view of the ways in which patterns of sexual behaviour and desire are learned. Jeffreys, for example, will have no truck whatsoever with any psychoanalytic view of the nature of desire and fantasy. Instead she adopts a view that sexual mores and sexual desire are learned by a process of 'conditioning', in which notions of female subordination are imprinted on a relatively passive subject. Hence the implausible notion that simply substituting a different 'input' (in this case a feminist one) might be enough to bring about processes of radical change of the deep structures of fantasy and eroticism. Third, the supposition that all fantasies ought to toe a morally and politically correct 'line'—even supposing that this were possible—is bound to be judgmental, divisive, and coercively alienating of those who seem to fall short of a (mythical) ideal.

So whereas Jeffreys would set P the moral task of changing her fantasies and her desire, Bartky suggests that whilst this is a reasonable goal for her to have, it is unlikely that she will get very far in doing so. Bartky's arguments against sexual voluntarism seem to me to be on the mark; but they leave P in an apparently unfortunate dilemma. And I think that despite Bartky's disagreements with many of the sorts of arguments put forward by writers such as Jeffreys, the whole debate is underpinned by some unexamined presuppositions and key terms; and it is these that I should now like to explore a little further. I want to offer some thoughts about fantasy and desire, about the nature of eroticism, and finally about the whole project of self-transformation envisaged both by Bartky and by Jeffreys.

Fantasy and Desire

The first thing to note here is that there is at times what I think is a problematic conflation between fantasy and desire in Bartky's argument. Bartky writes in what seems to be an undifferentiated way about fantasy and desire—about sadomasochistic sexual practices and about the fantasies of humiliation and the like which she ascribes to P. But 'desire' is a difficult term here, since it is plain that there are elements in many fantasies which are not connected with desire in the sense that one would like them to happen in real life. The connection between desire and fantasy is a complex one. Thus fantasies (of the kind which one would not like actually to happen) may prompt or facilitate desire for that which one would. So the notion that P should 'change her desires' is not at all as clear as it may seem at first sight. Suppose that a fantasy involving bondage or humiliation leads not to a desire to be bound or whipped but to a desire for more 'conventional' sex; what is it exactly that Bartky supposes should be changed?

Even more interesting and problematic, however, is the concept of 'fantasy' itself. Many writers on the subject of sexual fantasies do not stop to explore what they mean by 'fantasy'. Most commonly, they seem to assume that having a fantasy always involves a clear conception of one's own desires in relation to the fantasy, and a clear conception of one's own role in it; what one imagines doing, or having done to oneself. But this view of fantasy needs challenging.

In an essay entitled 'A Child Is Being Beaten', Freud (1979)[4] described a fantasy experienced by one of his patients. The interesting thing about the fantasy—indicated in the title itself—is that it was not clear to the patient *who* was being beaten or who was doing the beating. Sometimes, the patient might appear in the narrative as the child; sometimes as the person doing the beating; sometimes as a third party watching the event. In other words, the fantasy presented a scenario, but one in which the role of the person having the fantasy could shift or be quite unclear. I speculate here—but perhaps it is the case that in this kind of fantasy scenario, the persons involved are more likely to be 'strangers', anonymous, ciphers even, who interchange in the particular narrative. The point I am making is that the nature of fantasy, and its connection with desire, is often highly indeterminate; fantasies commonly offer open, rather than closed narratives, or hints of narratives, in which the question of identification with the position of victim, agent, voyeur, etc. may be undecidable or shifting. Empirical studies which try to establish whether or not there is a connection between fantasy (e.g. whilst reading or watching pornography), and what people then go out and do, frequently tend to miss this point. They assume without argument, for example, that if a man watches or fantasises a pornographic scene he is automatically 'identifying' with the man in the picture or the narrative, and desiring to 'do the same', or have the same done to him. Recent critiques of certain earlier psychoanalytic theories of the positioning of film viewers have also noted that one cannot assume that men will 'identify' with the male hero, or women with the female heroine.

I am inclined to think that the term 'fantasy' should be reserved for such narratives or scenarios in which the question of 'identification' may be shifting or indeterminate. Sometimes, however, the term 'fantasy' is used to refer to things such as passing thoughts which may indeed involve another specific person; imagining momentarily, for example, that someone whose voice one cannot stand is being smothered. Even here, however, I speculate that it is more likely that the fantasy (if it is one) will be of 'the person being smothered', rather than of I myself doing the smothering.

But there is another extremely important consideration. It should not be supposed that all fantasies have a clear and obvious meaning which can just be read off from some account of the salient features of the narrative. Apart from the complexity of the structures of identification that may be involved, and the undecidability of the positioning of the characters in the scenario, if we are to give any credence at all to psychoanalytic (or poststructuralist) views of meaning, then the unconscious or psychically important meaning of a fantasy may not be that which a naive reading would suggest. It might, in fact, even be its complete opposite. When considering the 'dreamwork', Freud argued that the latent meaning as opposed to the manifest content of a dream could only be arrived at by a process of considering the elements of the dream and discovering the ways in which their meaning was subject to processes or condensation and displacement. One thing might symbolise something else, or several other things; the manifest content might conceal the latent dream wish; in the process of displacement, meaning is 'shifted' from one thing to another. Condensation and displacement may be thought of, in a more linguistic turn, as metaphor and metonymy. Given the constant slippage of meaning, there is no way in which the 'real meaning' of a fantasy can simply be read off from a first account of the narrative or scenario. And in fact, some psychoanalytic uses of the term phantasy (spelt with a 'ph' to distinguish it from conscious fantasies) suggest that there are phantasies which are wholly unconscious, and whose meaning is radically inaccessible.

The indeterminacy of fantasy is linked, I think, to the profoundly unsettled, disparate and often decentred nature of sexual desire. An obvious point to make, for example, about Jeffreys' analysis of sexual ideology and pornography as wholly orientated towards male dominance and female submission is that she does not even seem to note the importance of the fact that many men, too, have masochistic fantasies involving various forms of domination (often by women), and of pain and submission. Flagellation was, apparently, one of the most common Victorian male fantasies (and practices when visiting prostitutes). And, given the indeterminacy of fantasy as well as evidence from women's sexual practices, it is plain that women may fantasise themselves in a dominant role. Jeffreys, and to some extent Bartky, seem to write as if there were no ambiguities and tensions around identification with 'subordinate' or 'dominant' roles in fantasy scenarios, and as if it can normally be assumed that the man will identify with the dominant role and the woman with the subordinate one. Jeffreys, in particular, writes as if the *sole* things that turn men on are having power over women and women's submitting to that power. This seems to me plainly false. Even Freud, for example, who, despite his own critique of the identification of masculinity with sexual activity and femininity with passivity, in the end consigns women to what he describes as 'passive' aims in intercourse, nevertheless constantly stressed the ways in which human desire is never irrevocably 'fixed' on any one set of aims, and the ways in which 'normal' heterosexuality and desire for intercourse is only precariously achieved.

Jeffreys would, I think, say that in so far as women had fantasies of
or desire for domination in sex, this would merely show that they had
accepted the dominant ideology and were behaving like men. I've suggested, rather, that identifications in fantasy are often radically indeterminate, and that the prevalence of any set of sexual aims or desires in
any human being is always precarious.

Eroticism

I would now like to make some tentative suggestions about the nature of
eroticism. Jeffreys' view of sexual desire and sexual fantasy is that it is
learned in a process of indoctrination or conditioning; she is totally
sceptical, for example, of all psychoanalytic or other models which trace
some of the deepest sexual impulses of human beings to the experiences
of childhood. The result is, I think, that her view of sexuality is curiously
disembodied. Sexual desire is simply a matter of social 'conditioning'—
and we might be able to reprogramme it by substituting a new sort of
conditioning. Now indeed the extent to which specific adult sexual pro-
clivities and fantasies can be traced directly back to particular childhood
experiences seems likely to remain a contentious issue. Nevertheless, it
seems to me that without a background of early infantile experience and
embodiment, it would be difficult to make much sense of adult human
sexuality at all.

There are two aspects of human sexuality which are, I think, particularly interesting in this context: issues of power and issues concerning
selfhood and the loss of self. Eroticism, in one sense, does indeed involve
power; the power to give pleasure, to dominate the senses of the other,
temporarily to obliterate the rest of the world; the power involved in being the person who is desired, the power to demand one's own pleasure.
And along with this power go forms of 'submission' (of surrendering, letting go, receiving), or of self-abnegation, of focusing entirely for a while
on the pleasure of the other. I suggest that these things are among the
constitutive elements of human eroticism. In addition, the erotic seems
to me frequently to involve some sense of 'loss' of the boundaries of self;
the temporary erosion of the bodily boundaries between one person and
another, and the temporary obliteration of one's normal or everyday
sense of oneself. One reason for the banality (and lack of eroticism!) of
many sex advice manuals is that they treat sexuality as if it were a matter
of 'button-pushing' between two wholly self-conscious human beings who
simply 'do' things to each other; they miss the dimension of sexuality in
which one gets lost and the frontiers of one's self temporarily dissolve.

Jeffreys suggests that we should rid sexuality and sexual desire of all
overtones of power, or of domination and subordination. But this fails

to recognize either the crucial slippages and tensions in the meaning of a word like 'power', or the ways in which, I have suggested, certain forms of power and submissiveness seem constitutive of human sexuality and sexual desire. This constitutive sort of role of submission and powerfulness can all too easily get overlaid, however, with more malign structures of gender, class or race-based forms of domination and exploitation. But in the desire to purge sexuality of the oppressive features of certain kinds of power, I think it is important not to lapse into a vision of 'mutuality' which seems unable to analyse the power of human eroticism adequately at all.

Some accounts of human sexuality have suggested that all adult human sexual desire aims unconsciously to 'replay' aspects of early infancy; the early symbiotic relationship to the (all-powerful) mother, or the first stages of life in which consciousness of self as separate was not really developed. Whilst I am suspicious of the reductionism of such accounts, it is nevertheless true that long before 'social conditioning' of the sort envisaged by Jeffreys can seriously come into play, our lives are often governed by, or at the mercy of, strong and often painful bodily desires and longings, and profound ambivalence towards those who are our caretakers. These surely form a background to adult human sexuality. No human being is totally without the desire to hurt and harm those whom he or she both loves but also may at times perceive as threatening or engulfing. No-one is wholly without the desire at times to have others in their power, if only to be the object of their desire; or without the desire to regress, to submit, to be protected and overwhelmed by the power of the other. The problem in thinking about sexuality, eroticism and power is how to give an account of these kinds of 'power' and 'submissiveness' which both recognizes their constitutive role but does not build into that constitutive role the sorts of power that come along with other forms of exploitation and domination.

The Project of Self-transformation

I now want to return to P's dilemma, as expressed by Bartky; should she or should she not attempt to change her desires and her fantasies, and should she feel shame at them?

The above discussion has suggested, I hope, that the dilemma is not quite as straightforward as it may at first have appeared to be. The meaning of P's desires and fantasies, the role she plays in them, and the significance they have in her life may itself not be clear at all. Bartky in fact recognizes herself, in her critique of sexual voluntarism, that when it comes to the roots of sexuality in the human psyche, self-knowledge often fails, and we are pretty much in the dark. But if this is acknowledged, then it should also be acknowledged that precisely *what* should be changed, and why, is also highly unclear. In the light, too, of the fact that the relation between fantasy and desire is a highly complex one, setting out to 'change her desires' is not at all a clear project on which P could embark, since their nature and meaning may be very obscure to her. So my own first piece of advice to P would be not to assume that there is an obvious 'meaning' to all her fantasies, or that their narratives indicate in any way at all what her 'real' desires or the deep structures of her own eroticism are.

Nevertheless, it might be argued that despite all the ambiguities and unclarities surrounding the interpretation of fantasy, surely there are *some* cases which are clear enough for P to be worried about and to want to try to change. Suppose, for example, that she persistently has a fantasy involving a scenario of a gang rape—even if it is unclear whether she is a participant or a voyeur—and that she can at times find this fantasy erotic. Suppose, even, that she finds it difficult to get sexually aroused with her partner at all if she does not fantasise such a scenario. Might she not feel morally guilty at such a fantasy and want to get rid of it? I want to end by asking whether she can and whether (and if so why) she should.

On the grounds that 'ought' implies 'can', P can only sensibly be advised to try to change her desires and fantasies if it is possible for her to do so. Here I think one has to steer a course between two paths. The first is the crude kind of sexual voluntarism which suggests that all that is needed is to keep away from men, acquire a feminist circle of friends, and use your will power. At a certain level, it may well be possible not to 'dwell' on fantasies that irrupt into one's mind; unless they are hopelessly obsessional, it may be possible to exercise control and to prevent them from lingering too long. But the 'deep structures' of human fears and human desires are both so opaque and so deep-rooted that the notion that one could voluntarily change them, as the result of a short-term effort of will-power, is surely wrong. Nevertheless, one wants also to say that the structures of human eroticism, whilst owing much to the general conditions of human infancy and human embodiment, also owe a great deal to the particular ways in which our desires and our imaginations are formed by the social relationships that help to create our personalities. Surely, if we saw the world differently, and if the social relationships under which we live were different, it might be expected that the structures of human desire and fantasy would be somewhat different.

In *The Sovereignty of Good*, Iris Murdoch (1970) writes about the ways in which we might attempt to change our feelings about someone, by a process of learning, painstakingly and sometimes painfully, to see someone differently.[5] Thus, if I learn more about a person's situation, I might come to see them as downtrodden and oppressed, and the anger I felt at their behaviour might shift in the direction of tolerance or pity. Similarly, if I learn about the ways in which I have been exploited myself, or about the ways in which certain social practices have worked against my own interests or those of other women, I might come to feel angered rather than flattered, say, by certain forms of male attention. Changes in one's emotions are frequently a result of changes in one's perceptions of the world, and in some circumstances these changes in perception may only result from a sustained collective endeavour to understand things differently, in which one is supported by others. Similarly, perhaps, it might be that new ways of seeing and understanding the world (which themselves could probably only come about in the context of changed social practices) could result, eventually, in profound shifts in patterns of desire and fantasy. We could, I think, only wait on events to know.

But suppose that we had some reason to hope and believe that in a different world, and with different understandings of our situation, our erotic life and our fantasies might be rather different. Why should this be a matter of concern to us? Provided that exploitation and harm to others are avoided, what does it matter what fantasy scenarios people play out in their heads, given that the meaning of these is in any case so unclear?

More than one answer might be given to this question. The first might be that even though many fantasies are unclear and difficult to interpret, some are *so* horrible that one would not want to countenance them as harmless in any human being, since the harm they envisage being done to another is so intolerable. One might instance here, for example, some of the fantasies described by Klaus Theweleit in his book *Male Fantasies* (1987), where he gives an account of the sexual fantasies he analysed in the letters, diaries and novels of a group of mercenary soldiers, the Freikorpsmen, in Germany between the two world wars.[6] These frequently involved the violent murder and mutilation of 'The Red Woman'—a mythical and over-sexualized figure of the communist woman whom the Freikorpsman wanted to obliterate to a bloody pulp. The fantasies are indeed horrifying, and closely related to a transparent fear of female sexuality. Theweleit speculates rather unsatisfactorily on the social background to these exaggerated fears of women, which spawned such hatred and desire for vengeance; but beyond doubt the fantasies are troubling and horrifying.

Perhaps if a person was prone to dwell obsessively on fantasy scenarios such as those described by Theweleit, it might be a cause for alarm. But the sorts of fantasies that Bartky envisages P as having are not as extreme and horrifying as this. Nor does Bartky suggest that having them is likely to make P commit acts of atrocity or violent harm to others. Why, then, should P attempt to get rid of them (even if she is likely to fail)? Part of the answer is that Bartky sees them as causing her suffering and feelings of shame. I've suggested that one way of coping with the shame, if it is painful, might be to overcome it by recognising the complex and indeterminate nature of fantasy, and not letting oneself assume that there necessarily *is* any deep conflict between one's desires and one's politics. But this is only part of the answer because at bottom, I think the reason why Bartky would like P to embark on the project of changing her desires is what I shall call an ethical vision of self and community. Bartky writes (1990, 51):

> liberals ignore the extent to which a person may experience her own sexuality as arbitrary, hateful and alien to the rest of her personality. Each of us is in pursuit of an inner integration and unity, a sense that the various aspects of self form a harmonious whole. But when the parts of the self are at war with one another, a person may be said to suffer from self-estrangement. That part of P which is compelled to produce sexually charged scenarios of humiliation is radically at odds with the P who devotes much of her life to the struggle against oppression. Now perfect consistency is demanded of no one, and our little inconsistencies may even lend us charm. But it is no small thing when the form of desire is disavowed by the personality as a whole.

In addition, in what I think is a telling comment, she says (1990, 61):

> The order of the psyche, here and now, in a world of pain and oppression, is not identical to the ideal order of a feminist political vision. We can teach a woman how to plan a demonstration, how to set up a phone bank, or how to lobby. We can share what we have learned about starting up a women's studies program or a battered women's shelter. But we cannot teach P . . . how to decolonize the imagination.

The problem with the imagery of decolonization is that it suggests that somewhere there might be an 'authentic' female imagination, free of all the influence of male domination. But this is to fall too far back into the coercive language of political 'correctness' of which Bartky herself is critical. It also supposes that we have some clear means of telling what is and is not politically 'correct'—that the meaning of desires and fantasies is, as it were, written on their face, and that we can clearly separate those which are authentically feminine from those which are masculine, or the effect of social subordination.

There is a need here to look critically at Bartky's vision of coherence, integration and unity. It has two aspects. First, Bartky envisages a (utopian) situation in which the structure of the human psyche might 'mirror' the ideal form of a community. I am not entirely clear what this might mean. If it means that all the desires of all individual members of a community might simply reflect or be wholly in tune with the larger political goals which a community set itself, then I can see no reason for supposing that this could be possible. One important reason for this is that I can see no possibility of a final elimination of potential conflict between individual aspirations, desires and interests, and broader social goals. In this sense, the personal can *not* always sit happily alongside the political. To suppose that it might seems to me to amount to imagining a kind of Platonic Utopia of the most coercive kind.

The other kind of 'coherence' that Bartky sees as a fundamental human goal is a coherence *within* the psyche. It would need another paper to explore this idea adequately, and I do not have space to discuss here, for example, Lacanian versus other psychoanalytic views of the 'fragmented' or 'split' nature of the human psyche. But even supposing (which I am inclined to do) that there *is* some sense of 'coherence' or 'integration' which is of central importance to human life and selfhood, it is also important not to assume that one can easily identify 'parts' of the personality or make quick judgements about what coheres or conflicts with what, or what the nature of the conflict is. For this reason, my second piece of advice to P, if she is distressed about what she feels to be a conflict, and if she desires more coherence within herself, would be this. Don't assume that 'conflict' can easily be identified, or that the only possible meaning of 'coherence' in one's life must be the impossible dream that all elements of thought, fantasy, imagination, desire and action might fit together into a seamless whole.

Notes

1. Snitow, A. 1979. 'Mass Market Romance: Pornography for Women is Different', *Radical History Review*, 20:141–61.

2. Jeffreys, S. 1990. *Anti-Climax: A Feminist Perspective on the Sexual Revolution.* London: The Women's Press.

3. Bartky, S. 1990. 'Feminine Masochism and the Politics of Personal Transformation', in *Femininity and Domination.* London: Routledge, 45–62.

4. Freud, S. 1979. 'A Child Is Being Beaten', in *Selected Writings,* vol. 10. Harmondsworth: Pelican.

5. Murdoch, I. 1970. *The Sovereignty of the Good.* London: Routledge.

6. Theweleit, K. 1987. *Male Fantasies,* vol. 1. Cambridge: Cambridge University Press.

Chapter 16

RETHINKING SADOMASOCHISM: FEMINISM, INTERPRETATION, AND SIMULATION

Patrick D. Hopkins

Sadomasochism has often been considered by feminists to be a major epistemological and behavioral structure of male-dominated societies.[1] Most often, this structure has manifested itself in the form of dominant males coercing and controlling females for their own aims. This manifestation has not been limited to blatant sexual activity, but has included, even more importantly, pervasive, hidden beliefs about the proper, "natural" relationships between men and women—beliefs which have allowed men to control the behavior and attitudes of women for their own economic, political, religious, as well as sexual purposes. It has been one of the primary goals of feminists to articulate, and then eradicate, the model of dominance and submission upon which so much of human behavior in patriarchal society is based. In particular, radical, separatist, and lesbian feminists have focused on eliminating this model as key to any hope for women's liberation, resisting instances of the dominance/submission model as expressed in pornography, rape, battery, and various 'malestream' media.

It was then both shocking and horrifying for many radical and politically active feminists in the late 1970s and early 1980s to discover that there were women who called themselves both feminists *and* sadomasochists.

Reprinted from *Hypatia* 9:1 (1994), pp. 116–41 with the permission of Patrick D. Hopkins. © 1994, Patrick D. Hopkins.

These were not women who believed that male domination was a good thing. They were not reactionary anti-feminists. These women were lesbians and radicals and feminist activists and scholars who claimed that one could be *both* a radical feminist committed to the liberation of women *and* a sadomasochist who enjoyed sexual activity based on the dominant/submissive model.

An unusual kind of altercation ensued—a battle among feminists about what feminism meant and what sadomasochism meant, with tremendous anger and hostility and incredulity on both sides. Although the so-called feminist "sex wars" were at their most pitched during the late 1970s and first half of the 1980s, it is not an issue that has been settled (if any issue is ever settled).[2] Radical feminists, and other feminists, continue to deplore and reject the arrival of "feminist," "lesbian" sadomasochism, though fewer articles are published on the subject these days. Lesbian feminist sadomasochists on the other hand, undaunted, have moved on to developing and articulating a sadomasochist community, culture, and literature. Prominent lesbian SM advocates and theorists have published pornographic novels, magazines, histories of SM, and how-to sex manuals, as well as joining a broader SM community in some publishing projects, editing new volumes on SM culture and practice in conjunction with SM advocates in gay male, bisexual, even heterosexual communities.[3] Why haven't anti-SM radical feminists kept up their active resistance? Perhaps because they feel they have said all that can really be said. Perhaps because they feel it would be a waste of feminist energy to continue working against SM, energy that would be better spent on other feminist projects. Perhaps, as one radical feminist teacher of my own has suggested, because they believe lesbian SM is a fad that will eventually go away.

The decline of published resistance to lesbian SM and the rise of pro-SM literature, theory, and history might lead one to think that SM is more accepted in the 1990s. I doubt this is true although perhaps some people have become habituated to the presence of SM. I think that among many radical feminists, lesbian or otherwise, it is not the case that SM has become more acceptable. Rather, it just does not seem worthwhile to waste energy on SM when so many other feminist tasks remain. The SM advocates have basically the same libertarian arguments, while all the radical counterarguments still stand.

But do the anti-SM arguments still stand? Did they ever stand? Can anti-SM feminists rest secure in their position?

It is true that the SM advocates still use many of the same arguments that they used during their political inception—basically libertarian arguments focusing on personal freedom, the right to privacy, anti-censorship, etc. However, SM defenders have not merely been repeating the same old message, and as such, the old anti-SM defenses may no longer be adequate. SM has moved beyond its initial focus on absolute, personal privacy, in which SM was defended as a private sexual activity which was strictly limited to the bedroom (metaphorically speaking) and has moved into the realms of political identity, spirituality, and epistemology. Previous radical counterarguments reacting to the absolute privatization of sexual experience and to traditional liberal claims of the inviolability of consensual sexual activity are unlikely to be adequate, if they ever were, for countering evolving SM.

In what follows, I want to engage the original criticisms of sadomasochism put forth by radical anti-SM feminists, assessing their relevance for dealing with contemporary SM epistemology and ethics as I see them. My premise in this paper is not that current SM activists have developed stunning new defenses of SM which sweep away the former radical critiques. Rather, my premise is that with the increased radicalization and communitization of SM, it becomes apparent that SM activity must be interpreted with a greater degree of subtlety and attention to context, both internal and external, than has previously been employed. To that end I will first look at the arguments against traditional concepts of SM. I will reinterpret SM in light of its recent articulation, and in turn, question the applicability of established counterarguments.

I. Anti-SM Feminist Oppositional Strategies

Generally, radical feminist opposition to lesbian SM can be characterized in terms of three primary strategies: 1. Lesbian SM replicates patriarchal relationships; 2. Consent to activities which eroticize dominance, submission, pain, and powerlessness is structurally impossible or ethically irrelevant; 3. Lesbian SM validates and supports patriarchy, though perhaps unintentionally.

First: The claim with which most anti-SM feminists begin, and which is probably the first reaction to hearing about the practice of lesbian "feminist" SM, is that SM replicates patriarchy. It seems an obvious inference to make, at least at first. Patriarchal society allows or encourages the sexual, economic, and psychological abuse of women, largely at the hands of men and for men's purposes. Lesbians who derive pleasure from humiliating or causing pain to other women seem blatantly to be reproducing the implicit values of patriarchal cultures, probably as a result of having internalized the view that women are sexual objects to be used for pleasure. Pleasure is to be had at the expense of women's pain.

The emphasis in this criticism is clear. Sadomasochism is a core structure of male-dominated culture. The fact that women engage in SM with other women does not obscure this fact. Indeed, it brings it into greater relief. Women, lesbians, even purported feminists, can internalize the degradation of women into sexual objects as a value without realizing that they have bought into patriarchal culture.

Bat-Ami Bar On:

> The primary claim of [feminist opposition] is that the erotization of violence or domination, and of pain or powerlessness, is at the core of sadomasochism and, consequently, that the practice of sadomasochism embodies the same values as heterosexual practices of sexual domination in general and sexually violent practices like rape in particular. (Bar On 1982, 75)

Jessie Meredith:

> When women practice dominance and submission in their sexual relationships, does this perpetuate the values of the patriarchal ruling class, whose stock-in-trade is dominance and submission? I believe that it does. (Meredith 1982, 97)

Diana Russell:

> Sadomasochism results in part from the internalization of heterosexual dominant-submissive role playing. Sadomasochism among lesbians involves, in addition, the internalization of a homophobic heterosexual view of lesbians. (Russell 1982, 176)

Second: SM advocates often claim that since participants in an SM activity consent to the act, they are not doing anything wrong. It is something that they themselves desire, even seek out. But radical feminists disagree. They claim that consent has long been used to justify treating women as lesser creatures, and the fact that women often say that they consent to certain patterns of male domination does not prove that they are acting freely. Women, like men, typically learn and internalize patriarchal values and think of them as natural. Consent to abuse cannot be considered justification of abuse. The purported "consent" is just an example of how deeply the internalization of oppression goes. In fact, even if a certain woman's assent to engage in a painful sexual activity can be considered consent, this does not mean that it can be considered a feminist activity, nor even can it be considered non-oppressive. The fact that an activity is merely consensual does not suggest that it should be considered morally permissible, non-pathological, and certainly not politically practical. Consent, therefore, can be seen as either a structural impossibility in the context of eroticized dominance/submission or as a hopelessly conflated irrelevancy.

Diana Russell:

> Women have been reared to be submissive, to anticipate and even want domination by men. But wanting or consenting to domination and humil-

iation does not make it nonoppressive. It merely demonstrates how deep and profound the oppression is. Many young Brahmin women in the nineteenth century "voluntarily" jumped into the funeral pyres of their dead husbands. What feminist would argue that these women were not oppressed? . . . Such consent does not mean that power has not been abused. (Russell 1982, 177)

Karen Rian:

I think the issue of "mutual consent" is utterly beside the point. The prosadomasochism argument often justifies lesbian sadomasochism as a matter of mutual consent and therefore, beyond reproach. However, I find this argument as irrelevant and unconvincing as the anti-feminist argument from women who claim that their greatest satisfaction is in "consenting" to sexual subservience to men. Since our sexuality has been for the most part constructed through social structures over which we have had no control, we *all* "consent" to sexual desires and activities which are alienating to at least some degree. However, there's a vast difference between consent and self-determination. (Rian 1982, 49)

Judith Butler:

What is problematic is that sm takes a non-reflective attitude toward sexual desire. Professing to embrace "consensual choice," and abstracting themselves from the real, shared world, sm lesbians leave behind the possibility for concrete personal and political choice. . . . That sm requires consent does not mean that it has overcome heterosexual power dynamics. Women have been consenting to heterosexual power dynamics for thousands of years. (Butler 1982, 172)

Third: As a result of replicating patriarchal values, desires, and behaviors, and by employing a naive conception of consent as defense, promoting and practicing sadomasochism actually ends up supporting patriarchy. SMists validate patriarchy's activities and undercut the power of feminist opposition by claiming that enjoying women's pain and humiliation can be conjoined with feminism itself. This is stronger than merely the claim that SM replicates patriarchy; this is the claim that SM actually furthers patriarchy, promotes patriarchy, and as such, inhibits the development of feminism and actively interferes with the liberation of women. Lesbian "feminist" SM reinforces the oppression of women.
Hilde Hein:

To degrade someone, even with that person's expressed consent, is to *endorse* the degradation of persons. It is to affirm that the abuse of persons is *acceptable*. For if some people may be humiliated and despised, all may be. (Hein 1982, 87)

Audre Lorde:

> Sadomasochism is an institutionalized celebration of dominant/subordi-
> nate relationships. And, it *prepares* us either to accept subordination or to
> enforce dominance. *Even in play,* to affirm that the exertion of power over
> powerlessness is erotic, is empowering, is to set the emotional and social
> stage for the continuation of that relationship, politically, socially and eco-
> nomically. (Lorde and Star 1982, 68)

Diana Russell:

> Proponents of sadomasochism espouse violence, pain and torture as long
> as they are consensual. But images of women being bound, beaten and hu-
> miliated foster ideas that this behavior may be acceptable, or at least excit-
> ing and legitimate, regardless of whether or not the recipients of this vio-
> lence are portrayed as consenting. (Russell 1982, 179)

I thus find that the charges of replicating patriarchy, the irrelevancy
or impossibility of consent, and the validation of patriarchy are recurring argument strategies. But are these charges accurate? Are they even
applicable? Are radical critics even talking about the same things that
the SM advocates are talking about?

Before making any interpretive sense of these questions or indeed of
the supposed object of interest—SM—it will be necessary to explore the
internal interpretive context of sadomasochistic activity. This will be critical in answering the question of whether or not SM replicates patriarchy
and will situate questions of the relevancy of consent and the validation of
patriarchy. In terms of the question of replication, I find two parallel, apparently similar, but largely discontinuous discourses operating regarding
SM—one interpreting the "internal" context of SM encounters from the
perspective of non-participating spectator, the other interpreting the "internal" context of SM encounters from the perspective of participant.

II. Replication Versus Simulation: Interpretive Contexts of SM

Radical critics often treat SM activities as if they were contextually and
performatively identical with any other "sadistic" or "masochistic" act occurring anywhere, anytime. The working assumption seems to be that
within patriarchal context (and perhaps beyond it), certain behaviors
possess an "essence" of their own, an intrinsic meaning, that cannot genuinely be altered by participant consent, community specification, or
conscious negotiation. Diana Russell says: "I consider the infliction or receiving of pain and/or humiliation for sexual pleasure, even within a
consensual relationship, as incompatible with feminism, because a 'mas-

ter-slave' . . . relationship or encounter is *inherently* unequal. Feminism rejects unequal sexual and love relationships" (Russell 1982, 177) [italics added].

Activities that eroticize submission and dominance are interpreted as operating exactly on the model of submission/dominance characteristic of male-dominated cultures. Any such activity, therefore, is thought to replicate patriarchal value, patriarchal desire, patriarchal behavior. That such activity might include the participation of lesbians does nothing to alter the interpretation—it still replicates the structure of masculinist desire. SM behavior is essentially no different from any other occurrence of the rape, beating, humiliation, exploitation, or degradation of women.

Sarah Hoagland writes: "What I've found quite jolting in several communities is the impulse to silence and ostracize Lesbian batterers while at the same time providing a forum for Lesbian sadists. This is significant because most batterers do not think that beating and humiliating another Lesbian is a positive thing to do, while sadists not only think it is alright but advocate it in the name of feminism, sisterhood and trust" (Hoagland 1982, 156). But is it the case that SM thinking and activity is really indistinguishable from apparently similar behavior in coercive, patriarchal context? Is it really even "apparently similar"? Is the meaning of the activities the same in SM and lesbian battery? Sarah Hoagland seems to think so, and by implication suggests that SM lesbians are encouraging the *kind* of activity that occurs in lesbian domestic violence.

SM advocates, as one might predict, explicitly reject any notion that they support or condone such violence. They don't even consider what they practice as violent. The problem is, they say, radicals have no sense of context. In their drive to expose the universal and eternal grip of patriarchy on every aspect of human experience, they ignore obvious differences in experience. For instance, in criticizing a slide presentation made by a feminist anti-pornography group, Pat Califia says:

> Their definition of porn was circular and sloppy. They defined any sexist or violent image as pornography, then turned around and used that assumption to "prove" that all pornography was violent and sexist. Lesbian sexuality was not discussed. Some vague distinction was made between "erotica" and "porn," but no examples of "erotica" were shown. This made me especially uncomfortable since many heterosexuals were present, and one of the favorite images of "violent" pornography was soft-core, glossy images of women kissing or going down on each other. The presenters' definition of violence was as tautological as their definition of pornography. There was no sense of context or scale. The lesbian porn was presented as being just as violent as a woman getting stabbed. Wearing high heels or being tied up was described with as much horror as getting raped. Corsets were condemned with as much vehemence as wife-beating. Anal sex was apparently a violent practice. Teenage girls apparently couldn't have sex without being

violated. And women in the sex industry were apparently being raped by the camera, not by the vice squad. . . . Anybody who questioned [the anti-pornography activists'] definition of porn or violence was accused of having bad consciousness about violence against women. (Califia 1987, 256–257)

The oft-repeated defense of SM that is supposed to demonstrate that SM activity is not just patriarchal violence is that SM activity is consensual. Consent to beating, humiliation, or role-playing is thought to justify such activity. Radicals question both the existence or relevance of consent. But is consent the only defense? I think not. I think that SM practitioners, as well as their radical critics, have not read with sufficient subtlety the dynamics of SM encounters. The interpretive context of SM has much more to offer as a defense.

That defense is this: SM sexual activity does not replicate patriarchal sexual activity. It simulates it. Replication and simulation are very different. Replication implies that SM encounters merely reproduce patriarchal activity in a different physical area. Simulation implies that SM selectively replays surface patriarchal behaviors onto a different contextual field. That contextual field makes a profound difference.

SM participants do not rape, they do rape scenes. SMists do not enslave, they do slave scenes. SMists do not kidnap, they do capture and bondage scenes. The use of the term "scenes" exposes a critical, central aspect of SM culture. SM is constructed as a performance, as a staging, a production, a simulation in which participants are writers, producers, directors, actors, and audience. Importantly, this is a simulation recognized as such. Participants know they are doing a scene. They have sought out other performers.

As with other kinds of performances, other kinds of simulations, there appear to be many similarities between the "real" activity and the staged activity. In the case of SM, there is strong emotion. There is tension. And there may be real, genuine pain.[4]

But similarity is not sufficient for replication.[5] Core features of real patriarchal violence, coercive violence, are absent. In real rapes, the victim is not a participant. She is not a subject. She is object, sport, commodity, disposable. She has little or no power. In an SM rape scene, however, the "victim" of a "rapist" is no replication of the victim of a rapist. This "victim" has negotiated with her "rapist" ahead of time to establish the design, production, duration, and performance of the "rape." She might establish "safe words" she can use during the scene to slow down or stop the action if it gets too intense, or too fast, or if it's just not stimulating enough. Often, safe words like "yellow" for slow down, or "red" for stop, are used (Weinberg, Williams, and Moser 1984, 385). True to the context of performance and simulation, however, sometimes the safe word is simply "safe word," a self-reflective signification of simulation (Truscott 1991, 19).

In real slavery, the slave is commodity and possession; the master may need fear, but not approval. The slave is capital resource, and often a threat—to be purchased, or bred, and acted upon. In SM "slave" and "master" scenes, however, the "slave" may reject the "master" (or "mistress") because she is not dominant enough, not experienced enough, not skillful enough to satisfy the "slave's" desires.[6] The "slave" may establish a time limit on her "slavery" because she has to get up and go to work at six o'clock the next morning. The "slave" may compliment (or criticize) the "master's" whipping technique and set up a time to meet her again next weekend.

It is certainly not absurd that critics of SM see replication of patriarchal roles and activities in SM. The surfaces seem similar to out-group observers. But though patriarchal violence may appear to parallel SM "violence," the parallel is unstable. The interpretive context is different. The material conditions are different. All the behaviors I mentioned—negotiation, safe words, mutual definition—take place in a self-defined community. SM communities, in their diversity—lesbian, gay, bisexual, heterosexual—have their own gathering places, their own publications, their own rules, their own senses of identity. This context of community is one aspect of SM that makes the charge of replicating patriarchal activity contestable.

In fact, SM scenes gut the behaviors they simulate of their violent, patriarchal, defining features. What makes events like rape, kidnapping, slavery, and bondage evil in the first place is the fact that they cause harm, limit freedom, terrify, scar, destroy, and coerce. But in SM there is attraction, negotiation, the power to halt the activity, the power to switch roles, and attention to safety. Like a Shakespearean duel on stage, with blunted blades and actors' training, violence is simulated, but is not replicated.

But what about another level of the problem of possible replication? Even if some critics of SM might agree that the material conditions and the interpretive context of SM are significantly different from genuine violence, perhaps they would suggest that this in no way eliminates the initial problem that the SM practitioner is attracted to violence, revels in the dominant/submissive model of sexuality, and derives pleasure from the suffering of women (herself or others). Even if such suffering is only simulated, not actually replicated, the sadomasochist still exhibits false consciousness, still engages in anti-feminist behavior, and still takes pleasure in abusing women or in being abused (albeit simulated).

But this criticism would fail to take the power of simulation into account. Certainly some people who enjoy the genuine suffering of women may make forays into the SM community before they are ferreted out. But it is not obvious that taking pleasure in the simulation of violence, domination, and submission is the same as or even indicative of taking pleasure in genuine violence, domination, and submission. Sexual desires do not always, perhaps not even predominantly, take as their objects isolated acts or isolated bodies. The context of the body and the act in an environment establishes the erotic interpretation. Thus, desire is not simply directed at certain specifiable bodies, but also at certain relatively specifiable environments. An entire context can be the "object" of desire. Not just an act, not just a body, not just a physiological reaction, but rather the entirety of bodies and circumstance and interpretation is desired. One can lust after a scene.[7]

In the case of SM, therefore, it should not be assumed that SM participants actually find pleasure in the torture of slaves, nor in the cries of a rape victim, nor in the humiliation of women, nor in the relentless assault of an attacker. In fact, it is a central ethical and political value of those SMists who also profess to be feminists that such events are indeed evil, deplorable, and repugnant. At the same time however, it is possible to desire the *simulation* of those events, to lust after the context of a negotiated and consensual "submission" or "domination." This does not mean that simulation is the closest the SM practitioner can get to her real desires. This does not mean that the simulation of rape is a legal stand-in for the real thing. Neither should it be taken for granted that the participants get their pleasure by getting so far into the fantasy that they feel like it is the real thing. Rather, the sadomasochist can *desire the simulation itself,* not as inferior copy of the real thing, not as copy of anything at all, but as simulation qua simulation. There is a specific sexual context. The real events of rape and attack may be the object of intense hatred, intense sorrow, intense resistance. Lesbian sadomasochists march in Take Back The Night marches, volunteer in rape crisis centers, and may even be victims of sexual assault themselves and speak out against it, bringing charges against their assailants. But this is not contradiction. For the actual desire of the SM participant may not be any form of real abuse. The desire may be for the simulation itself. Without limits, consent, ethical codes, safe words and community connection, the simulation would not be simulation. It would be replication or imitation—not the desired experience, and thus not erotic.

In significant ways, SM scenes parallel the experience of being on a roller coaster. There is intense emotion—fear, tension, anticipation, thrill. There is physiological arousal—adrenaline rush, headiness, gut twisting, a body high. All this because one has placed herself in the position of simulating plummeting to her death, of simulating flying off into space, of simulating the possibility of smashing into trees or metal railings. But is the best interpretation of the roller coaster rider's desire that she really would like to plummet to her death or collide with another train? Is it the case that she genuinely desires to be crushed against the ground, but because the law and conventional morality attempt to prevent it, alas, she is not able? Is riding a roller coaster just a matter of settling for the weaker imitation, for the copy of plummeting to her death?[8]

Of course not. In fact, the experience desired by the roller coaster rider is *precisely the simulation* of those lethal experiences—not because simulation is all she can get, but because *the simulation itself* is thrilling and satisfying. There is no actual desire to die, or fall, or crash. The simulation itself is the goal, not a lesser copy of the goal. So in the same way the roller coaster rider may find actually falling to her death repugnant and horrible, but finds simulation of that event thrilling and exciting, the SM practitioner may find actual violence and humiliation repugnant and horrible, but finds the simulation of that event thrilling and exciting—not as stand-in but as a goal in itself. It is simply not justified to assume that an SM participant finds real violence, real sexism, or real domination and submission desirable. As the lesbian feminist SM advocacy/support group Samois's Ministry of Truth put it: "Calling an S/M person sexist is like calling someone who plays Monopoly a capitalist" (Samois 1987, 151).

III. Consent and Content

For many SM practitioners, the belief that SM is not or cannot be genuinely consensual is part of a pervasive and false psychological stereotype of SM participants and encounters—an example of the kind of false stereotypes often attributed to minority groups. Experiences of their own autonomy and assertiveness in sexual scenes prove to SMists that they do in fact consent to SM activity and that their consent is not problematic. Gayle Rubin (herself a feminist scholar and sadomasochist) says: "The silliest arguments about S/M have been those which claim that it is impossible that people really consent to do it. . . . [T]he overwhelming coercion with regard to S/M is the way in which people are prevented from doing it. We are fighting for the freedom to consent to our sexuality without interference, and without penalty" (Rubin 1987, 224–25).

Rubin does not provide an argument defending the presence of consent in SM activities; she seems to think that she does not have to. Rubin largely treats the SM community like any other cultural minority, and suggests that the problem of questioning consent in SM lies not with SM practitioners, who experience the fullness of consent in every sought-after scene, but rather with radical feminist critics who are intent on attributing a set of unwarranted psychological traits to SMists. For Rubin, the case is no different from that of heterosexuals who claim that lesbians and gays can never be truly happy, even if they say they are.

This speaking from personal experience about the obviousness of genuine consent is quite at odds with radical critics. Radicals recognize that "consent" has been used against women many times—a claim with which SM feminists completely agree. Rubin acknowledges that "social relations of class, gender, race, and so forth in fact do limit the scope of possible decisions which can be made" (Rubin 1987, 224). What she disagrees with, however, is that SM is an obvious site at which the possibility of consent has been compromised.

In addition to the defense of personal experience in which masochists and sadists both have complete trust in their own consent, some SMists have claimed that the contractual nature of SM not only ensures consent but allows it to flourish. In fact, SM is thought to provide a radically honest, democratic model of consent that can be beneficially applied to other situations. Carol Truscott states:

> The starting point of all S/M relationships, then, is talk of the most intimate kind. The talk is about what S/M play gets the potential partners off; who will assume which role; whether other people may be included . . . ; what each person's limits are; whether or not "safe words" are allowed or required, and if so, what they are; the health of the partners . . . ; and, more mundanely, whether one or the other has to leave for work at five the next morning . . . traditional relationships don't usually begin with this intimate a discussion. Most couples never talk openly about what they want and what they are prepared to give in their sexual relationships. Communication about sexual activities is largely nonverbal: incoherent sounds combined with one partner seeking to move parts of the other's body in the hope that the "offending" partner will understand that something is amiss. . . . It is this, the negotiation preparatory to the new S/M relationship, that is the most important gift of contemporary consensual sadomasochism to the larger society. (Truscott 1991, 19)

Truscott goes on to say that the experience of many SM participants is that SM activity has taught them better how to handle conflicts and negotiations outside their sexual activities, suggesting that the skills of consent may actually be trained and improved.

But though this talk about consent sounds honest and arises from the kind of context feminists normally value—personal experience—there is still strong, gut-level resistance. A feminist cannot listen to claims about the joys of consenting to be tied down, whipped or urinated on, and claims that pretending to be a slave or a rape victim help teach independence and assertiveness, without remembering—remembering images of Chinese mothers "consenting" to have their daughters' feet bound, images of young girls "consenting" to be married to older men, images of women "consenting" unquestioningly to their husbands' will out of religious conviction, images of battered wives "consenting" to stay with their abusive husbands, images of fashion-conscious women "consenting" to endless and dangerous diets. Personal experience, while a powerful source of feminist insight and political truth, is also a potent site for the twisting of women's desires. Domination is not always achieved through physical and economic coercion alone. The imagination can be colonized as well. The personality can be coerced into constructing desires that serve other's interests. For some radical critics, the structure of certain choices themselves suggests that consent is doubtful.

Bat-Ami Bar On says: "The erotization of violence or domination and pain or powerlessness *necessarily* involves a violation of the right to determine what can be done with and to one's body" (Bar On 1982, 76) [italics added]. It seems that for Bar On, violence, domination, pain, and powerlessness are such clear and present evils that any notion of one "consenting" to such events must be read as the colonization of desires, not as the expression of autonomous attraction. Bar On's claim is central to the arguments of feminist detractors of SM. For her, this claim is the one that must be challenged if the defenders of SM are to make a successful case for genuine consent. She says: "This premise must be shown to be false in order to reject the opposition's argument. The burden of proof is on the vindicators of sadomasochism. . . . If one is to reject the opposition's argument, one must show that it is not necessarily the case that a sexual practice involving the erotization of violence or domination and of pain or powerlessness does not thereby also involve a violation of the right to determine what can be done with and to one's body" (Bar On 1982, 77).

Perhaps in light of what I have said about SM as simulation, a challenge can be brought forth. If it is possible, or maybe even probable, that SM participants desire the simulation itself, then the derivative eroticization would not be of "violence or domination and of pain or powerlessness" but of simulated violence, simulated domination, and simulated powerlessness. I leave out the term "pain" in this speculation because the pain experienced in SM can be very real indeed. While some role-playing activities use soft cloth "whips" or loose bondage, many activities involve real whips, restrictive bondage, and genuine pain (see footnote 4).

If the eroticization of *simulated* violence, domination, and submission is what is going on in SM scenes, then Bar On's claim would not seem to apply. Although the SM theorists whom I have read appear not to have thought about their sexual activities explicitly in terms of simulation, I think much of their rhetoric suggests that they would agree with Bar On that eroticizing violence, domination, and submission necessarily involves a violation of the right of bodily determination. However, many reject the claim that what goes on in SM relationships is violence. Carol Truscott rejects the claim that the notion of violence is even applicable to SM:

> The most common accusation leveled at practitioners of sadomasochism is
> that we are "violent." Consensual sadomasochism has nothing to do with vi-
> olence. Consensual sadomasochism is about *safely* enacting sexual fantasies
> with a *consenting* partner. Violence is the epitome of non-consensuality, an
> act perpetrated by a predator on a victim. A rapist lurking in the bushes is
> *not* going to ask me if I want to be raped. A person bent on killing me is not
> going to ask whether I have any objection to dying at her or his hands. . . .
> Consensual sadomasochism neither perpetuates violence nor serves as
> catharsis of the violent in the human spirit. Despite appearances, consen-
> sual sadomasochism has nothing to do with violence. (Truscott 1991, 30)

Interestingly, not only does Truscott claim that SMists do not equate
their sexual activity with violence, but also that their sexual activity is not
even a way to achieve catharsis of some desire toward genuine violence.
This is quite similar to my earlier claim that an SM practitioner may be attracted to the simulation *itself*, and not at all attracted to genuine violence.
The same line of thought may be applied to submission and dominance.

It is thus crucial in considering claims about consent in SM to ask the
following question: What is a sadomasochist consenting to? If the characterization of SM scenes as simulation is accurate, then one cannot
claim that a sadomasochist consents to genuine powerlessness, genuine
domination, or genuine submission. The SMist is instead consenting to
particular simulative performances negotiated beforehand among performers with equal power and equal say. As such, the radicals' critique of
consent fails to apply to the claims of consent employed in consensual
SM relationships. This is not a circular argument—consensual SM is by
consent so it is consensual. This is instead a re-cognition of the context
of SM as a practice of simulation in a specific and knowledgeable community.[9] It may be true that one cannot genuinely consent to powerlessness and domination, but this is not an argument against consenting to
simulated powerlessness and domination. The practices are different,
the contexts are different, the participants are different.

IV. Validation, Assimilation, and Public Relations

But even if we are to understand SM activity in terms of simulation and
recognize that consent to simulation is less problematic than consent to
genuine violence or powerlessness, SM still occurs in a patriarchal culture and cannot be uncomplicatedly extracted from that culture and analyzed or experienced strictly in its own terms. The fact remains that
genuine violence and domination do occur, and most representations of
such are not subject to the kind of consent ethics present in the SM community. The explicit characterization of fantasy, the self-conscious the-
atric model of the "scene," prior negotiation, sexual training, safe words,

attention to safety, and the potential switching of roles are rarely present in conventional media. When filtered through patriarchal interpretation, the simulative nature of SM may be ignored, thus contributing to the general context of the disempowerment and degradation of women by reinforcing the belief that all women's innermost erotic desire is to be dominated, controlled—a theme commonly echoed in violent, and even non-violent, films. Obviously this would interfere with most feminists' goals. There is a larger context to think about in regard to the presence of SM, a context which affects all women.

The fear, and often primary criticism, of most radical critics is that SM actually validates and supports the degradation of, and violence against, women. It is not obvious that this claim has been challenged by characterizing SM as consensual performances in contexts of simulation. The validation of violence against women, of seeing women as fantasy fodder and sexual fodder for heterosexual men, does not rest in any internal interpretation of an SM scene, but rather in the situatedness of that "scene" in broader patriarchal cultural context. Lesbian SM, like any other SM, still operates within the relatively uncritical larger field of sexism and the oppression of women. Can't it therefore still *function,* even unintentionally, as a representation, and thus validation, of the non-consensual domination model? This could occur in at least two ways. First, even if SM is primarily simulative rather than replicative, SM could validate patriarchy by condoning (perhaps unwittingly) the ideology of coercive sexual domination. Second, SM could be a destabilizing force within feminism itself, interfering with relations among feminists by scattering energy needed for specific projects and presenting feminism to the world as a movement of infighting and dissension.

In the first case, that of condoning a patriarchal ideology leading to violence against women, it should be made clear that this does not have to mean that any SM participant deliberately does this. Rather, just by taking place in patriarchal culture/context, SM will be seen as condoning the objectification of women's bodies, even if the dominant is herself a woman. It makes no difference if it really is simulation, even self-characterized subversive simulation.

Sarah Hoagland:

> The idea that nazi/Jew, master/slave scenes parody the Holocaust and slavery and therefore do not contribute to the context which allows such institutions to flourish, indicates a failure to understand a fundamental principle of separatism: to parody an institution is nevertheless to reinforce its world view (its Weltanschauung) and hence to validate it. To parody nazis may take some of the pompousness out of their ceremony, but the parody still validates nazism by perpetuating the language game, the conceptual framework, and thereby allows those who work with deadly earnest and intelligence toward fascism and slavery to exist in an ideological framework

necessary for their growth and development. It holds their foundation in-
tact, feeds it. (Hoagland 1982, 159)

The radicals' claim is that such imagery is not seen by viewers as rigidly
compartmentalized into a self-conscious fantasy, separated from male-
dominated culture, but is instead an uncritical reinforcement of the
fetishization of female submission and powerlessness central to the
structures of patriarchal sexual desire. Lesbian SM provides a particularly insidious reinforcement of that desire—it provides an image of assertive, even "feminist" women, who say that it really is their desire to be
dominated, and that sex based on dichotomies of power is what really
turns them on. Perhaps in a world where feminist critical insights
abounded and where a robust notion of simulation was active, a contextual interpretation of such claims would not be so dangerous, in the
sense of validating sexual desire focused on coercive or manipulative
sex. But in a world where feminist critical insights and self-conscious cinematic metaphoricity are the possession of a relatively small group, lesbian SM functions merely as a dumping of images into masculinist
context. One can easily imagine that those masculinist men who might
have access to such images will have little more critical insight than to defend their sexual desires or their version of women's sexual desires by
grunting "Well, she's a woman and *she* likes it" or "Well, she's a feminist
and *she* likes it."

The second way that lesbian SM is purported to validate patriarchy is by
hurting feminists and feminist projects. Again, this is not a charge of deliberate harm, but of inevitable harm. Audre Lorde worries that "sex wars"
in feminism disperse energy needed for other, important projects. She
says: "The question I ask, over and over, is *who is profiting from this?* When
sadomasochism gets presented on center stage as a conflict in the feminist
movement, I ask, what conflicts are *not* being presented?" (Lorde and Star
1982, 68), and later, "is this whole question of s/m sex in the lesbian community perhaps being used to draw attention and energies away from
other more pressing and immediately life-threatening issues facing us as
women in this racist, conservative and repressive period? A red herring? A
smoke screen for provocateurs?" (Lorde and Star 1982, 70).

In her short narrative *A Letter of the Times*, Alice Walker describes a
class in feminist theology in which students have been studying slave narratives. Students are encouraged to imagine what it would be like to be
enslaved or to be a mistress. Near the end of the class a television special
on sadomasochism airs in which a white "mistress" and her black "slave"
are presented. Walker's character writes: "All I had been teaching was
subverted by that one image, and I was incensed to think of the hard
struggle of my students to rid themselves of stereotype, to combat prejudice, to put themselves into enslaved women's skins, and then to see

their struggle mocked, and the actual enslaved *condition* of literally millions of our mothers trivialized—because two ignorant women insisted on their right to act out publicly a 'fantasy' that still strikes terror in black women's hearts" (Walker 1982, 207). Again, the chief indictment of lesbian SM is that it has the result of interfering with feminist projects and reinforces a patriarchal worldview.

I think it is clear, historically, that the presence of lesbian SM has created dissension and animosity among feminists. It has not, however, been demonstrated that SM, if accepted as an ethically permissible form of sexual activity, would in fact reinforce patriarchal beliefs about women's sexuality in the way radical critics claim it would. After all, sadomasochists who advocate understanding of and tolerance for the free exercise of their sexuality are constantly making it clear that consent, playfulness, safety, and the option of "role reversal" are central to their sexuality. But for purposes of this essay, let us assume that acknowledged SM sexuality *does* reinforce patriarchal beliefs in a significant number of persons as well as create problems for interfeminist relations—in spite of feminist SMists' attempts to prevent these effects. What political stance should feminist SMists take as a result of this knowledge? I do not think the answer is obvious.

Certainly the option radicals offer is that SMists renounce SM and stop living out their fantasies.[10] But this answer *is* politically, personally, and theoretically problematic, particularly for women informed by the critical insights of lesbian/radical feminism itself. In general, it sounds like SMists are being admonished to renounce, or at least hide, their sexual/political activities because they hurt "the movement" or because they "make things worse" by being so blatant and weird. For many SMists such a claim sounds suspiciously like the admonishments made by so-called "assimilationists"—admonishments radical feminists, and particularly lesbian feminists, typically reject.

Consider the advice given in the book *After the Ball*, which maps out a marketing/advertising strategy by which lesbians and gay men can achieve equality and acceptance in the U.S. The strategy focuses primarily on public relations for lesbians and gays and calls for the withdrawal of "fringe groups" that disturb the unity of the gay rights movement and reinforce harmful stereotypes. In describing a media campaign directed toward the goal of gay rights, Marshall Kirk and Hunter Madsen state:

> Persons featured in the media campaign should be wholesome and admirable by straight standards, and completely unexceptional in appearance; in a word, they should be indistinguishable from the straights we'd like to reach. In practical terms, this means that cocky mustachioed leathermen, drag queens, and bull dykes would not appear in gay commercials and other public presentations. . . . One could also argue that lesbians should be featured more prominently than gay men in the early stages of

the media campaign. Straights generally have fewer and cloudier precon-
ceptions about lesbians and may feel less hostile toward them. And *as women*
(generally seen as less threatening and more vulnerable than men), lesbians may be more credible objects of sympathy. (Kirk and Madsen 1989,
183–184)[11]

Of course, most radical feminists and especially lesbian separatist feminists vociferously reject the notion that they want to join mainstream
(malestream) U.S. culture (especially by making lesbians seem less
threatening) and that SMists are interfering with that goal. But this is not
my claim. Instead, I want to suggest a parallel between the kind of emo-
tional/political reaction SMists have to claims that they hurt feminism
and reinforce patriarchal culture, and the emotional/political reaction
separatists and other radicals have to the claim that they hurt the cause
of lesbian and gay liberation by disrupting the unity of "the movement."
In both cases, members of the impugned groups feel that their experiences, identities, and political aims will be ignored, repressed, or co-
opted for the "greater good," with little or no good for them. And in the
way that a mainstream, "assimilationist" gay rights movement would not
serve the political goals of radical lesbian feminists, an "assimilationist"
radical lesbian feminist movement may not serve the goals of sadomasochist feminists.

It is not by accident that the leading lesbian SM activist group Samois
chose as their slogan "The Leather Menace." The slogan is a play on
words of the phrase "The Lavender Menace" that was used to describe
the presence of lesbians in the National Organization for Women when
NOW was trying to purge lesbians from its membership (Califia 1987,
264). The parallel for SMists is obvious. NOW members thought that lesbians were hurting feminism and feminist projects and sought to expur-
gate them for purposes of political expediency. And of course, NOW was
not merely being reactionary. There was a contemporary political reality
to face. Lesbians really did pose more of a threat than straight, liberal
feminist women and really did possess the potential to disrupt NOW's
political goals and public relations campaigns. But the question for lesbians at the time was whether or not it was somehow their "feminist duty"
to shut up and get out, at least until society had been changed enough
to permit their presence later on. Obviously, many lesbians did not take
it as their feminist duty to shut up and get out. Many lesbians did not simply interpret their own situation as that of being feminists who happened
to like having sex with other women, and thus did not feel that they were
merely positing a liberal claim to sexual freedom somewhat beyond that
of NOW. Instead, they saw their sexuality intimately entwined with their
politics, identity and culture. They formed radical political associations
of their own because they no longer saw that the "feminist movement"
was particularly benefiting them and realized they had to form their own

theories and practices. Sadomasochists have been and are in a similar position.[12]

Gayle Rubin, in her influential paper *The Leather Menace: Comments on Politics and S/M,* makes it clear that she does not see activist sadomasochism as just another liberal call for sexual freedom. She says: "Sex is one of the few areas in which cultural imperialism is taken as a radical stance. . . . The idea that there is one best way to do sex afflicts radical as well as conservative thought on the subject. *Cultural relativism is not the same thing as liberalism"* (Rubin 1987, 226) [italics added].[13] Rubin takes sadomasochists to be structurally similar to other cultural minorities. As such, any group which repudiates SMists or seeks to silence them or change them will be seen as a cultural enemy. Hearing feminists decry SMists is strikingly similar, for feminist sadomasochists, to hearing feminists decry lesbians. And although many sadomasochists strongly feel that they are feminists, just like lesbians in NOW felt that they were feminists, many SMists have come to see radical feminists as agents of oppression. Rubin writes:

> When I came out as an S/M person, I got an unexpected lesson in how my gay ancestors must have felt. My youth as a sadomasochist has been spent at a time when, as part of a more general reconsolidation of anti-sex and anti-gay ideology, a new demonization of S/M is taking place. . . . Now that large parts of the feminist movement have similarly defined S/M as an evil product of patriarchy, it has become increasingly difficult for those of us who are feminists to maintain our membership in the women's community. . . . I used to read the feminist press with enthusiasm. Now I dread each new issue of my favorite periodicals wondering what vile picture of my sexuality will appear this month.
>
> There are many reasons why S/M has become such a *bête noire* in the women's movement, and most originate outside of feminism. With the glaring exception of monogamous lesbianism, the women's movement usually reflects the sexual prejudices prevailing in society. (Rubin 1987, 211–213)

It appears that in the context of an interpretation of SMists as a sexual minority developing and expressing their own culture, an appropriate response for SMists to the claim that SMists are hurting feminism is not necessarily to renounce SM, but to develop a politics which addresses their own needs and perspectives, including the continued identification as both feminists and sadomasochists. Part of such a politics, as in other movements, would be the continuing education of the public. SMists can provide information on the nature of consent, the nature of sexual play and fantasy, and information regarding stereotypes of SMists, thereby assuring that information about SM for SMists would be reflective of actual, considered practice, and not easily interpreted by others as a reinforcement, validation, or replication of patriarchal practice.

V. Conclusion

In conclusion, I would like to say something about the development of my own interest in SM as a philosopher and gender theorist. SM initially drew my attention because it seemed to be a site for the (partial) performative subversion of gender—one of the rare practices in which such subversion is often explicit (drag being another). Since I take great personal pleasure and great political hope in acts of gender subversion, SM seemed worthy of study.

Gender subversion appears to be taking place in a variety of ways. First, positions in a scene are determined by factors other than the "sex" of the participant. Pat Califia says: "We've made a major improvement on heterosexist mores by insisting that the bottom can be a man or a woman, has control, has the right to consent or refuse, and should always get off" (Califia 1991, 230). In terms of representation to the more general public, the pairing of a female dominant and a male submissive (a common occurrence in heterosexual and bisexual SM culture) could be an image subversive to patriarchal sexual ideology, one perhaps even more subversive than lesbian imagery in general.[14]

Second, even though the appearance of a power dichotomy is maintained in sex, it is not the same kind as in non-SM relationships. It is simulative, playful, funny, and all self-consciously so. Weinberg et al. relate: "at one commercial establishment, a scene put on for a male audience involved one dominant woman playing the role of interrogator and two submissives the role of captured spies. To obtain their 'secrets' the dominant tied the two submissives to a post and threatened punishment. The scene collapsed, however, as the two submissives had a fit of giggling and continued laughing no matter what script the dominant tried" (Weinberg, Williams, and Moser 1984, 384).

Third, the explicitly contractual and negotiative aspect of SM may represent a kind of postmodern democratic urge in which sex is treated as both a mutual contracting for sexual/emotional services and a self-conscious performance. I think that many non-SM sexual activities could use a heavy dose of this kind of democracy, honesty and negotiation. Needless frustration, abuse, and disappointment might be avoided. Sarah Keepers writes: "To me vanilla sex is as much about trust as leather folks attribute to S/M. In fact, I use safe words and I keep clear boundaries of do's and don'ts. The vanilla community should get hip to the fact that just because it's vanilla doesn't mean that safe words aren't necessary" (Keepers 1991, 7).

Fourth, the structure of the SM encounter seems to me to be, if not indicative of, at least consistent with the general late 20th century epistemological shift in a variety of cultures toward experiences of simulation, virtual realities, cinematic performances, applied mythologies. To the extent that sex and gender and sexual identities themselves are captured and manipulated and exposed by the "scene," they are made to seem less natural, less definite, less compulsory.

This is not to say that SM is the ultimate site of the final subversion of gender categories, nor that I find SM to have escaped traditional sexual categories. Many SMists still tend to be essentialists, interpreting their performative experiences in terms of their "SM souls" or "SM natures." SMists still tend to cling too strongly to binary structures as an intrinsic element of physical or biological reality which SM mirrors.[15] And of course, many SMists have made the predictable move into identity politics. Although I have said very little about identity in this essay, the very concept of an identity-based politics is rife with difficulty—difficulties that an SM identity politics would share.

But SM is in no way a static site. Pat Califia herself criticizes SM and acknowledges that it can be a dynamic site for the reconstruction of sex and desire: "But I sometimes wonder if we have not transferred many of our old gender patterns to the top/bottom dynamic. . . . We still assume that being penetrated is a submissive act and sticking it in is dominant. Pleasure is still assumed to degrade and disenfranchise women. This sounds too much like the values of the New Christian Right. . . . I think we should be challenging the very meanings that we assign *all* sexual acts. This is the truly radical potential of S/M. Are we frightened by the idea of having that much freedom?" (Califia 1991, 230).

It does seem to me that SM is a particularly heuristic site for sexual subversion and to the extent that patriarchy requires (natural) sexual categories, perhaps even a site for opposition to patriarchy. I find sites of hope in the epistemology of sadomasochism. I find freedom in the simulation. I find method in fetishism.

One last point: Judith Butler, in discussing how compulsory heterosexuality tends to assume that there are pregiven sexes which are expressed first through gender and then through sexuality, has suggested that the reversal of these assumptions might be useful for subverting gender. In seeing sex, gender, and sexualities as categories maintained by compulsory performances rather than the reverse, she asks: "How then to expose the causal lines as retrospectively and performatively produced fabrications, and to engage gender itself as an inevitable fabrication. . . . Perhaps this will be a matter of working sexuality *against* identity, even against gender" (Butler 1991, 29).

I find a similar subversive possibility in the method of SM—to work sexuality against identity. It is a method worth evaluating.

Notes

I would like to thank Marilyn Friedman for her helpful comments on this paper and for her considerable time in discussing the issues with me. My thanks also go to Jennifer McCrickerd, Virginia Ingram, and Perry Stevens for their suggestions and comments.

1. One passionate and eloquent example of this is certainly Mary Daly's *Gyn/Ecology: The Metaethics of Radical Feminism* (1978), particularly in her descriptions of Sado-Ritual Syndrome, Goddess Dismemberment, and of the "necrophilic" attraction males have for females.

2. I borrow the term "sex wars" from Ann Ferguson (1984). The "sex wars" issues continue to arise, lately in discussion of whether women's events such as women's music festivals should ban SM groups from participation (Saxe 1992).

3. For examples of SM fiction, see Pat Califia's books, *Macho Sluts* (1988) and *Doc and Fluff* (Califia 1990). For theory and history see Mark Thompson's edited anthology, *Leatherfolk: Radical Sex, People, Politics, and Practice* (Thompson 1991). The use of the term "radical" in the title of this second book points to the recent development in SM writing of conceiving SM as possessing a cultural/political identity. For a wide range of commentary, photography, and fiction see the magazines/journals *On Our Backs: Entertainment for the Adventurous Lesbian, Bad Attitudes, Outrageous Women: A Journal of Woman-To-Woman S/M,* and *Quim.*

4. Carol Truscott wants to make it very clear that real pain does occur in some SM situations. However, she also notes that an essential component of SM is the reconceptualizing of pain as "sensations of changing, sometimes increasing intensity, rather than considering it something to be avoided as we do under ordinary circumstances" (Truscott 1991, n. 24).

5. In no way do I present any full-fledged "theory" of simulation (as a broad construct) in this paper. I am not sure that I would even want to. I do, however, want to make some distinction between the kind of simulation I am talking about from some other theorists' use of "simulation." For example, when Baudrillard claims that "Of the same order as the impossibility of rediscovering an absolute level of the real, is the impossibility of staging an illusion. Illusion is no longer possible, because the real is no longer possible," he wants to demonstrate such by eliciting intuitions about a "simulated" theft and a "simulated" hold-up. He says:

> How to feign a violation and put it to the test? Go and simulate a theft in a large department store: how do you convince the security guards that it is a simulated theft? There is no "objective" difference: the same gestures and the same signs exist as for a real theft; in fact the signs incline neither to one side nor the other. As far as the established order is concerned, they are always of the order of the real. Go and organise a fake hold-up. Be sure that your weapons are harmless, and take the most trustworthy hostage, so that no life is in danger (otherwise you risk committing an offence). Demand ransom, and arrange it so that the operation creates the greatest commotion possible—in brief, stay close to the "truth," so as to test the reaction of the apparatus to a perfect simulation. But you won't succeed: the web of artificial signs will be inextricably mixed up with real elements (a police officer will really shoot . . .)—in brief, you will unwittingly find yourself immediately in the real, one of whose functions is precisely to devour every attempt at simulation, to reduce everything to some reality—that's exactly how the established order is. (Baudrillard 1983, 38–39)

Baudrillard is certainly right in claiming that the "repressive apparatus" does react to the simulation as though it were real. In relation to SM this has been demonstrated by the responses of both radical feminists and the judicial system. Gayle Rubin has reported that SM activity has sometimes been prosecuted under sexual assault laws. Because "sexual assault" is a felony, the state can press charges even when the purported "victim" of the assault objects. As a result, some tops/sadists have been convicted of sexual assault and sentenced to prison even when their partners protested that the sexual activity (e.g., a riding-crop spanking) was consensual (Rubin 1987, 199–200).

The disanalogy between SM and the examples Baudrillard gives rests in the degree of participation. In the fake theft and the fake hold-up, not everyone involved knows that the robbery is not real. The security guards do not know, the bank employees do not know, and so on. In SM, however, all participants are fully aware of the simulative nature of the activities. This is one of the primary points of significance in realizing that SM occurs in a community setting—not necessarily meaning that participants belong to formal SM organizations, but that participants are aware of others identifying as sadomasochists and are aware of community support structures such as magazines, books, political debates, etc. In fact, some SM sexual partners meet through some kind of SM community channel—bars, dungeon parties, phone connection lines, computer bulletin boards, magazine ads. Thus, while Baudrillard's examples clearly mix the signs of the real and of the simulative, this occurs because some people in the event know the guns are not real, for example, while other people do not know. In consensual SM, however, all the participants share an interpretation of the signs and so everyone knows that what is happening is not "real"—"real" meaning not that what is happening is false, but that it is not the same as the "original" from which it draws its images and scripts.

6. Pat Califia discusses the way in which tops' sexual and emotional needs are often ignored by thoughtless bottoms. She admonishes tops to "stop acting like a bunch of victimized codependents held hostage by rapacious bottoms" (Califia 1992, 19). It is revealing of the internal context of SM relations that bottoms can be considered manipulative, assertive, or insensitive, while tops can be considered inadequately assertive or inattentive to their own sexual satisfaction.

7. See Gilles Deleuze and Félix Guattari (1977). Also see Alphonso Lingis (1985). Lingis describes Deleuze and Guattari's position as one in which "sexual desire does not have as its objects persons or things at all. It is invested in whole environments, in vibrations and fluxes of all kinds; it is essentially nomadic. It is always with worlds that we make love" (Lingis 1985, 90).

8. My thanks go to Perry Stevens for this illuminating analogy.

9. The notion of community as applied to SM may be empirically somewhat problematic, at least in non-urban areas, for the simple reason that SM is still extremely vilified and as such, community visibility is dangerous. It is not, however, theoretically more problematic than any other community that serves persons whose "identifying" traits are stigmatized, unobvious behavioral and emotional interests, such as lesbians, gays, bisexuals, etc. Having said that, the very presence of a person in an SM community setting (provided it is not accidental) suggests a mutual recognition of desire. This is not to say that mere presence implies consent to any specific act, but a presence does suggest community affinity. Gayle

Rubin says:

> I came out as a lesbian in a small college town that had no visible lesbian
> community. . . . There was one mostly male gay bar called the Flame. I had
> heard for years it was the kind of place you wanted to stay away from. There
> were vague implications that if you went there, something bad would hap-
> pen. But it was the only gay bar in town, and I was drawn to it. I finally
> screwed up my courage and walked in. The minute I got past the front door
> I relaxed. It was full of very innocuous looking gay men and a couple of les-
> bians. I instantly realized that these were my people, and that I was one of
> the people I had been warned against. . . . Seven years later, I was again
> sweating in front of another tabooed threshold. This time it was the door
> to the Pleasure Chest in New York City. I must have walked up and down
> Seventh Avenue twenty times before I finally got a friend to go in with me.
> It took a little longer to get used to the S/M world than to the gay world.
> But by now I feel as at home in leather bars and sex toy shops as I do in les-
> bian bars and gay restaurants. Instead of the monsters and slimy perverts I
> had been led to expect, I found another hidden community. The S/M com-
> munity is not as large as the gay community, but it is complex, populated,
> and quite civilized. Most parts of the S/M community take a responsible at-
> titude to newcomers, teaching them how to do S/M safely, S/M etiquette,
> and acquired wisdom. Preconceived chimeras disappear in the face of ac-
> tual social practice. (Rubin 1987, 219–220)

10. Sandra Bartky has an interesting, but I think ultimately unsatisfactory,
analysis of this option. She believes that sadomasochistic desire is incompatible
with feminist principles but that it is extremely difficult to teach women how to
"decolonize the imagination." She seems to think that women who have SM desires but want to remain consistent with feminist principles are doomed to living
out a life of "existential unease" (Bartky 1990, 60–62).

11. I do not intend to make any judgment in this paper whatsoever regarding
the desirability or undesirability of Kirk and Madsen's position. Such a discussion is worthy of, at the very least, a separate and lengthy paper. I only use their
work as an example of what radical lesbians/gays/feminists often consider assimilationist.

12. It may be claimed that this analogy only holds in the end if SM really is
harmless for feminism. The problem with such a claim is knowing what should
and should not be considered to "harm feminism." One could make the claim
that the presence of lesbians really did harm the kind of feminism NOW was promoting at the time by giving conservatives support for their claims that feminism
threatened the traditional family, promoted homosexuality, etc. NOW's even-
tual move was not to defend their particular brand of feminism forever, but to
alter their feminism to include the struggle for lesbian visibility and rights. Sadomasochists, not surprisingly, could call for the same sort of inclusion, or at least
a halt to resistance, by claiming that their sexuality is no more harmful to a certain kind of inclusive feminism than lesbian sexuality was harmful to a certain
kind of inclusive feminism.

13. Gayle Rubin's claim concerning "one best way to do sex" may be a straw
person, but only in the sense that she might be attributing the notion of the "one

best way" to all radicals. Certainly there are some radicals who would allow a variety of sexual activity while still rejecting SM as an ethically permissible sexual activity. However, Rubin is responding to radicals who have chosen to publicly renounce her sexuality and fight its acceptance. Some of these radicals do seem to claim that the only ethical/politically permissible sexual activity for a feminist is egalitarian sex with another woman—where "egalitarian" is specified in terms of necessary, formal, physical requirements, ruling out the possibility of consensual SM activity regardless of the participants' interpretations of such activities.

14. And as Marilyn Friedman has pointed out, it is no accident that this staple of underground heterosexual pornography and professional SM sex services almost never appears in popular pornographic materials. It is curious that an activity that seems to be the fantasy of a significant number of heterosexual males is so underrepresented in mainstream heterosexual magazines and videos.

15. See again Carol Truscott (1991, 32).

References

Bar On, Bat-Ami. 1982. Feminism and sadomasochism: Self-critical notes. In *Against sadomasochism: A radical feminist analysis*. See Linden et al. 1982.

Bartky, Sandra. 1990. *Femininity and domination*. New York: Routledge.

Baudrillard, Jean. 1983. *Simulations*. New York: Semiotext(e).

Butler, Judith. 1982. Lesbian S & M: The politics of dis-illusion. In *Against sadomasochism: A radical feminist analysis*. See Linden et al. 1982.

―――. 1991. Imitation and gender insubordination. In *Inside/out: Lesbian theories, gay theories*, ed. Diana Fuss. New York: Routledge.

Califia, Pat. 1987. A personal view of the history of the lesbian S/M community and movement in San Francisco. In *Coming to power: Writings and graphics on lesbian S/M*. See Samois 1987.

―――. 1988. *Macho sluts*. Boston: Alyson Publications, Inc.

―――. 1990. *Doc and fluff: The dystopian tale of a girl and her biker*. Boston: Alyson Publications, Inc.

―――. 1992. The limits of the S/M relationship, or Mr. Benson doesn't live here anymore. In *Leatherfolk: Radical sex, people, politics, and practice*. See Thompson 1991.

Daly, Mary. 1978. *Gyn/Ecology: The metaethics of radical feminism*. Boston: Beacon Press.

Deleuze, Gilles, and Félix Guattari. 1977. *Anti-Oedipus*. Trans. Robert Hurley, Mark Seem and Helen R. Lane. New York: Viking.

Ferguson, Ann. 1984. Sex war: The debate between radical and libertarian feminists. *Signs* 10(1): 106–112.

Hein, Hilde. 1982. Sadomasochism and the liberal tradition. In *Against sadomasochism: A radical feminist analysis*. See Linden et al. 1982.

Hoagland, Sarah Lucia. 1982. Sadism, masochism and lesbian-feminism. In *Against sadomasochism: A radical feminist analysis*. See Linden et al. 1982.

Keepers, Sarah. 1991. Letter to the editor in *On our backs: Entertainment for the adventurous lesbian*, May/June.

Kirk, Marshall, and Hunter Madsen. 1989. *After the ball: How America will conquer its fear of gays in the 1990s*. New York: Doubleday.

Linden, Robin Ruth, Darlene R. Pagano, Diana E. H. Russell, and Susan Leigh Star, 1982. *Against sadomasochism: A radical feminist analysis*. East Palo Alto, Calif.: Frog In The Well.

Lingis, Alphonso. 1985. *Libido: The French existential theories*. Bloomington: Indiana University Press.

Lorde, Audre, and Susan Leigh Star. 1982. Interview with Audre Lorde. In *Against sadomasochism: A radical feminist analysis*. See Linden et al. 1982.

Meredith, Jesse. 1982. A Response to Samois. In *Against sadomasochism: A radical feminist analysis*. See Linden et al. 1982.

Rian, Karen. 1982. Sadomasochism and the social construction of desire. In *Against sadomasochism: A radical feminist analysis*. See Linden et al. 1982.

Rubin, Gayle. 1987. The leather menace: Comments on politics and S/M. In *Coming to power: Writings and graphics on lesbian S/M*. See Samois 1987.

Russell, Diana E. H. 1982. Sadomasochism: A contra-feminist activity. In *Against sadomasochism: A radical feminist analysis*. See Linden et al. 1982.

Samois. 1987. *Coming to power: Writings and graphics on lesbian S/M*. Boston: Alyson Publications, Inc.

Saxe, Lorena Leigh. 1992. Sadomasochism and exclusion. *Hypatia* 7(4): 59–72.

Thompson, Mark, ed. 1991. *Leatherfolk: Radical sex, people, politics, and practice*. Boston: Alyson Publications, Inc.

Truscott, Carol. 1991. S/M: Some questions and a few answers. In *Leatherfolk: Radical sex, people, politics, and practice*. See Thompson 1991.

Walker, Alice. 1982. A letter of the times, or should this sadomasochism be saved? In *Against sadomasochism: A radical feminist analysis*. See Linden et al. 1982.

Weinberg, Martin S., Colin J. Williams, and Charles Moser. 1984. The social constituents of sadomasochism. *Social Problems* 3(4): 379–389.

Chapter 17

REPLY TO PATRICK HOPKINS

Melinda Vadas

Patrick Hopkins claims that doing SM scenes may be compatible with feminist principles because such scenes are mere "simulations" of rape and other sexual atrocities. He compares such SM simulations to roller coaster rides. Hopkins says that roller coaster rides can be understood as simulations of falling to one's death. Hopkins points out that from the fact that one desires to ride a roller coaster it does not follow that one desires to fall to one's death or that one has a pro-attitude toward others falling to their deaths. Similarly, he says, from the fact that one desires to engage in a simulation of a rape it does not follow that one desires to be raped or that one has a pro-attitude toward rape.

I would like to point out to Hopkins that the situated disanalogies between roller coaster rides and SM scenes are many. In our lifeworld it is not the case that women are frequently murdered by men who push them to their deaths from roller coasters. If it were the case that every few seconds a woman was murdered by a man who pushed her to her death from a roller coaster, then the social meaning of a woman's choosing to go on such a ride would be very different from what it is now, and choosing to go on such a ride might then be more analogous to choosing to simulate a rape. As it is, however, in our lifeworld the differences between riding a roller coaster and simulating a rape are differences between different *sorts* of activities.

In recommending SM scenes to us, Hopkins overlooks the ways in

Reprinted from *Hypatia* 10:2 (1995), pp. 159–61, with the permission of Melinda Vadas. © 1995, Melinda Vadas.

which social and/or linguistic meaning does or does not connect simulations and that which they simulate, as well as the ways in which some
simulations conceptually require the actual existence of that which they
simulate while others do not. The thrill of roller coaster riding is not intrinsically a function of the existence or occurrence of actual deaths
produced by falls from high places. The experience of the ride is not mediated by the meaning, if any, of such actual deaths. The experience
would be thrilling even if no deaths from falling had ever occurred. In
fact, it would be thrilling even if no deaths *could* occur (because we all
bounced when dropped). People who ride roller coasters typically make
no connection at the level of meaning between deaths from falls and
their experience. Being dropped quickly through space produces an
adrenaline rush whether or not anyone ever dies or has died from such
a process. (In fact, and for these reasons, it is misleading to say that riding a roller coaster is a simulation of falling to one's death. It is not experienced, *de dicto*, as such.)

In contrast to the above, the thrill produced by doing SM scenes is relevantly different. The kick they give is a direct function of the actual, historical occurrence or existence of the death camps, rapes, and racist
enslavements they simulate. If these historical events had never occurred
or *could* not occur (because we all had a kindness gene), the simulation
would not only not be thrilling to the SMer, there would be no simulation at all because there would be nothing to simulate. The existence or
occurrence of the SM simulation both conceptually and empirically requires the existence or occurrence of actual injustice. The experience of
the simulation is mediated by the meaning of the injustices simulated.
To take pleasure in the simulation is to make one's pleasure contingent
on the actual occurrence and meanings of rape, racist enslavement, and
so on. Pleasures taken in this way are not feminist, and cannot be.

The claim that a new context produces new meanings for such SM
phrases as "Lick my boots, you nigger slut" and SM scenes of racist, sexist, and homophobic domination is disingenuous. If the new meaning
has overtaken the old, why then does doing the scene or saying the
words produce a specifically *sadomasochistic* thrill? If the old meaning is
gone, so would be the sadomaschistic pleasure. If the sadomasochistic
pleasure is not gone, neither is the old meaning.

The claim that a new context or practice can produce a new meaning
for what might appear to be "the same" object or event is true—a raised
hand can be a Nazi salute or a request for a teacher's recognition—but
such a new context is not produced, as Hopkins suggests it is, through
the good intentions or good characters of the participants, nor through
their adoption of meaning-irrelevant rules and procedures. The context
that gives the meaning of rape to rape is the context of sexualized dominance and submission—of dominance and submission as sex itself—

and it is this context that is purposely and seamlessly reproduced by SM practitioners in their simulations of rape and other unjust acts. When such simulations are employed, like rape itself, to produce sexual pleasure, the claim of a new context is baseless. Thus, the meaning of SM simulations is nothing new—the SM text consists of the same old words and scenes and oppressions. That is why SM simulations work sexually—and that is why their sexual use is not feminist.

Note

The publication of this reply has not changed my view that *Hypatia* is ableist and is to that degree anti-feminist. [This essay is a reply to Patrick Hopkins's "Rethinking Sadomasochism," this volume, pp. 189–214.]

PART 5

RAPE AND HARASSMENT

Chapter 18

IS *THIS* SEXUAL HARASSMENT?

Robin Warshaw

Sexual harassment? Not you. You're the new breed of male, sensitive to the age-old gender stereotypes women have had to battle as they gain the equality and respect rightfully theirs in a male-dominated business world. As far as you're concerned, bartering promotions for sexual favors is inappropriate office conduct of the worst sort—the kind of behavior that not only demeans co-workers but also tarnishes your own character and diminishes managerial effectiveness.

No. In this matter your conscience is as shiny and clean as Sir Galahad's shield.

So throughout the long media blizzard precipitated by Anita Hill, Clarence Thomas and the Senate judiciary peanut gallery, you sat snug and cozy, hands warming by the fire of your own morally appropriate behavior. But when the storm subsided, you may have found a new America waiting to challenge your conduct.

It is an America in which women, overcoming their fear of reprisal and disbelief, are bringing their grievances to court in record numbers. In the first half of 1992 alone, reports of harassment made to the Equal Employment Opportunity Commission increased more than 50 percent over the previous year.

It is also an America that is finally ready to take these grievances seriously. And while you may applaud this trend that's finally packing

---

Reprinted from *Exec* (Summer 1993), pp. 62–65, by permission of Robin Warshaw. © 1993, Robin Warshaw.

muscle onto what was formerly a pleasant but ineffective civil rights sentiment, the bottom line is that you may get caught in the crossfire.

The problem faced by men in this new environment is twofold: First, while most media-worthy cases of sexual harassment involve spectacularly colorful instances of inappropriate behavior, the majority of unheralded arguments currently being heard in the nation's courts don't fit so neatly into the public's perceptions of right and wrong. Harassment sometimes is in the eye of the beholder, and what may be one man's clumsy attempt at friendship or even honest romance may be one woman's sheer hell.

Complicating the whole matter are the hazy boundaries of the law. Except in cases of actual assault, there's still no steadfast uniformity regarding the type of behavior the courts and mediating agencies should judge to be harassing.

The following cases have all been culled from legal battles and disputes brought before public hearing examiners. Each has been chosen because it explores in some fashion the gray areas that lie just outside the realm of obviously inoffensive and threatening behavior. As you read them, ask yourself: Are the women involved simply too sensitive? Or are these in fact bona fide cases of harassment? Before you read the verdict, make your own judgment and see whether your behavioral gyroscope is guiding you straight and true—or wobbling dangerously.

CASE #1:
Is Sex Between Consenting Adults Harassment?

The Securities and Exchange Commission office was a sociable place to work—sociable, that is, if you were one of several employees, including supervisors, having romantic affairs with each other, holding frequent parties and leaving the office during the day to go drinking.

But one female attorney who did not participate in the carousing found her co-workers' behavior repulsive. She claimed she was harassed by the environment in which she had to work. Moreover, she said, women who had affairs with male supervisors were rewarded with bonuses and promotions. The woman conceded that no one had pressured her for sex or denied her any promotions because she wasn't one of the crowd.

Was she being too touchy?

The decision: Although the woman wasn't harassed on a quid pro quo (give something to get something) basis, a judge ruled that the "pervasive" behavior in the SEC office had created an offensive work environment. She was awarded back pay, a promotion and her choice of two jobs. The SEC also agreed to an outside review of its personnel practices.

The expert analysis: "That's a hostile work environment—no question about it," says Thomas A. McGinn, a human-resources consultant in Charlottesville, Virginia, and co-author (with Nancy Dodd McCann) of *Harassed: 100 Women Define Inappropriate Behavior in the Workplace* (Business One Irwin).

Socializing at work has its limits, and those limits certainly were crossed in the Roman Empire–type revels at that SEC office. Federal guidelines warn specifically that an employer who gives benefits to anyone in exchange for sex may be held liable for discriminating against other workers. But any affairs within an office—even among peers—can raise the potential for unequal treatment of nonparticipants.

CASE #2:
That's Entertainment?

Few things are as boring as most corporate meetings. In an attempt to liven up the presentations, an oil company brought a barely clad woman on a motorcycle to a regional meeting, according to a sexual-harassment complaint filed by a female supervisor for the company.

Moreover, she charged, when the corporation held a sales meeting at a restaurant, the entertainment was provided by strippers. And at a slide show held for employees, one slide featured the female supervisor's clothed rear end.

Was the woman harassed?

The decision: The federal judge presiding over this case noted that the incidents were without question inappropriate but weren't "sufficiently severe or pervasive to constitute a hostile environment." That noted, he found that no harassment had taken place.

The expert analysis: Surely there are other ways to entertain and inform employees, suggests Anthony M. Micolo, a human-resources representative with Eastman Kodak in New York City. As for the incidents in the case: "I would probably feel myself, as a man, uncomfortable with this stuff," he says.

More to the point is that while a "hostile environment" charge often needs more than one or two incidents to substantiate it, other judges might find episodes such as the preceding sufficient to establish a pervasive climate of harassment. Micolo points out that corporations need to consider what conduct will be deemed acceptable. "Above and beyond sales goals and operational goals, there have to be people goals," he says. "You have to view the work environment as one that's productive to employees, not oppressive to them."

CASE #3:
Just a Friendly Ride

A midwinter snowstorm hit so hard that one Virginia corporation sent its workers home early. A female word-processing technician needed a ride, which was readily offered by a male engineer for whom she had done some work. He assured her that his four-wheel drive vehicle would have no trouble navigating the storm.

Indeed, it didn't. When they arrived, he entered her apartment. He says he only kissed her. She says he tried to kiss and fondle her, despite her protestations. When she complained to their employer, the man was reprimanded and warned he would be fired if he committed another such act.

Was he simply a clumsy guy looking for companionship or a threatening menace?

What happened: The woman's lawyers showed in court that the corporation had received previous complaints from other women about the man's behavior. After a ruling determined that the company had a legal responsibility to prevent the incident, the employer made an out-of-court settlement.

The expert analysis: According to Louise Fitzgerald, a psychologist and researcher on sexual harassment at the University of Illinois at Champaign, such a scenario is common but not innocuous. "This is unwanted sexual attention of a predatory nature and is a violation of someone's right to bodily integrity." In research Fitzgerald conducted among working women, 15 percent had been victims at work of undesired attempts at touching, fondling, grabbing or kissing.

CASE #4:
The Chummy Boss

The new secretary thought it strange that her boss walked her to her car every night, but she believed it was to offer security. She couldn't explain why he walked her to the bathroom, hovered over her desk, left her personal notes about her appearance or bought her gifts. She complained about this to her friends, but not to management.

She hoped that by letting her boss know she was happily married, the unwanted attention would stop. Instead, when she was hospitalized for back surgery, he called frequently, visited, sent notes and brought flowers. When she returned to work, he tried to give her back rubs whenever he noticed her stretching. She told him to stop. Finally, she spoke to a supervisor, who told her to talk to her boss again. Ultimately, she quit the job after her boss accused her of having an affair with a male co-worker and threatened to withhold a promised raise if it was true.

Was the boss anything more than an annoying pest?

What happened: A local human-relations commission ruled in the woman's favor and the company offered a $6,700 settlement. She declined the settlement and went to court.

Then a federal judge asserted that no harassment had taken place. He ruled that the boss's conduct "would not have interfered with a reasonable person's work performance or created an intimidating, hostile or offensive working environment." He added that the woman's protests to her boss "were not delivered with any sense of urgency, sincerity or force." Legal experts say such cases will now more often be decided by juries, with verdicts increasingly likely to favor complainants.

The expert analysis: Some argue that in order to dispel any hint of sexual harassment in an office, all friendly interactions would have to stop. However, Jonathan A. Segal, a management attorney in Philadelphia who advises companies on sexual harassment issues, disputes that dour view. "An occasional compliment is not harassment," he says, "but an excessive interest in an employee's private life is."

Segal spends most of his time providing employers with preventive education on how to avoid situations such as the one above. "Any thorough training program would make clear that what this individual did was wrong," he says. Moreover, he adds, complaints should never be handled by the individuals charged with harassment.

CASE #5:
The Writing on the Wall

A woman learned that obscene cartoons about her had been posted in the men's room of her office building. The graffiti sketches depicted various sex acts and mentioned her name.

The lewd illustrations remained on display in the public bathroom for a week, even after the company's chief executive had seen them. It was only after he learned the woman was upset about the cartoons that they were removed.

Was the office worker sexually harassed or was she just the target of crude, yet childish, pranksters?

What happened: The court sided with the woman, determining that the cartoons were "highly offensive to a woman who seeks to deal with her fellow employees and clients with professional dignity." The employer agreed to pay her full salary and psychiatric bills until she found new employment.

In a similar case, a federal judge in Jacksonville, Florida, determined that pinup calendars and posters of women's genitals that were displayed at a shipyard were a "visual assault on the sensibilities of female workers," constituted sexual harassment and kept women out of jobs there.

The expert analysis: Where certain men might feel flattered or amused to have their names attached to sexually explicit cartoons, most women would likely feel shame and humiliation. Joan Lester, director of the Equity Institute, an Emeryville, California, consultancy in multicultural issues, points out that for a woman to be chosen for such treatment is "chilling and intimidating." It's also potentially dangerous: "The cartoons could be an incitement to sexual violence." For the targeted woman, that fear—coupled with the ridicule—could quickly destroy her work world.

It would have been far better if a male co-worker had taken the pictures down immediately, but such allies for women are often rare in work settings. "There's the fear [for a male co-worker] of breaking rank, that his masculinity will be questioned," says Lester. The situation was worsened by the company president's knowledge of the drawings. "It shows he didn't have an understanding of the human consequences and the legal issues," Lester adds.

CASE #6:
What Is Reasonable

Two office employees, female and male, worked at desks just a few yards away from each other. One day they went to lunch together.

When the man later asked the woman out for yet another lunch (and perhaps a drink), she turned him down. After that rebuff, he began sending her love letters, including one that was three pages long and single-spaced. The woman became increasingly frightened about the unwanted attention and filed a sexual harassment complaint.

Was the man just doing some harmless, old-fashioned courting?

What happened: The woman's case was dismissed at first by a judge who called the man's behavior "trivial," but an appellate court, in a precedent-setting decision, found that sexual harassment should be viewed as a "reasonable woman" might experience it and remanded it back to the lower court. More and more future cases will be decided using this "reasonable woman" standard.

The expert analysis: In a society in which sexual assault is not uncommon, such persistent, unwelcome advances from a man are frightening. "Physical size and physical well-being have a lot to do with it," says San Francisco labor attorney Cliff Palefsky, who represents plaintiffs in sexual harassment cases. That's why, Palefsky explains, if a man is subjected to excessive staring by a woman, he might think, "So what?" But when the situation is reversed, "it's enough to give a woman the creeps." Most men, he adds, have never experienced such scary intrusiveness.

Because of men's and women's disparate views, the evaluation of sexual harassment charges is now moving away from the legal tradition of using a "reasonable man's" (or "reasonable person's") interpretation of an incident to judgments based on how a "reasonable woman" might view an event. Palefsky says the concept has received quick acceptance. "This isn't paternalistic protection for women," he says. "It's a reality. There's such a huge difference in perspective."

Chapter 19

SEXUAL HARASSMENT IN THE LAW: THE DEMARCATION PROBLEM

Mane Hajdin

1. Introduction

This paper presupposes that the law about sexual harassment in the work place,[1] if it is to be acceptable, ought to provide a workable criterion of demarcation between sexual harassment and those forms of sexual interaction between people who work together that do not constitute sexual harassment. It also presupposes that the law ought to do so without leaving the latter class empty or almost empty, and without becoming a vehicle of legal moralism (for example, the fact that a certain act involves adultery should not in itself constitute a reason for classifying it as an act of sexual harassment). I do *not* presuppose that the demarcation ought to be sharp: it can be as fuzzy as similar legal demarcations usually are.

I believe that the overwhelming majority of people, including the overwhelming majority of those who strongly support the present sexual harassment law, can accept these presuppositions, and that it is therefore safe to take them as one's starting point. Most people also believe that the present sexual harassment law in fact satisfies the conditions that I have presupposed. The aim of this paper is to show that it does not,

Sections 1–6 of this essay are an abridged reprint of "Sexual Harassment in the Law: The Demarcation Problem," *Journal of Social Philosophy* 25:3 (1994), pp. 102–22; sections 7–8 are an abridged reprint of "Sexual Harassment and Negligence," *Journal of Social Philosophy* 28:1 (1997), pp. 37–53. Reprinted by permission of Mane Hajdin and the *Journal of Social Philosophy*.

to examine why it does not, and to explore how it might be modified so that it does.

2. Consent

However, before we start that examination of the law itself, it will be instructive to look briefly at the way the problem of demarcation is treated in some nonlegal writings on the topic.

One widely quoted book on sexual harassment, for example, raises the question of demarcation by acknowledging that

> Sexual give-and-take—the friendly verbal interaction between colleagues, the acknowledged attraction between coworkers, the accepted physical gesturing of male and female—is a healthy behavior in which individuals of various ages and stations choose to engage.
>   . . . The humor and affection in sexual give-and-take may be a way to reduce sexual tensions. It may relieve the monotony of routine work. It may even be preliminary courtship, a kind of testing before proceeding with a more serious relationship.[2]

This book offers the following as the solution: " 'Choice' is the critical concept. . . . Whatever the intent, sexual give-and-take is based on mutual *consent* of equals. This is obviously not the case in sexual harassment."[3]

Relying on the word "consent" to mark the boundary between sexual harassment and other forms of sexual interaction[4] appears natural both because of the widespread use of the phrase "consenting adults" in connection with other sex-related matters and because the word "consent" usually marks the boundary between rape and sexual intercourse that is not rape, and analogies between sexual harassment and rape readily suggest themselves. Another popular book on the topic thus says that "sexual harassment is not synonymous with all sexual activity any more than rape is synonymous with intercourse."[5]

The actual law explicitly[6] rejects the presence of consent as the criterion of demarcation, but the idea that the presence of consent *could* be the criterion is nevertheless a tempting one. Showing, within this section, why that idea is misguided will facilitate our discussion of the actual law, in the sections that follow.

People, in general, have no difficulty understanding the requirement that one should seek the consent of one's intended partner before engaging in sexual intercourse. It is notorious that cases occasionally arise in which one's general understanding of that requirement may be difficult to apply, but such cases are exceptional. In the overwhelming majority of cases, people know how to go about complying with this requirement, and find it relatively easy to pursue their sexual interests without violating it.

There is also no deep difficulty about understanding how the requirement of consent applies not only to sexual intercourse itself, but also to many other forms of physical contact aimed at sexual satisfaction.

The law about sexual harassment, however, applies not only to activities of this kind, but also to acts such as "requests for sexual favors" and "sexual advances." Those who think about sexual harassment in terms of consent seem to believe that this is simply an *extension* of the range of activities to which the requirement of consent applies and that the requirement can still be understood by analogy with the requirement of consent for sexual intercourse.

This is not so. The analogy breaks down because requests for sexual favors and sexual advances *are* precisely the acts of seeking consent for sexual interaction. To say that one should seek consent for these acts is to say that one should seek consent for seeking consent for sexual interaction. Thinking about sexual harassment in this way thus introduces *iterated* requirements of consent, which is something that is absent from the straightforward requirement of consent that is embodied in the law about rape.

This is not in itself an argument against looking at sexual harassment in terms of consent. *Sometimes* it makes perfect sense to say that one should not even seek consent for something unless one is in the appropriate relationship with the person whose consent one intends to seek, and that one can be in such a relationship only as a result of having sought and obtained consent to be in it. In the matter at hand, for example, it makes sense to say that one should never straightforwardly ask for someone's consent to sexual intercourse, unless that person has already consented to be in a certain kind of personal relationship in which consent for sexual intercourse may be sought. Whatever one might think about the wisdom of making this into a legal rule, one cannot claim that the fact that this rule involves iterated requirements of consent in any way impairs its intelligibility, or that it would make it unduly difficult to comply with it. In fact, most people have always followed some such rule as a matter of social convention anyway.

One could easily think of other examples, in which there are three, four, and perhaps many more iterated requirements of consent, and in which that still does not cause any serious problem. There is, however, a serious problem when we have *infinitely* many iterated requirements of consent, and this is precisely what we end up having if we think about sexual harassment in terms of consent. An act of seeking consent for sexual interaction of any kind can, namely, always be aptly described as a sexual advance itself, and this is what generates the infinite regress. If there were a requirement that one seek consent for every sexual advance one intends to make, then one could comply with that requirement only by making another, prior, sexual advance. But given that the requirement applies to all advances, it applies to that prior advance too: in order to legitimize it, one has to make another, still earlier sexual advance. The requirement, however, applies to *it* as well and so on, *ad infinitum.*

The requirement that one seek consent prior to engaging in any form of behavior that is currently within the scope of the sexual harassment law would therefore be in principle impossible to comply with, except by never engaging in *any* form of sexual interaction with the people one works with.

Every relationship of sexual nature, as a matter of logic, begins with a first step, and that first step is, again as a matter of logic, bound to be non-consensual. To prohibit all non-consensual sexual interaction is thus to prohibit the first step of every relationship of sexual nature, and to prohibit the first step of something is to prohibit the whole of it. The prohibition of all non-consensual sexual interaction would therefore amount to a prohibition of *all* sexual interaction.

3. Unwelcomeness

Having thus disposed of the suggestion that the term "consent" could play a role in providing the criterion of demarcation, we should now examine whether the criteria that the law actually uses fare any better. According to the Supreme Court, "the gravamen of any sexual harassment claim is that the alleged sexual advances were 'unwelcome'."[7] The term "unwelcome" comes from the well-known federal EEOC Guidelines on Sexual Harassment, where it is used in a way that appears to provide a criterion of demarcation.

We can all probably think of clear-cut cases of unwelcome sexual advances and clear-cut cases of welcome sexual advances, and it therefore seems unquestionable that the word "unwelcome" marks a genuine distinction here. This, however, is not enough, because if the rules about sexual harassment are to be legitimate legal rules, they have to be capable not only of being applied by various observers after the fact, but also of playing a role in guiding potential harassers before they act.

In order to comply with a rule that prohibits unwelcome sexual advances, one has to find out, of each sexual advance that one considers making, whether it would be unwelcome or not. Given that people's preferences in sexual matters tend to vary greatly from one individual to another, and that they usually do not advertise them, readily available information about a given person typically does not provide sufficient ground for concluding whether that person would, under the given circumstances, welcome a sexual advance from such-and-such other person or not. Broad generalizations, such as the generalization that a married person is less likely to welcome an advance than an unmarried one, are far too broad to entail anything useful about individual cases. This means that, in a typical case, the only way to find out whether the sexual advance one is contemplating would be welcome is to ask whether it would be welcome. But asking whether something would be welcome is very similar to seeking consent for it. Therefore although the consent-based and welcomeness-based demarcation may look different from the viewpoint of an after-the-fact observer, they are very similar from the viewpoint of a person who is trying to comply with the prohibition of sexual harassment. This similarity makes a welcomeness-based attempt at the demarcation liable to the same argument that was used in the preceding section.

Asking whether a sexual advance would be welcome need not, of course, take the form of a straightforward verbal inquiry: our culture provides numerous nonverbal and roundabout verbal ways of accomplishing the same purpose. But in whatever way it may be carried out, it remains true that this prior inquiry itself constitutes a sexual advance. The prohibition of unwelcome sexual advances therefore applies to it as well: the only way to comply is to find out whether it would be unwelcome, and one can find that out only if one undertakes another, still earlier, inquiry, which inquiry, in turn, is going to constitute yet another sexual advance, and so forth. The same infinite regress gets generated again.

Someone may try to respond to this argument by claiming that an *inquiry* as to whether X would be (un)welcome is, in general, *less likely* to be unwelcome than X itself. On that basis, one could argue that the likelihood of unwelcomeness keeps diminishing as we follow the regress, and that after a certain *finite* number of steps it becomes so low as not to create any practical difficulty. Therefore, he could claim, for most ends and purposes, the regress need not be regarded as infinite, after all.

This counterargument is however mistaken: the likelihood of unwelcomeness does *not* diminish along the regress. An inquiry as to whether X would be unwelcome, other things being equal, has *exactly* the same likelihood of being unwelcome as X itself. This is because whenever X itself would be unwelcome, an inquiry as to whether X would be (un)welcome is bound to be unwelcome too. If I would not welcome X, then I have no reason whatsoever to welcome an inquiry about it (viewed as such) and at least some reasons not to welcome it, namely that answering it requires expenditure of my time and energy (not to mention that it might be disruptive).

For some values of X, I may have further reasons for not welcoming any inquiries as to whether X would be welcome, but we do not need to discuss these, because the reason based on expenditure of time and energy is sufficient to establish the connection between the unwelcomeness of X and the unwelcomeness of inquiries about it, for all values of

$X.$[8] We therefore have to conclude that the word "unwelcome" does generate the same kind of infinite regress as the word "consent."

To make this point still clearer, I should emphasize that the "logic" of the word "unwelcome" is different from that of some other words for negative attitudes, such as "repugnant" and "outrageous." The appeal that the above objection to my infinite regress argument may, at first sight, have is probably due to not appreciating that difference.

From the fact that I would find X repugnant it does not, in general, follow that I would find an inquiry about it repugnant. This is because the *intensity* of my negative attitude towards the inquiry is often lower than the intensity of my negative attitude towards X, and it is thus possible that it would fall below the threshold for application of the word "repugnant." The crucial difference between "repugnant" and "unwelcome" is that "repugnant" is not simply a word for a negative attitude, but a word for a negative attitude above a certain threshold of intensity, while the meaning of "unwelcome" does not involve the intensity of the attitude. As long as the attitude *is* negative, rather than positive, the word "unwelcome" is appropriate, no matter how low the intensity of that negative attitude might be. It is quite possible that, as we follow the regress that my argument presents, the intensity of the negative attitude is diminishing, but the likelihood of the applicability of the word "unwelcome" to describe that attitude is not thereby diminishing, because the meaning of that word is indifferent to intensity. If one attempted to create such a regress with the word "repugnant," the intensity threshold that is built into the meaning of *that* word could prevent the regress from becoming infinite. There is no such threshold to stop the regress with the word "unwelcome."

4. Offensiveness

The argument that I have just presented shows that the word "unwelcome" is incapable of playing any useful role in providing the criterion of demarcation. This, however, does not constitute a complete argument against the present law, because the law, following the EEOC Guidelines, does not treat the unwelcomeness of a sexual advance as a sufficient condition for its being an instance of sexual harassment: the criterion of unwelcomeness is supposed to work together with a number of other criteria.

The relevant part of the Guidelines reads:

> Unwelcome sexual advances, requests for sexual favors, and other verbal or physical conduct of a sexual nature constitute sexual harassment when (1) submission to such conduct is made either explicitly or implicitly a term or condition of an individual's employment, (2) submission to or rejection of

such conduct by an individual is used as the basis for employment decisions affecting such individual, or (3) such conduct has the purpose or effect of unreasonably interfering with an individual's work performance or creating an intimidating, hostile, or offensive working environment.

As can be seen, this formulation has the structure of a complex disjunction. The rate of incidence and the intuitive moral gravity of the behavior described vary considerably from one disjunct to another.

Because of its complexity, one cannot tell, just by glancing at it, whether this formulation is capable of providing the criterion of demarcation. However, for my purposes, it might not be necessary to examine all elements of the formulation. In order to prove that a disjunctively structured criterion of demarcation is defective, it is enough to show that one of its disjuncts "leaks." Showing that there is no workable criterion of demarcation between the conduct covered by *one* disjunct that purports to spell out *a* sufficient condition for sexual harassment and sexual interaction that does not constitute sexual harassment is, therefore, sufficient to prove that the Guidelines, as a whole, do not provide the criterion of demarcation we are looking for.

According to the quoted part of the EEOC Guidelines, a sufficient reason for regarding something as sexual harassment is that it is an instance of

unwelcome sexual advances or other verbal conduct of a sexual nature which has the effect of creating an offensive working environment.

Suppose one wishes to avoid engaging in this kind of conduct. How does one go about that?

Given that we have already seen that the word "unwelcome" is not doing any useful job here, the only thing that remains to be done is to try to predict whether the conduct that one is contemplating will actually have the effect of "creating an offensive working environment" for the person (or persons) in question. Now, again, given that people tend to differ greatly[9] in what they find offensive in sexual matters, this is often very difficult to predict on the basis of the readily available information about the person.[10] The only way to arrive at such a prediction seems to be to ask the person. But to do that is to engage in "sexual advances or other verbal conduct" that may well turn out to contribute to creating "an offensive working environment." So we seem to have the regress again.

However, the argument I used above cannot be transposed here completely. This is because the word "offensive" seems to be, in the relevant respect, more similar to the word "repugnant" than to "unwelcome." It is quite possible to make inquiries as to whether X is offensive in a way that will not be offensive even to those who find X itself offensive. For example, the question "Do you find it offensive if someone tells sexual jokes in your presence?" (asked in a serious tone of voice) is unlikely to be offensive even to those who find actual sexual jokes offensive.

Such cautious inquiries may indeed stop the infinite regress, but they give rise to another problem. They purchase their relative inoffensiveness at the price of imprecision. If I put to someone the above question about sexual jokes, that person may well answer "no," having in mind some mildly off-color jokes, and then nevertheless feel offended by a particularly gross joke that I proceed to tell. If the person is more thoughtful, the answer may end up being true but unhelpful: "it all depends on the joke." In order to get the information one needs, one has to make one's inquiry more specific. But the more specific, precise, or unambiguous such an inquiry is, the more similar to its subject matter it becomes. This similarity entails increased likelihood of offensiveness. If one makes the inquiry about jokes more specific by asking, "Do you find it offensive if, in your presence, people tell sexual jokes that contain the following features: . . . ?," one reduces the probability of misunderstanding, but also creates the risk that the listing of the features of sexual jokes that one has in mind will itself be offensive to one's interlocutor. An increase in the precision of such inquiries thus goes together with an increase in the likelihood of their being offensive. The limiting case would be to ask something like, "Do you find it offensive if, in your presence, people tell jokes like this one: '. . .'?," which is bound to trigger the same reaction as if the joke had been straightforwardly told.

If one is to be reasonably certain that one's preliminary inquiry, as to whether one's contemplated course of behavior would be offensive, will not itself be offensive, one has to formulate it in vague general terms, which means that it becomes unlikely to accomplish its purpose. If one is to ensure that it does accomplish its purpose, one has to make it specific, unambiguous, precise, but in sexual matters such a specific, unambiguous, precise inquiry is almost as likely to cause offense as the behavior that it is about. Because of this dilemma, compliance with the requirement presented by the EEOC Guidelines is *impossible*, except by abstaining from *all* sexual advances and other verbal conduct of a sexual nature.

5. Pervasiveness

There is, however, an important objection that can be raised against my argument. The Supreme Court has held that sexual harassment of the kind I have been considering is actionable only if it is "sufficiently *severe or pervasive* 'to alter the conditions of [the victim's] employment and create an abusive working environment'."[11] This means that (except for *severe* incidents) a single act is not sufficient to give rise to liability: viable action has to be based on "incidents, comments, or conduct that occurred with some frequency."[12] Someone may try to argue that, when the requirement of pervasiveness is taken into account, the law about sexual harassment turns out to be much less absurd than my argument has made it appear.

In order to see why the requirement of pervasiveness does not detract from the argument I have presented, we need to remind ourselves of the fact that the mechanism by means of which the harassment law is intended to prevent harassment has two stages. With certain exceptions, the law does *not* directly require individual potential harassers to abstain from harassment. Rather, the law requires *employers* to *see to it* that there is no harassment in their businesses. Employers normally comply with that requirement by enacting and enforcing internal regulations that require individual potential harassers to abstain from harassment.

Now, the threshold of pervasiveness belongs to the first stage: it is a condition of employers' legal liability. If A's harassment of B crosses the threshold of pervasiveness, then their employer becomes legally liable for having allowed this to happen. This means that the employer cannot afford to wait until the threshold is crossed. In order to avoid liability, the employer has to have in place mechanisms that will make it possible to interfere with A's conduct *before* it gets to the threshold. The regulations of the employer's business therefore have to make internally actionable any conduct that *contributes* to creating an offensive working environment, even if that conduct is, on its own, neither severe nor pervasive.

That the employer has to prohibit its individual employees from engaging in any such acts becomes particularly vivid in the light of the Fifth Circuit decision in *Waltman v. International Paper Co.*[13] According to that decision it is not necessary that the threshold be crossed by the cumulative effect of the acts of one harasser or a group of harassers acting in concert. The threshold may, instead, be crossed by the cumulative effect on one person of the acts of different harassers who are acting independently of each other. Thus, if A_1 performs one and only one act that is offensive to B, and A_2 then independently performs another, but again only one, act that is offensive to B, and $A_3 \ldots A_n$ each independently performs one act offensive to B, the threshold may be crossed and the employer liable. Given that A_1, A_2, . . . , A_n are *ex hypothesi* acting independently of each other, the employer can prevent this from occurring only if each individual act of $A_1, A_2, \ldots, A_n$ is prohibited by its regulations.

From the viewpoint of individual potential harassers, the operation of sexual harassment law therefore, in spite of the severe-or-pervasive test, amounts to a prohibition of *all* offensive acts of a sexual nature. This prohibition is subject to my argument according to which it, in turn, amounts to a prohibition of all conduct of a sexual nature.

6. Reasonableness

Up to this point, I have been treating the criterion of demarcation set out in the EEOC Guidelines as a *subjective* standard, which is what it, on its face, appears to be. Courts, however, often make the standard partially objective by introducing into their deliberations the perspective of a *reasonable person*[14] or, more recently, of a *reasonable woman*.[15]

The presence of the notion of reasonableness in the case law on sexual harassment, however, does not significantly affect the arguments of the preceding sections. Central to these arguments was the simple observation that people differ greatly in what they find unwelcome and offensive in sexual matters. That observation remains true even if one restricts one's attention to reasonable people. For most examples of conduct of a sexual nature, one can find some reasonable people who would find it unwelcome and offensive, *and* other reasonable people who would not. Some reasonable people find deeply offensive the same sexual jokes that other, equally reasonable, people find highly entertaining. Some reasonable people would be offended by the same sexual advances that other reasonable people would be happy to receive.

The same is true if one focuses on reasonable women. The kinds of sexual advances that offend some reasonable women make other women, who satisfy all the usual criteria of reasonableness, happy. Some reasonable women find offensive the same sexual jokes that other reasonable women find entertaining. The question as to whether a reasonable woman would be offended by such-and-such sexual joke is thus analogous to the question whether a reasonable woman would like anchovies on her pizza. The only answer that can be given to such questions is: "Some reasonable women would, some would not."

Because of such huge differences among reasonable people, and among reasonable women, when it comes to sexuality, invoking the notion of reasonableness is of no help in solving the demarcation problem.

7. Deliberate Insults vs. *Bona Fide* Sexual Advances

What the preceding sections show is that the sexual harassment law is incapable of providing a workable criterion of demarcation between sexual harassment and other forms of sexual interaction, without leaving the latter class empty or almost empty. The prohibition of sexual harassment thus amounts to a prohibition of all sexual interaction between people who work together. The argument was not that the law makes the demarcation at the wrong place, or that it makes a demarcation that is fuzzy, but rather that it makes no real demarcation at all.

The root of the demarcation problem is that defining sexual harassment in terms of the unwelcomeness and offensiveness of the conduct to its recipient jumbles together two very different kinds of conduct: deliberate insults of a sexual nature and *bona fide* sexual advances that happen to end up offending their recipients.

The aim of a deliberate insult of a sexual nature is to give some kind of satisfaction to the person who is making it *at the expense* of the person insulted. In other words, its aim is to increase the well-being of the person making it by decreasing the well-being of the person subjected to it. And not only are deliberate insults intended to produce the decrease in the well-being of the persons to whom they are directed, but they almost always do in fact produce it.

A *bona fide* sexual advance is, on the other hand, aimed at increasing the well-being of the person making it without decreasing the well-being of the person to whom it is directed. In making a sexual advance, one normally hopes that it will lead to interaction that will be satisfying not only to oneself but also to the other person. In technical terminology, this important difference between sexual advances and deliberate insults can be expressed by saying that *bona fide* sexual advances are aimed at producing a Pareto improvement (at least so far as the people directly involved are concerned), while deliberate insults most definitely are not.

Needless to say, sexual advances do not always produce the hoped-for Pareto improvements. All too often a sexual advance ends up being directed to a person who is in fact disinclined, sometimes quite strongly disinclined, to pursue sexual interaction of the kind that is being proposed, with the person who is proposing it. Instead of leading to a mutually fulfilling experience, a sexual advance may thus result in making the person to whom it is directed feel offended, humiliated, annoyed, uncomfortable, or otherwise displeased. This *is* a serious problem for everyone concerned, but it is a problem that is rather different from the problem posed by deliberate insults of a sexual nature.

Moreover, although sexual advances do not always produce the results that those who make them hope for, it is important not to forget that they sometimes do. Sometimes, sexual advances do lead to mutually fulfilling sexual interaction that brings a great deal of happiness to those involved. The kind of fulfillment and happiness that mutually satisfying sexual relationships bring cannot be achieved except by someone making some steps toward its being achieved—steps that can always be characterized as sexual advances. In other words, sexual advances sometimes do lead to Pareto improvements, and the Pareto improvements to which they lead cannot be realized without sexual advances being made. This makes sexual advances very different from deliberate insults of a sexual nature, which practically never lead to any Pareto improvements. Indeed, deliberate insults of a sexual nature typically lead to a net decrease in total well-being, because the decrease in the well-being of the person insulted is typically greater than the increase in the well-being of the person making the insult. This difference is supremely relevant to determining how the problems caused by these kinds of conduct should be dealt with, and yet it often ends up being swept under the carpet in discussions of sexual harassment.

In the literature on sexual harassment one frequently finds the idea that "sexual harassment has always been primarily about power, only rarely about sex, and never about romance."[16] As one writer has elaborated it:

> Sexual harassment has nothing whatsoever to do with libido and lust. It has everything to do with exploiting, objectifying, and dominating women. It is a manifestation of the extreme loathing so many men bear toward women.[17]

These claims are fairly plausible as an analysis of what goes on in deliberate insults of a sexual nature, but it is difficult to see how the claim that sexual harassment is about power and not sex is supposed to apply to *bona fide* sexual advances that turned out to have bad effects on the person receiving them. Consider, for example, the case of Sterling Gray writing a note to co-worker Kerry Ellison, in which he said

> I cried over you last night and I'm totally drained today. . . . Thank you for talking with me. I could not stand to feel your hatred for another day.[18]

This note did make Ms. Ellison "shocked and frightened"[19] and a federal court of appeals held that writing such notes may constitute sexual harassment. But to say that in writing these words Mr. Gray was somehow asserting his power over Ms. Ellison stretches the meaning of the word "power" beyond recognition. It is also difficult to see how this note could be interpreted as an expression of Mr. Gray's "extreme loathing" either toward women in general or toward Ms. Ellison in particular.

Many of those who write about sexual harassment proceed as if the whole problem posed by the conduct that is currently so classified amounted to a straightforward clash of interests. They seem to assume that on one side is the interest that harassers have in pursuing harassment, and that on the other side is the interest that the potential victims have in not being subjected to harassment. On that assumption, if harassment takes place, it is the interests of the harassers that are satisfied; if it does not take place, it is the interests of those who otherwise would have been its victims that are satisfied. To those who view sexual harassment in that way it appears that the main issue we are facing in deciding what kinds of laws we should have about it is whether we should have the laws that support the interests of harassers in harassing, or the laws that support the interests of potential victims in not being harassed. Once that is taken to be the main issue, the answer seems obvious: of course we should support the interests of potential victims and not of the harassers. This way of framing the issue leads those who accept it to advocate the laws that will restrict behavior classified as sexual harassment as much as possible.

This model fits well the harassment that consists in deliberate insults of a sexual nature. The problem posed by such insults can be treated as amounting to the clash between the interest that those who are inclined to make such insults have in the satisfaction that they get out of making them and the interest that the potential victims have in not being insulted.

The reliance on this model, however, seriously distorts the problem posed by *bona fide* sexual advances that, contrary to what those who are making them are hoping for, turn out to be offensive to those to whom they are directed. That problem does not amount to such a straightforward clash of interests. To be sure, those who may be subjected to such advances do have an interest in not being subjected to them. But those who make the advances that turn out to be offensive do not have any interest in making *them*. What they want is to make advances that will be accepted, not advances that will be offensive. The outcome of a *bona fide* advance that turned out to be offensive is not only against the interests of the recipient of the advance, but also against the interests of the maker of the advance. The advances that turn out to be offensive are usually a source of at least some embarrassment to those who make them. Moreover, such advances are undesirable even from the viewpoint of those advance-makers who are sufficiently thick-skinned not to suffer such embarrassment, because they constitute a waste of their time and energy. Given that what happens in such advances is against the interests of both parties, the problem posed by it cannot be regarded as a matter of straightforward clash between the interests of the two parties involved.

If the outcomes of such advances are against the interests of those who make them, why do they make them? The answer is that, in making them, they are driven by the interest that they have in making successful advances, advances that will be accepted and lead to some kind of fulfillment and happiness. It is in the nature of the kind of cases we are looking at that the makers of offensive advances, at the moment when they are making them, do not know that they are making unsuccessful advances; they are hoping that their advances will turn out to be successful. And when a sexual advance is successful, that is, when it leads to a fulfilling sexual relationship, its outcome is not only in the interests of the maker of the advance, but also in the interests of its recipient.

We thus have, on one side, offensive sexual advances, which are against the interests of both parties and, on the other side, successful sexual advances, leading to mutually satisfying sexual relationships, which are in the interests of both parties. When these two kinds of cases are considered separately, in neither of them do we have any clash of interests. The problem that we have here does not arise out of anything that could be seen by considering the two kinds of cases separately, but out of the fact that the two kinds of cases are inextricably bound together. What binds them together is the ignorance of the makers of advances as to whether their advances are going to turn out to be successful or unwelcome, offensive, and so forth. Successful advances and offensive advances do not result from decisions of different kinds; they both result from decisions of one and the same kind, namely the decisions to make sexual advances, of which one hopes that they will turn out to be successful, but which may turn out to be offensive. Because both kinds of advances result from decisions of the same kind, it is impossible to have laws, or rules of any other sort, that would regulate successful and offensive advances separately. Any rule that by its wording purports to be about advances of only one of the two kinds will still, inevitably, end up regulating the other kind as well.

Even if we focus only on the potential makers and recipients of sexual advances and set aside any interests of third parties, we need to take into account at least four sets of interests in order to understand the workings of any rule that tries to regulate such advances. These four sets of interests are:

(1)   the interests of potential makers of sexual advances in making advances that will lead to mutually satisfying sexual relationships;

(2)   the interests of potential makers of sexual advances in not making advances that will turn out to be unwelcome, offensive, and so forth, to their recipients;

(3)   the interests of potential recipients of sexual advances in receiving advances that will lead to mutually satisfying sexual relationships; and

(4)   the interests of potential recipients of sexual advances in not receiving advances that will be unwelcome, offensive, and so forth, to them.

Makers of *bona fide* sexual advances have interests of both the first and the second kind. Those who have interests of the third kind normally also have interests of the fourth kind. Given that one and the same person is often both a potential maker and potential recipient of sexual advances, it is often the case that one and the same person has interests of all four kinds.

There are also quite a few people who are not, at a given moment, interested in establishing any new sexual relationships, and who thus have interests of the fourth kind without having interests of any of the other three kinds. But although an individual may have interests of the fourth kind only, at a typical contemporary work place the interests of all four kinds are likely to be represented in some way.

Much of the literature about sexual harassment is written as if the interests of the fourth kind were somehow decisive, as if they were obviously more worthy of legal protection than the interests of the other kinds. This bias is probably a result of the distorting influence of trying to deal with *bona fide* sexual advances that went wrong by using the same model that is used for dealing with deliberate insults of a sexual nature. It needs to be emphasized that this bias in favor of the interests of the fourth kind is unfair not only to the makers of sexual advances, but also to all the potential recipients of sexual advances who have interests of the third kind. Unless one believes that sexual relationships are somehow intrinsically suspect, it is not clear why the interests of the fourth kind should be more important than the interests of the third kind.

The absurdity of treating the interests of the fourth kind as decisive becomes even more obvious if we compare sexual advances to other activities that involve a similar pattern of interests. For example, although we do think that the interests of potential victims of traffic accidents deserve legal protection, we do not think that they are the only interests relevant to our deciding what kind of legal rules to have about motor traffic. If we thought that these interests were decisive, we would have to prohibit completely motor traffic, because that is the only way to ensure that no one will ever suffer a traffic accident. The reason why no one would support such a prohibition is that motor traffic is something that brings considerable benefits to both motorists and non-motorists. In determining what kind of legal regime to have about motor traffic we take into account both the interests that people have in not being victims of accidents and the interests that they (both motorists and non-motorists) have in the benefits that the existence of motor traffic brings (together with other interests they may have in its being cheap, quick, and readily available).

8. How We Might Try to Solve the Demarcation Problem

In determining what kind of legal rules should govern a particular kind of activity, we normally take into account both the interests that people have in the benefits that the activity brings when it goes well and the interests they have in avoiding the consequences that appear when it does not. We base our decisions on comparing the expected social utility of a practice (the magnitude of the benefits multiplied by the probability of their occurrence) with the expected social disutility or the expected social cost (the magnitude of the harms multiplied by the probability of their occurrence). We are thus not tempted to prohibit all motor traffic, since it is far more probable that an individual car trip will be successful than that it will result in an accident. But we do prohibit particular kinds of driving that significantly increase the probability of accidents, such as driving at very high speeds or under the influence of alcohol.

What rules about sexual harassment would emerge if we took into account all the relevant interests, the same way we do in all other areas of life? One thing that we immediately notice is that, in most everyday circumstances, the probability that a given sexual advance someone is considering making will be unsuccessful is quite high, far higher than, say, the probability that a given car trip will end in an accident. However, we need to also take into account the fact that, although the probability of a given advance being successful might not be all that high, the magnitude of the benefit that is achieved when it is successful is high indeed. For most people, successful personal relationships that have a sexual component are a source of more intense happiness and sense of fulfillment than anything else.

In comparison with the benefits that result from successful sexual advances, the harms that result from unsuccessful, unwelcome, sexual advances are usually minor. Having to turn down a sexual advance is annoying, but in most cases it is not anything more than mildly annoying. Much of the literature on sexual harassment emphasizes that unwelcome sexual advances sometimes cause very serious harm to their recipients. That this is so is undoubtedly true, and that is a fact that needs to be taken into account in any deliberations as to what kind of rules there should be about sexual harassment. The literature, however, tends to obscure the fact that it is only *sometimes* that unwelcome sexual advances cause such serious harm and that receiving an unwanted sexual advance and turning it down is usually not a deeply traumatic experience.

When we apply to these facts the patterns of reasoning that we use in other areas of life, we are forced to conclude that sexual advances are often worthwhile and ought to be legally permitted. The fact that the magnitude of the benefits (to both parties taken together) of a successful sexual advance is typically much greater than the magnitude of the harms (to both parties taken together) of an unsuccessful sexual advance entails that sexual advances are typically worthwhile, even when they are not particularly likely to be successful. For example, in most situations it is quite plausible to say that, taking into account the interests of both parties, a sexual advance that has only 10 percent probability of being successful is still worthwhile, because the benefits that will obtain if it is successful are more than ten times greater than the harms that will result if it is unsuccessful.

This pattern of reasoning also enables us, at least in principle, to isolate the kinds of sexual advances that are not worthwhile. A crude sexual advance may still have some probability of being successful and bringing happiness to the people concerned but, in assessing whether it is worthwhile, we need to also take into account that it has considerable probability of causing serious harm (and not just mere annoyance). For at least some crude or aggressive advances we will have to conclude that the magnitude of the harm, multiplied by its probability, is so great that the advances in question are not worthwhile, and that it may be desirable to have rules that prohibit them.

Moreover, in determining whether sexual advances of a particular kind would be worthwhile we need to compare the making of such advances not only with not making any advances, but also with making other kinds of advances that can be made under the circumstances. Suppose, for example, that under certain circumstances one kind of a sexual advance has 10 percent probability of being successful, 88 percent probability of being unsuccessful and causing mild annoyance, and 2 percent probability of causing serious offense. Considered on its own, such an advance may well seem worthwhile. Suppose, however, that there is a different kind of advance that one can make under these circumstances that also has 10 percent chance of being successful, but only 1 percent probability of causing serious offense (and 89 percent probability of causing mild annoyance), and that is not any more burdensome to make than the first kind. Surely, if we knew all that, we would want to encourage people to make advances of the latter kind: the risk of harm is decreased without anything else being affected. Or suppose that there is a third kind of advance that can be made under the same circumstances, one that would increase the probability of success from 10 percent to 11 percent, but that would at the same time increase the probability of offense to 20 percent. In that case the relevant question to ask would not be whether the 11 percent probability of success outweighs the 20 percent probability of offense (together with 69 percent probability of mild annoyance), but rather whether the *additional* 1 percent probability of success justifies the *additional* 19 percent probability of offense. If the answer to that question is "no," as it may well be (that depends on the precise intensity of the offense), then we may want to discourage people from making advances of this third type and encourage them to make the advances that are less risky instead. This is exactly analogous to the reasoning that leads us to impose speed limits on motor traffic. We ask ourselves whether any extra benefits that would be gained by people driving at a high rather than moderate speed are worth the extra risk of accidents; if it turns out they are not, we impose the speed limit that prohibits driving at high speed.

The pattern of reasoning about sexual advances that has just been sketched is also analogous to the reasoning expressed, within the context of torts, in the celebrated Learned Hand's formula. According to that formula, the duty that the law of torts imposes on a potential tortfeasor is the duty to undertake every precaution against causing injuries that satisfies the condition that the burden of undertaking it is less than the gravity of the injury that is at stake, multiplied by the probability of its occurrence[20] (or, more precisely, by the reduction in the probability that would be achieved by the precautions). There is, according to the formula, no duty to undertake any precautions that would be more burdensome than that. Those who omit to undertake the precautions required by the formula are liable for any damages that do occur, but those who have undertaken such precautions have secured themselves against liability.

Making a crude, aggressive, sexual advance, which is fairly likely to offend, when a more polite, less likely to offend, advance could have been made, is analogous to omitting to take precautions that could have been made. Just as Learned Hand's formula imposes on potential tortfeasors the duty to take precautions that are not excessively burdensome, the way of thinking about sexual advances that has been sketched above would lead to the duty to opt for polite rather than crude sexual advances whenever doing so is not excessively burdensome. The burden may, in the case of sexual advances, include the reduction of the probability of success, and whether it is excessive would depend, as in Learned Hand's formula, on whether it exceeds the magnitude of the harm multiplied by the reduction in the probability of its occurrence that would result from opting for the polite advance. Just like Learned Hand's formula, this way of thinking would, however, not lead to any duty regarding sexual advances that would be too burdensome. It would not, for example, lead to the duty to abstain from sexual advances altogether simply because people might be offended by them, which is what the present law about sexual harassment amounts to.

A rule that would say that sexual advances are prohibited if they are not worthwhile in the sense that has been explained above, and that they are permitted if they are, would thus be a considerable improvement over the rules embodied in the present law about sexual harassment. Saying that *bona fide* sexual advances that are not worthwhile in that sense constitute sexual harassment (together with *quid pro quo* harassment, deliberate insults of a sexual nature and similar acts), but that worthwhile sexual advances do not, fits fairly well the ordinary meaning of the word "harassment": a body of law that would be centered around such a rule could thus be quite naturally called the law about sexual harassment, in spite of being rather different from the present sexual harassment law.

Such a rule would, unlike the present sexual harassment law, remain neutral among the four kinds of interests that are at stake in sexual advances: it would take them all into account, without treating some of them as more worthy of protection than others. Such neutrality among specific interests that are at stake is precisely what we generally expect from the legal system.

Notes

1. This paper is *worded* as a paper about sexual harassment in the work place, but its argument *mutatis mutandis* applies to sexual harassment in higher education as well.

2. Billie Wright Dziech and Linda Weiner, *The Lecherous Professor: Sexual Harassment on Campus* (Boston: Beacon Press, 1984), 25.

3. *Ibid.*, italics added.

4. Throughout this paper, the phrase "sexual interaction" should be understood as an abbreviation for "sexual interaction between people who work together."

5. Lin Farley, *Sexual Shakedown: The Sexual Harassment of Women on the Job* (New York: Warner Books, 1978), 188.

6. " 'Voluntariness' in the sense of consent is not a defense to such a claim" (*Meritor Savings Bank v. Vinson*, 477 U.S. 57, 69 [1986]).

7. *Meritor Savings Bank v. Vinson*, 477 U.S. 57, 68 (1986).

8. The above reasoning is of course concerned with inquiries as to whether *X* would be (un)welcome only *as such:* an inquiry that is unwelcome as such may well turn out to be welcome because of some special circumstances.

9. Notice that the only thing that the language of the quoted part of the Guidelines makes relevant is whether the conduct *actually* has the required kind of effect on the *plaintiff;* it is irrelevant that it might have different effects on others. Cf. *Morgan v. Hertz Corp.,* 542 F. Supp. 123, 128 (1981), where the court noted that some of the women at Hertz who were exposed to the same conduct as the plaintiffs "did not mind, or even participated in the comments and remarks," but dismissed that as irrelevant.

10. For example, married people who have strict views about adultery may be offended by *any* sexual advance directed at them, no matter how it is formulated, because they regard it as implying that they are immoral, while some married people are longing for affairs. Yet, the two may be indistinguishable in terms of the general information that is likely to be available to those who work with them.

11. *Meritor Savings Bank v. Vinson*, 477 U.S. 57, 67 (1986), italics added, quoting *Henson v. City of Dundee*, 682 F.2d 897, 904 (1982).

12. *Rabidue v. Osceola Refining Co.*, 805 F.2d 611, 620 (1986).

13. 875 F.2d 468 (1989).

14. "To accord appropriate protection to both plaintiffs and defendants in a hostile and/or abusive work environment sexual harassment case, the trier of fact, when judging the totality of the circumstances impacting upon the asserted abusive and hostile environment placed in issue by the plaintiff's charges, must adopt the perspective of a reasonable person's reaction to a similar environment under essentially like or similar circumstances" (*Rabidue v. Osceola Refining Co.*, 805 F.2d 611, 620 [1986]).

15. The case of *Ellison v. Brady* (924 F.2d 872 [1991]) has achieved notoriety for having "introduced" the reasonable woman standard, although it can be found in the somewhat earlier case *Andrews v. City of Philadelphia*, 895 F.2d 1469, 1482–1483 (1990).

16. Louise F. Fitzgerald, "Science v. Myth: The Failure of Reason in the Clarence Thomas Hearings," *Southern California Law Review* 65 (1992): 1399–1410, at 1399.

17. Kerry Segrave, *The Sexual Harassment of Women in the Workplace, 1600 to 1993* (Jefferson, N.C.: McFarland, 1993), 2.

18. *Ellison v. Brady,* 924 F.2d 872, 874 (1991).

19. *Ibid.*

20. *United States v. Carroll Towing Co.*, 159 F.2d 169, 173 (1947).

Chapter 20

HOW BAD IS RAPE?

H. E. Baber

Rape is bad. This is uncontroversial.[1] It is one of the many wrongs committed against women. But *how* bad is rape, more particularly, how bad is it vis-à-vis other gender-based offenses? I shall argue that while rape is very bad indeed, the work that most women employed outside the home are compelled to do is more seriously harmful insofar as doing such work damages the most fundamental interests of the victim, what Joel Feinberg calls "welfare interests," whereas rape typically does not.[2]

It may be suggested that the very question of which of these evils is the more serious is misconceived insofar as the harms they induce are so different in character as to be incommensurable. Nevertheless, for practical purposes we are often obliged to weigh interests in diverse goods against one another and to compare harms which are very different in nature. Feinberg's account of how we may assess the relative seriousness of various harms, in *Harm to Others* and elsewhere, provides a rational basis for such comparisons and for my consideration of the relative seriousness of rape and work. In addition, my comparison of these harms brings to light a lacuna in Feinberg's discussion which I propose to fill by providing an account of the way in which the duration of a harmed state contributes to its seriousness.

Reprinted from *Hypatia* 2:2 (1987), pp. 125–38, with the permission of H. E. Baber. © 1987, H. E. Baber.

H. E. Baber

Why Rape Is Bad

Rape is bad because it constitutes a serious harm to the victim. To harm a person is to thwart, set back or otherwise interfere with his interests. Understood in this sense, "harm" is not synonymous with "hurt." We typically have an interest in avoiding chronic, distracting physical pain and psychic anguish insofar as we require a certain degree of physical and emotional well-being to pursue our projects, hence hurts are often harmful (e.g., root canal work). Arguably, there are also harms which are not hurtful. Our interests extend to states of affairs beyond immediate experience. I have an interest, for example, in my reputation so that if I am slandered I am harmed even if I am altogether unaware of what is being said about me. Names can never hurt me but they can, even without my knowledge, harm me insofar as I have an interest in others' thinking well of me. Harms are thus to be understood in terms of the interests or stakes that persons have in states of affairs.

Virtually everyone has an interest in avoiding involuntary contact with others, particularly unwanted contacts which are intimate or invasive. Being raped violates this interest, hence, quite apart from any further consequences it may have for the victim or for others, it constitutes a harm. In addition, people have an interest in not being used as mere means for the benefit of others, an interest which is violated by rape. Finally, all persons can be presumed to have an interest in going about their business free of restriction and interference. Rape, like other crimes of violence, thwarts this interest. Since rape sets back some of the victim's most important interests, the victim of rape is in a harmed condition.

Furthermore, the condition of being raped is a *harmful* condition as well as a *harmed* condition insofar as it has a tendency to generate further harms—anxiety, feelings of degradation and other psychological states which may interfere with the victim's pursuit of other projects. In these respects rape is no different from other violent crimes. The victim of assault or robbery is violated and this in and of itself constitutes a harm. In addition, being assaulted or robbed is harmful insofar as victims of assault and robbery tend to suffer from fears and psychological traumas as a result of their experience which may interfere with their pursuit of other projects.

Now there is a tendency to exaggerate the *harmfulness* of rape, that is, to make much of the incapacitating psychological traumas that some victims suffer as a result of being raped. One motive for such claims is the recognition that the harm of rape *per se* is often underestimated and hence that, in some quarters, rape is not taken as seriously as it ought to be taken. Rape has not been treated in the same way as other crimes of violence. A person, whether male or female, who is mugged is not asked to produce witnesses, to provide evidence of his good character or display bodily injuries as evidence of his unwillingness to surrender his wallet to his assailant. In the past, however, the burden of proof has been placed wrongfully on the victims of rape to show their respectability and their unwillingness, the assumption being that (heterosexual) rape is merely a sexual act rather than an act of violence and that sex acts can be presumed to be desired by the participants unless there is strong evidence to the contrary. This is not so. Writers who stress the traumas rape victims suffer cite the deleterious consequences of rape in response to such assumptions.

It is, however, quite unnecessary to exaggerate the harmfulness of rape to explain its seriousness. Women are not merely sexual resources whose wants and interests can be ignored—and women do not secretly want to be raped. Like men, women have an important interest in not being used or interfered with, hence being raped is a harm. Even if it did not hurt the victim physically or psychologically or tend to bring about any *further* harms it would still be a harm in and of itself. A person who is assaulted or robbed does not need to produce evidence of the psychological trauma he suffers as a consequence in order to persuade others that he has been harmed. We recognize that, quite apart from the consequences, the act of assault or robbery is itself a harm. The same should be true of rape. If we recognize rape for what it is, a violent crime against the person, we shall not take past sexual activity as evidence that the victim has not "really" been raped any more than we should take a history of habitual charitable contributions as evidence that the victim of mugging has not "really" been robbed, neither shall we feel compelled to stress the psychological consequences of rape to persuade ourselves that rape is in and of itself a harm.

If this is made clear, there is no compelling reason to harp on the suffering of rape victims. Furthermore, arguably, on balance, it may be undesirable to do so. First, making much of the traumas rape victims allegedly suffer tends to reinforce the pervasive sexist assumption that women are cowards who break under stress and are incapable of dealing with physical danger or violence. Secondly, it would seem that conceiving of such traumas as normal, expected consequences of rape does a disservice to victims who might otherwise be considerably less traumatized by their experiences.

The Relative Seriousness of Harms

Everyone agrees that rape is bad. The disagreement is over how bad. This raises a more general question, namely that of ranking harms with regard to their relative seriousness.

Given our understanding of harm as the thwarting of a being's interests and our assumption that a person's interests extend beyond immediate experience, it will not do to rank harms strictly according to the amount of disutility they generate for the victim or the extent to which they decrease his utility. A person is harmed when his interests are impeded regardless of whether he suffers as a consequence. Persons have an interest in liberty, for example, and are harmed when deprived of liberty even if they do not *feel* frustrated as a consequence. The advice of stoics has a hollow ring; projects for "adjusting" people to severely restrictive conditions strike most of us as unacceptable precisely because we recognize that even if self-cultivation or conditioning can prevent us from being hurt or feeling frustrated by the thwarting of our most fundamental interests, such practices cannot prevent us from being harmed.

Intuitively, the seriousness of a harm is determined by the importance of the interest which is violated within the network of the victim's interests.

> Some interests are more important than others in the sense that harm to them is likely to lead to greater damage to the whole economy of personal (or as the case may be, community) interests than harm to the lesser interest will do, just as harm to one's heart or brain will do more damage to one's bodily health than an "equal degree" of harm to less vital organs. Thus, the interest of a standard person in X may be more important than his interest in Y in that it is, in an analogous sense, more "vital" in his whole interest network than is his interest in Y. A person's welfare interests tend to be his most vital ones, and also to be equally vital. (Feinberg, 204–5)

A person's "welfare interests" are those which are typically most vital in a personal system of interests, e.g., interests in minimally decent health and the absence of chronic distracting pain, a tolerable environment, economic sufficiency, emotional stability, the absence of intolerable stress and minimal political liberty—all those things which are required for the "standard person" to pursue any further projects effectively.

> These are interests in conditions that are generalized means to a great variety of possible goals and whose joint realization, in the absence of very special circumstances, is necessary for the achievement of more ultimate aims. . . . When they are blocked or damaged, a person is very seriously harmed indeed, for in that case his more ultimate aspirations are defeated too; whereas setbacks to a higher goal do not to the same degree inflict damage on the whole network of his interests. (Feinberg, 37)

Three points should be noted here. First, we decide which interests are to count as welfare interests by reflecting upon the needs and capacities of the "standard person." Some people indeed are more capable than the standard person—and we have all heard their inspirational stories *ad nauseam.* The standard person, however, cannot be expected to produce saleable paintings with a brush held in his mouth if paralyzed nor can the standard person be expected to overcome grinding poverty and gross discrimination to achieve brilliant success at the very pinnacle of the corporate ladder.

Secondly, welfare interests are interests in having minimally tolerable amounts of good things, just enough to enable their possessor to pursue his ulterior interests. Empirical questions may be raised as to what sort of environment is "tolerable" to the standard person, what degree of political liberty he needs to pursue his goals and how much material security he requires. Nevertheless a person who lives under conditions of extreme political oppression, who ever fears the midnight visit of the secret police, or one who spends most of his time and energy scratching to maintain the minimal material conditions for survival is effectively blocked from pursuing other ends.

Now persons have an interest in having more of goods such as health, money and political liberty than they require for the pursuit of their ulterior interests since such surplus goods are a cushion against unforeseen reverses. In hard times, a middle class family may have to cut its entertainment and clothing budget—a working class family, however, may be reduced to chill penury while the truly poor are forced out onto the street. Nevertheless the interest in having money, health and the like in excess of the tolerable minimum is not itself a *welfare* interest.

Finally it should be noted that "welfare interests, taken together, make a chain that is no stronger than its weakest link." There are few, if any, tradeoffs possible among welfare interests: an excess of one good cannot compensate for the lack of a minimally tolerable level of another. "All the money in the world won't help you if you have a fatal disease, and great physical strength will not compensate for destitution or imprisonment" (Feinberg, 57)—nor, one might add, will fringe benefits, company picnics, impressive titles or even high pay compensate for dull, demeaning work in an all but intolerable environment.

The greatest harms which can come to persons are those which affect their most vital interests. To maim or cripple a person is to do him a great harm insofar as one's interest in physical health is a very vital interest, indeed, a welfare interest. Stealing a sum of money from a rich man is less harmful than stealing the same sum of money from a pauper insofar as depriving a person of his means of survival sets back a welfare interest whereas depleting his excess funds does not.

Now in light of these considerations it should be apparent, first, that rape is a serious harm but, secondly, that it is not among the most serious harms that can befall a person. It is a serious offense because everyone has an interest in liberty construed in the broadest sense not merely as freedom from state regulation but as freedom to go about one's business without interference. Whenever a person's projects are impeded, whether by a public agency or a private individual, he is, to that extent, harmed. Rape interferes with a person's freedom to pursue his own projects and is, to that extent, a harm. It does not, however, render a person altogether incapable of pursuing his ulterior interests. Having a certain minimally tolerable amount of liberty is a welfare interest without which a person cannot pursue any further projects. While rape diminishes one's liberty, it does not diminish it to such an extent that the victim is precluded from pursuing other projects which are in his interest.

No doubt most rape victims, like victims of violent crime generally, are traumatized. Some rape victims indeed may be so severely traumatized that they incur long-term, severe psychological injury and are rendered incapable of pursuing other projects. For the standard person, however, for whom sexuality is a peripheral matter on which relatively little hinges,[3] being raped, though it constitutes a serious assault on the person, does not violate a welfare interest. There is no evidence to suggest that most rape victims are permanently incapacitated by their experiences nor that in the long run their lives are much poorer than they otherwise would have been. Again, this is not to minimize the harm of rape: rape is a grave harm, nevertheless some harms are graver still and, in the long run, more harmful.

Times, Interests, Harms

What can be worse than rape? A number of tragic scenarios come to mind:

(1) A person is killed in the bloom of youth, when he has innumerable projects and plans for the future. Intuitively death is always a bad thing, though it is disputed whether it is a harm, but clearly untimely death is a grave harm insofar as it dooms the victim's interest in pursuing a great many projects.

(2) A person is severely maimed or crippled. The interests of a person who is mentally or physically incapacitated are thwarted as the range of options available to him in his impaired state is severely limited.

(3) A person is destitute, deprived of food, clothing and shelter. Here one thinks of the victims of famine in Africa or street people reduced to sleeping in doorways in our otherwise affluent cities. Persons in such circumstances have not the resources to pursue their ulterior interests.

(4) A person is enslaved. He is treated as a mere tool for the pursuit of his master's projects and deprived of the time and resources to pursue his own.

Each of these misfortunes is worse than rape. And the list could be continued.

Notice that all of the harmed conditions described are not merely painful or traumatic but chronic rather than episodic. They occupy large chunks of persons' histories—or, in the case of untimely death, actually obliterate large segments of their *projected* histories. To this extent such harmed conditions interfere more with the pursuit of other projects which are conducive to persons' well-being than does rape.

Now it is not entirely clear from Feinberg's discussion how the temporal extent of harms figure into calculations of their relative seriousness. Feinberg (45ff.) suggests that transitory hurts, whether physical or mental, do not harm the interests of the standard person, for whom the absence of pain is not a focal aim, whereas chronic, distracting pain and emotional instability set back persons' most vital interests insofar as they preclude them from pursuing their goals and projects.

Nevertheless, intense pain, however transitory, may be all-encompassing and completely distracting for the extent of its duration. It is not entirely clear from Feinberg's discussion, however, why, given his account of interests and harms, we should not be forced to conclude that some transitory hurts are harms not because they violate an interest in not being hurt but because they preclude the victim from pursuing other interests, albeit for a very short time. Indeed, it is not clear why we should not be compelled to regard some very transitory pains, traumas, and inconveniences as set-backs to welfare interests. If we agree that being imprisoned for a number of years impedes a welfare interest insofar as it precludes the prisoner from pursuing his ulterior interests while imprisoned, why should we not say that being locked in the bathroom for twenty minutes is a harm of equal, if not greater magnitude, though of shorter duration? After all, while locked in the bathroom, I am, if anything, in a worse position to pursue my ulterior interests than I should be if I were in prison.

Intuitively, however, the duration of a harmed state figures importantly in assessments of its seriousness. Being locked in the bathroom for twenty minutes is not, we think, a great harm of short duration—it is simply a trivial harm insofar as it makes no significant difference to the victim's total life plan. Being imprisoned for several years, on the contrary, does make an important difference to the victim's biography: all other things being equal it precludes him from realizing a great number of aims that he should otherwise have accomplished. All is not as it was after the prisoner has served his sentence. After his release, the prisoner has much less time to accomplish his ends. A large chunk of his life has been blanked out and most likely his total life history will be poorer for it.

Imprisonment impedes a welfare interest insofar as it deprives the prisoner of the minimal amount of liberty requisite for the pursuit of a great many of his ulterior interests. Furthermore, the deprivation of liberty imposed upon the prisoner, like other harms to welfare interests, cannot be truly compensated by an abundance of other goods. Even the lavish banquets and luxurious accommodations imagined by self-proclaimed advocates of law and order who deplore the "soft treatment" of offenders could not compensate for the restriction of individual liberty imposed upon prisoners. Furthermore, benefits conferred *after* the prisoner's release cannot truly compensate him either. A person who has been falsely imprisoned may be "compensated" after a fashion with a monetary settlement but we all recognize that this does not really set things right: he has, after all, lost that many years off of his life and as a consequence he will *never* achieve a great many things that he would otherwise have achieved.

We might capture our intuitions about the role that the duration of harmed states plays in determining their seriousness in the following way: Typically, people's focal aims are, as it were, timeless. Some people, indeed, may have the ambition to accomplish certain feats at certain times of their lives, e.g., to make a million by age thirty, but in most cases the objects of our desires are not temporally tagged and timing is not, in the strict sense, essential to their realization. I can no longer make-a-million-by-age-thirty though I still can make a million. Of course I would prefer to have the million sooner than later. If, however, my aim is merely to make a million at some time or other I can afford to sit tight. Though the circumstances that prevail at some times may be more conducive to the achievement of my goal than those which prevail at other times, it is not essential to the realization of my ambition that it occur at any special time. My aim is not essentially time-bound.

Because most of persons' focal aims are not time-bound, persons by and large can afford to sit tight. Barring the occasional Man from Porlock, our interests are not seriously set back by transitory pains or other relatively short-lived distractions. A momentary twinge may prevent me from starting to write my paper at 12:05. No matter: I shall start it at 12:06, and the delay is unlikely to have any significant effect on my total opus. My interest is in producing a certain body of work during my lifetime and this interest is sufficiently robust to withstand a good many temporary set-backs. Nevertheless, while most people's interests are relatively robust, insofar as they are not time-bound, they are not impregnable. Long-term or chronic distractions can seriously impede even those interests which are not time-bound. If I suffer from chronic, distracting pain or emotional instability for a number of years I may *never* write my paper or realize many of my other ambitions. Art is long but life, alas, is short.

Now when it comes to assessing the relative seriousness of various harms we consider them with respect to their tendency to interfere with our typically "timeless" aims. The most serious harms are those which interfere with the greatest number of interests for the longest time, those which are most likely to prevent us from ever achieving our goals. The greatest harms, those which damage welfare interests, therefore, bring about harmed states which are chronic rather than episodic.

Working Is Worse Than Being Raped

On this account being obliged to work is, for many people, a very serious harm indeed insofar as work is chronic: it occupies a large part of the worker's waking life for a long time. For the fortunate few, work in and of itself contributes to the worker's well-being. For many workers, however, work provides few satisfactions. For the least fortunate, whose jobs are dull, routine and regimented, work provides no satisfactions whatsoever and the time devoted to work prevents them from pursuing any other projects which might be conducive to their well-being.

As a matter of fact, women figure disproportionately though not exclusively in this group. Discrimination is not only unfair—and this in itself constitutes a harm—it is harmful insofar as many women as a result of discriminatory employment practices are compelled to take very unpleasant, underpaid, dead-end jobs and, as a consequence, to spend a substantial part of their waking lives at tedious, regimented, mind-killing toil. A great many men have equally appalling jobs. I suggest, however, that anyone, whether male or female, who spends a good deal of time at such work is in a more seriously harmed state than one who is raped. Women however have an additional grievance insofar as such jobs fall disproportionately to them as a consequence of unfair employment practices.

A few hours or even a week of typing statistics or operating a switchboard, however unpleasant, may not be seriously harmful. For most women in the workforce, however, such unpleasantness occupies a substantial part of their waking hours for years. Currently most women can look forward to spending the greater part of their adult lives typing, hash-slinging, cashiering or assembling small fiddly mechanisms. To be compelled to do such work is to be harmed in the most serious way. Doing such work impedes a welfare interest: it deprives the worker of the minimal degree of freedom requisite for the pursuit of a number of other interests. As with other such deprivations, the harm done cannot be undone by other benefits. Sexists may suggest that women in such positions gain satisfaction from selfless service to their employers and families and some self-proclaimed feminists may suggest that the satisfaction of financial independence makes up for the drudgery. This is, however, plainly false. The amount of time workers must spend at their jobs deprives them of the freedom necessary to the effective pursuit of their other projects. For this there can be no true compensation.

Rape, like all crimes against the person, is bad in part because it deprives the victim of some degree of freedom; being compelled to work is worse in this regard insofar as it chronically deprives the victim of the minimal amount of freedom requisite to the pursuit of other important interests which are conducive to his well-being.

Work is worse than rape in other respects as well. The pink-collar worker, like the rape victim, is used as a mere means to the ends of others, but arguably, in being used the worker is violated in a more intimate, more detrimental way than the rape victim. Rape is an emotionally charged issue insofar as it has become a symbol of all the ways in which women are violated and exploited, but rape *per se* merely violates the victim's sexual integrity. The work that most women do, however, violates their integrity as intellectual beings. The routine clerical work which falls almost exclusively to women precludes the worker's thinking about other matters: she is fettered intellectually for the greater part of her day. Such work occupies the mind just enough to dominate the worker's inner life but not enough to be of any interest. One does not have to buy questionable Cartesian doctrines about the nature of the self to recognize that persons have a greater stake in their mental and emotional lives than they do in their sexuality. Recognizing this, it seems reasonable to suggest that being "raped" intellectually violates a more vital interest than being raped sexually.

Now there are indeed certain disanalogies between the harms of rape and pink-collar work. First, arguably, persons have a right not to be raped but they do not have a right to avoid unpleasant work. Secondly, while rapists clearly harm their victims it is not so clear that employers, particularly if they have not engaged in unfair hiring practices, harm their employees. Thirdly, it may be suggested that the rape victim is *forced* into a compromising position whereas the pink-collar worker is not. Finally, it will be suggested that the work most women do is not so grim as I have suggested. None of these suggestions, however, seriously damages my case.

First, I have not argued that being compelled to do unpleasant work is a *wrong* but only that it is a *harm,* and a grave one. To be harmed is not necessarily to be wronged, nor do persons have a right absolute not to be harmed in any way. It may be, in some cases, that the advancement of the interests of others outweighs the harm that comes to the victim so that, on balance, the harm to the victim does not constitute an injustice or a wrong. As consumers, all of us, men and women alike, have an interest in retaining women as a source of cheap clerical and service work. It may be that, on balance, this outweighs the interest of women as potential workers in not being exploited—though I doubt it. If this is so, then the exploitation of women in these positions is not a wrong. It is, nevertheless, a harm.

Secondly, on Feinberg's account, natural disasters—and not merely persons who omit to aid victims—cause great harm. More generally, to be in a harmed state is not necessarily to be harmed by some moral agent. To suggest that workers are seriously harmed by the work they do is not to say that their employers are harming them. Indeed, it seems that most supervisors, managers and owners of businesses are rather like carriers of harmful diseases: they are causally responsible for persons' coming to harm, but we should not want to say that they *harm* anyone.

Thirdly, most women in the pink-collar sector are compelled to work: the myth that most women enter the workforce to get out of the house and make pin money has long been exploded. Now intuitions about what constitutes coercion differ radically. Some suggest, for example, that a woman who cannot display bruises or wounds as evidence of a desperate struggle has not really been forced to have sex with her assailant. I, however, go with the commonsensical meaning of coercion, without pretending to know the analysis. On this account a woman with a knife to her throat is forced to engage in sexual intercourse and a woman with no other adequate means of support for herself and her family is forced to work. An exceptional person indeed may pull herself up by the bootstraps; the standard person, however, cannot.

Fourthly, a growing sociological literature on women in the workforce, observation, and personal experience all suggest that the work most women do is every bit as harmful as I have suggested. A "phenomenology" of womenswork is beyond the scope of this paper, and beyond my competence as an analytic philosopher. Even if I should succeed in conveying the dull misery of the working day, the stress at other times, knowing that another day of work is getting closer, and beyond this, the knowledge that there is no way out, it would not be entirely to the point. As Feinberg notes, except for Epicureans, for whom the absence of pain is a focal aim, neither physical pain nor psychic anguish is in and of itself a harm: they are harms only insofar as they impede the agent's interests. It is not the misery of working *per se* but the extent to which most work precludes one's pursuit of other ends which makes work the grave harm that it is. Even if many workers avoid the hurt, all endure the harm insofar as their interests are impeded and their lives are impoverished.

Finally, I recognize that many men are forced to do demeaning, dull, often dangerous work. Again, this is hardly a criticism of my case. I grant that men are harmed in the most serious way by being forced into such drudgery. My suggestion is merely that a person, whether male or female, who spends a good deal of time doing such work is in a more seriously harmed state than one who is raped. Rape is bad, indeed, very bad. But being a keypunch operator is worse.

I recognize that this conclusion will be met with considerable hostility. Beyond the harm that rapists inflict upon their victims, rape is a powerful symbol of the oppression women suffer and thus naturally arouses the wrath and indignation of virtually all women who are aware of their situation. Still, to the vast numbers of single parents who are unable to provide a minimally decent standard of living for their families on the wages paid for "women's work," to all women who do pink-collar work, and to all who recognize that they are in danger of being compelled to take such work—and virtually all of us are in danger—the shift of emphasis by some feminist organizations from activities geared to end sex discrimination in employment to a range of other projects is extremely irritating.

Why Rape Is Considered the Supreme Evil—a Postscript

In light of the fact (which should be apparent to all reasonable people) that spending the better part of one's waking hours over a period of years at boring, regimented work is worse than being the victim of violent crime, one wonders why it is so often assumed that rape is the supreme evil. Two conjectures come to mind.

First, it is generally assumed that women are largely incapable of dealing with danger or physical violence. Since rape is a crime against women primarily, given this assumption, it would follow that most rape victims would be more traumatized than victims of other violent crimes. This is an insult to women: it is incumbent upon us to show that we are as macho as anyone!

Secondly, women are traditionally viewed primarily in connection with concerns which center around their sexuality—in terms of their roles as lovers, wives and mothers. Because women are seen in this way, it is commonly assumed that they have a greater stake in matters concerning sexuality in the broadest sense than do men. So, for example, all issues concerning reproduction are thought of as "women's issues" despite the recognition by all but the most primitive peoples that men play an essential role in the reproductive process. Indeed, it is often assumed that women have more of a stake in sexual matters than they do in any other concerns.

Given these assumptions it would follow that any violation of sexual integrity would be extremely harmful to women. Arguably if rape is considered among the gravest of harms it is largely because women are regarded as beings whose welfare is tied up most intimately with sexual concerns and relationships, persons to whom other matters, such as intellectual stimulation and professional achievement, are relatively peripheral.

Most women take strong exception to being regarded as "sex objects." What is often thought to be objectionable about this role is the suggestion of passivity, the implication that one is an *object* which is used for sexual purposes rather than a *subject* of sexual experience. But there is something even more objectionable about the idea of being a "sex object," namely the suggestion that one is primarily a sexual being, a person whose most important interests are connected to the genital area and the reproductive system and with roles that are tied up with one's sexuality.

I suggest that the primary reason why rape is regarded as one of the most serious harms that can befall a woman is precisely because women are regarded as sex objects, beings who have little of value beyond their sexuality. Further I suggest that women who would regard being raped as the supreme violation and humiliation are implicitly buying into this view.

If these are indeed the reasons why rape is seen as supremely harmful to women, as I suggest they are, then it follows that the suggestion that rape is the worst harm that can befall a woman is a consequence of sexist assumptions about the character and interests of women. Rape, like all other crimes of violence, constitutes a serious harm to the victim. Nevertheless, I have suggested that to consider it the most serious of all harms is no less sexist than to consider it no harm at all.

Notes

1. Everyone agrees that rape is bad. The controversy concerns the criteria for counting an act as an instance of rape in the first place, including the relevance of the victim's prior sexual conduct, and the trustworthiness of victims' testimony. The recent reopening of the Dotson case, for example, represents a threat to feminist gains insofar as it tends to undermine the credibility of victims—not because it suggests that rape is less serious than is commonly supposed.

The core meaning of "rape" is "forcible or fraudulent sexual intercourse especially imposed on women" (*The Little Oxford Dictionary*); but, given the elaborate and confusing rules of sexual etiquette that have traditionally figured in human courtship rituals, it has not always been clear what constituted fraud or coercion in these matters. In particular, it has been assumed that female coyness is simply part of the courtship ritual so that women who acquiesce to the sexual demands of acquaintances under protest are merely playing the game and thus have not in fact been forced into anything. That is to say it is assumed that under such conditions the sexual act is *not an instance of rape at all*, hence that a woman who claims she has been raped in such circumstances is disingenuous and may be assumed to have malicious motives.

It is to these assumptions that women should object—not to my suggestion that rape is a less serious harm than has commonly been thought. What sexists underestimate is not the seriousness of rape but rather the frequency with which it occurs.

2. See especially chapters 1 and 5 in Joel Feinberg, *Harm to Others* (Oxford, Eng.: Oxford Univ. Press, 1984).

3. My argument rests on the assumption that very little hangs on sexuality issues, that persons' focal aims, and hence their interests, have to do primarily with matters which are quite separate and not much affected by sexual activities, whether voluntary or involuntary. In spite of popular acceptance of Freudian doctrines, this does seem to be the case.

In a society where people's most important aims were tied up with sexual activities, things would be different and rape would be even more serious than it is among us. Imagine, for example, a society in which women were excluded entirely from the workforce and marriage was their only economic option so that a woman's sexuality, like the cowboy's horse, was her only means of livelihood; imagine that in this society sexual purity were highly valued (at least for women) and a woman who was known to be "damaged goods" for whatever reason, was as a result rendered unmarriageable and subjected to constant humiliation by her relatives and society at large. In such circumstances rape would indeed violate a welfare interest and would be among the most serious of crimes, rather like horsetheft in the Old West. There are no doubt societies in which this is the case. It is not, however, the case among us.

Again, some people may regard their sexual integrity as so intimately wrapped up with their self-concept that they would be violated in the most profound way if forced to have sexual intercourse against their will. There are no doubt persons for whom this is the case. It is not, however, the case for the standard person.

Admittedly, this is an empirical conjecture. But we do recognize that it is the case for the standard male person, and the assumption that women are different seems to be a manifestation of the sexist assumption that women are primarily sexual beings.

Chapter 21

THE HARMS OF CONSENSUAL SEX

Robin West

A re consensual, non-coercive, non-criminal, and even non-tortious, heterosexual transactions ever harmful to women? I want to argue briefly that many (not all) consensual sexual transactions are, and that accordingly we should open a dialogue about what those harms might be. Then I want to suggest some reasons those harms may be difficult to discern, even by the women sustaining them, and lastly two ways in which the logic of feminist legal theory and practice itself might undermine their recognition.

Let me assume what many women who are or have been heterosexually active surely know to be true from their own experience, and that is that some women occasionally, and many women quite frequently, consent to sex even when they do not desire the sex itself, and accordingly have a good deal of sex that, although consensual, is in no way pleasurable. Why might a woman consent to sex she does not desire? There are, of course, many reasons. A woman might consent to sex she does not want because she or her children are dependent upon her male partner for economic sustenance, and she must accordingly remain in his good graces. A woman might consent to sex she does not want because she rightly fears that if she does not her partner will be put into a foul humor, and she simply decides that tolerating the undesired sex is less burdensome than tolerating the foul humor. A woman might consent to sex

Reprinted, with the permission of Robin West and The American Philosophical Association, from *The American Philosophical Association Newsletters* 94:2 (1995), pp. 52–55.

she does not want because she has been taught and has come to believe that it is her lot in life to do so, and that she has no reasonable expectation of attaining her own pleasure through sex. A woman might consent to sex she does not want because she rightly fears that her refusal to do so will lead to an outburst of violence behavior some time following—only if the violence or overt threat of violence is *very* close to the sexual act will this arguably constitute a rape. A woman may consent to sex she does not desire because she *does* desire a friendly man's protection against the very real threat of non-consensual violence rape by other more dangerous men, and she correctly perceives, or intuits, that to gain the friendly man's protection, she needs to give him, in exchange for that protection, the means to his own sexual pleasure. A woman, particularly a young woman or teenager, may consent to sex she does not want because of peer expectations that she be sexually active, or because she cannot bring herself to hurt her partner's pride, or because she is uncomfortable with the prospect of the argument that might ensue, should she refuse.

These transactions may well be rational—indeed in some sense they all are. The women involved all trade sex for something they value more than they value what they have given up. But that doesn't mean that they are not harmed. Women who engage in unpleasurable, undesired, but consensual sex may sustain real injuries to their sense of selfhood, in at least four distinct ways. First, they may sustain injuries to their capacities for self-assertion: the "psychic connection," so to speak, between pleasure, desire, motivation, and action is weakened or severed. *Acting* on the basis of our own felt pleasures and pains is an important component of forging our own way in the world—of "asserting" our "selves." Consenting to *un*pleasurable sex—acting in spite of displeasure—threatens that means of self-assertion. Second, women who consent to undesired sex many injure their sense of self-*possession*. When we consent to undesired penetration of our physical bodies we have in a quite literal way constituted ourselves as what I have elsewhere called "giving selves"—selves who cannot be violated, because they have been defined as (and define themselves as) being "for others." Our bodies to that extent no longer belong to ourselves. Third, when women consent to undesired and unpleasuarable sex because of their felt or actual dependency upon a partner's affection or economic status, they injure their sense of autonomy: they have thereby neglected to take whatever steps would be requisite to achieving the self-sustenance necessary to their independence. And fourth, to the extent that these unpleasurable and undesired sexual acts are followed by contrary to fact claims that they enjoyed the whole thing—what might be called "hedonic lies"—women who engage in them do considerable damage to their sense of integrity.

These harms—particularly if multiplied over years or indeed over an entire adulthood—may be quite profound, and they certainly may be serious enough to outweigh the momentary or day-to-day benefits garnered by each individual transaction. Most debilitating, though, is their circular, self-reinforcing character: the more thorough the harm—the deeper the injury to self-assertiveness, self-possession, autonomy and integrity—the greater the likelihood that the woman involved will indeed *not* experience these harms as harmful, or as painful. A woman utterly lacking in self-assertiveness, self-possession, a sense of autonomy, or integrity will not experience the activities in which she engages that reinforce or constitute those qualities *as harmful*, because she, to that degree, lacks a self-asserting, self-possessed self who *could* experience those activities as a threat to her selfhood. But the fact that she does not experience these activities as harms certainly does not mean that they are not harmful. Indeed, that they are not felt as harmful is a consequence of the harm they have already caused. This phenomenon, of course, renders the "rationality" of these transactions tremendously and even tragically misleading. Although these women may be making rational calculations in the context of the particular decision facing them, they are, by making those calculations, sustaining deeper and to some degree unfelt harms that undermine the very qualities that constitute the capacity for rationality being exercised.

Let me quickly suggest some reasons that these harms go so frequently unnoticed—or are simply not taken seriously—and then suggest in slightly more detail some ways that feminist legal theory and practice may have undermined their recognition. The first reason is cultural. There is a deep-seated U.S. cultural tendency to equate the legal with the good, or harmless: we are, for better or worse, an anti-moralistic, anti-authoritarian, and anti-communitarian people. When combined with the sexual revolution of the 1960s, this provides a powerful cultural explanation for our tendency to shy away from a sustained critique of the harms of consensual sex. Any suggestion that legal transactions to which individuals freely consent may be harmful, and hence *bad*, will invariably be met with skepticism—*particularly* where those transactions are sexual in nature. This tendency is even further underscored by more contemporary postmodern skeptical responses to claims asserting the pernicious consequences of false consciousness.

Second, at least our legal-academic discourses, and no doubt academic political discourses as well, have been deeply transformed by the "exchange theory of value," according to which, if I exchange A for B voluntarily, then I simply must be better off after the exchange than before, having, after all, agreed to it. If these exchanges *are* the source of value, then it is of course impossible to ground a *value* judgment that some voluntary exchanges are harmful. Although stated baldly this theory of value surely has more critics than believers, it nevertheless in some way perfectly captures the modern zeitgeist. It is certainly, for example, the starting and ending point of normative analysis for many, and perhaps most, law students. Obviously, given an exchange theory of value, the harms caused by consensual sexual transactions simply fade away into definitional oblivion.

Third, the exchange theory of value is underscored, rather than significantly challenged, by the continuing significance of liberal theory and ideology in academic life. To the degree that liberalism still rules the day, we continue to valorize individual choice against virtually anything with which it might seem to be in conflict, from communitarian dialogue to political critique, and continue to perceive these challenges to individual primacy as somehow on a par with threats posed by totalitarian statist regimes.

Fourth, and perhaps most obvious, the considerable harms women sustain from consensual but undesired sex must be downplayed if the considerable pleasure men reap from heterosexual transactions is morally justified—*whatever* the relevant moral theory. Men do have a psycho-sexual stake in insisting that voluntariness alone ought be sufficient to ward off serious moral or political inquiry into the value of consensual sexual transactions.

Let me comment in a bit more detail on a further reason why these harms seem to be underacknowledged, and that has to do with the logic of feminist legal theory, and the efforts of feminist practitioners, in the area of rape law reform. My claim is that the theoretical conceptualizations of sex, rape, force, and violence that underscore both liberal and radical legal feminism undermine the effort to articulate the harms that might be caused by consensual sexuality. I will begin with liberal feminism and then turn to radical feminism.

First, and entirely to their credit, liberal feminist rape law reformers have been on the forefront of efforts to stiffen enforcement of the existing criminal sanction against rape, and to extend that sanction to include non-consensual sex which presently is not cognizable legally as rape but surely should be. This effort is to be applauded, but it has the *almost* inevitable consequence of valorizing, celebrating, or, to use the critical term, "legitimating" consensual sexual transactions. If rape is bad *because* it is non-consensual—which is increasingly the dominant liberal-feminist position on the badness of rape—then it seems to follow that *consensual* sex must be good because it is consensual. But appearances can be misleading, and this one certainly is. That non-consensual transactions—rape, theft, slavery—are bad because non-consensual does *not* imply the value, worth or goodness of their consensual counterparts— sex, property, or work. It only follows that consensual sex, property, or work are not bad in the ways that non-consensual transactions are bad; they surely may be bad for some other reason. We need to explore, in the case of sex (as well as property and work), what those other reasons might be. Non-consensuality does not exhaust the types of harm we inflict on each other in social interactions, nor does consensuality exhaust the list of benefits.

That the liberal-feminist argument for extending the criminal sanction against rape to include non-consensual sex *seems* to imply the positive value of consensual sex is no doubt in part simply a reflection of the powers of the forces enumerated above—the cultural, economic, and liberal valorization of individualism against communal and authoritarian controls. Liberal feminists can obviously not be faulted for that phenomenon. What I want to caution against is simply the ever present temptation to *trade* on those cultural and academic forces in putting forward arguments for reform of rape law. We need not trumpet the glories of consensual sex *in order to* make out a case for strengthening the criminal sanction against coercive sex. Coercion, violence, and the fear under which women live because of the threat of rape are sufficient evils to sustain the case for strengthening and extending the criminal law against those harms. We need not and should not supplement the argument with the unnecessary and unwarranted celebration of consensual sex—which, whatever the harms caused by coercion, does indeed carry its own harms.

Ironically, radical feminist rhetoric—which *is* aimed at highlighting the damage and harm done to women by ordinary, "normal" heterosexual transactions—*also* indirectly burdens the attempt to articulate the harms done to women by consensual heterosexual transactions, although it does so in a very different way. Consider the claim, implicit in a good deal of radical feminist writing, explicit in some, that "all sex is rape," and compare it for a moment with the rhetorical Marxist claim that "all property is theft." Both claims are intended to push the reader or listener to a reexamination of the ordinary, and both do so by blurring the distinction between consent and coercion. Both seem to share the underlying premise that that which is coerced—and perhaps *only* that which is coerced—is bad, or as a strategic matter, is going to be perceived as bad. Both want us to re-examine the value of that which we normally think of as good or at least unproblematic because of its apparent consensuality—heterosexual transactions in the first case, property transactions in the second—and both do so by putting into doubt the reality of that apparent consensuality.

But there is a very real difference in the historical context and hence the practical consequences of these two rhetorical claims. More specifically, there are two pernicious, or at least counter-productive, consequences of the feminist claim which are not shared, at least to the same degree, by the Marxist. First, and as any number of liberal feminists have noted, the radical feminist equation of sex and rape runs the risk of undermining parallel feminist efforts in a way not shared by the Marxist equation of property and theft. Marxists are for the most part not engaged in the project of attempting to extend the existing laws against *theft* so as to embrace non-consensual market transactions that are currently not covered by the laws against larceny and embezzlement. Feminists, however, *are* engaged in a parallel effort to extend the existing laws against rape to include all non-consensual sex, and as a result, the radical feminist equation of rape and sex is indeed undermining. The claim that all sex is in effect non-consensual runs the real risk of "trivializing," or at least confusing, the feminist effort at rape reform so as to include all truly non-consensual sexual transactions.

There is, though, a second cost to the radical feminist rhetorical claim, which I hope these comments have by now made clear. The radical feminist equation of rape and sex, no less than the liberal rape reform movement, gets its rhetorical force by trading on the liberal, normative-economic, and cultural assumptions that whatever is coercive is bad, and whatever is non-coercive is morally non-problematic. It has the effect, then, of further burdening the articulation of harms caused by consensual sex by forcing the characterization of those harms into a sort of "descriptive funnel" of non-consensuality. It requires us to say, in other words, that consensual sex is harmful, if it is, only because or to the extent that it shares in the attributes of non-consensual sex. But this might not be true—the harms caused by consensual sex might be just as important, just as serious, but nevertheless *different* from the harms caused by non-consensual sex. If so, then women are disserved, rather than served, by the equation of rape and sex, even were that equation to have the rhetorical effect its espousers clearly desire.

Liberal feminist rape reform efforts and radical feminist theory both, then, in different ways, undermine the effort to articulate the distinctive harms of consensual sex; the first by indirectly celebrating the value of consensual sex, and the latter by at least rhetorically denying the existence of the category. Both, then, in different ways, underscore the legitimation of consensual sex effectuated by non-feminist cultural and academic forces. My conclusion is simply that feminists could counter these trends in part by focusing attention on the harms caused women by consensual sexuality. Minimally, a thorough-going philosophical treatment of these issues might clear up some of the confusions on both sides of the "rape/sex" divide, and on the many sides of what have now come to be called the intra-feminist "sex wars," which continue to drain so much of our time and energy.

PART 6

PORNOGRAPHY AND PROSTITUTION

Chapter 22

TALK DIRTY TO ME

Sallie Tisdale

Once or twice a month I visit my neighborhood adult store, to rent a movie or buy a magazine. I am often the only woman there, and I never see another woman alone. Some days there may be only a single clerk and a few customers; at other times I see a dozen men or more: heavyset working men, young men, businessmen. In their midst I often feel a little strange, and sometimes scared. To enter I have to pass the flashing lights, the neon sign, the silvered windows, and go through the blank, reflecting door.

It takes a certain pluck simply to enter. I can't visit on days when I am frail or timid. I open the door feeling eyes on me, hearing voices, and the eyes are my mother's eyes, and, worse, my father's. The voices are the voices of my priest, my lover, my friends. They watch the little girl and chide her, a naïf no more.

I don't make eye contact. Neither do the men. I drift from one section of the store to the other, going about my business. I like this particular store because it is large and well-lit; there are no dark corners in which to hide or be surprised. The men give me sidelong glances as I pass by, and then drop their eyes back to the box in their hands. Pornography, at its roots, is about watching; but no one here openly watches. This is a place of librarian silences. As I move from shelf to shelf, male customers gather at the fringes of where I stand. I think they would like to know which movies I will choose.

In the large front room with the clerks are glass counters filled with vibrators, promising unguents, candy bowls filled with condoms. On the
wall behind the counter where you ask for help are giant dildos, rubber
vaginas, rubber faces with slit eyes, all mouth. Here are the more mainstream films, with high production values and name stars. Near the door
are the straight movies, the standard hard core you can find these days
in most urban video-rental stores. Here is the large and growing amateur
section: suburban porn. Here is a small section of straight Japanese
movies, a section of gay male films, and the so-called lesbian films, directed toward the male viewer: *Dildo Party* and *Pussy Licker*.

The first time I came here alone I dressed in baggy jeans and a
pullover sweater, and tied my long hair up in a bun. After a while I was
approached by a fat man with a pale, damp face and thinning hair.

"Excuse me," he said. "I'm not trying to come on to you or anything,
but I can't help noticing you're, you know, female."

I could only nod.

"And I wonder," he continued, almost breathless, "if you like this
stuff"—and he pointed at a nearby picture of a blonde woman in red lingerie. "You see, my girlfriend, she broke up with me, and I'd bought her
all this stuff—you know, sex clothes—and she didn't like it." He paused.
"I mean, it's out in the back of my truck right now. If you just want to
come outside you can have it."

I turned my back in polite refusal, and left before it could grow completely dark outside. He didn't follow; I've never been approached there
again.

Another day, when I asked for my movies by number, I didn't want the
clerk to glance at the titles, and I tried to distract him with a question. I
asked if any women still work here. He was young, effeminate, with a
wispy mustache and loose, shoulder-length hair, and he apologized
when he said no.

"Even though we're all guys now, we try to be real sensitive," he said,
pulling my requests off the shelf without a glance. "If anyone gives you a
hard time, let us know. You let us know right away, and we'll take care of
it." He handed me my choices in a white plastic bag.

"Have a nice day."

Later. I am home, with my movies. I drink a glass of wine, my lover eats
from a silver bowl of popcorn he put beside us on the couch. We are
watching a stylish film with expensive sets and a pulsing soundtrack. The
beautiful actresses wear sunglasses in every scene, and the wordless scenes
shift every few minutes. Now there are two women together; now two
women and an adoring man, a tool of the spike-heeled women. A few
scenes later there is only one woman, blonde, with a luxuriant body. She
reaches one hand slowly down between her legs and pulls a diamond

necklace from between her vaginal lips, jewel by jewel. She slides it up her abdomen, across her breast, to her throat, and into her mouth.

Some of my women friends have never seen or read pornography—by which I mean expressions of explicit sex. That I don't find strange; it's a world of women which sometimes seems not to be about women at all. What is odd to me is that I know women who say they never think about it, that they are indifferent, that such scenes and stories seem meant for other people altogether. They find my interest rather curious, I suppose. And a little awkward.

The images of pornography are many and varied; some are fragmented and idealized. Some are crude and unflattering. I like the dreamy, psychedelic quality of certain scenes; I like the surprises in others, and I like the arousal, the heat which can be born in my body without warning, in an instant. I have all the curiosity of the anthropologist and the frank hope of the voyeur. Pornography's texture is shamelessness; it maps the limits of my shame.

At times I find it harder to talk about pornography than my own sexual experience; what I like about pornography is as much a part of my sexuality as what I do, but it is more deeply psychological. What I *do* is the product of many factors, not all of them sexually motivated. But what I *imagine* doing is pure—pure in the sense that the images come wholly from within, from the soil of the subconscious. The land of fantasy is the land of the not-done and the wished-for. There are private lessons there, things for me to learn, all alone, about myself.

I feel bashful watching; that's one small surprise. I am self-conscious, prickly with the feeling of being caught in the act. I can feel that way with friends, with my lover of many years, and I can feel that way alone. Suddenly I need to shift position, avert my eyes. Another surprise, and a more important one: These images comfort me. Pornography reflects the obsessions of the age, which is my age. Sex awakens my unconscious; pornography gives it a face.

When I was ten or eleven my brother shared his stolen *Playboy* with me. The pneumatic figurines seemed magnificent and unreal. Certainly they seemed to have nothing at all to do with me or my future. I was a prodigious reader, and at an early age found scenes of sex and lasciviousness in many books: *The French Lieutenant's Woman,* which granted sex such power, and William Kotzwinkle's *Nightbook,* blunt and unpredictable.

I was not *taught,* specifically, much of anything about sex. I knew, but I knew nothing that counted. I felt arousal as any child will, as a biological state. And then came adolescence: real kisses, and dark, rough fumblings, a rut when all the rules disappeared. Heat so that I couldn't speak to say yes, or no, and a boy's triumphant fingers inside my panties was a glorious relief, and an awful guilt.

I entered sex the way a smart, post-Sixties teenager should, with fore-thought and contraception and care. My poor partner: "Is that all?" I said out loud when it was over. Is that really what all the fuss was about? But the books and magazines seemed a little more complicated to me af-ter that. I learned—but really just information. I had little enough un-derstanding of sex, and very little wisdom.

At the age of twenty, when I was, happily, several months' pregnant, the social work office where I was employed held a seminar on sexuality. We were determinedly liberal about the whole thing; I believe the point was to support clients in a variety of sexual choices. We were given a homework assignment on the first day, to make a collage that expressed our own sexuality. I returned the next morning and saw that my col-leagues, male and female both, had all made romantic visions of can-dlelight and sunsets. I was the youngest by several years, heavy-bellied, and I had brought a wild vision of masked men and women, naked tor-sos, skin everywhere, darkness, heat.

I knew I was struggling, distantly and through ignorance, with a deep shame. It was undirected, confusing; for years I had been most ashamed of the shame itself. Wasn't sex supposed to be free, easy? What was wrong with me, that I resisted? Why did I feel so afraid of the surrender, the sex-ual depths? And yet I was ashamed of what I desired: men and women both. I wanted vaguely to try . . . *things,* which no one spoke about; but surely people, somewhere, did. I was ashamed of all my urges, the small details within the larger act, the sudden sounds I made. I could hear that little voice: *Bad girl. Mustn't touch.*

I was a natural feminist; I knew the dialectic, the lingo. And all my se-crets seemed to wiggle free no matter what, expand into my unfeminist consciousness. I didn't even know the words for some of what I imag-ined, but I was sure of this: Liberated women didn't even *think* about what I wanted to do. My shame was more than a preoccupation with sex—everyone I knew was preoccupied with sex. It was more than being confused by the messy etiquette of the 1970s, more than wondering just how much shifting of partners I should do. It was shame for my own unasked-for appetites, which would not be still.

I was propelled toward the overt—toward pornography. I needed in-formation not about sex but about sexual parameters, the bounds of the normal. I needed reassurance, and blessing. I needed permission.

Several years ago, now in my late twenties, I began to watch what I at first called "dirty movies" and to read what were undoubtedly dirty books: *The Story of O* and *My Secret Life.* I went with the man I was living with, my arm in his and my eyes down, to a theater on a back street. It was very cold and dark inside the movie house, so that the other patrons were only dim shadows, rustling nearby. The movie was grainy, half-blurred, the sound muddy, the acting awful. At the same time I felt as though I'd crossed a line: There was a world of sexual material to see, and I was very curious to see it. Its sheer mass and variety reassured me. I couldn't imagine entering this world alone, though, not even for a quick foray into the screened-off section of the local video store, behind the sign reading OVER 18 ONLY. There were always men back there, and only men.

Watching, for the first time, a man penetrate another woman was like leaving my body all at once. I was outside my body, watching, because she on the screen above me *was* me; and then I was back in my body very much indeed. My lust was aroused as surely and uncontrollably by the sight of sex as hunger can be roused by the smell of food. I know how naive this sounds now, but I had never quite believed, until I saw it, that the sex in such films was *real,* that people fucked in front of cameras, eyes open. I found it a great shock: to see how different sex could be, how many different things it could mean.

Not all I felt was arousal. There are other reasons for a hurried blush. A woman going down on a man, sucking his cock as though starving for it, the man pulling away and shooting come across her face, the woman licking the come off her lips. I felt a heady mix of disgust and excitement, and confusion at that mix. Layers peeled off one after the other, because sometimes I disliked my own response. I resist it still, when something dark and forbidden emerges, when my body is provoked by what my mind reproves.

Inevitably, I came across something awful, something I really hated. The world of pornography is indiscriminate; boundaries get mixed up. Some stories are violent, reptilian, and for all their sexual content aren't about sex. I was reminded of a story I had found by accident, a long time ago, in a copy of my father's *True* magazine. I was forbidden to read *True,* for reasons unexplained. Before I was caught at it and the magazine taken away, I had found an illustration of a blood-splattered, nearly naked woman tied to a post in a dim basement, and had read up to the place in the text where the slow flaying of her legs had begun. It was gothic and horrible, and haunted me for years. Of course, I make my own definitions, everyone does; and to me that sort of thing has nothing to do with pornography. It *is* obscene, though, a word quite often applied to things that have nothing to do with sex. Pornography is sex, and sex is consensual, period. Without consent, the motions of sex become violence, and that alone defines it for me.

I realize this is not the opinion of conservative feminists such as the lawyer Catharine MacKinnon, who believes that violence, even murder, is the end point of all pornography. Certainly a lot of violent material has sexual overtones; the mistake is assuming that anything with sex in it is primarily about sex. The tendency to assume so says something about the person making the assumption. One important point about this distinction is that the one kind of material is so much more readily available than the other: *True* and slasher films and tabloids are part of the common culture. My father bought *True* at the corner tobacco store. Scenes of nothing but mutual pleasure are the illicit ones.

I fall on a line of American women about midway between the actresses whose films I rent and the housewife in Des Moines who has never seen such a film at all. My female friends fall near me, to either side, but most of them a little closer to Des Moines. The store I frequent for my books and films reflects the same continuum: For all its blunt variety, that store is clean, well-lit, friendly, and its variety of materials reflects a variety of hoped-for customers. There are many places I will not go, storefronts and movie houses that seem to me furtive and corrupt. Every society has its etiquette, its rules; so does the world of pornography.

I am deep into thinking about these rules; my cheeks are bright and my palms damp, and the telephone rings. Without thinking I plunge my caller into such thoughts. I chatter a few minutes into a heavy, shifting silence, and then suddenly realize how ill-bred I must seem. Out here, in the ordinary world, such things are not talked about at all. It's one definition of pornography: whatever we will not talk about.

I know I break a rule when I enter the adult store, whether my entrance is simply startling or genuinely unwelcome. The sweaty-lipped man with lingerie wouldn't, couldn't approach me in a grocery store or even a bar. Not like that, and perhaps not at all. Pornography degrades the male vision of women in this way. When I stand among the shelves there I am standing in a maze of female images, shelf after shelf of them, hundreds of naked women smiling or with their eyes closed and mouths open or gasping. I am just one more image in a broken mirror, with its multiple reflections of women, none of them whole.

I am still afraid. These days I am most aware of that fear as a fear of where I will and will not go, what I think of as *possible* for me. But, oh— I'm curious. I can be so curious. A while ago I recruited two friends, one man and one woman, and the three of us went to a peep show together like a flying wedge, parting the crowds of nervy young men, them jostling each other with elbows in the ribs, daring each other, *g'wan.* We changed bills for quarters, leaned together in the dim hallways, elbowed each other in the ribs—*g'wan.* There were endless film loops in booths for singles, various movie channels from which to choose in booths for two people, tissues provided, and a live show. One minute for twenty-five cents, and the signs above each booth flashing on and off, on and off again in the dark, from a green VACANT to a red IN USE and back again.

I pulled a door shut and disappeared into the musky dark; I could hear muffled shouts from the young men in booths on either side. The panel slid up on my first quarter to a brightly lit, mirrored room with three women, all simulating masturbation. The one in the center was right in front of me, and she caught my eye and grinned at me, in black leather just like her. I think she sees few women in the booths, and many men.

Men—always the Man who is the standard-bearer for what is obscene and forbidden. That Man, the one I fear whether I mean to or not, in elevators and parking lots and on the street, is the man who will be inflamed by what he sees. I fear he will be *persuaded* by it, come to believe it, learn my fantasy and think I want him to make it come true. When I haven't the temerity to go through one of these veiled doors, it's because I am afraid of the men inside: afraid in a generic, unspoken way, afraid of Them.

Susan Sontag, exhaustively trying to prove that certain works of pornography qualify as "literature"—a proof almost laughably pointless, I think—notes its "singleness of intention" as a point against its inclusion. I am interested in literature, pornographic and otherwise, by my responses to any given piece; and my responses to pornography are layered and complex and multiple.

Some pieces bore me: They are cheesy or slow, badly written or mechanical. Others disturb me by the unhappiness I sense, as though the actors and actresses wished only to be somewhere else. There are days when I am saturated and feel weary of the whole idea. Sometimes I experience a kind of ennui, a *nausea* from all that grunting labor, the rankness of the flesh. I get depressed, for simple enough reasons. I rented a movie recently that opened with a scene of two naked women stroking each other. One of the women had enormous breasts, hard balloons filled with silicone riding high on her ribs and straining the skin. She looked mutilated, and the rest of the movie held no interest for me at all.

I wish for more craft, a more artful packaging. I tire of browsing stacks of boxes titled *Fucking Brunettes* and *Black Cocks and Black Cunts* and *Monumental Knockers*. The mainstream films, with their happy, athletic actors, can leave me a little cold. That's how I felt watching a comfortable film called *The Last Resort*. The plot, naturally, is simple: A woman with a broken heart accompanies her friends, a couple, to a resort. Over the next twenty-four hours she has vigorous sex with a waiter, a cook (he in nothing but a chef's hat and apron), a waitress, a waitress and a maintenance man together. The other guests cavort cheerfully, too. I found it all so earnest and wholesome. A friend and fellow connoisseur deplores these films where everyone has a "penis-deflatingly good time squirting sperm about with as much passion as a suburban gardener doing his lawn." These movies are too hygienic. They're not dirty enough.

And now women are making films for women viewers. The new films by and for lesbians can be nasty and hot. But the heterosexual films, heavy on relationships and light on the standard icons of hard core, seem ever so soft to me. (They're reminiscent of those social worker collages.) They're tasteful and discreet. I'm glad women have, so to speak, seized the means of production. I'm glad women are making pornographic films, writing pornographic books, starting pornographic magazines; I'm happier still when the boundaries in which women create expand. I don't believe there are limits to what women can imagine or enjoy. I don't want limits, imposed from within or without, on what women can see, or watch, or do.

Any amateur psychologist could have a field day explaining why I prefer low-brow, hard-core porn to feminine erotica. I've spent enough time trying to explain things to myself: why I prefer *this* to *that*. There are examples of pornography, films and stories both, that genuinely scare me. They are no more bizarre or extreme than books or movies that may simply excite or interest me, but the details affect me in certain specific ways. The content touches me, just there, and I'm scared, for no reason I can explain, or excited by a scene that repels me. It may be nothing more than sound, a snap or thwack or murmur. And I want to keep watching those films, reading those books; when I engage in my own fears, I learn about them. I may someday master a few. When I happen upon such scenes, I try to look directly. Seeing what I don't like can be as therapeutic as seeing what I do.

Feminists against pornography (as distinct from other anti-pornography camps) hold that our entire culture is pornographic. In a pornographic world all our sexual constructions are obscene; sexual materials are necessarily oppressive, limited by the constraints of the culture. Even the act of viewing becomes a male act—an act of subordinating the person viewed. Under this construct, I'm a damaged woman, a heretic.

I take this personally, the effort to repress material I enjoy—to tell me how wrong it is for me to enjoy it. Anti-pornography legislation is directed at me: as a user, as a writer. Catharine MacKinnon and Andrea Dworkin—a feminist who has developed a new sexual orthodoxy in which the male erection is itself oppressive—are the new censors. They are themselves prurient, scurrying after sex in every corner. They look down on me and shake a finger: *Bad girl. Mustn't touch.*

That branch of feminism tells me my very thoughts are bad. Pornography tells me the opposite: that *none* of my thoughts are bad, that anything goes. Both are extremes, of course, but the difference is profound. The message of pornography, by its very existence, is that our sexual selves are real.

Always, the censors are concerned with how men *act* and how women are portrayed. Women cannot make free sexual choices in that world; they are too oppressed to know that only oppression could lead them to sell sex. And I, watching, am either too oppressed to know the harm that my watching has done to my sisters, or—or else I have become the Man. And it is the Man in me who watches and is aroused. (Shame.) What a misogynistic worldview this is, this claim that women who make such choices cannot be making free choices at all—are not free to make a choice. Feminists against pornography have done a sad and awful thing: *They* have made women into objects.

I move from the front of the adult store I frequent to the back. Here is the leather underwear, dildos of all sizes, inflatable female dolls, shrink-wrapped fetish magazines. Here are movies with taboo themes—older movies with incest plots, newer ones featuring interracial sex, and grainy loops of nothing more than spanking, spanking, spanking. Here are the films of giant breasts, or all-anal sex, food fights, obese actresses, and much masturbation. This is niche marketing at its best.

In the far back, near the arcade booths, are the restraints, the gags and bridles, the whips and handcuffs, and blindfolds. Here are dildos of truly heroic proportions. The films here are largely European, and quite popular. A rapid desensitization takes me over back here, a kind of numbing sensory overload. Back here I can't help but look at the other customers; I find myself curious about which movies each of *them* will rent.

Women who have seen little pornography seem to assume that the images in most films are primarily, obsessively, ones of rape. I find the opposite theme in American films: that of an adolescent rut, both male and female. Its obsession is virility, endurance, lust. Women in modern films are often the initiators of sex; men in such films seem perfectly content for that to be so.

Power fantasies, on the other hand, are rather common for men and women both. I use the term "power" to describe a huge continuum of images: physical and psychological overpowering of many kinds, seduction and bondage and punishment, the extremes of physical control practiced by S&M enthusiasts. The word "rape" for such scenes is inappropriate; the fact of rape has nothing to do with sex, or pornography. Power takes a lot of forms, subtle, overt. Out of curiosity I rented a German film called *Discipline in Leather*, a film, I discovered, without sex, without nudity. Two men are variously bound, chained, laced, gagged, spanked, and ridden like horses by a Nordic woman. "Nein!" she shouts. "Nicht so schnell!" The men lick her boots, accept the bridle in cringing obeisance. I found it laughably solemn, a Nazi farce, and then I caught myself laughing. This is one of many similar films, and I never want to laugh at the desires of another. A lot of people take what I consider trifling or silly to be terribly important. I want never to forget the bell curve of human desire, or that few of us have much say about where on the curve we land. I've learned this from watching porn: By letting go of judgments I hold against myself, and my desires, I let go of judgments about the desires and the acts of others.

I recently saw a movie recommended by one of the clerks at the adult store, a send-up called *Wild Goose Chase*. In the midst of mild arousal, I found a scene played for laughs, about the loneliness taken for granted in the pornographic world. The actor is Joey Silvera, a good-looking man with blond hair and startling dark eyes. In this film he plays a detective; the detective has a torrid scene with his secretary, who then walks out on him. He holds his head in his hands. "I don't need her," he mumbles. "I got women. I got my *own* women!" He stands and crosses to a file cabinet. "I got plenty of women!" He pulls out a drawer and dumps it upside down, spilling porn magazines in a pile on the floor. He crawls over them, stroking the paper cunts, the breasts, the pictured thighs, moaning, kissing the immobile faces.

The fantasies of power are shame-driven, I think: When I envision my own binding, my submission, I am seeing myself free. Free of guilt, free of responsibility. So many women I've known have harbored these fantasies, and grown more guilty for having them. And so many of those women have been strong, powerful, self-assured. Perhaps, as one school of feminist thought says, we've simply "eroticized our oppression." I know I berated myself a long while for that very thing, and tried to make the fantasies go away. But doing so denies the fact of my experience, which includes oppression and dominance, fear and guilt, and a hunger for surrender. This is the real text of power fantasies: They are about release from all those things. A friend who admits such dreams herself gave me Pat Califia's collection of dominance stories, *Macho Sluts*. I opened at random and was rooted where I stood: The stories are completely nasty, well written, and they are smart. "I no longer thought about the future," one character says, spread-eagle and bound in front of mirrors during sex. "I did not exist, except as a response to her touch. There was nothing else, no other reality, and no whim of my own will moved me." Such dreams transcend mere sex and enter, unexpectedly, the world of relationship. I could not read such stories, watch such films, with anyone but a lover. I couldn't act them out except with the person whom I trusted most of all.

It was only last year when I stopped making my lover go with me to the adult store. I make myself go alone now, or not at all; if I believe this should be mine for the choosing, then I want to get it myself. Only alone will that act of choosing be a powerful act. So I went yesterday, on a Wednesday in the middle of the morning, and found a crowd of men. There was even a couple, the young woman with permed hair and a startled look, like a deer caught in headlights. She kept her hands jammed in the pockets of her raincoat, and wouldn't return my smile. There was an old man on crutches huddled over a counter, and a herd of clerks, playing bad, loud rock music. I was looking for a few specific titles, and a clerk directed me to the customers' computer, on a table in the amateur section. It's like the ones at the library, divided by title, category (fat girl, Oriental, spanking, hetero, and so on), or a particular star.

The big-bellied jovial clerk came over after a few minutes.

"That working for you?" he sang out. "I tell you, I don't know how the hell that works."

I tell him I'm looking for a movie popular several years ago, called *Talk Dirty to Me*.

"Hey, Jack," he yells. "We got *Talk Dirty to Me*?" In a few minutes four clerks huddle around me and the computer, watching me type in the title, offering little suggestions. From across the store I can still hear the helpful clerk. "Hey, Al," he's shouting. "Lady over there wants *Talk Dirty to Me*. We got that?"

I still blush; I stammer to say these things out loud. Sex has eternal charm that way—a perpetual, organic hold on my body. I am aroused right now, writing this. Are you, dear reader? Do you dream, too?

A friend called this story my "accommodation," as though I'd made peace with the material. I have never had to do that. I have always just been trying to make peace with my abyssal self, my underworld. Pornography helps; that's simple. I became sexual in a generation that has explored sex more thoroughly and perhaps less well than any before. I live with myself day to day in a sex-drenched culture, and that means living with my own sex. After exposing myself truly to myself, it's surprisingly easy to expose myself to another.

I want not to accommodate to pornography but to claim it. I want to be the agent of sex. I want to *own* sex, as though I had a right to these depictions, these ideas, as though they belonged to us all. The biggest surprise is this one: When I am watching—never mind what. I am suddenly restless, shifting, crossing my legs. And my perceptive lover smiles at me and says, "You like that, don't you? See—*everyone* does that."

Chapter 23

OBJECTIFICATION

Martha C. Nussbaum

It is true, and very much to the point, that women are objects, commodities, some deemed more expensive than others—but it is only by asserting one's humanness every time, in all situations, that one becomes someone as opposed to something. That, after all, is the core of our struggle.

Andrea Dworkin, *Woman Hating*

Sexual objectification is a familiar concept. Once a relatively technical term in feminist theory, associated in particular with the work of Catharine MacKinnon and Andrea Dworkin, the word "objectification" has by now passed into many people's daily lives. It is common to hear it used to criticize advertisements, films, and other representations, and also to express skepticism about the attitudes and intentions of one person to another, or of oneself to someone else. Generally it is used as a pejorative term, connoting a way of speaking, thinking, and acting that the speaker finds morally or socially objectionable, usually, though not always, in the sexual realm. Thus, Catharine MacKinnon writes of pornography, "Admiration of natural physical beauty becomes objectification. Harmlessness becomes harm."[1] The portrayal of women "dehumanized as sexual objects, things, or commodities" is, in fact, the first category of pornographic material made actionable under MacKinnon and Dworkin's proposed Minneapolis ordinance.[2] The same sort of pejora-

---

Nussbaum, Martha C., "Objectification," *Philosophy and Public Affairs* 24:4 (1995), pp. 249–91. Copyright © 1995 by Princeton University Press. Reprinted by permission of Princeton University Press.

tive use is very common in ordinary social discussions of people and events.

Feminist thought, moreover, has typically represented men's sexual objectification of women as not a trivial but a central problem in women's lives, and the opposition to it as at the very heart of feminist politics. For Catharine MacKinnon, "women's intimate experience of sexual objectification . . . is definitive of and synonymous with women's lives as gender female."[3] It is said to yield an existence in which women "can grasp self only as thing."[4] Moreover, this baneful experience is, in MacKinnon's view, unavoidable. In a most striking metaphor, she states that "All women live in sexual objectification the way fish live in water"—meaning by this, presumably, not only that objectification surrounds women, but also that they have become such that they derive their very nourishment and sustenance from it. But women are not fish, and for MacKinnon objectification is bad because it cuts women off from full self-expression and self-determination—from, in effect, their humanity.

But the term "objectification" can also be used, somewhat confusingly, in a more positive spirit. Indeed, one can find both of these apparently conflicting uses in the writings of some feminist authors: for example, legal theorist Cass Sunstein, who has been generally supportive of Mac-Kinnon's critique of sexuality. Throughout his earlier writings on pornography, Sunstein speaks of the treatment of women as objects for the use and control of men as the central thing that is bad in pornographic representation.[5] On the other hand, in a mostly negative review of a recent book by Nadine Strossen defending pornography,[6] Sunstein writes the following:

> People's imaginations are unruly. . . . It may be possible to argue, as some people do, that objectification and a form of use are substantial parts of sexual life, or wonderful parts of sexual life, or ineradicable parts of sexual life. Within a context of equality, respect, and consent, objectification—not at all an easy concept to define—may not be so troublesome.[7]

To be sure, Sunstein expresses himself very cautiously, speaking only of an argument that might be made and not indicating his own support for such an argument. Nonetheless, to MacKinnon and Dworkin, who have typically represented opposition to objectification as at the heart of feminism, this paragraph might well seem puzzling. They might well wish to ask: What does Sunstein wish to defend? Why should "objectification and a form of use" ever be seen as "wonderful" or even as "ineradicable" parts of sexual life? Wouldn't it always be bad to use a "someone" as a "something"? And why should we suppose that it is at all possible to combine objectification with "equality, respect, and consent"? Isn't this precisely the combination we have shown to be impossible?

My hunch, which I shall pursue, is that such confusions can arise because we have not clarified the concept of objectification to ourselves, and that once we do so we will find out that it is not only a slippery, but also a multiple, concept. Indeed, I shall argue that there are at least seven distinct ways of behaving introduced by the term, none of which implies any of the others, though there are many complex connections among them. Under some specifications, objectification, I shall argue, is always morally problematic. Under other specifications, objectification has features that may be either good or bad, depending upon the overall context. (Sunstein was certainly right to emphasize the importance of context, and I shall dwell on that issue.) Some features of objectification, furthermore, I shall argue, may in fact in some circumstances, as Sunstein suggests, be either necessary or even wonderful features of sexual life. Seeing this will require, among other things, seeing how the allegedly impossible combination between (a form of) objectification and "equality, respect, and consent" might after all be possible.

I am going to begin with a series of examples, to which I shall return in what follows. All are examples of what might plausibly be called the objectification of one person by another, the seeing and/or treating of someone as an object. In all cases the objectified person is a sexual partner or would-be sexual partner, though the sexual context is not equally prominent in all of the cases. Deliberately, I have chosen examples from a wide variety of styles; and I have not restricted my sample to the male objectification of women, since we need to be able to ask how our judgments of the cases are influenced by larger issues of social context and social power.

(1.) His blood beat up in waves of desire. He wanted to come to her, to meet her. She was there, if he could reach her. The reality of her who was just beyond him absorbed him. Blind and destroyed, he pressed forward, nearer, nearer, to receive the consummation of himself, be received within the darkness which should swallow him and yield him up to himself. If he could come really within the blazing kernel of darkness, if really he could be destroyed, burnt away till he lit with her in one consummation, that were supreme, supreme.

D. H. Lawrence, *The Rainbow*

(2.) yes because he must have come 3 or 4 times with that tremendous big red brute of a thing he has I thought the vein or whatever the dickens they call it was going to burst though his nose is not so big after I took off all my things with the blinds down after my hours dressing and perfuming and combing it like iron or some kind of a thick crowbar standing all the time he must have eaten oysters I think a few dozen he was in great singing voice no I never in all my life felt anyone had one the size of that to make you feel full up he must have eaten a whole sheep after whats the idea making us like that with a big hole in the middle of us like a Stallion driving it up into you because thats all they want out of you with that determined vicious look in his eye I had to halfshut my eyes still he hasn't such a tremendous amount of spunk in him.

James Joyce, *Ulysses*

(3.) She even has a sheet over her body, draped and folded into her contours. She doesn't move. She might be dead, Macrae thinks. . . . Suddenly a desire to violate tears through his body like an electric shock, six thousand volts of violence, sacrilege, the lust to desecrate, destroy. His thumbs unite between the crack of her ass, nails inwards, knuckle hard on knuckle, and plunge up to the palms into her. A submarine scream rises from the deep green of her dreaming, and she snaps towards waking, half-waking, half-dreaming with no sense of self . . . and a hard pain stabbing at her entrails. . . . Isabelle opens her eyes, still not knowing where or what or why, her face jammed up against the cracking plaster . . . as Macrae digs deeper dragging another scream from her viscera, and her jerking head cracks hard on the wall, . . . and her palms touch Macrae's hands, still clamped tight around her ass, kneading, working on it, with a violence born of desperation and desire, desire to have her so completely . . . that it seems as if he would tear the flesh from her to absorb it, crush it, melt it into his own hands. . . . And Isabelle . . . hears a voice calling out "don't stop; don't stop," a voice called from somewhere deep within her from ages past, ancestral voices from a time the world was young, "don't stop, don't stop." It's nearer now, this atavistic voice, and she realises with surprise that it is coming from her mouth, it is her lips that are moving, it is her voice.

"Laurence St. Clair," *Isabelle and Véronique: Four Months, Four Cities*

(4.) Three pictures of actress Nicollette Sheridan playing at the Chris Evert Pro-Celebrity Tennis Classic, her skirt hiked up to reveal her black underpants. Caption: "Why We Love Tennis." *Playboy*, April 1995

(5.) At first I used to feel embarrassed about getting a hard-on in the shower. But at the Corry much deliberate excitative soaping of cocks went on, and a number of members had their routine erections there each day. My own, though less regular,

were, I think, hoped and looked out for. . . . This naked min-
gling, which formed a ritualistic heart to the life of the club,
produced its own improper incitements to ideal liaisons, and
polyandrous happenings which could not survive into the
world of jackets and ties, cycle-clips and duffel-coats. And how
difficult social distinctions are in the shower. How could I now
smile at my enormous African neighbour, who was responding
in elephantine manner to my own erection, and yet scowl at
the disastrous nearly-boy smirking under the next jet along?

Alan Hollinghurst, *The Swimming-Pool Library*

(6.) She had passed her arm into his, and the other objects in the
room, the other pictures, the sofas, the chairs, the tables, the
cabinets, the 'important' pieces, supreme in their way, stood
out, round them, consciously, for recognition and applause.
Their eyes moved together from piece to piece, taking in the
whole nobleness—quite as if for him to measure the wisdom of
old ideas. The two noble persons seated, in conversation, at tea,
fell thus into the splendid effect and the general harmony: Mrs.
Verver and the Prince fairly 'placed' themselves, however unwittingly, as high expressions of the kind of human furniture
required, aesthetically, by such a scene. The fusion of their
presence with the decorative elements, their contribution to
the triumph of selection, was complete and admirable; though
to a lingering view, a view more penetrating than the occasion
really demanded, they also might have figured as concrete at-
testations of a rare power of purchase. There was much indeed
in the tone in which Adam Verver spoke again, and who shall
say where his thought stopped? '*Le compte y est.* You've got some
good things.'

Henry James, *The Golden Bowl* [8]

Most of the works and authors are familiar. Hollinghurst's novel of gay
London before AIDS has been widely hailed as one of the most important
pieces of erotic writing in the 1980s. To those who are unfamiliar with
the *oeuvre* of Laurence St. Clair, it is probably sufficient to point out that
St. Clair is a pseudonym of James Hankinson, scholar in ancient Greek
philosophy and Professor of Philosophy at the University of Texas at
Austin, who wrote this novel for a standard hard-core pornographic series, and was later publicized as its author.

So: we have six examples of conduct that seems to deserve, in some
sense, the name of "objectification." In each case, a human being is regarded and/or treated as an object, in the context of a sexual relationship. Tom Brangwen sees his wife as a mysterious inhuman natural force,

a "blazing kernel of darkness." Molly reduces Blazes Boylan to his genital dimensions, regarding him as somewhat less human than the stallion
to which she jokingly compares him. Hankinson's hero Macrae treats
the sleeping Isabelle as a prehuman, preconscious being ripe for invasion and destruction, whose only quasi-human utterance is one that confirms her suitability for the infliction of pain. The *Playboy* caption
reduces the young actress, a skilled tennis player, to a body ripe for male
use: it says, in effect, she thinks she is displaying herself as a skilled athletic performer, but all the while she is actually displaying herself to *our*
gaze as a sexual object. Hollinghurst's hero represents himself as able to
see his fellow Londoners as equal interchangeable bodies or even body
parts, under the sexual gaze of the shower room, a gaze allegedly independent of warping considerations of class or rank. Maggie and Adam
contemplate their respective spouses as priceless antiques whom they
have collected and arranged.

In all such analyses of literary works, we need to distinguish the objectification of one character by another character from the objectification
of persons by a text taken as a whole. Both are of interest to me as examples of morally assessable human conduct, and, given the connections of
my analysis to the debate over pornography, I shall be concerned with the
morality of the conduct that consists in representing,[9] as well as with the
morality of represented conduct. Both sorts of conduct can be morally assessed, but they should be kept separate. Frequently it is difficult to do
this, but the attempt must be made, since important moral issues clearly
turn on the difference, and in dealing with literary examples we must
grapple with it. Fortunately, ethical criticism of literature has by now developed a rich set of distinctions to assist us. Especially helpful is Wayne
Booth's threefold distinction between (a) the *narrator* of a text (and/or
its other characters); (b) the *implied author,* that is, the sense of life embodied in the text taken as a whole; and (c) the *real-life author,* who has
many properties lacked by the implied author, and may lack some that
the implied author has.[10] Booth argues, and I agree, that the ethical criticism of the action represented in a text is one thing, and criticism of the
text as a whole another; to get to the second we need to focus on the *implied author,* asking ourselves what sort of interaction the text as a whole
promotes in us as readers, what sorts of desires and projects it awakens
and constructs. In this way, ethical criticism of texts can be both sensitive
to literary form and continuous with the ethical appraisal of persons.[11]

Here what we should probably say is that Brangwen's way of viewing his
wife is exemplary of attitudes that Lawrence advocates in his text taken as
a whole, and in other related texts; that Molly Bloom's attitude to Boylan
is far from being the only attitude to sexual relations that Joyce depicts,
even in his portrayal of Molly's imagining; that Hankinson's entire text
objectifies women in the manner of the passage cited, which is but the

first of a sequence of increasingly violent episodes that, strung together, constitute the whole of the "novel";[12] that *Playboy*'s typical approach to women's bodies and achievements is well captured in my example; that Henry James's novel, by contrast, awakens serious moral criticism of its protagonists by portraying them as objectifiers. Hollinghurst is the most puzzling example, and it remains to me quite unclear what attitude the text as a whole invites us to assume to its protagonist and his fantasies.

To give a suggestion of my reaction to the texts: I think that while none of them is without moral complexity, and none will be to everyone's taste, two examples of conduct in them, perhaps three, stand out as especially sinister. (The James characters are the ones of whom I would be most ready to use the term "evil.") At least one of the texts shows how objectification of a kind might be quite harmless and even pleasant; and at least one, perhaps more than one, shows what might lead someone to suggest that it could be a wonderful part of sexual life. Taken as a group, the examples invite us to distinguish different dimensions of objectification and to notice their independence from one another. When we do so, I shall argue, we discover that all types of objectification are not equally objectionable; that the evaluation of any of them requires a careful evaluation of context and circumstance; and that, once we have made the requisite distinctions, we will see how at least some of them might be compatible with consent and equality, and even be "wonderful" parts of sexual life.

1. Seven Ways to Treat a Person as a Thing

Now we need to begin the analysis. I suggest that in all cases of objectification what is at issue is a question of treating one thing as another: One is treating *as an object* what is really not an object, what is, in fact, a human being. The notion of humanity is involved in quite a Kantian way in the Dworkin quotation that is my epigraph, and I think that it is implicit in most critiques of objectification in the MacKinnon/Dworkin tradition. Beyond this, however, we need to ask what is involved in the idea of treating *as an object*. I suggest that at least the following seven notions are involved in that idea:

1. *Instrumentality:* The objectifier treats the object as a tool of his or her purposes.

2. *Denial of autonomy:* The objectifier treats the object as lacking in autonomy and self-determination.

3. *Inertness:* The objectifier treats the object as lacking in agency, and perhaps also in activity.

4. *Fungibility:* The objectifier treats the object as interchangeable (a) with other objects of the same type, and/or (b) with objects of other types.

5. *Violability:* The objectifier treats the object as lacking in boundary-integrity, as something that it is permissible to break up, smash, break into.

6. *Ownership:* The objectifier treats the object as something that is owned by another, can be bought or sold, etc.

7. *Denial of subjectivity:* The objectifier treats the object as something whose experience and feelings (if any) need not be taken into account.[13]

Each of these is a feature of our treatment of things, though of course we do not treat all things as objects in all of these ways. Treating things as objects is not objectification, since, as I have suggested, objectification entails making into a thing, treating *as* a thing, something that is really not a thing. Nonetheless, thinking for a bit about our familiar ways of treating things will help us to see that these seven features are commonly present, and distinct from one another. Most inanimate objects are standardly regarded as tools of our purposes, though some are regarded as worthy of respect for their beauty, or age, or naturalness. Most inanimate objects are treated as lacking autonomy, though at times we do regard some objects in nature, or even some machines, as having a life of their own. Many objects are inert and/or passive, though not by any means all. Many are fungible with other objects of a similar sort (one ballpoint pen with another), and also, at times, with objects of a different sort (a pen with a word processor), though many, of course, are not. Some objects are viewed as "violable"[14] or lacking in boundary-integrity, though certainly not all: We will allow a child to break and destroy relatively few things in the house. Many objects are owned, and are treated as such, though many again are not. (It is interesting that the unowned among the inanimate objects—parts of nature for the most part—are also likely to be the ones to which we especially often attribute a kind of autonomy and an intrinsic worth.) Finally, most objects are treated as entities whose experiences and feelings need not be taken into account, though at times we are urged to think differently about parts of the natural environment, whether with illicit anthropomorphizing or not I shall not determine here. In any case, we can see on the list a cluster of familiar attitudes to things, all of which seem to play a role in the feminist account of the objectification of persons. What objectification is, is to treat a human being in one or more of these ways.

Should we say that each is a sufficient condition for the objectification of persons? Or do we need some cluster of the features, in order to have a sufficient condition? I prefer not to answer this question, since I believe that use is too unclear. On the whole, it seems to me that "objectification" is a relatively loose cluster-term, for whose application we sometimes treat any one of these features as sufficient, though more often a plurality of features is present when the term is applied. Clearly there are other ways we standardly treat things—touching them, seeing them—that do not suggest objectification when we apply the same mode of treatment to persons, so we have some reason to think that these seven items are at least signposts of what many have found morally problematic. And there are some items on the list—especially denial of autonomy and denial of subjectivity—that attract our attention from the start because they seem to be modes of treatment we wouldn't bother discussing much in the case of mere things, where questions of autonomy and subjectivity do not arise; they seem most suited to the thinglike treatment of persons. This suggests that they may be of special interest to us in what follows, suggesting that we are going to be at least as interested in the treatment that is denied to persons as in the treatment that is accorded them.[15]

How are the features connected? It will be helpful to turn, first, to two examples from the thing-world: a ballpoint pen, and a Monet painting. The way in which a ballpoint pen is an object involves, it would seem, all the items on this list, with the possible exception of violability. That is, it might be thought inappropriate or at least wasteful to break up ballpoint pens, but I don't think that worry would rise to great moral heights. Certainly it seems that to treat the pen as a tool, as nonautonomous, as inert, as fungible (with other pens and at times with other instruments or machines), as owned, and as lacking in subjectivity—all this is exactly the standard and appropriate way to treat it. The painting, on the other hand, is certainly nonautonomous, owned, inert (though not passive), and lacking in subjectivity; it is definitely not fungible, either with other paintings or, except in the limited sense of being bought and sold, which doesn't imply thoroughgoing fungibility, with anything else either; its boundaries are precise, and there is a real question whether it is simply a tool for the purposes of those who use and enjoy it. What this tells us already is that objects come in many kinds. Some objects are precious objects, and these will usually lack fungibility and possess some boundary-integrity (inviolability).[16] Others are not so precious, and are both fungible and all right to break up.

The items on the list come apart in other ways as well. We see from the case of the painting that lack of autonomy does not necessarily imply instrumentality, though treating as instrumental may well imply treating as nonautonomous; the fact that most objects are inert should not conceal from us, for our later purposes, the fact that inertness is not a necessary condition of either lack of autonomy or instrumentality. Precisely what is useful about my word processor, what makes it such a good tool for my purposes, is that it is not inert. Nor does instrumentality entail lack of consideration for feelings and subjectivity—for one's purpose in using a tool may turn out to require concern for its experiences (as our porno-graphic examples will clearly show). As for violability, it is not entailed, it would seem, by any of the other six items. Even fungible items are not generally regarded as all right to break or smash, though the ones that are all right to smash are usually of the fungible sort, perhaps because it seems clear that they can be replaced by others of the kind.

Again, the fact that most objects are owned should not conceal from us the fact that ownership is not entailed by any of the other items on the list. Does it entail any of the others? Not fungibility, as is shown by the case of the painting. Not violability, not inertness, and probably not in-strumentality, as our attitudes to household pets and even plants show us clearly. (We don't think they are just tools of our own purposes.) But probably ownership does entail lack of self-determination and auton-omy; indeed it seems conceptually linked to that absence, though an item may certainly lack autonomy without being owned.

Finally, a thing may be treated as something whose experiences and feelings need not be taken into account without being treated as a mere tool, without being treated as fungible, without being seen as violable—all these are shown in the Monet painting case; also, without being seen as owned (the Grand Canyon, the Mojave Desert), and, it seems clear, without being seen as inert (my word processor). If one treats an object as something whose feelings and experiences need not be taken into ac-count, is that consistent with treating as autonomous? I think very likely not. Again, it seems that there is a conceptual connection here.

In fact, what we are discovering is that autonomy is in a certain sense the most exigent of the notions on our list. It seems difficult if not im-possible to imagine a case in which an inanimate object is treated as au-tonomous, though we can certainly imagine exceptions to all the others. And treating an item as autonomous seems to entail treating it as non-instrumental, as not simply inert, as not owned, and as not something whose feelings need not be taken into account. The only kind of objec-tification that seems clearly consistent with treating-as-autonomous, in fact, seems to be treating-as-fungible, and this in the limited sense of treating as fungible with other autonomous agents. This turns out to be highly pertinent to Hollinghurst, and to a well-developed ideology of gay male promiscuity, best exemplified, perhaps, in Richard Mohr's *Gay Ideas,* where fungibility-objectification is linked with democratic equal-ity.[17] To this I shall return. Treating-as-violable, as lacking boundary-integrity, may well also be consistent with treating-as-autonomous, and it is a prominent claim of defenders of consensual sadomasochism, for example lesbian and gay writers Gayle Rubin and Richard Mohr, that this is so. Interestingly enough, the same claim has been defended by conservative political philosopher Roger Scruton, in an eloquent and surprising argument.[18] (In fact, Scruton's entire analysis has a great deal to offer the person who tries to think about this subject, and it is certainly the most interesting philosophical attempt as yet to work through the moral issues involved in our treatment of persons as sex partners.)

On the other hand, there is one way in which *instrumentality* seems to be the most morally exigent notion. We can think of many cases in which it is permissible to treat a person or thing as nonautonomous (the Monet painting, one's pets, one's small children), and yet inappropriate to treat the object merely or primarily as a tool of our own purposes. That, I have said, would be a bad attitude to the painting, even though the painting hardly displays autonomy. What is interesting is to see how few of the other forms of object-treatment are clearly ruled out by the decision not to treat a thing as instrumental. What more, in fact, is entailed by the decision to treat a thing as, to use the Kantian phrase, an end in itself? Not treating-as-autonomous, I have said; though this does not rule out the possibility that treating-as-autonomous would be a necessary feature of the noninstrumental treatment *of adult human beings*. Not treating as noninert, in the case of the painting; though again, it is at least arguable that noninstrumentality for adult humans entails recognition of agency and activity. Not treating as nonfungible, or at least not clearly so. I may view each one of many pieces of fine silver flatware as precious for its own sake, and yet view them as exchangeable one for another. Not treating as having subjectivity, or not generally (the painting again); though once again, it might turn out that to treat an adult human being as an end in him- or herself does entail recognition of subjectivity. And, finally, it seems quite unclear whether treating as an end in itself requires seeing as inviolable. That all seems to depend on the nature of the object. (Some experimental artworks, for example, invite breakage.) On the whole, though, there may be a conceptual connection between treating as an end in itself and treating as inviolable, in the sense that to break up or smash an object is usually to use it in accordance with one's own purposes in ways that negate the natural development and may even threaten the existence of the object.

I now pass over the fascinating issues of objectification raised by our treatment of plants and other animals, and move on to some cases involving the treatment of human beings by human beings. Let us for the moment avoid the sexual realm. And let us consider first of all the relationship between parent and child. The treatment of young children by their parents almost always involves a denial of autonomy; it involves some aspects of ownership, though not all. On the other hand, in almost all times and places it has been thought bad for parents to treat their children as lacking in bodily integrity—battery and sexual abuse, though common, are more or less universally deplored. Nor would it be at all common to find children treated as inert and lacking in activity. On the other hand, the extent to which children may be used as tools of their parents' purposes, as beings whose feelings need not be taken into account, and even as fungible,[19] has varied greatly across place and time. Modern American views of child rearing would view all three of these forms of objectification as serious moral wrongs; in other times and places, they have not been so regarded.

Let us now consider Marx's account of the objectlike treatment of workers under capitalism (abstracting from the question of its truth).[20] Absence of true autonomy is absolutely crucial to the analysis, as is also instrumentality and absence of concern for experiences and feelings (although Marx seems to grant that workers are still treated with some lingering awareness of their humanity, and are not regarded altogether as tools or even animals).[21] Workers are also treated as quite thoroughly fungible, both with other able-bodied workers and at times with machines. They are not, however, treated as inert: Their value to the capitalist producer consists precisely in their activity. Nor, whatever other flaws Marx finds with the system, does he think they are treated as physically violable. The physical safety of workers is at least nominally protected, though of course it is not all that well protected, and the gradual erosion of health through substandard living conditions may itself be regarded as a kind of slow bodily violation. Spiritual violation, on the other hand, lies at the heart of what Marx thinks is happening to workers, when they are deprived of control over the central means of their self-definition as humans. Finally, workers are not exactly owned, and are certainly morally different from slaves, but in a very profound sense the relationship is one of ownership—in the sense, namely, that what is most the worker's own, namely the product of his labor, is what is most taken away from him. MacKinnon has written that sexuality is to feminism what work is to Marxism: In each case something that is most oneself and one's own is what is seen by the theory to have been taken away.[22] We should remember this analogy, when we enter the sexual domain.

Now let us think of slavery. Slavery is defined as a form of ownership. This form of ownership entails a denial of autonomy, and it also entails the use of the slave as a mere tool of the purposes of the owner. (Aristotle defines the slave as "an animate tool.") This is true so far as the institution is concerned, and (as even Aristotle granted) is not negated by the fact that on occasion noninstrumental friendships may exist between slave and owner. (As Aristotle says, in that case the friendship is not with the slave *qua* slave, but with the slave *qua* human.[23]) Why so, given that I have noted that in the case of paintings, and house plants, and pets, treating-as-owned need not entail treating-as-instrumental? I believe that it is something about the type of ownership involved in slavery, and its relation to the humanity of the slave, that makes this connection. Once one treats a human being as a thing one may buy or sell, one is *ipso facto* treating that human being as a tool of one's own purposes. Perhaps this is because, as I have suggested, the noninstrumental treatment of adult human beings entails recognition of autonomy, as is not the case for paintings and plants; and ownership is by definition incompatible with autonomy.

On the other hand, slaves are certainly not treated as inert, far from it. Nor are they necessarily treated as fungible, in the sense that they may be specialized in their tasks. Yet the very toollike treatment inherent in the institution entails a certain sort of fungibility, in the sense that a person is reduced to a set of body parts performing a certain task, and under that understanding can be replaced by another similar body, or by a machine. Slaves are not necessarily regarded as violable; there may even be laws against the rape and/or bodily abuse of slaves. But it is easy to see how the thinglike treatment of persons inherent in the institution led, as it so often did, to the feeling that one had a right to use the body of that slave in whatever way one wished. Once one treats as a tool and denies autonomy, it is difficult to say why rape or battery would be wrong, except in the sense of rendering the tool a less efficient tool of one's purposes. Slaves, finally, are not always denied subjectivity; one may imagine them as beings mentally well suited to their lot; one may also think with a limited empathy about their pleasure or pain. On the other hand, once again, the very decision to treat a person as not an end in him- or herself, but as a mere tool, leads rather naturally to a failure of imagination. Once one makes that basic move it is very easy indeed to stop asking the questions morality usually dictates, such as, What is this person likely to feel if I do X? What does this person want, and how will my doing X affect her with respect to those wants? And so on.

This example prepares us for the MacKinnon/Dworkin analysis of sexuality, since it shows us how a certain sort of instrumental use of persons, negating the autonomy that is proper to them as persons, also leaves the human being so denuded of humanity, in the eyes of the objectifier, that he or she seems ripe for other abuses as well—for the refusal of imagination involved in the denial of subjectivity,[24] for the denial of individuality involved in fungibility, and even for bodily and spiritual violation and abuse, if that should appear to be what best suits the will and purposes of the objectifier. The lesson seems to be that there is something especially problematic about instrumentalizing human beings, something that involves denying what is fundamental to them as human beings, namely, the status of being ends in themselves. From this one denial, other forms of objectification that are not logically entailed by the first seem to follow.

Notice, however, that instrumentalization does not seem to be problematic in all contexts. If I am lying around with my lover on the bed, and use his stomach as a pillow,[25] there seems to be nothing at all baneful about this, provided that I do so with his consent (or, if he is asleep, with a reasonable belief that he would not mind), and without causing him pain, provided, as well, that I do so in the context of a relationship in which he is generally treated as more than a pillow.[26] This suggests that what is problematic is not instrumentalization per se, but treating someone *primarily* or *merely* as an instrument. The overall context of the relationship thus becomes fundamental, and I shall return to it.

II. Kant, Dworkin, and MacKinnon

We are now beginning to get a sense of the terrain of this concept, and to see how slippery, and how multiple, it is. We are also beginning to approach, I think, the core idea of MacKinnon's and Dworkin's analysis. As Barbara Herman has argued in a remarkable article,[27] this core notion is Kantian. Central to Kant's analysis of sexuality and marriage is the idea that sexual desire is a very powerful force that conduces to the thinglike treatment of persons, by which he meant, above all, the treatment of persons not as ends in themselves, but as means or tools for the satisfaction of one's own desires.[28] That kind of instrumentalizing of persons was very closely linked, in his view, to both a denial of autonomy—one wishes to dictate how the other person will behave, so as to secure one's own satisfaction—and also to a denial of subjectivity—one stops asking how the other person is thinking or feeling, bent on securing one's own satisfaction. It would appear that these three notions are the ones in which Kant is interested. Inertness, fungibility, ownership, and even violability don't seem to interest him, although one can easily see how the instrumentalization he describes might lead, here as in the case of the slave, to the view that the other body can be violated or abused, so long as that secures the agent's own pleasure. Certainly Dworkin, when she follows him, does make this connection, tracing the prevalence of sex abuse and sadistic violence to the initial act of denying autonomy and endlike status.[29]

Why does Kant think that sex does this? His argument is by no means clear, but we can try to elaborate it. The idea seems to be that sexual desire and pleasure cause very acute forms of sensation in a person's own body; that these sensations drive out, for a time, all other thoughts, including the thoughts of respect for humanity that are characteristic of the moral attitude to persons. Apparently he also thinks that they drive out every endlike consideration of the pleasure or experience of the sex partner, and cause attention to be riveted in on one's own bodily states. In that condition of mind, one cannot manage to see the other person as anything but a tool of one's own interests, a set of bodily parts that are useful tools for one's pleasure, and the powerful urge to secure one's own sexual satisfaction will ensure that instrumentalization (and therefore denial of autonomy and of subjectivity) continue until the sexual act has reached its conclusion. At the same time, the keen interest both parties have in sexual satisfaction will lead them to permit themselves to be treated in this thinglike way by one another, indeed, to volunteer eagerly to be dehumanized in order that they can dehumanize the other in turn.[30] Kant clearly believes this to be a feature of sexuality generally, not just of male sexuality, and he does not connect his analysis to any issues of social hierarchy or the asymmetrical social formation of erotic desire. He seems to think that in a typical sex act both parties eagerly desire both to be objectifiers and to be objects.

MacKinnon and Dworkin in a way follow Kant, but in a very important way depart from him. Like Kant, they start from the notion that all human beings are owed respect, and that this respect is incompatible with treating them as instruments, and also with denials of autonomy and subjectivity.[31] Unlike Kant, however, they do not believe that these denials are intrinsic to sexual desire itself. They do not have a great deal to say about how sexual desire can elude these problems, but the more overtly erotic parts of Dworkin's fiction suggest that it is possible to aim, in sex, at a mutually satisfying fused experience of pleasure in which both parties temporarily surrender autonomy in a good way (a way that enhances receptivity and sensitivity to the other) without instrumentalizing one another or becoming indifferent to one another's needs. Since she is clearly much influenced by Lawrence, I shall return to these issues when I discuss him later. Moreover, in her discussions of James Baldwin in *Intercourse*,[32] Dworkin makes it clear that she thinks that the lovemaking of gay men can right now, in our society, exemplify these good characteristics. The problem derives not from any obtuseness in sexual desire itself, but from the way in which we have been socialized erotically, in a society that is suffused with hierarchy and domination. Men learn to experience desire in connection with paradigm scenarios of domination and instrumentalization. (The fact that pornography is, for both MacKinnon and Dworkin, a primary source of these paradigm scenarios is what explains the importance of pornography in their thought.) Women learn to experience desire in connection with these same paradigm scenarios, which means that they learn to eroticize being dominated and being turned into objects. Thus objectification for MacKinnon and Dworkin is asymmetrical: on the one side the objectifier, on the other side, the volunteer for object-status. And this means that it is only the female for whom sex entails a forfeiture of humanity, being turned into something rather than someone. MacKinnon and Dworkin sometimes suggest that this objectification involves elements of inertness,[33] fungibility, and ownership;[34] but it seems to me clear that the central core of the concept, as they use it, is in fact that of instrumentality, connected in a Kantian way to denials of autonomy and subjectivity, and in a related way to the possibility of violation and abuse.[35]

Kant's solution to the problem of sexual objectification and use is marriage.[36] He argues that objectification can be rendered harmless only if sexual relations are restricted to a relationship that is structured institutionally in ways that promote and, at least legally if not morally, guarantee mutual respect and regard. If the two parties are bound to support one another in various ways, this ensures a certain kind of respect for personhood that will persist undestroyed by the ardors of lovemaking, though it is apparently Kant's view that this respect and "practical love" can never color or infuse the lovemaking itself.[37] Characteristically, Kant is not very much worried about the asymmetrical or hierarchical nature of marriage, or about its aspects of ownership and denial of autonomy. These aspects he sees as fitting and proper, and he never suggests that sexual objectification derives support from these institutional arrangements.

For Dworkin and MacKinnon, by contrast, hierarchy is at the root of the problem. The lack of respect that much lovemaking displays is not, as I have argued, a feature of sexuality in itself; it is created by asymmetrical structures of power. Marriage, with its historical connotations of ownership and nonautonomy, is one of the structures that makes sexuality go bad. We see this, for example, in Dworkin's *Mercy,* in which the mutually satisfying passionate sexual relationship between Andrea and the young revolutionary turns sour as soon as they are man and wife. Encouraged by the institution, he begins to need to assert his dominance sexually, and the relationship degenerates into a terrible saga of sadism and abuse. In this morality tale Dworkin illustrates her belief that institutions maim us despite our best intentions, causing the eroticization of forms of sexual conduct that dehumanize and brutalize. The remedy for this state of affairs, it is suggested, is no single institution, but rather the gradual undoing of all the institutional structures that lead men to eroticize power. Thus the critiques of sexual harassment, of domestic violence, and of pornography hang together as parts of a single program of Kantian moral/political reform.

Failure to sort out the different aspects of the concept of objectification leads at times to obscurity in MacKinnon's and Dworkin's critique. Consider, for example, the following passage from Dworkin's analysis of *The Story of O:*

> O is totally possessed. That means that she is an object, with no control over her own mobility, capable of no assertion of personality. Her body is *a* body, in the same way that a pencil is a pencil, a bucket is a bucket, or, as Gertrude

Stein pointedly said, a rose is a rose. It also means that O's energy, or power, as a woman, as Woman, is absorbed. . . . The rings through O's cunt with Sir Stephen's name and heraldry, and the brand on her ass, are permanent wedding rings rightly placed. They mark her as an owned object and in no way symbolize the passage into maturity and freedom. The same might be said of the conventional wedding ring.[38]

Here we have inertness, fungibility, and ownership, all treated as if they are more or less inevitable consequences of an initial denial of autonomy (mixed up, clearly, with instrumentalization). It may be true that the novel makes these connections, and that the particular way in which Sir Stephen possesses O is in fact incompatible with active agency, with qualitative individuality, or with nonownership. But it is important to insist that these are logically independent ideas. One may deny autonomy to a beloved child without these other consequences. So what we want to know is: How are they connected here? What should make us believe that a typical male way of relating to women as non-autonomous brings these other consequences in its train? (For it is clear, as the wedding-ring remark indicates, that for Dworkin *The Story of O* is a paradigm of a pattern of relationship prevalent in our culture.) If we are contemplating institutional and/or moral change, we need to understand these connections clearly, so that we will have a sense of where we might start.

What brings these different aspects of the concept together is, I believe, a certain characteristic mode of instrumentalization and use that is alleged to lie behind the male denial of autonomy to women. For Sir Stephen, O exists only as something to be used to gratify his own pleasure (and, as Dworkin perceptively points out, as a surrogate for the male René whom he loves, but will not approach physically). Apart from that, she is O, zero. So she is not like a beloved child, who may be denied autonomy but retain individuality and agency. She is just a set of bodily parts, in particular a cunt and an anus[39] to be entered and used, with nothing of salience over and above them, not even the individuality and agency of those parts. It is in this way, I believe, that Dworkin (and at times MacKinnon) makes the further step from the core concepts of instrumentalization and denial of autonomy to the other aspects of the concept of objectification. They believe that these connections are ubiquitous. This, they suggest, is the sum total of what women are under male domination. But once we have noticed that the connections are not as conceptually tight as they suggest, we are led to ask how pervasive in fact they are. And we are led to ask whether and to what extent women and men can combine these features in different ways in their lives, uncoupling passivity from instrumentality, for example, or fungibility from the denial of autonomy.

III. A Wonderful Part of Sexual Life?

Before returning to the passages, we must observe one fundamental point: In the matter of objectification, context is everything. MacKinnon and Dworkin grant this when they insist, correctly, that we assess male-female relations in the light of the larger social context and history of female subordination, and insist on differentiating the meaning of objectification in these contexts from its meaning in either male-male or female-female relations. But they rarely go further, looking at the histories and the psychologies of individuals. (In fact, in judging literary works they standardly refuse appeal to the work-as-a-whole test; even where narrative is concerned, context is held to be irrelevant.[40]) In a sense the fine details of context are of little interest to them, involved as they are in a political movement; on the other hand, such details are of considerable interest to us; for I shall argue that in many if not all cases, the difference between an objectionable and a benign use of objectification will be made by the overall context of the human relationship in question.

This can easily be seen if we consider a simple example. W, a woman, is going out of town for an important interview. M, an acquaintance, says to her, "You don't really need to go. You can just send them some pictures." If M is not a close friend of W, this is almost certain to be an offensively objectifying remark. It reduces W to her bodily (and facial) parts, suggesting, in the process, that her professional accomplishments and other personal attributes do not count. The remark certainly seems to slight W's autonomy; it treats her as an inert object, appropriately represented by a photograph; it may suggest some limited sort of fungibility. It may also, depending on the context, suggest instrumentalization: W is being treated as an object for the enjoyment of the male gaze. Suppose, now, M is W's lover, and he says this to her in bed. This changes things, but we really don't know how, because we don't know enough. We don't know what the interview is for (a modelling job? a professorship?). And we don't know enough about the people. If M standardly belittles her accomplishments, the remark is a good deal worse than the same remark made by a stranger, and more deeply suggestive of instrumentalization. If, on the other hand, there is a deeply understood mutual respect between them, and he is simply finding a way of telling her how attractive she is, and perhaps of telling her that he doesn't want her to leave town, then things become rather different. It may still be a risky thing to say, far more risky than the very same thing said by W to M, given the social history that colors all such relationships. Still, there is the sense that the remark is not reductive—that instead of taking away from W, the compliment to her appearance may have added something. (Much depends on tone of voice, gesture, sense of humor.) Consider, finally, the same remark made to W by a close friend. W knows that this friend respects her accomplishments, and has great confidence in his attitude toward her in all respects pertinent to friendship; but she wishes he would notice her body once in a while. In this case, the objectifying remark may come as a pleasant surprise to W, a joke embodying a welcome compliment. Though we still need to know more about what the interview is all about, and how it is related to W's capacities (and though we still should reflect about the fact that it is extremely unlikely, given the way our society currently is, that such a remark will ever be made by W to M), it may well seem to her as if the remark has added something without taking anything away. It is possible, of course, that W reacts this way because she has eroticized her own submission. Such claims, like all claims of false consciousness, are difficult to adjudicate. But it seems to me implausible that all such cases are of this sort. To these human complexities Dworkin and MacKinnon frequently seem to me insufficiently sensitive.

Let us now turn to the passages. Lawrence focuses, here as often, on the willing resignation of autonomy and, in a sense, of subjectivity. The power of sexuality is most authentically experienced, in his view, when the parties do put aside their conscious choice-making, and even their inner life of self-consciousness and articulate thought, and permit themselves to be, in a sense, objectlike, natural forces meeting one another with what he likes to call "blood knowledge." Thus Brangwen feels his blood surging up in a way that eclipses deliberation, that makes him "blind and destroyed." His wife at this moment does appear to him as a mysterious thinglike presence—in the striking metaphor, a "blazing kernel of darkness" (indicating that the illumination that comes from sexuality requires, first, the blinding of the intellect). This thinglike presence summons him—not, however, to instrumental use of it, but to a kind of surrender of his own personhood, a kind of yielding abnegation of self-containment and self-sufficiency. This sort of objectification has its roots, then, in a mutual denial of autonomy and subjective self-awareness. It has links with inertness, understood as passivity and receptivity, since both surrender agency before the power of the blood. It has links, as well, with fungibility: For in a certain sense Lydia's daily qualitative individuality does vanish before his desire, as she becomes an embodiment of something primal; and he puts aside his daily ways of self-definition, his own idiosyncrasies, before the dark presence that summons him. And that is also a link with violability: For in the sway of desire he no longer feels himself clearly individuated from her, he feels his boundaries become porous, he feels the longing to be "destroyed" as an individual, "burnt away."[41] Lawrence, like (and influenced by) Schopenhauer, sees a connection between the ascendancy of passion and the loss of definite boundaries, the loss of what Schopenhauer calls the *principium individuationis*.

All this is objectification. And whether or not one finds Lawrence's prose, or even his ideas, to one's taste, it seems undeniable that it captures some profound features of at least some sexual experiences. (As I have said, it is this very idea of sexuality that animates the fiction of Andrea Dworkin, and it is this wonderful possibility that she hates sexism for destroying.) If one were to attribute a sense to Sunstein's remark that objectification might be argued to be a wonderful part of sexual life, one might begin to do so along these lines. Indeed, one might go so far as to claim, with Schopenhauer, that it is a necessary feature of sexual life—though Lawrence seems to me to make a more plausible claim when he indicates that such resignation of control is not ubiquitous, and can in fact be relatively rare, especially in a culture very much given to self-conscious aloofness and the repression of feeling.

It is worth noting that Lawrentian objectification is frequently connected with a certain type of reduction of persons to their bodily parts, and the attribution of a certain sort of independent agency to the bodily parts. Consider this scene from *Lady Chatterley:*

"Let me see you!"

He dropped the shirt and stood still, looking towards her. The sun through the low window sent a beam that lit up his thighs and slim belly, and the erect phallus rising darkish and hot-looking from the little cloud of vivid gold-red hair. She was startled and afraid.

"How strange!" she said slowly. "How strange he stands there! So big! and so dark and cocksure! Is he like that?"

The man looked down the front of his slender white body, and laughed. Between the slim breasts the hair was dark, almost black. But at the root of the belly, where the phallus rose thick and arching, it was gold-red, vivid in a little cloud.

"So proud!" she murmured, uneasy, "And so lordly! Now I know why men are so overbearing. But he's lovely, really, like another being! A bit terrifying! But lovely really! And he comes to me—" She caught her lower lip between her teeth, in fear and excitement.

The man looked down in silence at his tense phallus, that did not change. . . . "Cunt, that's what tha'rt after. Tell lady Jane tha' wants cunt. John Thomas, an' th' cunt o' lady Jane!—"

"Oh, don't tease him," said Connie, crawling on her knees on the bed towards him and putting her arms round his white slender loins, and drawing him to her so that her hanging swinging breasts touched the top of the stirring erect phallus, and caught the drop of moisture. She held the man fast.

Here there is a sense in which both parties put aside their individuality and become identified with their bodily organs. They see one another in terms of those organs. And yet Kant's suggestion that in all such focusing on parts there is denial of humanity seems quite wrong. Even the suggestion that they are *reducing* one another to their bodily parts seems quite wrong, just as I think it seemed wrong in my simple photograph example. The intense focusing of attention on the bodily parts seems an addition, rather than a subtraction, and the scene of passion, which is fraught for Constance with a sense of terror, and the fear of being overborne by male power, is rendered benign and loving, is rendered in fact liberating, by this very objectification, in the manner in which Mellors undertakes it, combining humor with passion.

Why is Lawrentian objectification benign, if it is? We must point, above all, to the complete absence of instrumentalization, and to the closely connected fact that the objectification is symmetrical and mutual—and in both cases undertaken in a context of mutual respect and rough social equality.[42] The surrender of autonomy and even of agency and subjectivity are joyous, a kind of victorious achievement in the prison-house of English respectability. Such a surrender constitutes an escape from the prison of self-consciousness that, in Lawrence's quite plausible view, seals us off from one another and prevents true communication and true receptivity. In the willingness to permit another person to be this close, in a position where the dangers of being dominated and overborne are, as Constance knows, omnipresent, one sees, furthermore, enormous trust, trust that might be thought to be impossible in a relationship that did not include at least some sort of mutual respect and concern—although in Lawrence's depictions of a variety of more or less tortured male/female relationships we discover that this is complex. Where there is loss of autonomy in sex, the context is, or at least can be, one in which, on the whole, autonomy is respected and promoted; the success of the sexual relationship can have, as in Constance's case, wide implications for flourishing and freedom more generally. We do not need to find every single idea of Lawrence's about sexuality appealing in order to see in the scene something that is of genuine value. Again, where there is a loss in subjectivity in the moment of lovemaking, this can be and frequently is accompanied by an intense concern for the subjectivity of the partner at other moments, since the lover is intensely focused on the moods and wishes of that one person, whose states mean so much for his or her own. Brangwen's obsession with his wife's fluctuating moods shows this very clearly.

Finally, we see that the kind of apparent fungibility that is involved in identifying persons with parts of their bodies need not be dehumanizing at all, but can coexist with an intense regard for the person's individuality, which can even be expressed in a personalizing and individualizing of the bodily organs themselves, as in the exchange between Mellors and Constance. Giving a proper name to the genital organs of each is a way of signifying the special and individual way in which they desire one another, the nonfungible character of Mellors's sexual intentionality.[43] It is Mellors's way of telling Constance what she did not know before (and what MacKinnon and Dworkin seem at times not to know), that to be identified with her genital organs is not necessarily to be seen as dehumanized meat ripe for victimization and abuse, but can be a way of being seen more fully as the human individual she is. It is a reminder that the genital organs of people are not really fungible, but have their own individual character, and are in effect parts of the person, if one will really look at them closely without shame.[44]

We are now in a position to notice something quite interesting about Kant. He thinks that focusing on the genital organs entails the disregard of personhood—because he apparently believes that personhood and humanity, and, along with them, individuality, do not reside in the genital organs; the genital organs are just fungible nonhuman things, like so many tools. Lawrence says that is a response that itself dehumanizes us, by reducing to something animal what properly is a major part of the humanity in us, and the individuality as well. We have to learn to call our genital organs by proper names—that would be at least the beginning of a properly complete human regard for one another.

Thinking about Lawrence can make us question the account of the deformation of sexuality given by MacKinnon and Dworkin. For Lawrence suggests that the inequality and, in a sense, dehumanization of women in Britain—which he does frequently acknowledge, not least in *Lady Chatterley*—rests upon and derives strength from the denial of women's erotic potentiality, the insistence that women be seen as sexless things and not identified also with their genital organs. Like Audre Lorde among contemporary feminists,[45] Lawrence shows how a kind of sexual objectification—not, certainly, a commercial sort, and one that is profoundly opposed to the commercialization of sex[46]—can be a vehicle of autonomy and self-expression for women, how the very surrender of autonomy in a certain sort of sex act can free energies that can be used to make the self whole and full.[47] In effect, Mellor is the only character in that novel who sees Connie as an end in herself, and this noninstrumentalization, and the attendant promotion of her autonomy, is closely connected to his sexual interest.

MacKinnon and Dworkin would surely object that both Lawrence and Lorde are somewhat naive in their assumption that there is a domain of "natural" sexuality behind cultural constructions, that can be liberated in a sex act of the right sort. They would argue that this underestimates the depth to which sexual roles and desires are culturally shaped, and therefore infected by the ubiquitous distortions of gender roles. It is beyond the scope of this article to adjudicate this large controversy, but I can at least indicate the direction my reply would take. I believe that it is correct that Lawrence's romantic rhetoric of nature and blood knowledge probably is naive, underestimating the depth of socialization and, more generally, of cognitive awareness, in sexual life. Nor do I sympathize with Lawrence's idea that sexuality is better the freer it is of both culture and thought. On the other hand, I think that his larger case for the value of a certain type of resignation of control, and of both emotional and bodily receptivity, does not depend on these other theses, and that one can defend a kind of Lawrentian sexuality (as, indeed, Andrea Dworkin herself does, in the early chapters of *Mercy* and in her essays on Baldwin) without accepting them. Such a stance does involve the recognition that our culture is more heterogeneous, and allows us more space for negotiation and personal construction, than MacKinnon and Dworkin usually allow.[48]

We turn now to Molly Bloom. Molly regards Blazes Boylan as a collection of outsized bodily parts. She does so with humor and joy, though at the same time with certain reservations about the quality of Boylan's humanity. Her objectification of Boylan has little to do with either denial of his autonomy or instrumentalization and use—certainly not with inertness either, or ownership, or violability. It focuses on features of denial of subjectivity (she never in the entire monologue wonders about what he feels, as she so frequently does about Poldy), fungibility (he is just an especially large penis, "all right to spend time with as a joke," almost interchangeable with a stallion, or an inanimate dildolike crowbar). This is far from being a profound Lawrentian experience. It is a little unsatisfying, in its absence of depth, to Molly herself—whose ambiguous use of the word "spunk" to mean both "semen" and "character" shows us throughout the monologue her own confusion about the importance of this physical joy by comparison to her physically unsatisfying but loving relationship with Poldy. On the other hand, it seems that Molly's delight in the physical aspects of sex (which was found especially shocking by prudish attackers of the novel) is at least a part of what Lawrence and Audre Lorde want women to be free to experience, and it seems wrong to denigrate it because of its incompleteness. (Indeed, one might say that the theme of the novel as a whole is the acceptance of incompleteness, and what Joyce would most profoundly be opposed to would be a moralizing Lawrentian romantic denigration of Molly's pleasure on account of the fact that it was not especially earthshaking.[49]) So here we have quite a different way in which objectification may be a joyous part of sexual life—and maybe this sort of mythic focusing on body parts is even a regular or necessary feature of it, though Molly's comic exaggeration is not.

What is especially important to notice, for our purposes, is the way in which our reaction to Molly's objectification of Boylan is conditioned by context. Molly is socially and personally quite powerless, except through her powers of seduction. She is also aware that Boylan does not have an especially high regard for her—he is, like so many other men, using her

as a sex object—"because thats all they want out of you." There is a re-
taliatory self-protective character to her denial of subjectivity that makes
it seem right and just in a way that it might not be if it were Boylan thinking about Molly.

Hankinson's hard-core "novel" is both a typical example of the genre at-
tacked by MacKinnon and Dworkin and, in itself, quite an interesting
case in its pseudo-literary aspects. For if one holds this passage up next
to *The Rainbow,* as the customer of the Blue Moon Press is not very likely
to do, one notices the way in which Hankinson has borrowed from
Lawrence, and has incorporated into his narrative of violence and abuse
features of the Lawrentian "blood-knowledge" and denial of autonomy
that serve as legitimating devices for the violence that ensues. We said
that Lawrentian sexuality involves the surrender of individuation, and a
certain sort of porousness of boundaries that can border on violability.
Lawrence certainly depicts the willingness to be penetrated as a valuable
aspect of sexual receptivity. The questions then are, (a) can sadomasochistic sexual acts ever have a simply Lawrentian character, rather
than a more sinister character? and (b) is Hankinson's narrative a case
of that benign sort? (Here I shall not be able to say much about the characters and their conduct without focusing on the way in which the "implied author" has structured the narrative as a whole, since the "novel"
is exceedingly formulaic and lacking in complex characterization.)
    There seems to be no a priori reason why the answer to (a) cannot be
"yes." I have no very clear intuitions on this point, and here I'm going to
have to own to limits of experience and desire; but it would seem that
some narrative depictions of sadomasochistic activity do plausibly attribute to its consensual form a kind of Lawrentian character, in which
the willingness to be vulnerable to the infliction of pain, in some respects a sharper stimulus than pleasure, manifests a more complete trust
and receptivity than could be found in other sexual acts. Pat Califia's disturbing short story "Jenny" is one example of such a portrayal.[50] And
Hankinson certainly positions his narrative this way, suggesting that
there is a profound mutual desire that leads the two actors to seek an absence of individuation. The Lawrentian "atavistic voice" speaking from
within Isabelle asks for the continuation of violence, and Hankinson suggests that in asking this she is making contact with some depth in her being that lies beneath mere personality. All this is Lawrence, and
Schopenhauer, in Blue Moon Press clothing.
    What make the difference, clearly, are context and intention. For the
answer to (b) is clearly "no." Not only the character Macrae, but Hankinson's text as a whole, represent women as creatures whose autonomy
and subjectivity don't matter at all, insofar as they are not involved in the
gratification of male desire. The women, including whatever signs of hu-

manity they display, are just there to be used as sex objects for men in whatever way suits them. The eroticization of the woman's inertness, her lack of autonomy, her violability—and the assuaging fiction that this is what she has asked for, this is what nature has dictated for her—all these features, which make the example a textbook case of MacKinnon's views and a classic candidate under the Minneapolis and the Indianapolis version of the MacKinnon/Dworkin ordinance, also make it crucially unlike Lawrence, in which vulnerability and risk are mutually assumed and there is no malign or destructive intent.[51] In Lawrence, being treated as a cunt is a permission to expand the sphere of one's activity and fulfillment. In Hankinson, being treated like a cunt is being treated as something whose experiences don't matter at all. The entire novel, which is nothing but a succession of similar scenes, conceals the subjectivity of women from the reader's view, and constructs women as objects for male use and control. There is a ghastly way in which subjectivity does figure: For Macrae's desire is a desire "to violate . . . to desecrate, destroy." It is a desire that would not have been satisfied by intercourse with a corpse, or even an animal. What is made sexy here is precisely the act of turning a creature whom in one dim corner of one's mind one knows to be human into a thing, a something rather than a someone. And to be able to do that to a fellow human being is sexy because it is a dizzying experience of power.

J. S. Mill vividly described the distorted upbringing of men in England, who are taught every day that they are superior to one half of the human race, even though at the same time they see the fine achievements and character of women daily before their eyes. They learn that just in virtue of being male they are superior to the most exalted and talented woman, and they are corrupted by this awareness.[52] Consider in this light the education of Hankinson's reader, who learns (in the visceral way in which pornography leaves its impress, forming patterns of arousal and response[53]) that just in virtue of being male he is entitled to violate half of the human race, whose humanity is at the same time dimly presented to his vision. To the extent that he immerses himself in such works and regularly finds easy and uncomplicated satisfaction in connection with the images they construct, he is likely to form certain patterns of expectation regarding women—that they are for his pleasure, to be taken in this way. The work as a whole, which contains no episodes that are not of this kind, strongly encourages such projections.[54] Unlike MacKinnon and Dworkin, I do not favor any legal restrictions on such work, even the civil ordinance they propose, since I believe that any such proposal would jeopardize expressive interests that it is important to protect.[55] I also think that its availability has moral value, since we learn a lot about sexism from studying it. But I would certainly take it away from any young boy I know, I would protest against its inclusion on a reading list or syllabus—except in the way I recommend our reading it here[56]—and I would think that an ethical critique of it, which needs to be given again and again, is indeed, as Andrea Dworkin says in my epigraph, "at the heart of struggle."

Playboy is more polite, but ultimately similar. Here again I agree with MacKinnon and Dworkin, who have repeatedly stressed the essential similarity between the soft-core and the hard-core pornography industries. The message given by picture and caption is, "whatever else this woman is and does, for us she is an object for sexual enjoyment." Once again, the male reader is told, in effect, that he is the one with subjectivity and autonomy, and on the other side are things that look very sexy and are displayed out there for his consumption, like delicious pieces of fruit, existing only or primarily to satisfy his desire.[57] The message is more benign, because, as a part of the *Playboy* "philosophy," women are depicted as beings made for sexual pleasure, rather than for the infliction of pain, and their autonomy and subjectivity are given a nodding sort of recognition. In a sense *Playboy* could be said to be part of the movement for women's liberation, in the sense suggested by Lawrence and Lorde. Insofar as women's full autonomy and self-expression are hindered by the repression and denial of their sexual capacities, thus far the cheery liberationist outlook of *Playboy* might be said to be feminist.

However, the objectification in *Playboy* is in fact a profound betrayal not only of the Kantian ideal of human regard but also, and perhaps especially, of the Lawrence/Lorde program. For *Playboy* depicts a thoroughgoing fungibility and commodification of sex partners, and, in the process, severs sex from any deep connection with self-expression or emotion. Lorde argues plausibly when she suggests that this dehumanization and commercialization of sex is but the modern face of an older puritanism, and the apparent feminism of such publications is a mask for a profoundly repressive attitude toward real female passion.[58] Indeed, Hankinson could argue that *Playboy* is worse than his novel, for his novel at least connects sexuality to the depths of people's dreams and wishes (both female and male) and thus avoids the reduction of bodies to interchangeable commodities, whereas in *Playboy* sex is a commodity, and women become very like cars, or suits, namely, expensive possessions that mark one's status in the world of men.

Who is objectified in *Playboy*? In the immediate context, it is the represented woman who is being objectified and, derivatively, the actress whose photograph appears. But the characteristic *Playboy* generalizing approach ("why we love tennis," or "women of the Ivy League")—assisted in no small measure by the magazine's focus on photographs of real women, rather than on paintings or fictions—strongly suggests that real-life women relevantly similar to the tennis player can easily be cast in the roles in which *Playboy* casts its chosen few. In that way it constructs for the reader a fantasy objectification of a class of real women. Used as a masturbatory aid, it encourages the idea that an easy satisfaction can be had in this uncomplicated way, without the difficulties attendant on recognizing women's subjectivity and autonomy in a more full-blooded way.[59]

We can now observe one further feature of Lawrence that marks him as different from the pornographer. In Lawrence the men whose sexual behavior is approved are always remarkably unconcerned with worldly status and honor. The last thing they would think of would be to treat a woman as a prize possession, an object whose presence in their lives, and whose sexual interest in them, enhances their status in the world of men. (Indeed, that sort of status-centered attitude to women is connected by Lawrence with sexual impotence, in the character of Clifford Chatterley.) One cannot even imagine Mellors boasting in the locker room of the "hot number" he had the previous night, or regarding the tits and ass, or the sexual behavior, of Connie as items of display in the male world. What is most characteristic of Mellors (and of Tom Brangwen) is a profound indifference to the worldly signs of prestige; and this is a big part of the reason why both Connie Chatterley and the reader have confidence that his objectification of her is quite different from commodification (in my vocabulary, instrumentalization/ownership).

Playboy, by contrast, is just like a car magazine, only with people instead of cars to make things a little sexier—in the Hankinson way in which it is sexier to use a human being as a thing than simply to have a thing, since it manifests greater control, it shows that one can control what is of such a nature as to elude control. The magazine is all about the competition of men with other men, and its message is the availability of a readily renewable supply of more or less fungible women to men who have achieved a certain level of prestige and money—or rather, that fantasy women of this sort are available, through the magazine, to those who can fantasize that they have achieved this status. It is not in that sense very different from the ancient Greek idea that the victorious warrior would be rewarded with seven tripods, ten talents of gold, twenty cauldrons, twelve horses, and seven women.[60] Objectification means a certain sort of self-regarding display.

The one further thing that needs to be said about the picture is that in the *Playboy* world it is sexier, because more connected with status, to have a woman of achievement and talent than an unmarked woman, in the way that it is sexier to have a Mercedes than a Chevrolet, in the way that Agamemnon assures Achilles that the horses he is giving him are prize-winning racehorses and the women both beautiful and skilled in weaving. But a sleek woman is even more sexy than a sleek car, which cannot really be dominated since it is nothing but a thing. For what *Playboy* repeatedly says to its reader is, Whoever this woman is and whatever she has achieved, for you she is cunt, all her pretensions vanish before your sexual power. For some she is a tennis player—but you, in your mind, can dominate her and turn her into cunt. For some, Brown students are Brown students. For you, dear reader, they are *Women of the Ivy League* (an issue in preparation as I write, and the topic of intense controversy among my students[61]). No matter who you are, these women will (in masturbatory fantasy) moan with pleasure at your sexual power. This is the great appeal of *Playboy* in fact: It satisfies the desires of men to feel themselves special and powerful, by telling them that they too can possess the signs of exalted status that they think of as in real life reserved for such as Donald Trump. This, of course, Lawrence would see as the sterile status-seeking of Clifford Chatterley, in a modern guise.

Playboy, I conclude, is a bad influence on men[62]—hardly a surprising conclusion. I draw no legal implications from this judgment, but, as in the case of Hankinson, I think we should ponder this issue when we educate boys and young men, and meet the prevalence of that style of objectification with criticism—the most powerful form of which is, as Andrea Dworkin said, the assertion of one's own humanity at all times.

Hollinghurst is a case full of fascinating ambiguity. On its surface, this scene, like many in the novel, manifests the exuberant embrace of sexual fungibility that characterized parts of the male gay subculture in the pre-AIDS era. It seems like a very different sort of eroticizing of bodily parts from the sort that goes on in Hankinson and *Playboy*, more like Molly Bloom, in fact, in its delight in the size of organs, coupled with a cheerful nonexploitative attitude, albeit an emotionally superficial one, to the people behind the parts. Richard Mohr has written eloquently of this sort of promiscuous sexuality that it embodies a certain ideal of democracy, since couplings of the anonymous bathhouse sort neglect distinctions of class and rank. In a rather Whitmanesque burst of enthusiasm, he concludes that "Gay sexuality of the sort that I have been discussing both symbolizes and generates a kind of fundamental equality—the sort of fundamental equality that stands behind and is necessary for justifications of democracy."[63] The idea is that anonymous couplings establish that in an especially fundamental matter everyone really is equal to everyone else. Mohr makes it very clear that this can happen among men because they are already acknowledged socially as more than just bodies, because the social meaning of objectification among men is altogether different from its meaning between men and women. This being the case, promiscuous and anonymous sex can exemplify a norm of equality.

Mohr does seem to have gotten at something important about democracy, something about the moral role of the fungibility of bodies that is probably important in both the utilitarian and the Kantian liberal traditions. Certainly the fact that all citizens have similar bodies subject to similar accidents has played an important role in the thought of democratic theorists as diverse as Rousseau and Walt Whitman. Some such egalitarian idea animates Hollinghurst as well, at some moments. On the other hand, it is a little hard to know how the sexual scene at issue really is supposed to show the sort of equal regard for bodily need that underlies this democratic tradition. Notice how distinctions of class and rank are omnipresent, even in the prose that pushes them aside. The narrator is intensely conscious of racial differences, which he tends, here as elsewhere, to associate with stereotypes of genital organ size. Nor are the cycle-clips and duffel-coats that mark the lower-middle classes ever out of mind, even when they are out of sight—and the disdainful description of the small genitalia of the "smirking" neighbor strongly suggests the disdain of the "jacket and tie" for these signs of inferiority. We notice, in fact, that all the genitalia described are stereotypes, and none is personalized with the regard of Mellor for the "cunt of Lady Jane."

Now the question is, how is this connected with the emphasis on fungibility? Mohr would say, presumably, that there is no connection—that this narrator, an upper-class Englishman, has just not managed to enter fully enough into the democratic spirit of the bathhouse world. But the suspicion remains that there may after all be some connection between the spirit of fungibility and a focus on these superficial aspects of race and class and penis size, which do in a sense dehumanize, and turn people into potential instruments. For in the absence of any narrative history with the person, how can desire attend to anything else but the incidental, and how can one do more than use the body of the other as a tool of one's own states?[64] The photographs used by Mohr to illustrate his idea focus intently on hypermasculine characteristics of musculature and penis size, which presumably are not equally distributed among all citizens of this world, and indeed one imagines that the world so constructed is likely to be one in which morally irrelevant characteristics count for everything, rather than nothing, an extremely hierarchical world, rather than one without hierarchy. Maybe this just means that people are not after all treated as fungible, and that if they were to be more fully treated as fungible things would be well. But the worry is that in a setting which, in order to construct a kind of fungibility, denies all access to those features of personhood at the heart of the real democratic equality of persons, it is hard to see how things could turn out otherwise. This is not a knock-down argument showing that Mohr's Whitmanesque ideal is doomed to failure. The connection between fungibility and instrumentality is loose and causal, rather than conceptual. But it is a worry that would, I think, be shared by MacKinnon and Dworkin with Lorde and Lawrence: Can one really treat someone with the respect and concern that democracy requires if one has sex with him in the anonymous spirit of Hollinghurst's description?

We arrive, finally, at the end of *The Golden Bowl*. This is, to my mind, the most sinister passage on my list, if we focus on the conduct of the characters rather than the implied author, and the one that most clearly depicts a morally blameworthy instrumentalization of persons—though of course it is the business of the novel as a whole to question this behavior. Treating their respective spouses as fine antique furniture is, for Adam and Maggie, a way of denying them human status and asserting their right to the permanent use of those splendidly elegant bodies. This use involves denial of autonomy—Charlotte has to be sent off to the museum in America to be "buried," the Prince has to be turned into an elegant if flawed domestic object—and also denial of subjectivity. To appreciate them as antique furniture is to say, we don't have to ask ourselves whether they are in pain. We can just look at them and neglect the claims that they actively make. The *sposi* are rendered inert, morally and emotionally, and as in a sense, fungible—for from the outset Maggie has noted that to treat her husband as a work of art is to neglect his personal uniqueness.[65] In fact, we see every item on our list except physical violability—and emotional violation is amply attested.

This should tell us that the dehumanization and objectification of persons has many forms. It is not obvious that the "core" of such objectification is sexual, or that its primary vehicle is the specifically erotic education of men and women. Mill tells us that the entire education of men in his society teaches the lesson of domination and use; he does not put the blame at the door of the specifically sexual education. Here we are reminded that there can be morally sinister objectification without any particular connection to sex, or even to gender roles. Maggie and Adam learned their attitudes to persons by being rich collectors. Their attitude probably has consequences for sex, but it has its roots elsewhere, in an attitude to money and to other things that James associates with America. All things, in the rich American world, are regarded as having a price, as being essentially controllable and usable, if only one is wealthy enough. Nothing is an end in itself, because the only end is wealth.[66]

The skeptical incursion of the narrator, with his "lingering view, a view more penetrating than the occasion demanded," points out that what we really see here is the "concrete attestatio[n]" of "a rare power of purchase."

This complicates our question—for it tells us that we should question the claim of Kant, Dworkin, and MacKinnon that the deformation of sexual desire is prior to, and causes, other forms of objectification of the sexual partner. It also seems possible that in many cases an antecedent deformation of attitudes to things and persons infiltrates and poisons desire.[67] I shall not be able to pursue this question further. I leave it on the table, in order to suggest the next chapter that would need to be written in any story of sexual objectification in our world.

To conclude, let me return to the seven forms of objectification and summarize the argument. It would appear that Kant, MacKinnon, and Dworkin are correct in one central insight: that the instrumental treatment of human beings, the treatment of human beings as tools of the purposes of another, is always morally problematic; if it does not take place in a larger context of regard for humanity, it is a central form of the morally objectionable. It is also a common feature of sexual life, especially, though not only, in connection with male treatment of women. As such, it is closely bound up with other forms of objectification, in particular with denial of autonomy, denial of subjectivity, and various forms of boundary-violation. In some forms, it is connected with fungibility and ownership or quasi-ownership: the notion of "commodification."

On the other hand, there seems to be no other item on the list that is always morally objectionable. Denial of autonomy and denial of subjectivity are objectionable if they persist throughout an adult relationship, but as phases in a relationship characterized by mutual regard they can be all right, or even quite wonderful in the way that Lawrence suggests. In a closely related way, it may at times be splendid to treat the other person as passive, or even inert. Emotional penetration of boundaries seems potentially a very valuable part of sexual life, and some forms of physical boundary-penetration also, though it is less clear which ones these are. Treating-as-fungible is suspect when the person so treated is from a group that has frequently been commodified and used as a tool, or a prize; between social equals these problems disappear, though it is not clear that others do not arise.

As for the aetiology of objectification, we have some reasons by now to doubt Kant's account, according to which the baneful form of use is inherent in sexual desire and activity themselves. We have some reason to endorse MacKinnon and Dworkin's account, according to which social hierarchy is at the root of the deformation of desire; but Lorde and Lawrence show us that the deformation is more complicated than this, working not only through pornography but also through puritanism and the repression of female erotic experience.[68] In that sense it may be plausible to claim, as Lawrence does, that a certain sort of objectifying attention to bodily parts is an important element in correcting the deformation and promoting genuine erotic equality. Finally, we should grant that we do not really know how central sexual desire is in all these problems of objectification and commodification, by comparison, for example, to economic norms and motives that powerfully construct desire in our culture.

There is no particular logical place to end what has been intended as an initial exploration of a concept whose full mapping will require many more investigations. So it may be fitting enough to end with the juxtaposition of two literary scenes involving what might well be called objectification. One is a vivid reminder, courtesy of James Hankinson, of what motivates the Kantian project of MacKinnon and Dworkin. The other is a passage in which Lawrence indicates the terms on which objectification, of a kind, can be a source of joy—mentioning a possibility that Kant, MacKinnon, and Dworkin, in different ways and for different reasons and with different degrees of firmness and universality, would appear to deny:

> She feels the sole of his foot on her waist, then waits for what seems like an eternity for him to bring the crop down onto her flesh, and when eventually the blow falls squarely across her buttocks and the pain courses through her, she feels a burning thrill of salvation as if the pain will cauterize her sins and make her whole again, and as Macrae bring the crop down on her again and again, she feels the sin falling from her, *agnus dei qui tollis peccata mundi,* and she finds in the mortifying a vision of the road to paradise lined with the grateful souls who have been saved from fire by fire, and she too is grateful to Macrae for beating her clean again.

> "But what do you believe in?" she insisted.
> "I believe in being warm hearted. I especially believe in being warm hearted in love, in fucking with a warm heart. . . ."
> She softly rubbed her cheek on his belly, and gathered his balls in her hand. . . .
> All the while he spoke he exquisitely stroked the rounded tail, till it seemed as if a slippery sort of fire came from it into his hands. . . .
> "An' if tha shits an' if tha pisses, I'm glad. I don't want a woman as couldna shit nor piss. . . ."
> With quiet fingers he threaded a few forget-me-not flowers in the fine brown fleece of the mount of Venus.[69]

Notes

1. Catharine MacKinnon, *Feminism Unmodified* (Cambridge, Mass.: Harvard University Press, 1987), p. 174.

2. See MacKinnon, *Feminism,* p. 262 n. 1. The Indianapolis ordinance struck down in *American Booksellers, Inc. v. Hudnut* (598 F. Supp. 1316 [S.D. Ind. 1984]) uses the related category: "women are presented as sexual objects for domination, conquest, violation, exploitation, possession, or use. . . ."

3. MacKinnon, *Toward a Feminist Theory of the State* (Cambridge, Mass.: Harvard University Press, 1989), p. 124.

4. Ibid.

5. Cass Sunstein, *The Partial Constitution* (Cambridge, Mass.: Harvard University Press, 1993), pp. 257–90; also "Neutrality in Constitutional Law (with Special Reference to Pornography, Abortion, and Surrogacy)," *Columbia Law Review* 92 (1992): 1–52.

6. *Defending Pornography: Free Speech, Sex, and the Fight for Women's Rights* (New York: Scribner, 1995).

7. Sunstein, review of Strossen, *The New Republic,* 9 January 1995.

8. Passages are taken from: D. H. Lawrence, *The Rainbow* (London: Penguin, 1989; first publication 1915), pp. 132–33; James Joyce, *Ulysses* (New York: Modern Library, 1961; first copyright 1914), p. 742; "Laurence St. Clair," *Isabelle and Véronique: Four Months, Four Cities* (New York: Blue Moon Books, Inc., 1989), pp. 2–4 (of 181 pages); Alan Hollinghurst, *The Swimming-Pool Library* (New York: Vintage, 1989; first published 1988), p. 20; Henry James, *The Golden Bowl* (New York: Penguin Books, 1985; first published 1904), p. 574.

9. On the artist's creative activity as an example of morally assessable conduct, see my discussion of Henry James in " 'Finally Aware and Richly Responsible': Literature and the Moral Imagination," in *Love's Knowledge* (New York: Oxford University Press, 1990).

10. See Booth, *The Company We Keep: An Ethics of Fiction* (Berkeley: University of California Press, 1988).

11. See Booth, *Company,* chap. 3. He uses Aristotle's account of friendship to ask about the ethical value of spending time in the company of texts of different sorts.

12. I want to emphasize that I speak only of the text, and make no claim about the motives and views of Hankinson himself, who may for all we know have had any number of different motives for writing in this genre. We should scrupulously observe Booth's distinction between the "implied author" and the "real-life author."

13. Each of these seven would ultimately need more refinement, in connection with debates about the proper analysis of the core notions. There are, for example, many theories of what autonomy and subjectivity are.

14. I put this in quotes because I am conscious that the word is not ideal; it is too anthropomorphic for things like ballpoint pens.

15. The same is true of "violability"—see n. 14 above—although if I had chosen a term such as "breakability" it would not be.

16. It is interesting to consider in this regard the legal doctrine of "moral rights" of the creators of artworks, which, in much of Europe and increasingly in the United States, protects creators against objectionable alterations in an artwork even after they have relinquished ownership. Technically speaking, these are rights of the artist, not of the artwork, and may be waived by the artist, though not, in a jointly produced work, by one artist without the consent of the others; but the resulting situation is one in which the work itself has, in effect, rights against being defaced or destroyed or in nonpermitted ways altered. For a good summary of the doctrine, see Martin A. Roeder, "The Doctrine of Moral Right: A Study in the Law of Artists, Authors and Creators," *Harvard Law Review* 53 (1940): 554–78; see also Peter H. Karlen, "Joint Ownership of Moral Rights," *Journal, Copyright Society of the U.S.A.* (1991): 242–75; for criticism of some recent U.S. state laws, see Thomas J. Davis, Jr., "Fine Art and Moral Rights: The Immoral Triumph of Emotionalism," *Hofstra Law Review* 17 (1989): 317 ff. I am grateful to William Landes for these references.

17. Richard D. Mohr, *Gay Ideas: Outing and Other Controversies* (Boston: Beacon Press, 1992), especially the essay " 'Knights, Young Men, Boys': Masculine Worlds and Democratic Values," pp. 129–218.

18. See Rubin, "Thinking Sex," in *The Lesbian and Gay Studies Reader*, ed. H. Abelove et al. (New York: Routledge, 1993); Mohr, " 'Knights, Young Men,'" cited above. See Scruton's *Sexual Desire: A Moral Philosophy of the Erotic* (New York: The Free Press, 1986).

19. In an interesting sense, the norm of unconditional love of children may lead love to disregard the particularizing qualities of the individual, and this may be seen as a good feature of parental love. See Gregory Vlastos, "The Individual as Object of Love in Plato," in *Platonic Studies* (Princeton: Princeton University Press, 1973).

20. For MacKinnon's account of the relation between this account and her feminist account of objectification, see *Feminist Theory*, p. 124; cf. also pp. 138–39. It is fairly clear from this discussion that the term "objectification" is intended by MacKinnon to correspond to Marx's language of "Versachlichung" or "Verdinglichung" in *Das Kapital*, and is closely connected with the notion of "Entaüsserung," closely linked by Marx to "Entfremdung," usually translated "alienation." MacKinnon explains Marx's argument that the "realization" of the self in private property is really a form of alienation of the self, and then says that in the case of property "alienation is the socially contingent distortion" of a process of realization, whereas in sexuality as currently realized, women's objectification just *is* alienation: ". . . from the point of view of the object, women have not authored objectifications, they have been them."

21. One might certainly wonder whether Marx has underestimated the distinction between the worker's situation, based on a contract in which there is at least some kind of consent, and the situation of the slave, which lacks any sort of consent. This tendency to equate relations that may be subtly distinct is closely related to MacKinnon and Dworkin's tendency to efface distinctions among different types of sexual relations.

22. *Feminism Unmodified* (Cambridge, Mass.: Harvard University Press, 1987), p. 48. See also *Feminist Theory*, pp. 124, 138–39. MacKinnon understands Marx to mean that the worker puts his selfhood into the "products and relationships" he creates, "becomes embodied in" these products. So read, Marx's idea is a version of Diotima's idea, in Plato's *Symposium*, that human beings seek to create items in which their identity may be extended and prolonged.

23. This is also the way in which I would regard the incentive of manumission as a reward for hard work: It is an incentive that is not exactly part of the institution, offered to the slave as human. Other incentives for hard work do not involve a recognition of autonomous agency and purpose.

24. Though, once again, we shall see that a certain sort of keen attention to subjective experience may be entailed by certain sorts of instrumental use of persons.

25. I owe this example to Lawrence Lessig.

26. One way of cashing this out further would be to ask to what extent my use of him as a pillow prevented him from either attaining or acting on important capacities with which he identifies his well-being. Am I preventing him from getting up to eat? From sleeping? From walking around? From reading a book? And so forth.

27. "Could It Be Worth Thinking About Kant on Sex and Marriage?" in Louise Antony and Charlotte Witt, eds., *A Mind of One's Own: Feminist Essays on Reason and Objectivity* (Boulder: Westview, 1993), pp. 49–67.

28. See *Lectures on Ethics*, esp. the following passage, quoted by Herman, p. 55: "Taken by itself [sexual love] is a degradation of human nature; for as soon as a person becomes an Object of appetite for another, all motives of moral relationship cease to function, because as an Object of appetite for another a person becomes a thing and can be treated and used as such by every one."

29. See *Intercourse* (New York: Free Press, 1987), pp.122–23: "There is a deep recognition in culture and in experience that intercourse is both the normal use of a woman, her human potentiality affirmed by it, and a violative abuse, her privacy irredeemably compromised, her selfhood changed in a way that is irrevocable, unrecoverable. . . . By definition, she [has] a lesser privacy, a lesser integrity of the body, a lesser sense of self, since her body can be physically occupied and in the occupation taken over."

30. Thus sex for Kant is not like a contractual relation in which one can use the other person as a means in an overall context of mutual respect: For sexual desire, according to his analysis, drives out every possibility of respect. This is so even in marriage (see below), although there the legal context ensures that at least in other parts of the relationship respect will be present.

31. See, for a very Kantian example, Dworkin's *Intercourse*, pp. 140–41: "It is especially in the acceptance of the object status that her humanity is hurt: it is . . . an implicit acceptance of less freedom, less privacy, less integrity. In becoming an object so that he can objectify her so that he can fuck her, she begins a political collaboration with his dominance; and then when he enters her, he confirms for himself and for her what she is: that she is something, not someone; certainly not someone equal."

32. Pp. 47–61.

33. See, for example, MacKinnon, *Feminist Theory*, p. 124: "Women have been the nature, the matter, the acted upon to be subdued by the acting subject seeking to embody himself in the social world"; and p. 198: "The acting that women are allowed is asking to be acted upon."

34. Both fungibility and ownership, for example, are implicit in MacKinnon's description of males as "consumers" and "women as things for sexual use" (ibid., pp. 138–39).

35. See the convincing discussion of MacKinnon's ideas in Sally Haslanger, "On Being Objective and Being Objectified," in *A Mind of One's Own*, pp. 85–125, esp. p. 111, where she argues that instrumentality is at the heart of MacKinnon's concept of objectification.

36. See Herman's excellent discussion, pp. 62–63: "The rules are not so much to restrain or oblige action as to construct moral regard. That is, they make the sexual interest in another person possible only where there is secure moral regard for that person's life, and they do this by making the acceptance of obligations with respect to that person's welfare a condition of sexual activity."

37. Compare MacKinnon, *Feminist Theory*, pp. 138–39: ". . . objectification itself, with self-determination ecstatically relinquished, is the apparent content of women's sexual desire and desirability."

38. Andrea Dworkin, *Woman Hating* (New York: E. P. Dutton, 1974), pp. 58, 62.

39. Dworkin points to the prevalence of anal penetration in the novel as evidence that O is a surrogate for René.

40. See, for example, MacKinnon, *Feminist Theory*, p. 202, objecting that the "as a whole" test legitimates publications such as *Playboy*: ". . . legitimate settings diminish the injury perceived to be done to the women whose trivialization and objectification it contextualizes. Besides, if a women is subjected, why should it matter that the work has other value? Perhaps what redeems a work's value among men enhances its injury to women."

41. In the particular case, this does not seem to be connected with a willingness to be broken or smashed, but one should see, I think, a close link between this sort of boundary-surrender and the boundary-surrender involved in at least some sadomasochistic relationships.

42. I mean here to say that a working-class man in England of that time is roughly comparable in social power to an upper-class woman. As for Brangwen and his wife, her higher-class origins and her property give her a rough parity with him.

43. This point is only slightly weakened by the fact that "John Thomas" is a traditional name for the penis, and is not original with Mellors. The entire exchange has a very personal character, and it is at any rate clear that this is the first time that Constance has heard the name, and that for her it is a fully proper name. The fact that the genital organ is given a personal proper name, and yet a name distinct from the name of the rest of Mellor is itself complexly related to my earlier point about loss of individuality: For it alludes to the fact that in allowing this part to take over, one does cease to be oneself.

What should one make of the fact that Constance's cunt is not given a proper name, but is simply called "the cunt of Lady Jane," with a joking allusion to the tension between sex and class? One could, of course, argue that Mellors is treating her genitals less personally than he treats his own; but then I think it would be a jarring note in the scene if he did simply invent a name for her cunt—presumably that is a game in which she ought to play a role, and she is too frightened at this point to play that game.

44. I think that this position is subtly different from the position developed in Scruton's *Sexual Desire*. Scruton holds that in a good sexual encounter the individual people encounter one another in one another's bodies, because they allow their respective bodies to be illuminated by their own personalities—"the body of the other becomes the other self, and is illuminated in the moment of arousal by the 'I' " (Scruton, letter of 1 April 1995). I feel that in Scruton's attitude to the body there is always a sense that just as it is, it is not a part of our personhood—it needs to be transfigured, and in a sense redeemed from mere animality, by a momentary and mysterious "illumination." The view I share with Lawrence holds, instead, that it was always, just as it is, a part of personhood, and doesn't need to be transfigured, or rather, that the only transfiguration it needs is shame-free attention and love. The difference comes out clearly in our respective attitudes to the bodies of animals—on which see my review of *Sexual Desire* in *The New York Review of Books*, December 18, 1986.

45. Audre Lorde, "The Uses of the Erotic," in *Sister Outsider* (Freedom, Calif.: Crossing Press, 1984), pp. 53–59.

46. See also Lorde, ibid., p. 54: "The erotic . . . has been made into the confused, the trivial . . . the plasticized sensation."

47. Ibid., p. 57: "For once we begin to feel deeply all the aspects of our lives,

we begin to demand from ourselves and from our life-pursuits that they feel in accordance with that joy which we know ourselves to be capable of."

48. In that sense, the proposal is in the spirit of the attitude to sexuality expressed in the writings of the late John J. Winkler, especially *The Constraints of Desire: The Anthropology of Sex and Gender in Greece* (New York: Routledge, 1990).

49. See my discussion in "The Transfiguration of Everyday Life," *Metaphilosophy* 25 (1994): 238–61.

50. "Jenny," in Pat Califia, *Macho Sluts: Lesbian Erotic Fiction* (Boston: Alyson, 1984). See also Roger Scruton, *Sexual Desire*.

51. Things are made more complex by the fact that the two Hankinson *characters* are in a sense quite Lawrentian—it is the implied author, not Macrae, who seems to be proceeding in bad faith, ascribing to the woman a subjectivity desirous of pain and humiliation. Why, then, do I move so quickly in the Hankinson case to a critique of the construction of the fiction as a whole, given that both cases are apparently equally fictional? The answer lies in the formulaic character of the Hankinson text, which invites us to see the characters as mere pretexts for the implied author's expression of a view about women's sexuality. It seems pointless to discuss their conduct independently of a discussion of the genre, and the author's participation in it.

52. Mill, *The Subjection of Women*, ed. Susan Okin (Indianapolis: Hackett, 1988), pp. 86–87: "Think what it is to a boy, to grow up to manhood in the belief that without any merit or any exertion of his own, though he may be the most frivolous and empty or the most ignorant and stolid of mankind, by the mere fact of being born a male he is by right the superior of all and every one of an entire half of the human race: including probably some whose real superiority to himself he has daily or hourly occasion to feel. . . . Is it imagined that all this does not pervert the whole manner of existence of the man, both as an individual and as a social being?"

53. For MacKinnon's accounts of this, see refs. in *Feminism Unmodified* and *Only Words*. See also Joshua Cohen, "Freedom, Equality, Pornography," in *Justice and Injustice in Legal Theory*, ed. Austin Sarat and Thomas Kearns (Ann Arbor: University of Michigan Press, 1996). Compare Mill's account of the way in which domination is "inoculated by one schoolboy upon another" (*Subjection*, ibid.), though with no explicit reference to specifically erotic education.

54. One might complain about the possible bad influence of the unrepresentative portrayal of women even in a narrative that contextualized the portrayal in a way inviting criticism or distancing; thus it is not obviously mistaken of MacKinnon and Dworkin to reject appeal to context in defense of objectionable passages. But their ideas about the construction of desire take on more power when the work as a whole encourages the belief that this is the way all male-female relations are, or can be. This point about the unrepresentative portrayal of women is logically independent of and has implications beyond the objectification issue: For one could, similarly, object to a work that, without objectifying women in any of the senses discussed here, portrayed all its female characters as stupid, or greedy, or unreliable.

55. My reasons are those given by Joshua Cohen in "Freedom, Equality, Pornography," presented at an APA Central Division session along with the present article, and forthcoming in *Justice and Injustice in Legal Theory*, ed. Sarat and Kearns.

56. It is an interesting question to what extent a critical context of reading can impede the formation of the patterns of desire constructed by the work as it addresses its implied reader. The ancient Greek Stoics, unlike Plato, wanted to keep tragic poetry around as a source of moral warning about the pain that would ensue from the overestimation of the "goods of fortune"—as Epictetus defined tragedy, "What happens when chance events befall fools." Rejecting Plato's banishment of the poets, they thought they could domesticate them by moral critique. Were they right? See Nussbaum, "Poetry and the Passions: Two Stoic Views," in J. Brunschwig and M. Nussbaum, eds., *Passions & Perceptions* (Cambridge: Cambridge University Press, 1993), pp. 97–149.

57. See the very good discussion in Alison Assiter, "Autonomy and Pornography," in *Feminist Perspectives in Philosophy,* ed. Morwenna Griffiths and Margaret Whitford (London: Macmillan, 1988), pp. 58–71, who argues that the person who frequently experiences satisfaction in connection with such limited relationships is less likely to seek out less distorting, more complicated relationships. Assiter's article contains a valuable parallel to Hegel's Master-Slave dialectic.

58. Lorde, "Uses of the Erotic," p. 54: "But pornography is a direct denial of the power of the erotic, for it represents the suppression of true feeling. Pornography emphasizes sensation without feeling."

59. See Assiter, "Autonomy and Pornography," pp. 66–69. One may accept this criticism of *Playboy* even if one is not convinced that its portrayal of women is sufficiently depersonalizing to count as objectification.

60. See Homer, *Iliad* IX.121–30; this is the offer Agamemnon makes to assuage the anger of Achilles.

61. The essence of the controversy was over the ethical question whether women should allow themselves to be hired as models, given that they would be cast in the role of representing Brown women generally, and given that Brown women generally didn't want to be represented in that way. Issues were also raised about whether the student newspaper should have run an ad for the recruitment, given that campus sentiment was against it; and students sponsored a forum to discuss the more general ethical and legal issues involved. Since the actual recruitment took place off campus, there was nothing else to say, and in fact Brown produced the largest number of applicant models of any Ivy League campus.

62. I am thinking of bad influence in Wayne Booth's way (*The Company We Keep,* see above), as a bad way of spending one's time thinking and desiring during the time one is reading. I make no claims in this article about causal connections between those times and other times, though I do find convincing Assiter's claim that the habit of having pleasure in connection with fantasies of this type is likely to lead one to seek out such undemanding relationships in life, rather than those involving a fuller recognition of women's subjectivity and autonomy.

63. *Gay Ideas,* p. 196.

64. I think that this is the point made by Roger Scruton in *Sexual Desire,* when he holds that a context of intimacy and mutual regard promote the sexual attention to individuality.

65. See Chap. I, Pt. i (Maggie to the Prince): "You're a rarity, an object of

beauty, an object of price. You're not perhaps absolutely unique, but you're so curious and eminent that there are very few others like you. . . . You're what they call a *morceau de musée*."

66. See the impressive Marxist reading of the novel in Ed Ahearn, *Marx and Modern Fiction* (New Haven: Yale University Press, 1989), pp. 76–99.

67. See Ahearn, *Marx*, p. 99: ". . . the celebration of the aesthetic and the misuse of persons, two forms of acquisition, are rooted in that original accumulation, the money of the amiable Adam Verver."

68. This double aetiology is suggested in some parts of Dworkin's *Intercourse*, especially "Dust/Dirt"; and in the episode in *Mercy* in which the Greek lover of Andrea abuses her after discovering that she has been having sex with other men.

69. I am grateful to many people for comments that have helped me revise the article, among them: Mary Becker, Joshua Cohen, Richard Craswell, David Estlund, Robert Goodin, John Hodges, Robert Kaster, William Landes, Lawrence Lessig, Charles Nussbaum, Rachel Nussbaum, Richard Posner, Roger Scruton, Cass Sunstein, Candace Vogler. Above all, I am grateful to the students in my Feminist Philosophy class at Brown University, who discussed the article with relentless critical scrutiny, and especially to: Kristi Abrams, Lara Bovilsky, Hayley Finn, Sarah Hirshman, James Maisels, Gabriel Roth, Danya Ruttenberg, Sarah Ruhl, and Dov Weinstein.

Chapter 24

SHOULD FEMINISTS OPPOSE
PROSTITUTION?

Laurie Shrage

Because sexuality is a social construction, individuals as individuals are not free to experience *eros* just as they choose. Yet just as the extraction and appropriation of surplus value by the capitalist represents a choice available, if not to individuals, to society as a whole, so too sexuality and the forms taken by *eros* must be seen as at some level open to change.

Nancy Hartsock, *Money, Sex and Power*[1]

Introduction

Prostitution raises difficult issues for feminists. On the one hand, many feminists want to abolish discriminatory criminal statutes that are mostly used to harass and penalize prostitutes, and rarely to punish johns and pimps—laws which, for the most part, render prostitutes more vulnerable to exploitation by their male associates.[2] On the other hand, most feminists find the prostitute's work morally and politically objectionable. In their view, women who provide sexual services for a fee submit to sexual domination by men, and suffer degradation by being treated as sexual commodities.[3]

Reprinted from *Ethics* 99:2 (1989), pp. 347–61, with the permission of Laurie Shrage and the University of Chicago Press. © 1989 by The University of Chicago.

My concern, in this paper, is whether persons opposed to the social subordination of women should seek to discourage commercial sex. My goal is to marshal the moral arguments needed to sustain feminists' condemnation of the sex industry in our society. In reaching this goal, I reject accounts of commercial sex which posit cross-cultural and trans-historical causal mechanisms to explain the existence of prostitution or which assume that the activities we designate as "sex" have a universal meaning and purpose. By contrast, I analyze mercenary sex in terms of culturally specific beliefs and principles that organize its practice in contemporary American society. I try to show that the sex industry, like other institutions in our society, is structured by deeply ingrained attitudes and values which are oppressive to women. The point of my analysis is not to advocate an egalitarian reformation of commercial sex, nor to advocate its abolition through state regulation. Instead, I focus on another political alternative: that which must be done to subvert widely held beliefs that legitimate this institution in our society. Ultimately, I argue that nothing closely resembling prostitution, as we currently know it, will exist, once we have undermined these cultural convictions.

Why Prostitution Is Problematic

A number of recent papers on prostitution begin with the familiar observation that prostitution is one of the oldest professions.[4] Such 'observations' take for granted that 'prostitution' refers to a single trans-historical, transcultural activity. By contrast, my discussion of prostitution is limited to an activity that occurs in modern Western societies—a practice which involves the purchase of sexual services from women by men. Moreover, I am not interested in exploring the nature and extension of our moral concept "to prostitute oneself"; rather, I want to examine a specific activity we regard as prostitution in order to understand its social and political significance.

In formulating my analysis, I recognize that the term 'prostitute' is ambiguous: it is used to designate both persons who supply sex on a commercial basis and persons who contribute their talents and efforts to base purposes for some reward. While these extensions may overlap, their relationship is not a logically necessary one but is contingent upon complex moral and social principles. In this paper, I use the term 'prostitute' as shorthand for 'provider of commercial sexual services,' and correspondingly, I use the term 'prostitution' interchangeably with 'commercial sex.' By employing these terms in this fashion, I hope to appear consistent with colloquial English, and not to be taking for granted that a person who provides commercial sexual services "prostitutes" her- or himself.

Many analyses of prostitution aim to resolve the following issue: what would induce a woman to prostitute herself—to participate in an impersonal, commercial sexual transaction? These accounts seek the deeper psychological motives behind apparently voluntary acts of prostitution. Because our society regards female prostitution as a social, if not natural, aberration, such actions demand an explanation. Moreover, accepting fees for sex seems irrational and repugnant to many persons, even to the woman who does it, and so one wonders why she does it. My examination of prostitution does not focus on this question. While to do so may explain why a woman will choose prostitution from among various options, it does not explain how a woman's options have been constituted. In other words, although an answer to this question may help us understand why some women become sellers of sexual services rather than homemakers or engineers, it will not increase our understanding of why there is a demand for these services. Why, for example, can women not as easily achieve prosperity by selling child-care services? Finding out why there is a greater market for goods of one type than of another illuminates social forces and trends as much as, if not more than, finding out why individuals enter a particular market. Moreover, theorists who approach prostitution in this way do not assume that prostitution is "a problem about the women who are prostitutes, and our attitudes to them, [rather than] a problem about the men who demand to buy them."[5] This assumption, as Carole Pateman rightly points out, mars many other accounts.

However, I do not attempt to construct an account of the psychological, social, and economic forces that presumably cause men to demand commercial sex, or of the factors which cause a woman to market her sexual services. Instead, I first consider whether prostitution, in all cultural contexts, constitutes a degrading and undesirable form of sexuality. I argue that, although the commercial availability of sexuality is not in every existing or conceivable society oppressive to women, in our society this practice depends upon the general acceptance of principles which serve to marginalize women socially and politically. Because of the cultural context in which prostitution operates, it epitomizes and perpetuates pernicious patriarchal beliefs and values and, therefore, is both damaging to the women who sell sex and, as an organized social practice, to all women in our society.

Historical and Cross-cultural Perspectives

In describing Babylonian temple prostitution, Gerda Lerner reports: "For people who regarded fertility as sacred and essential to their own survival, the caring for the gods included, in some cases, offering them sexual services. Thus, a separate class of temple prostitutes developed. What seems to have happened was that sexual activity for and in behalf of the god[s] or goddesses was considered beneficial to the people and sacred."[6] Similarly, according to Emma Goldman, the Babylonians believed that "the generative activity of human beings possessed a mysterious and sacred influence in promoting the fertility of Nature."[7] When the rationale for the impersonal provision of sex is conceived in terms of the promotion of nature's fecundity, the social meaning this activity has may differ substantially from the social significance it has in our own society.

In fifteenth-century France, as described by Jacques Rossiaud, commercial sex appears likewise to have had an import that contrasts with its role in contemporary America. According to Rossiaud:

> By the age of thirty, most prostitutes had a real chance of becoming reintegrated into society. . . . Since public opinion did not view them with disgust, and since they were on good terms with priests and men of the law, it was not too difficult for them to find a position as servant or wife. To many city people, public prostitution represented a partial atonement for past misconduct. Many bachelors had compassion and sympathy for prostitutes, and finally, the local charitable foundations of the municipal authorities felt a charitable impulse to give special help to these repentant Magdalens and to open their way to marriage by dowering them. Marriage was definitely the most frequent end to the career of communal prostitutes who had roots in the town where they have publicly offered their bodies.[8]

The fact that prostitutes were regarded by medieval French society as eligible for marriage, and were desired by men for wives, suggests that the cultural principles which sustained commercial exchanges of sex in this society were quite different than those which shape our own sex industry. Consequently, the phenomenon of prostitution requires a distinct political analysis and moral assessment vis-à-vis fifteenth-century France. This historically specific approach is justified, in part, because commercial sexual transactions may have different consequences for individuals in an alien society than for individuals similarly placed in our own. Indeed, it is questionable whether, in two quite different cultural settings, we should regard a particular outward behavior—the impersonal provision of sexual services for fees or their equivalent—as the same practice, that is, as prostitution.

Another cross-cultural example may help to make the last point clear. Anthropologists have studied a group in New Guinea, called the Etoro, who believe that young male children need to ingest male fluid or semen in order to develop properly into adult males, much like we believe that young infants need their mother's milk, or some equivalent, to be properly nurtured. Furthermore, just as our belief underlies our practice of breast-feeding, the Etoro's belief underlies their practice of penis-feeding, where young male children fellate older males, often their relatives.[9] From the perspective of our society, the Etoro's practice involves behaviors which are highly stigmatized—incest, sex with children, and homosexuality. Yet, for an anthropologist who is attempting to interpret and translate these behaviors, to assume that the Etoro practice is best subsumed under the category of "sex," rather than, for example, "child rearing," would reflect ethnocentrism. Clearly, our choice of one translation scheme or the other will influence our attitude toward the Etoro practice. The point is that there is no practice, such as "sex," which can be morally evaluated apart from a cultural framework.

In general, historical and cross-cultural studies offer little reason to believe that the dominant forms of sexual practice in our society reflect psychological, biological, or moral absolutes that determine human sexual practice. Instead, such studies provide much evidence that, against a different backdrop of beliefs about the world, the activities we designate as "sex"—impersonal or otherwise—have an entirely different meaning and value. Yet, while we may choose not to condemn the "child-rearing" practices of the Etoro, we can nevertheless recognize that "penis-feeding" would be extremely damaging to children in our society. Similarly, though we can appreciate that making an occupation by the provision of sex may not have been oppressive to women in medieval France or ancient Babylon, we should nevertheless recognize that in our society it can be extremely damaging to women. What then are the features which, in our culture, render prostitution oppressive?

The Social Meaning of Prostitution

Let me begin with a simple analogy. In our society there exists a taboo against eating cats and dogs. Now, suppose a member of our society wishes to engage in the unconventional behavior of ingesting cat or dog meat. In evaluating the moral and political character of this person's behavior, it is somewhat irrelevant whether eating cats and dogs "really" is or isn't healthy, or whether it "really" is or isn't different than eating cows, pigs, and chickens. What is relevant is that, by including cat and dog flesh in one's diet, a person may really make others upset and, therefore, do damage to them as well as to oneself. In short, how actions are widely perceived and interpreted by others, even if wrongly or seemingly irrationally, is crucial to determining their moral status because, though such interpretations may not hold up against some "objective reality," they are part of the "social reality" in which we live.

I am not using this example to argue that unconventional behavior is wrong but, rather, to illustrate the relevance of cultural convention to how our outward behaviors are perceived. Indeed, what is wrong with prostitution is not that it violates deeply entrenched social conventions—ideals of feminine purity, and the noncommoditization of sex—but precisely that it epitomizes other cultural assumptions—beliefs which, reasonable or not, serve to legitimate women's social subordination. In other words, rather than subvert patriarchal ideology, the prostitute's actions, and the industry as a whole, serve to perpetuate this system of values. By contrast, lesbian sex, and egalitarian heterosexual economic and romantic relationships, do not. In short, female prostitution oppresses women, not because some women who participate in it "suffer in the eyes of society" but because its organized practice testifies to and perpetuates socially hegemonic beliefs which oppress all women in many domains of their lives.

What, then, are some of the beliefs and values which structure the social meaning of the prostitute's business in our culture—principles which are not necessarily consciously held by us but are implicit in our observable behavior and social practice? First, people in our society generally believe that human beings naturally possess, but socially repress, powerful, emotionally destabilizing sexual appetites. Second, we assume that men are naturally suited for dominant social roles. Third, we assume that contact with male genitals in virtually all contexts is damaging and polluting to women. Fourth, we assume that a person's sexual practice renders her or him a particular "kind" of person, for example, "a homosexual," "a bisexual," "a whore," "a virgin," "a pervert," and so on. I will briefly examine the nature of these four assumptions, and then discuss how they determine the social significance and impact of prostitution in our society. Such principles are inscribed in all of a culture's communicative acts and institutions, but my examples will only be drawn from a common body of disciplinary resources: the writings of philosophers and other intellectuals.

The universal possession of a potent sex drive.—In describing the nature of sexual attraction, Schopenhauer states:

> The sexual impulse in all its degrees and nuances plays not only on the stage and in novels, but also in the real world, where, next to the love of life, it shows itself the strongest and most powerful of motives, constantly lays claim to half the powers and thoughts of the younger portion of mankind, is the ultimate goal of almost all human effort, exerts an adverse influence on the most important events, interrupts the most serious occupations every hour, sometimes embarrasses for a while even the greatest minds, does not hesitate to intrude with its trash interfering with the negotiations of statesmen and the investigation of men of learning, knows how to slip its love letters and locks of hair even into ministerial portfolios and philosophical manuscripts, and no less devises daily the most entangled and the worst actions, destroys the most valuable relationships, breaks the firmest

bonds, demands the sacrifice sometimes of life or health, sometimes of wealth, rank, and happiness, nay robs those who are otherwise honest of all conscience, makes those who have hitherto been faithful, traitors; accordingly to the whole, appears as a malevolent demon that strives to pervert, confuse, and overthrow everything.[10]

Freud, of course, chose the name "libido" to refer to this powerful natural instinct, which he believed manifests itself as early as infancy.

The assumption of a potent "sex drive" is implicit in Lars Ericsson's relatively recent defense of prostitution: "We must liberate ourselves from those mental fossils which prevent us from looking upon sex and sexuality with the same naturalness as upon our cravings for food and drink. And, contrary to popular belief, we may have something to learn from prostitution in this respect, namely, that coition resembles nourishment in that if it cannot be obtained in any other way it can always be bought. And bought meals are not always the worst."[11] More explicitly, he argues that the "sex drive" provides a noneconomic, natural basis for explaining the demand for commercial sex.[12] Moreover, he claims that because of the irrational nature of this impulse, prostitution will exist until all persons are granted sexual access upon demand to all other persons.[13] In a society where individuals lack such access to others, but where women are the social equals of men, Ericsson predicts that "the degree of female frustration that exists today . . . will no longer be tolerated, rationalized, or sublimated, but channeled into a demand for, inter alia, mercenary sex."[14] Consequently, Ericsson favors an unregulated sex industry, which can respond spontaneously to these natural human wants. Although Pateman, in her response to Ericsson, does not see the capitalist commoditization of sexuality as physiologically determined, she nevertheless yields to the assumption that "sexual impulses are part of our natural constitution as humans."[15]

Schopenhauer, Freud, Ericsson, and Pateman all clearly articulate what anthropologists refer to as our "cultural common sense" regarding the nature of human sexuality. By contrast, consider a group of people in New Guinea, called the Dani, as described by Karl Heider: "Especially striking is their five year post-partum sexual abstinence, which is uniformly observed and is not a subject of great concern or stress. This low level of sexuality appears to be a purely cultural phenomenon, not caused by any biological factors."[16] The moral of this anthropological tale is that our high level of sexuality is also "a purely cultural phenomenon," and not the inevitable result of human biology. Though the Dani's disinterest in sex need not lead us to regard our excessive concern as improper, it should lead us to view one of our cultural rationalizations for prostitution as just that—a cultural rationalization.

The "natural" dominance of men.—One readily apparent feature of the sex industry in our society is that it caters almost exclusively to a male clientele. Even the relatively small number of male prostitutes at work serve a predominantly male consumer group. Implicit in this particular division of labor, and also the predominant division of labor in other domains of our society, is the cultural principle that men are naturally disposed to dominate in their relations with others.

Ironically, this cultural conviction is implicit in some accounts of prostitution by feminist writers, especially in their attempts to explain the social and psychological causes of the problematic demand by men for impersonal, commercial sex. For example, Marxist feminists have argued that prostitution is the manifestation of the unequal class position of women vis-à-vis men: women who do not exchange their domestic and sexual services with the male ruling class for their subsistence are forced to market these services to multiple masters outside marriage.[17] The exploitation of female sexuality is a ruling-class privilege, an advantage which allows those socially identified as "men" to perpetuate their economic and cultural hegemony. In tying female prostitution to patriarchy and capitalism, Marxist accounts attempt to tie it to particular historical forces, rather than to biological or natural ones. However, without the assumption of men's biological superiority, Marxist feminist analyses cannot explain why women, at this particular moment under capitalism, have evolved as an economic under-class, that is, why capitalism gives rise to patriarchy. Why did women's role in production and reproduction not provide them a market advantage, a basis upon which they could subordinate men or assert their political equality?

Gayle Rubin has attempted to provide a purely social and historical analysis of female prostitution by applying some insights of structuralist anthropology.[18] She argues that economic prostitution originates from the unequal position of men and women within the mode of reproduction (the division of society into groups for the purpose of procreation and child rearing). In many human cultures, this system operates by what Lévi-Strauss referred to as "the exchange of women": a practice whereby men exchange their own sisters and daughters for the sisters and daughters of other men. These exchanges express or affirm "a social link between the partners of the exchange . . . confer[ring] upon its participants a special relationship of trust, solidarity, and mutual aid."[19] However, since women are not partners to the exchange but, rather, the objects traded, they are denied the social rights and privileges created by these acts of giving. The commoditization of female sexuality is the form this original "traffic in women" takes in capitalist societies. In short, Rubin's account does not assume, but attempts to explain, the dominance of men in production, by appealing to the original dominance of men in reproduction. Yet this account does not explain why women are the objects of the original affinal exchange, rather than men or opposite sex pairs.[20]

In appealing to the principle that men naturally assume dominant roles in all social systems, feminists uncritically accept a basic premise of patriarchy. In my view such principles do not denote universal causal mechanisms but represent naturally arbitrary, culturally determined beliefs which serve to legitimate certain practices.

Sexual contact pollutes women.—To say that extensive sexual experience in a woman is not prized in our society is to be guilty of indirectness and understatement. Rather, a history of sexual activity is a negative mark that is used to differentiate kinds of women. Instead of being valued for their experience in sexual matters, women are valued for their "innocence."

That the act of sexual intercourse with a man is damaging to a woman is implicit in the vulgar language we use to describe this act. As Robert Baker has pointed out, a woman is "fucked," "screwed," "banged," "had," and so forth, and it is a man (a "prick") who does it to her.[21] The metaphors we use for the act of sexual intercourse are similarly revealing. Consider, for example, Andrea Dworkin's description of intercourse: "The thrusting is persistent invasion. She is opened up, split down the center. She is occupied—physically, internally, in her privacy."[22] Dworkin invokes both images of physical assault and imperialist domination in her characterization of heterosexual copulation. Women are split, penetrated, entered, occupied, invaded, and colonized by men. Though aware of the nonliteralness of this language, Dworkin appears to think that these metaphors are motivated by natural, as opposed to arbitrary, cultural features of the world. According to Ann Garry, "Because in our culture we connect sex with harm that men do to women, and because we think of the female role in sex as that of harmed object, we can see that to treat a woman as a sex object is automatically to treat her as less than fully human."[23] As the public vehicles for "screwing," "penetration," "invasion," prostitutes are reduced to the status of animals or things—mere instruments for human ends.

The reification of sexual practice.—Another belief that determines the social significance of prostitution concerns the relationship between a person's social identity and her or his sexual behavior.[24] For example, we identify a person who has sexual relations with a person of the same gender as a "homosexual," and we regard a woman who has intercourse with multiple sexual partners as being of a particular type—for instance, a "loose woman," "slut," or "prostitute." As critics of our society, we may find these categories too narrow or the values they reflect objectionable. If so, we may refer to women who are sexually promiscuous, or who have sexual relations with other women, as "liberated women," and thereby show a rejection of double (and homophobic) standards of sexual morality. However, what such linguistic iconoclasm generally fails to challenge is that a person's sexual practice makes her a particular "kind" of person.

I will now consider how these cultural convictions and values structure the meaning of prostitution in our society. Our society's tolerance for commercially available sex, legal or not, implies general acceptance of principles which perpetuate women's social subordination. Moreover, by their participation in an industry which exploits the myths of female social inequality and sexual vulnerability, the actions of the prostitute and her clients imply that they accept a set of values and beliefs which assign women to marginal social roles in all our cultural institutions, including marriage and waged employment. Just as an Uncle Tom exploits noxious beliefs about blacks for personal gain, and implies through his actions that blacks can benefit from a system of white supremacy, the prostitute and her clients imply that women can profit economically from patriarchy. Though we should not blame the workers in the sex industry for the social degradation they suffer, as theorists and critics of our society, we should question the existence of such businesses and the social principles implicit in our tolerance for them.

Because members of our society perceive persons in terms of their sexual orientation and practice, and because sexual contact in most settings—but especially outside the context of a "secure" heterosexual relationship—is thought to be harmful to women, the prostitute's work may have social implications that differ significantly from the work of persons in other professions. For instance, women who work or have worked in the sex industry may find their future social prospects severely limited. By contrast to medieval French society, they are not desired as wives or domestic servants in our own. And unlike other female subordinates in our society, the prostitute is viewed as a defiled creature; nonetheless, we rationalize and tolerate prostitutional sex out of the perceived need to mollify men's sexual desires.

In sum, the woman who provides sex on a commercial basis and the man who patronizes her epitomize and reinforce the social principles I have identified: these include beliefs that attribute to humans potent, subjugating sex drives that men can satisfy without inflicting self-harm through impersonal sexual encounters. Moreover, the prostitute cannot alter the political implications of her work by simply supplying her own rationale for the provision of her services. For example, Margo St. James has tried to represent the prostitute as a skilled sexual therapist, who serves a legitimate social need.[25] According to St. James, while the commercial sex provider may be unconventional in her sexual behavior, her work may be performed with honesty and dignity. However, this defense is implausible since it ignores the possible adverse impact of her behavior on herself and others, and the fact that, by participating in prostitution, her behavior does little to subvert the cultural principles that make her work harmful. Ann Garry reaches a similar conclusion about pornography: "I may not think that sex is dirty and that I would be a harmed object; I may not know what your view is; but what bothers me is that this is the view embodied in our language and culture. . . . As long as sex is connected with harm done to women, it will be very difficult not to see pornography as degrading to women. . . . The fact that audience attitude is so important makes one wary of giving whole-hearted approval to any pornography seen today."[26] Although the prostitute may want the meaning of her actions assessed relative to her own idiosyncratic beliefs and values, the political and social meaning of her actions must be assessed in the political and social context in which they occur.

One can imagine a society in which individuals sought commercial sexual services from women in order to obtain high quality sexual experiences. In our society, people pay for medical advice, meals, education in many fields, and so on, in order to obtain information, services, or goods that are superior to or in some respect more valuable than those they can obtain noncommercially. A context in which the rationale for seeking a prostitute's services was to obtain sex from a professional— from a person who knows what she is doing—is probably not a context in which women are thought to be violated when they have sexual contact with men. In such a situation, those who supplied sex on a commercial basis would probably not be stigmatized but, instead, granted ordinary social privileges.[27] The fact that prostitutes have such low social status in our society indicates that the society in which we live is not congruent with this imaginary one; that is, the prostitute's services in our society are not generally sought as a gourmet item. In short, if commercial sex was sought as a professional service, then women who provided sex commercially would probably not be regarded as "prostituting" themselves—as devoting their bodies or talents to base purposes, contrary to their true interests.

Subverting the Status Quo

Let me reiterate that I am not arguing for social conformism. Rather, my point is that not all nonconformist acts equally challenge conventional morality. For example, if a person wants to subvert the belief that eating cats and dogs is bad, it is not enough to simply engage in eating them. Similarly, it is unlikely that persons will subvert prevalent attitudes toward gender and sexuality by engaging in prostitution.

Consider another example. Suppose that I value high quality child care and am willing to pay a person well to obtain it. Because of both racial and gender oppression, the persons most likely to be interested in and suitable for such work are bright Third World and minority First World women who cannot compete fairly for other well-paid work. Suppose, then, I hire a person who happens to be a woman and a person of color to provide child care on the basis of the belief that such work requires a high level of intelligence and responsibility. Though the belief on which this act is based may be unconventional, my action of hiring a "sitter" from among the so-called lower classes of society is not politically liberating.[28]

What can a person who works in the sex industry do to subvert widely held attitudes toward her work? To subvert the beliefs which currently structure commercial sex in our society, the female prostitute would need to assume the role not of a sexual subordinate but of a sexual equal or superior. For instance, if she were to have the authority to determine what services the customer could get, under what conditions the customer could get them, and what they would cost, she would gain the status of a sexual professional. Should she further want to establish herself as a sexual therapist, she would need to represent herself as having some type of special technical knowledge for solving problems having to do with human sexuality. In other words, experience is not enough to establish one's credentials as a therapist or professional. However, if the industry were reformed so that all these conditions were met, what would distinguish the prostitute's work from that of a bona fide "sexual therapist"? If her knowledge was thought to be only quasilegitimate, her work might have the status of something like the work of a chiropractor, but this would certainly be quite different than the current social status of her work.[29] In sum, the political alternatives of reformation and abolition are not mutually exclusive: if prostitution were sufficiently transformed to make it completely nonoppressive to women, though commercial transactions involving sex might still exist, prostitution as we now know it would not.

If our tolerance for marriage fundamentally rested on the myth of female subordination, then the same arguments which apply to prostitution would apply to it. Many theorists, including Simone de Beauvoir and Friedrich Engels, have argued that marriage, like prostitution, involves female sexual subservience. For example, according to de Beauvoir: "For both the sexual act is a service; the one is hired for life by one man; the other has several clients who pay her by the piece. The one is protected by one male against all others; the other is defended by all against the exclusive tyranny of each."[30] In addition, Lars Ericsson contends that marriage, unlike prostitution, involves economic dependence for women: "While the housewife is totally dependent on her husband, at least economically, the call girl in that respect stands on her own two feet. If she has a pimp, it is she, not he, who is the breadwinner in the family."[31]

Since the majority of marriages in our society render the wife the domestic and sexual subordinate of her husband, marriage degrades the woman who accepts it (or perhaps only the woman who accepts marriage on unequal terms), and its institutionalization in its present form oppresses all women. However, because marriage can be founded on principles which do not involve the subordination of women, we can challenge oppressive aspects of this institution without radically altering it.[32] For example, while the desire to control the sinful urges of men to fornicate may, historically, have been part of the ideology of marriage, it does not seem to be a central component of our contemporary rationalization for this custom.[33] Marriage, at present in our society, is legitimated by other widely held values and beliefs, for example, the desirability of a long-term, emotionally and financially sustaining, parental partnership. However, I am unable to imagine nonpernicious principles which would legitimate the commercial provision of sex and which would not substantially alter or eliminate the industry as it now exists. Since commercial sex, unlike marriage, is not reformable, feminists should seek to undermine the beliefs and values which underlie our acceptance of it. Indeed, one way to do this is to outwardly oppose prostitution itself.

Conclusions

If my analysis is correct, then prostitution is not a social aberration or disorder but, rather, a consequence of well-established beliefs and values that form part of the foundation of all our social institutions and practices. Therefore, by striving to overcome discriminatory structures in all aspects of society—in the family, at work outside the home, and in our political institutions—feminists will succeed in challenging some of the cultural presuppositions which sustain prostitution. In other words, prostitution needs no unique remedy, legal or otherwise; it will be remedied as feminists make progress in altering patterns of belief and practice that oppress women in all aspects of their lives. Yet, while prostitution requires no special social cure, some important strategic and symbolic feminist goals may be served by selecting the sex industry for criticism at this time. In this respect, a consumer boycott of the industry is especially appropriate.

In examining prostitution, I have not tried to construct a theory which can explain the universal causes and moral character of prostitution. Such questions presuppose that there is a universal phenomenon to which the term refers and that commercial sex is always socially deviant and undesirable. Instead, I have considered the meaning of commercial sex in modern Western cultures. Although my arguments are consistent with the decriminalization of prostitution, I conclude from my investigation that feminists have legitimate reasons to politically oppose prostitution in our society. Since the principles which implicitly sustain and organize the sex industry are ones which underlie pernicious gender asymmetries in many domains of our social life, to tolerate a practice which epitomizes these principles is oppressive to women.[34]

Notes

1. Nancy Hartsock, *Money, Sex and Power* (Boston: Northeastern University Press, 1985), p. 178.

2. See Rosemarie Tong, *Women, Sex, and the Law* (Totowa, N.J.: Rowman and Allanheld, 1984), pp. 37–64. See also Priscilla Alexander and Margo St. James, "Working on the Issue," National Organization for Women (NOW) National Task Force on Prostitution Report (San Francisco: NOW, 1982).

3. See Carole Pateman, "Defending Prostitution: Charges against Ericsson," *Ethics* 93 (1983): 561–65; and Kathleen Barry, *Female Sexual Slavery* (New York: Avon, 1979).

4. For example, see Gerda Lerner, "The Origin of Prostitution in Ancient Mesopotamia," *Signs: Journal of Women in Culture and Society* 11 (1986): 236–54; Lars Ericsson, "Charges against Prostitution: An Attempt at a Philosophical Assessment," *Ethics* 90 (1980): 335–66; and James Brundage, "Prostitution in the Medieval Canon Law," *Signs: Journal of Women in Culture and Society* 1 (1976): 825–45.

5. Pateman, p. 563.

6. Lerner, p. 239.

7. Emma Goldman, "The Traffic in Women," in *Red Emma Speaks*, ed. Alix Kates Shulman (New York: Schocken, 1983), p. 180.

8. Jacques Rossiaud, "Prostitution, Youth, and Society in the Towns of Southeastern France in the Fifteenth Century," in *Deviants and the Abandoned in French Society: Selections from the Annales Economies, Sociétés, Civilisations*, ed. Robert Forster and Orest Ranum (Baltimore: Johns Hopkins University Press, 1978), p. 21.

9. See Gilbert H. Herdt, ed., *Rituals of Manhood* (Berkeley and Los Angeles: University of California Press, 1982). Also see Harriet Whitehead, "The Varieties of Fertility Cultism in New Guinea: Part 1," *American Ethnologist* 13 (1986): 80–99. In comparing penis-feeding to breast-feeding rather than to oral sex, some anthropologists point out that both involve the use of a culturally erotic bodily part for parental nurturing.

10. Arthur Schopenhauer, "The Metaphysics of the Love of the Sexes," in *The Works of Schopenhauer*, ed. Will Durant (New York, Simon & Schuster, 1928), p. 333.

11. Ericsson, p. 355.

12. Ibid., p. 347.

13. Ibid., pp. 359–60.

14. Ibid., p. 360.

15. Pateman, p. 563.

16. Karl Heider, "Dani Sexuality: A Low Energy System," *Man* 11 (1976): 188–201.

17. See Friedrich Engels, *The Origin of the Family, Private Property and the State* (New York: Penguin, 1985); Goldman; Alison Jaggar, "Prostitution," in *The Philosophy of Sex*, ed. Alan Soble (Totowa, N.J.: Rowman & Littlefield, 1980), pp. 353–58.

18. Gayle Rubin, "The Traffic in Women: Notes on the 'Political Economy' of Sex," in *Toward an Anthropology of Women*, ed. Rayna Reiter (New York: Monthly Review Press, 1975).

19. Ibid., p. 172.

20. In his attempt to describe the general principles of kinship organization implicit in different cultures, Lévi-Strauss admits it is conceivable that he has over-emphasized the patrilineal nature of these exchanges: "It may have been noted that we have assumed what might be called . . . a paternal perspective. That is, we have regarded the woman married by a member of the group as acquired, and the sister provided in exchange as lost. The situation might be altogether different in a system with matrilineal descent and matrilocal residence. . . . The essential thing is that every right acquired entails a concomitant obligation, and that every renunciation calls for a compensation. . . . Even supposing a very hypothetical marriage system in which the man and not the woman were exchanged . . . the total structure would remain unchanged" (Claude Lévi-Strauss, *The Elementary Structures of Kinship* [Boston: Beacon, 1969], p. 132). A culture in which men are gifts in a ritual of exchange is described in Michael Peletz, "The Exchange of Men in Nineteenth-Century Negeri Sembilan (Malaya)," *American Ethnologist* 14 (1987): 449–69.

21. Robert Baker, " 'Pricks' and 'Chicks': A Plea for 'Persons,' " in *Philosophy and Sex*, ed. R. Baker and F. Elliston (Buffalo, N.Y.: Prometheus, 1984), pp. 260–66. In this section, Baker provides both linguistic and nonlinguistic evidence that intercourse, in our cultural mythology, hurts women.

22. Andrea Dworkin, *Intercourse* (New York: Free Press, 1987), p. 122.

23. Ann Garry, "Pornography and Respect for Women," in Baker and Elliston, eds., p. 318.

24. In "Defending Prostitution," Pateman states: "The services of the prostitute are related in a more intimate manner to her body than those of other professionals. Sexual services, that is to say, sex and sexuality, are constitutive of the body in a way in which the counseling skills of the social worker are not. . . . Sexuality and the body are, further, integrally connected to conceptions of femininity and masculinity, and all these are constitutive of our individuality, our sense of self-identity" (p. 562). On my view, while our social identities are determined by our outward sexual practice, this is due to arbitrary culturally determined conceptual mappings, rather than some universal relationship holding between persons and their bodies.

25. Margo St. James, Speech to the San Diego County National Organization for Women, La Jolla, California, February 27, 1982, and from private correspondence with St. James (1983). Margo St. James is the founder of COYOTE (Call Off Your Old Tired Ethics) and the editor of *Coyote Howls*. COYOTE is a civil rights organization which seeks to change the sex industry from within by gaining better working conditions for prostitutes.

26. Garry, pp. 318–23.

27. According to Bertrand Russell: "In Japan, apparently, the matter is quite

otherwise. Prostitution is recognized and respected as a career, and is even adopted at the insistence of parents. It is often a not uncommon method of earning a marriage dowry" (*Marriage and Morals* [1929; reprint, New York: Liveright, 1970], p. 151). Perhaps contemporary Japan is closer to our imaginary society, a society where heterosexual intercourse is not felt to be polluting to women.

28. This of course does not mean we should not hire such people for child care, for that would simply be to deny a good person a better job than he or she might otherwise obtain—a job which unlike the prostitute's job is not likely to hurt their prospects for other work or social positions. Nevertheless, one should not believe that one's act of giving a person of this social description such a job does anything to change the unfair structure of our society.

29. I am grateful to Richard Arneson for suggesting this analogy to me.

30. Simone de Beauvoir, *The Second Sex* (New York: Vintage, 1974), p. 619. According to Engels: "Marriage of convenience turns often enough into the crassest prostitution—sometimes of both partners, but far more commonly of the woman, who only differs from the ordinary courtesan in that she does not let out her body on piecework as a wage worker, but sells it once and for all into slavery" (p. 102).

31. Ericsson, p. 354.

32. Pateman argues: "The conjugal relation is not necessarily one of domination and subjection, and in this it differs from prostitution" (p. 563). On this I agree with her.

33. Russell informs us that "Christianity, and more particularly St. Paul, introduced an entirely novel view of marriage, that it existed not primarily for the procreation of children, but to prevent the sin of fornication. . . . I remember once being advised by a doctor to abandon the practice of smoking, and he said that I should find it easier if, whenever the desire came upon me, I proceeded to suck an acid drop. It is in this spirit that St. Paul recommends marriage" (pp. 44–46).

34. I am grateful to Sandra Bartky, Alison Jaggar, Elizabeth Segal, Richard Arneson, and the anonymous reviewers for *Ethics* for their critical comments and suggestions. Also, I am indebted to Daniel Segal for suggesting many anthropological and historical examples relevant to my argument. In addition, I would like to thank the philosophy department of the Claremont Graduate School for the opportunity to present an earlier draft of this paper for discussion.

Chapter 25

WHAT'S WRONG WITH PROSTITUTION?

Igor Primoratz

O ver the last three decades the sexual morality of many Western societies has changed beyond recognition. Most of the prohibitions
which made up the traditional, extremely restrictive outlook on sex that
reigned supreme until the fifties—the prohibitions of masturbation, premarital and extra-marital sex, promiscuity, homosexuality—are no longer
seen as very serious or stringent or, indeed, as binding at all. But one or
two traditional prohibitions are still with us. The moral ban on prostitution, in particular, does not seem to have been repealed or radically miti-
gated. To be sure, some of the old arguments against prostitution are
hardly ever brought up these days; but then, several new ones are quite
popular, at least in certain circles. Prostitution is no longer seen as the
most extreme moral depravity a woman is capable of; but the view that it
is at least seriously morally flawed, if not repugnant and intolerable, is still
widely held. In this paper I want to look into some of the main arguments
in support of this view and try to show that none of them is convincing.[1]

1. Positive Morality

The morality of this society and of most other societies today condemns
prostitution in no uncertain terms; the facts of the condemnation and
its various, sometimes quite serious and far-reaching consequences for

those who practise it, are too well known to need to be recounted here. But what do these facts prove? Surely not that prostitution *is* wrong, only that positive morality of this and many other societies *deems it* wrong. With regard to prostitution, as with regard to any moral issue, we must surely attend to the distinction between positive morality, the morality prevalent in a society and expressed in its public opinion, its laws, and the lives of its members, and critical morality, which is a set of moral principles, rules and values together with the reasoning behind them that an individual may adopt, not only to live by them, but also to apply them in judging critically the morality of any particular society, including his or her own.

To be sure, the importance, or even tenability, of this distinction has been denied; there have been authors (Emile Durkheim is a good example) who maintained that whatever a society holds to be right or wrong *is* right or wrong in that society. But the flaws of this position, which might be termed moral positivism or conventionalism, are obvious and fatal. One is that it implies that all philosophers, religious teachers, writers and social reformers who set out to criticize and reform the moral outlook of their societies were not merely wrong—all of them may, and some of them must have been wrong—but utterly misguided in what they were trying to do, for what they were trying to do logically cannot be done. There is no such thing as a radical moral critique of one's society (or any other society, for that matter). Another implausible implication of moral positivism is that the same action or practice can be both right (in one society) and wrong (in another). Thus prostitution was both morally unobjectionable (in ancient Greece) *and* a moral abomination (in nineteenth-century England). Finally, positive morality is often inconsistent. Prostitution is, again, a case in point. It has been pointed out time and again that there is no morally significant difference between the common prostitute and the spouse in what used to be called a marriage of convenience. This kind of marriage, said Friedrich Engels, for example, 'turns often enough into the crassest prostitution—sometimes of both partners, but far more commonly of the woman, who only differs from the ordinary courtesan in that she does not let out her body on piecework as a wage worker, but sells it once and for all into slavery.'[2] The word 'slavery' is too strong, and it may not be the spouse's body that is being sold, but otherwise the point is well taken. How can positive morality condemn mercenary sex in one case, but not in the other?

I am not saying that this inconsistency cannot be explained. It can, if we attend to the social meaning of marriage and prostitution.[3] Both can be called 'sexual institutions', as both have to do with sex, both are institutional frameworks for satisfying sexual desire. But their social meaning is not the same. Throughout history, the most important social function of sex has been reproduction. Marriage has always been seen as the best institutional set-up for procreating and socializing the young. Accordingly, marriage is the central, most respected and most strongly supported among the sexual institutions, while other such institutions, such as concubinage or wife exchange, are the less supported and respected the more they are removed from marriage. Prostitution is at the other end of this range, for in prostitution

> both parties use sex for an end not socially functional, the one for pleasure, the other for money. To tie intercourse to sheer physical pleasure is to divorce it both from reproduction and from the sentimental primary type of relation which it symbolizes. To tie it to money . . . does the same thing. . . . On both sides the relationship is merely a means to a private end. . . .[4]

Both money and pleasure may be very important to the individuals concerned but, as merely individual objectives, have no social significance. Therefore, society accords prostitution neither support nor respect. The traditional Western sexual ethic considers sex as in itself morally problematic if not downright bad or sinful, and thus legitimate only as a means of procreation, and perhaps also of expression and reinforcement of emotions and attitudes usually associated with procreation. It is easy to see how Western society came to condemn and despise the practice of prostitution.

However, the inconsistency of condemning mercenary sex outside marriage but not within it still has not been explained. The missing part is the fact that society is concerned with practices and institutions, not with individuals; social morality judges primarily practices and institutions, and deals with individuals simply, and solely, by subsuming them under the roles defined by practices and institutions. If it were otherwise, if social morality were interested in, and capable of, relating to the individual and his or her actions in their particularity and complexity, as all serious and discerning moral thinking does, it could not fail to condemn mercenary sex within marriage no less than outside it. For it does not consider marriage valuable in itself, but as the proper framework for reproduction and the upbringing of offspring, and also, perhaps, as the framework that best sustains the emotions and attitudes helpful in the performance of these tasks. Therefore marital sex is not legitimate simply as marital, but as sex that serves the social purpose of marriage. When a person engages in sex within marriage, but fails to live up to this normative conception of the institution and has sex merely in order to secure the economic benefits of the married state, that is no less mercenary than the sex sold on the street to all comers, and accordingly no less wrong from the point of view of the sexual ethic to which society adheres on the level of rules and roles, practices and institutions. Society does not see this because it cannot be bothered to look into the life, actions and motives of the individual. But that is surely reason enough not to bother with its pronouncements when attempting to settle an important moral question.

2. Paternalism

Paternalism is most commonly defined as 'the interference with a person's liberty of action justified by reasons referring exclusively to the welfare, good, happiness, needs, interests or values of the person being coerced.'[5] Philosophical discussions of paternalism have concentrated on paternalist legislation; for the most obvious, and often the most effective, kind of interference with an individual's liberty of action is by means of law. But paternalism can also be put forward as a moral position: one can argue that the wrongness of doing something follows from the fact that doing it has serious adverse effects on the welfare, good, etc. of the agent and, having made that judgment, exert the pressure of the moral sanction on the individuals concerned to get them to refrain from doing it. A popular way of arguing against prostitution is of this sort: it refers to such hazards of selling sex as (i) venereal diseases; (ii) unpleasant, humiliating, even violent behaviour of clients; (iii) exploitation by madams and pimps; (iv) the extremely low social status of prostitutes and the contempt and ostracism to which they are exposed. The facts showing that these are, indeed, the hazards of prostitution are well known; are they not enough to show that prostitution is bad and to be avoided?

A short way with this objection is to refuse to acknowledge the moral credentials of paternalism, and to say that what we have here is merely a prudential, not a moral argument against prostitution.

However, we may decide to accept that paternalist considerations can be relevant to questions about what is morally right and wrong. In that case, the first thing to note about the paternalist argument is that it is an argument from *occupational* hazards and thus, if valid, valid only against prostitution as an *occupation*. For in addition to the professional prostitute, whose sole livelihood comes from mercenary sex, there is also the amateur, who is usually gainfully employed or married and engages in prostitution for additional income. The latter—also known as the secret prostitute—need not at all suffer from (iii) and (iv), and stands a much lower chance of being exposed to (i) and (ii). A reference to (iii) actually is not even an argument against professional prostitution, but merely against a particular, by no means necessary way of practising it; if a professional prostitute is likely to be exploited by a madam or pimp, then she should pursue the trade on her own.

But it is more important to note that the crucial, although indirect cause of all these hazards of professional prostitution is the negative attitude of society, the condemnation of prostitution by its morality and its laws. But for that, the prostitute could enjoy much better medical protection, much more effective police protection from abusive and aggressive behaviour of clients and legal protection from exploitation by pimps and madams, and her social status would be quite different. Thus the paternalist argument takes for granted the conventional moral condemnation of prostitution, and merely gives an additional reason for not engaging in something that has already been established as wrong. But we can and should refuse to take that for granted, because we can and should refuse to submit to positive morality as the arbiter of moral issues. If we do so, and if a good case for morally condemning commercial sex has still not been made out, as I am trying to show in this paper, then all these hazards should be seen as reasons for trying to disabuse society of the prejudices against it and help to change the law and social conditions in general in which prostitutes work, in order radically to reduce, if not completely eliminate, such hazards.

However, there is one occupational hazard that has not been mentioned so far: one that cannot be blamed on unenlightened social morality, and would remain even if society were to treat prostitution as any other legitimate occupation. That is the danger to the sex life of the prostitute. As Lars Ericsson neatly puts it, 'Can one have a well-functioning sexual life if sex is what one lives by?'[6]

One way of tackling this particular paternalist objection is to say, with David A. J. Richards, that perhaps one can. Richards claims that there is no evidence that prostitution makes it impossible for those who practise it to have loving relationships, and adds that 'there is some evidence that prostitutes, as a class, are more sexually fulfilled than other American women.'[7] The last claim is based on a study in which 175 prostitutes were systematically interviewed, and which showed that 'they experienced orgasm and multiple orgasm more frequently in their personal, "non-commercial" intercourse than did the normal woman (as defined by Kinsey norms).'[8] Another, probably safer response is to point out, as Ericsson does, that the question is an empirical one and that, since there is no conclusive evidence either way, we are not in a position to draw any conclusion.[9]

My preferred response is different. I would rather grant the empirical claim that a life of prostitution is liable to wreck one's sex life, i.e. the minor premise of the argument, and then look a bit more closely into the major premise, the principle of paternalism. For there are two rather different versions of that principle. The weak version prevents the individual from acting on a choice that is not fully voluntary, either because the individual is permanently incompetent or because the choice in question is a result of ignorance of some important facts or made under

extreme psychological or social pressure. Otherwise the individual is
considered the sole qualified judge of his or her own welfare, good, happiness, needs, interests and values, and the choice is ultimately his or
hers. Moreover, when a usually competent individual is prevented from
acting on a choice that is either uninformed or made under extreme
pressure, and is therefore not fully voluntary, that individual will, when
the choice-impairing conditions no longer obtain, agree that the paternalist interference was appropriate and legitimate, and perhaps even be
grateful for it. Strong paternalism *is* meant to protect the individual
from his or her own voluntary choices, and therefore will not be legit-
imized by retrospective consent of the individual paternalized. The assumption is not that the individual is normally the proper judge of his or
her own welfare, good, etc., but rather that someone else knows better
where the individual's true welfare, good, etc. lie, and therefore has the
right to force the individual to act in accordance with the latter, even
though that means acting against his or her fully voluntary choice, which
is said to be merely 'subjective' or 'arbitrary'. Obviously, the weak version
of paternalism does not conflict with personal liberty, but should rather
be seen as its corollary; for it does not protect the individual from
choices that express his or her considered preferences and settled values, but only against his or her 'non-voluntary choices', choices the individual will subsequently disavow. Strong paternalism, on the other
hand, is essentially opposed to individual liberty, and cannot be accepted by anyone who takes liberty seriously. Such paternalism smacks
of intellectual and moral arrogance, and it is hard to see how it could
ever be established by rational argument.[10]

Accordingly, if the argument from the dangers to the prostitute's sex
life is not to be made rather implausible from the start, it ought to be put
forward in terms of weak rather than strong paternalism. When put in
these terms, however, it is not really an argument that prostitution is
wrong because imprudent, but rather that it is wrong if and when it is
taken up imprudently. It reminds us that persons permanently incompetent and those who still have not reached the age of consent should
not (be allowed to) take up the life of prostitution and thereby most
likely throw away the prospect of a good sex life. (They should not [be
allowed to] become prostitutes for other reasons anyway.) As for a competent adult, the only legitimate paternalist interference with the choice
of such a person to become a prostitute is to make sure that the choice
is a free and informed one. But if an adult and sane person is fully ap-
prised of the dangers of prostitution to the sex life of the prostitute and
decides, without undue pressure of any sort, that the advantages of prostitution as an occupation are worth it, then it is neither imprudent nor
wrong for that person to embark on the line of work chosen.[11] In such a
case, as Mill put it, 'neither one person, nor any number of persons, is

warranted in saying to another human creature of ripe years that he shall not do with his life for his own benefit what he chooses to do with it.'[12]

3. Some Things Just Are Not for Sale

In the eyes of many, by far the best argument against prostitution is brief and simple: some things just are not for sale, and sex is one of them.

It would be difficult not to go along with the first part of this argument. The belief that not everything can or should be bought and sold is extremely widespread, if not universal. The list of things not for sale is not exactly the same in all societies, but it seems that every society does have such a list, a list of 'blocked exchanges'.

The term is Michael Walzer's, and a discussion of such exchanges is an important part of his theory of justice. The central thesis of the theory is that there are several spheres of personal qualities and social goods, each autonomous, with its own criteria, procedures and agents of distribution. Injustice occurs when this autonomy is violated, when the borders are crossed and a sphere of goods becomes dominated by another in that the goods of the former are no longer distributed in accordance with its own criteria and procedures, but in accordance with those of the other sphere. The market is one such sphere—actually, the sphere with the strongest tendency to expand into, and dominate, other spheres of goods, at least in a modern capitalist society. But even this kind of society has an impressive list of things not for sale. The one Walzer offers as 'the full set of blocked exchanges in the United States today', but which would be valid for any contemporary liberal and democratic society, includes the sale of human beings (slavery), political power and office, criminal justice, freedom of speech, various prizes and honours, love and friendship, and more.[13] This is, obviously, a mixed lot. In some cases, the very nature of a good rules out its being bought and sold (love, friendship); in others, that is precluded by the conventions which constitute it (prizes); in still others, the dominant conception of a certain sphere of social life prohibits the sale, as, for instance, our conception of the nature and purpose of the political process entails that political power and office must not be bought and sold. (To be sure, some of the things listed as a matter of fact are bought and sold. But that happens only on the black market, and the fact that the market is 'black', and that those who buy and sell there do so in secret, goes to show both the illegitimacy and the secondary, parasitic character of such transactions.) There is, thus, no single criterion by reference to which one could explain why all these items appear on the list, and why no other does.

What of sex? It is not on the list; for sex, unlike love, can, as a matter of fact, be bought and sold, and there is no single, generally accepted conception of sex that prohibits its sale and purchase. 'People who believe that sexual intercourse is morally tied to love and marriage are likely to favour a ban on prostitution. . . . Sex can be sold only when it is understood in terms of pleasure and not exclusively in terms of married love. . . .'[14]

This is helpful, for it reminds us that the 'Not for sale' argument is elliptic; the understanding of sex that is presupposed must be explicated before the argument can be assessed. But the remark is also inaccurate, since it conflates two views of sex that are both historically and theoretically different: the traditional view, which originated in religion, that sex is legitimate only within marriage and as a means to procreation, and the more modern, secular, 'romantic' view that sex is to be valued only when it expresses and enhances a loving relationship. Let me look briefly into these two views in order to see whether a commitment to either does, indeed, commit one to favouring a ban on prostitution.

The first views sex as intrinsically inferior, sinful and shameful, and accepts it only when, and in so far as, it serves an important extrinsic purpose which cannot be attained by any other means: procreation. Moreover, the only proper framework for bringing up children is marriage; therefore sex is permissible only within marriage. These two statements make up the core of the traditional Christian understanding of sex, elaborated in the writings of St. Augustine and St. Thomas Aquinas, which has been by far the most important source of Western sexual ethics. To be sure, modern Christian thought and practice have broadened this view in various ways, in order to allow for the role of sex in expressing and enhancing conjugal love and care. Within the Catholic tradition this has been recognized as the 'unitive' function of sex in marriage; but that is a rather limited development, for it is still maintained that the two functions of sex, the unitive and the procreative, are inseparable.

Do those who are committed to this view of sex—and in contemporary Western societies, I suppose, only practising Catholics are—have to endorse the ban on prostitution? At a certain level, they obviously must think ill of it; for, as has often been pointed out, theirs is the most restrictive and repressive sexual ethics possible. It confines sex within the bounds of heterosexual, monogamous, exclusive, indissoluble marriage, and rules out sexual relations between any possible partners except husband and wife (as well as masturbation). Moreover, it restricts the legitimate sexual relations between the spouses to those that are 'by nature ordained' toward procreation. Prostitution or, more accurately, common prostitution, which is both non-marital and disconnected from procreation, would seem to be beyond the pale.

But then, even the legitimacy of marital and procreative sex is of a rather low order: as sex, it is intrinsically problematic; as marital and procreative, it is accepted as a necessary evil, an inevitable concession to fallen human nature. As St. Augustine says, 'any friend of wisdom and holy joys who lives a married life' would surely prefer to beget children without 'the lust that excites the indecent parts of the body', if it only were possible.[15] Therefore, if it turns out that accepting sex within marriage and for the purpose of procreation only is not concession enough, that human sexuality is so strong and unruly that it cannot be confined within these bounds and that attempts to confine it actually endanger the institution of marriage itself, the inevitable conclusion will be that further concession is in order. This is just the conclusion reached by many authors with regard to prostitution: it should be tolerated, for it provides a safety valve for a force which will otherwise subvert the institution of marriage and destroy all the chastity and decency this institution makes possible. My favourite quotation is from Mandeville, who, of course, sees that as but another instance of the general truth that private vices are public benefits:

> If Courtezans and Strumpets were to be prosecuted with as much Rigour as some silly People would have it, what Locks or Bars would be sufficient to preserve the Honour of our Wives and Daughters? For 'tis not only that the Women in general would meet with far greater Temptations, and the Attempts to ensnare the Innocence of Virgins would seem more excusable to the sober part of Mankind than they do now: But some Men would grow outrageous, and Ravishing would become a common Crime. Where six or seven Thousand Sailors arrive at once, as it often happens at *Amsterdam*, that have seen none but their own Sex for many Months together, how is it to be supposed that honest Women should walk the Streets unmolested, if there were no Harlots to be had at reasonable Prices? . . . There is a Necessity of sacrificing one part of Womankind to preserve the other, and prevent a Filthiness of a more heinous Nature.[16]

That prostitution is indispensable for the stability and the very survival of marriage has not been pointed out only by cynics like Mandeville, misanthropes like Schopenhauer,[17] or godless rationalists like Lecky[18] and Russell;[19] it was acknowledged as a fact, and as one that entails that prostitution ought to be tolerated rather than suppressed, by St. Augustine and St. Thomas themselves.[20] Moreover, it has been confirmed by sociological study of human sexual behaviour, which shows that the majority of clients of prostitutes are married men who do not find complete sexual fulfillment within marriage, but are content to stay married provided they can have extra-marital commercial sex as well.[21] Accordingly, even if one adopts the most conservative and restrictive view of sex there is, the view which ties sex to marriage and procreation, one need not, indeed should not condemn prostitution too severely. One should rather take a tolerant attitude to it, knowing that it is twice removed from the ideal state of affairs, but that its demise would bring about something incomparably worse.

Another view which would seem to call for the condemnation of prostitution is the 'romantic' view of sex as essentially tied to love; for mercenary sex is normally as loveless as sex can ever get. The important thing to note is that whatever unfavourable judgment on prostitution is suggested by this view of sex, it will not be a judgment unfavourable to prostitution as such, but rather to prostitution as a type of loveless sex. It is the lovelessness, not the commercial nature of the practice that the 'romantic' objects to.

One response to this kind of objection would be to take on squarely the view of sex that generates it. One could, first, take a critical look at the arguments advanced in support of the view that sex should always be bound up with love; second, bring out the difficulties of the linkage, the tensions between love and sex which seem to make a stable and fruitful combination of the two rather unlikely; finally, argue for the superiority of loveless, noncommittal, 'plain sex' over sex that is bound up with love. All this has already been done by philosophers such as Alan Goldman and Russell Vannoy,[22] and probably by innumerable non-philosophers as well.

Another response would be to grant the validity of the 'romantic' view of sex, but only as a personal ideal, not a universally binding moral standard. This is the tack taken by Richards,[23] who points out that it would be signally misguided, indeed absurd, to try to enforce this particular ideal, based as it is 'on the cultivation of spontaneous romantic feeling.'[24] My preferred response to the 'romantic' objection is along these lines, but I would like to go a bit further, and emphasize that it is possible to appreciate the 'romantic' ideal and at the same time not only grant that sex which falls short of it need not be wrong, but also allow that it can be positively good (without going as far as to claim that it is actually better than sex with love).

The 'romantic' typically points out the difference between sex with and without love. The former is a distinctively human, complex, rich and fruitful experience, and a matter of great importance; the latter is merely casual, a one-dimensional, barren experience that satisfies only for a short while and belongs to our animal nature. These differences are taken to show that sex with love is valuable, while loveless sex is not. This kind of reasoning has the following structure:

A is much better than B.
Therefore, B is no good at all.

In addition to being logically flawed, this line of reasoning, if it were to be applied in areas other than sex, would prove quite difficult to follow. For one thing, all but the very rich among us would die of hunger; for only the very rich can afford to take *all* their meals at the fanciest restaurants.[25]

Of course, B can be good, even if it is much less good than A. Loveless sex is a case in point. Moreover, other things being equal, it is better to be able to enjoy both loving and loveless sex than only the former. A person who enjoyed sex as part of loving relationships but was completely incapable of enjoying plain sex would seem to be missing out on something. To be sure, the 'romantic' rejection of plain sex often includes the claim that other things are not equal: that a person who indulges in plain sex thereby somehow damages, and ultimately destroys, his or her capacity for experiencing sex as an integral part of a loving relationship. This is a straightforward empirical claim about human psychology; and it is clearly false.

All this has to do with plain sex in general, rather than with its mercenary variety in particular. That is due to the general character of the 'romantic' objection to prostitution: prostitution is seen as flawed not on account of its commercial nature, but rather because it has nothing to do with love. Accordingly, as far as the 'romantic' view of sex is concerned, by exonerating plain sex, one also exonerates its commercial variety.

4. The Feminist Critique (a): Degradation of Women

In this section and the next I deal with what I have termed the 'feminist' objections to prostitution. This should not be taken to suggest that these objections are put forward only by feminists, nor that they are shared by all feminists. Contemporary discussion of the rights and wrongs of prostitution is for the most part a debate between those who hold that the sale of sex is just another service, in itself as legitimate as any other and not to be interfered with as long as no injustice, exploitation or fraud is involved, and those who deny this and claim that prostitution is essentially bound up with degradation or oppression of women. The particular concern for the role and status of women that motivates the latter position is clearly feminist; the former position can loosely be termed liberal. But there is a certain overlap: one of the currents of feminism is liberal feminism, and its adherents do not subscribe to the critique of prostitution advanced by feminists of other stripes, but rather think of it much as other liberals do, as morally unobjectionable in itself.[26] Incidentally, the position of liberal feminists seems to be more in tune with the way prostitutes themselves think of their occupation; but that may not count for much, as illiberal feminists are likely to dismiss the views of prostitutes as just another case of false consciousness.

One might want to take issue with the whole feminist approach to the question of prostitution as a question about women; for, after all, not all prostitutes are women. But this is not a promising tack; for, if not all, most of them are and always have been. So if prostitution involves either degradation or oppression, the great majority of those degraded or oppressed are women. But does it?

There is no denying that the belief that prostitution degrades those who practise it is very widespread. But this belief may be wrong. The question is: *Just why* should prostitution be considered degrading? There are four main answers: (i) because it is utterly impersonal; (ii) because the prostitute is reduced to a mere means; (iii) because of the intimate nature of the acts she performs for money; (iv) because she actually sells her body, herself. Let me look into each of these claims in turn.

(i) Prostitution is degrading because the relation between the prostitute and the client is completely impersonal. The client does not even perceive, let alone treat the prostitute as the person she is; he has no interest, no time for any of her personal characteristics, but relates to her merely as a source of sexual satisfaction, nothing more than a sex object.

One possible response to this is that prostitution need not be impersonal. There is, of course, the streetwalker who sells sex to all comers (or almost); but there is also the prostitute with a limited number of steady clients, with whom she develops quite personal relationships. So if the objection is to the impersonal character of the relation, the most that can be said is that a certain kind of prostitution is degrading, not that prostitution as such is. I do not want to make much of this, though. For although in this, as in many other services, there is the option of personalized service, the other, impersonal variety is typical.

My difficulty with the argument is more basic: I cannot see why the impersonal nature of a social transaction or relation makes that transaction or relation degrading. After all, the personal relations we have with others—with our family, friends and acquaintances—are just a small part (although the most important part) of our social life. The other part includes the overwhelming majority of our social transactions and relations which are, and have to be, quite impersonal. I do not have a personal relationship with the newspaper vendor, the bus driver, the shop assistant, and all those numerous other people I interact with in the course of a single day; and, as long as the basic decencies of social intercourse (which are purely formal and impersonal) are observed, there is nothing wrong with that. There is nothing wrong for me to think of and relate to the newspaper vendor as just that and, as far as I am concerned, nothing more. That our social relations must for the most part be impersonal may be merely a consequence of the scarcity of resources we invest in them. But it is inescapable in any but the smallest and simplest, so-called face-to-face society.

It may well be said that the selling and buying of newspapers and sex are quite different. While an impersonal attitude is unobjectionable in the former case, it is objectionable, because degrading, in the latter. But if this is the point, then the objection presupposes that sex ought to be personal; and that still has not been established. It need not be on any but the 'romantic' conception of sex; and I hope to have shown in the preceding section that the 'romantic' case against unromantic sex is not very strong.

The next two points are suggested in the following remarks by Russell:

> The intrusion of the economic motive into sex is always in a greater or lesser degree disastrous. Sexual relations should be a mutual delight, entered into solely from the spontaneous impulse of both parties. Where this is not the case, everything that is valuable is absent. To use another person in so intimate a manner is to be lacking in that respect for the human being as such, out of which all true morality must spring. . . . Morality in sexual relations, when it is free from superstition, consists essentially of respect for the other person, and unwillingness to use that person solely as a means of personal gratification without regard to his or her desires. . . . Prostitution sins against this principle. . . .[27]

(ii) Prostitution is said to degrade the prostitute because she is used as a means by the client. The client relates to the prostitute in a purely instrumental way: she is no more than a means to his sexual satisfaction. If so, is he not reducing her to a mere means, a thing, a sex object, and thereby degrading her?

If he were to rape her, that would indeed amount to treating her without regard to her desires, and thus to reducing, degrading her to a mere means. But as a customer rather than a rapist, he gets sexual satisfaction from her for a charge, on the basis of a mutual understanding, and she does her part of the bargain willingly. It is not true that he acts without regard to her desires. He does not satisfy her sexual desire; indeed, the prostitute does not desire that he should do so. But he does satisfy the one desire she has with regard to him: the desire for money. Their transaction is not 'a mutual delight, entered into solely from the spontaneous impulse of both parties', but rather a calculated exchange of goods of different order. But it does not offend against the principle of respect for human beings as such as long as it is free from coercion and fraud, and both sides get what they want.[28]

Most of our social transactions and relations are impersonal, and most are instrumental. There is nothing wrong with either impersonal or instrumental ways of relating to others as such. Just as the fact that A relates to B in a completely impersonal way is not tantamount to a violation of B's personhood, B's status as a person, so the fact that A relates to B in a purely instrumental way is not equivalent to A's reducing B to a mere means. In both cases B's informed and freely given consent absolves the relation of any such charge, and thereby also of the charge of degradation.

(iii) Sex is an intimate, perhaps the most intimate part of our lives. Should it not therefore be off limits to commercial considerations and transactions? And is it not degrading to perform something so intimate as a sex act with a complete stranger and for money?

It is not. As Ericsson points out,

> we are no more justified in devaluating the prostitute, who, for example, masturbates her customers, than we are in devaluating the assistant nurse, whose job it is to take care of the intimate hygiene of disabled patients. Both help to satisfy important human needs, and both get paid for doing so. That the harlot, in distinction to the nurse, intentionally gives her client pleasure is of course nothing that should be held against her![29]

It might be objected that the analogy is not valid, for there is an important asymmetry between pain and pleasure: the former has significantly greater moral weight than the latter. While it may be morally acceptable to cross the borders of intimacy in order to relieve pain or suffering, which is what the nurse does, that does not show that it is permissible to do so merely for the sake of giving pleasure, which is what the prostitute provides. But if so, what are we to say of a fairly good looking woman who undergoes plastic surgery and has her breasts enlarged (or made smaller) in order to become even more attractive and make her sex life richer and more pleasurable than it already is? Is she really doing something degrading and morally wrong?

(iv) Prostitution is degrading because what the prostitute sells is not simply and innocuously a service, as it may appear to a superficial look; actually, there is much truth in the old-fashioned way of speaking of her as a woman who 'sells herself'. And if *that* is not degrading, what is?

The point has been made in two different ways.

David Archard has recently argued that there is a sense in which the prostitute sells herself because of the roles and attitudes involved in the transaction:

> Sexual pleasure is not . . . an innocent commodity. Always implicated in such pleasure is the performance of roles, both willing and unwilling. These roles range from the possibly benign ones of doer and done-to, through superior and subordinate to abaser and abased. Thus, when a man buys 'sex' he also buys a sexual role from his partner, and this involves the prostitute in being something more than simply the neutral exchanger of some commodity.

More specifically,

> if I buy (and you willingly sell) your allegiance, your obsequiousness, your flattery or your servility there is no easy distinction to be made between you as 'seller' and the 'good' you choose to sell. Your whole person is implicated in the exchange. So it is too with the sale of sex.[30]

However, commercial sex need not involve obsequiousness, flattery or servility, let alone allegiance, on the part of the prostitute. These attitudes, and the 'role' they might be thought to make up, are not its constitutive parts; whether, when, and to what degree they characterize the transaction is an empirical question that admits of no simple and general answer. Indeed, those who, knowingly or not, tend to approach the whole subject of sex from a 'romantic' point of view often say that sex with prostitutes is an impoverished, even sordid experience because of the impersonal, quick, mechanical, blunt way in which the prostitute goes about her job.

Moreover, some services that have nothing to do with sex tend to involve and are expected to involve some such attitudes on the part of the person providing the service. Examples would vary from culture to culture; the waiter and the hairdresser come to mind in ours. Now such attitudes are undoubtedly morally flawed; but that does not tell against any particular occupation in which they may be manifested, but rather against the attitudes themselves, the individuals who, perhaps unthinkingly, come to adopt them, and the social conventions that foster such attitudes.

Another way to try to show that the prostitute sells herself, rather than merely a service like any other, is to focus on the concept of self-identity. This is the tack taken by Carole Pateman. She first points out that the service provided by the prostitute is related in a much closer way to her body than is the case with any other service, for sex and sexuality are constitutive of the body, while the labour and skills hired out in other lines of work are not. 'Sexuality and the body are . . . integrally connected to conceptions of femininity and masculinity, and all these are constitutive of our individuality, our sense of self-identity.'[31] Therefore, when sex becomes a commodity, so do bodies and selves.

But if so, what of our ethnic identity? When asked to say who they are, do not people normally bring up their ethnic identity as one of the most important things they need to mention? If it is granted that one's ethnic identity is also constitutive of one's individuality, one's sense of self-identity, what are we to say of a person who creates an item of authentic folk art and then sells it, or of a singer who gives a concert of folk music and charges for attendance? Are they also selling themselves, and thus doing something degrading and wrong?

The likely response will be to refuse to grant our ethnic identity the same significance for our self-identity that is claimed for gender. Although people typically refer to their ethnic identity when explaining who they are, there are also many exceptions. There are individuals who used to think of themselves in such terms, but have come to repudiate, not merely their particular ethnic affiliation, but the very idea that ethnicity should be part of one's sense of who one is. There are also persons who have always felt that way (perhaps because that is how they were brought up to feel). They do not think of their own sense of self-identity as somehow incomplete, and neither should we. There are no analogous examples with regard to gender; we all think of ourselves as either men or women, and whatever particular conception one has of one's gender, the conception is closely connected with one's sexuality. Gender is much more basic than ethnicity, much more closely related to our sense of self-identity than ethnicity and anything else that may be thought relevant.

Perhaps it is.[32] But if that is reason enough to say that the prostitute sells her body and herself, and thus does something degrading and wrong, will not we have to say the same of the wet nurse and the surrogate mother? Their bodies and gender are no less involved in what they do than the body and gender of the prostitute; and they charge a fee, just as the prostitute does. I do not know that anybody has argued that there is something degrading, or otherwise morally wrong, in what the wet nurse does, nor that what she does is selling her body or herself, so I think she is a good counterexample to Pateman's argument.

The surrogate mother might be thought a less compelling one, for there has been considerable debate about the nature and moral standing of surrogacy. I do not need to go into all that, though.[33] The one objection to surrogacy relevant in the present context is 'that it is inconsistent with human dignity that a woman should use her uterus for financial profit and treat it as an incubator for someone else's child.'[34] However, it is not explained just why it should be thought inconsistent with human dignity to do that. Indeed, it is not clear how it could be, if it is not inconsistent with human dignity that a woman should use her breasts for financial profit and treat them as a source of nourishment for someone else's child. And if it is not, why should it be inconsistent with human dignity that a woman should use her sex organs and skills for financial profit and treat them as a source of pleasure for someone else?

5. The Feminist Critique (b): Oppression of Women

The other main feminist objection to prostitution is that it exemplifies and helps to maintain the oppression of women. This objection is much more often made than argued. It is frequently made by quoting the words of Simone de Beauvoir that the prostitute 'sums up all the forms of feminine slavery at once';[35] but de Beauvoir's chapter on prostitution, although quite good as a description of some of its main types, is short on argument and does nothing to show that prostitution as such must be implicated in the oppression of women.

An argument meant to establish that with regard to our society has recently been offered by Laurie Shrage. She expressly rejects the idea of discussing commercial sex in a 'cross-cultural' or 'trans-historical' way, and grants that it need not be oppressive to women in every conceivable or, indeed, every existing society. What she does claim is that in our society prostitution epitomizes and perpetuates certain basic cultural assumptions about men, women and sex which provide justification for the oppression of women in many domains of their lives, and in this way harm both prostitutes and women in general.[36]

There are four such cultural assumptions, which need not be held consciously but may be implicit in daily behaviour. A strong sex drive is a universal human trait. Sexual behaviour defines one's social identity, makes one a particular 'kind' of person: one is 'a homosexual', 'a prostitute', 'a loose woman'. Men are 'naturally' dominant. In this connection, Shrage points out that the sex industry in our society caters almost exclusively to men, and 'even the relatively small number of male prostitutes at work serve a predominantly male consumer group.'[37] Finally, sexual contact pollutes and harms women.

The last claim is supported by a three-pronged argument. (i) In a woman, a history of sexual activity is not taken to suggest experience in a positive sense, expertise, high-quality sex. On the contrary, it is seen as a negative mark that marks off a certain kind of woman; women are valued for their 'innocence'. (ii) That sex with men is damaging to women is implicit in the vulgar language used to describe the sex act: 'a woman is "fucked", "screwed", "banged", "had", and so forth, and it is a man (a "prick") who does it to her.'[38] (iii) The same assumption is implicit in 'the metaphors we use' for the sex act. Here Shrage draws on Andrea Dworkin's book *Intercourse*, which invokes images of physical assault and imperialist domination and describes women having sexual intercourse with men as being not only entered or penetrated, but also 'split', 'invaded', 'occupied' and 'colonized' by men.

These cultural assumptions define the meaning of prostitution in our society. By tolerating prostitution, our society implies its acceptance of these assumptions, which legitimize and perpetuate the oppression of women and their marginality in all the main areas of social life. As for prostitutes and their clients, whatever their personal views of sex, men and women, they imply by their actions that they accept these assumptions and the practice they justify.

Now this argument is unobjectionable as far as it goes; but it does not go as far as Shrage means it to. In order to assess its real scope, we should first note that she repeatedly speaks of 'our' and 'our society's' toleration of prostitution, and refers to this toleration as the main ground for the conclusion that the cultural assumptions prostitution is said to epitomize in our society are indeed generally accepted in it. But toleration and acceptance are not quite the same; actually, toleration is normally defined as the putting up with something we *do not* accept. Moreover, prostitution is not tolerated at all. It is not tolerated legally: in the United States it is legal only in Nevada and illegal in all other states, while in the United Kingdom and elsewhere in the West, even though it is not against the law as such, various activities practically inseparable from it are. Some of these restrictions are quite crippling; for instance, as Marilyn G. Haft rightly says, 'to legalize prostitution while prohibiting solicitation makes as much sense as encouraging free elections but prohibiting campaigning.'[39] It certainly is not tolerated morally; as I pointed out at the beginning, the condemnation of prostitution is one of the very few prohibitions of the traditional sexual morality that are still with us. It is still widely held that prostitution is seriously morally wrong, and the prostitute is subjected to considerable moral pressure, including the ultimate moral sanction, ostracism from decent society. That the practice is still with us is not for want of trying to suppress it, and therefore should not be taken as a sign that it is being tolerated.

Furthermore, not all the cultural assumptions prostitution in our society allegedly epitomizes and reinforces are really generally accepted. The first two—that human beings have a strong sex drive, and that one's sexual behaviour defines one's social identity—probably are. The other two assumptions—that men are 'naturally' dominant, and that sex with men harms women—are more important, for they make it possible to speak of oppression of women in this context. I am not so sure about the former; my impression is that at the very least it is no longer accepted quite as widely as it used to be a couple of decades ago. And I think it is clear that the latter is not generally accepted in our society today. The evidence Shrage brings up to show that it is is far from compelling.

(i) It is probably true that the fact that a woman has a history of sexual activity is not generally appreciated as an indicator of experience and expertise, analogously to other activities. But whatever the explanation is—and one is certainly needed—I do not think that entails the other half of Shrage's diagnosis, namely that women are valued for their 'innocence'. That particular way of valuing women and the whole 'Madonna or harlot' outlook to which it belongs are well behind us as a society, although they characterize the sexual morality of some very traditional communities. A society which has made its peace with non-marital sex in general and adolescent sex in particular to the extent that ours has could not possibly have persisted in valuing women for their 'innocence'.

(ii) Shrage draws on Robert Baker's analysis of the language used to refer to men, women and sex. Baker's point of departure is the claim that the way we talk about something reflects our conception of it; he looks into the ways we talk about sex and gender in order to discover what our conceptions of these are. With regard to sexual intercourse, it turns out that the vulgar verbs used to refer to it, such as 'fuck', 'screw', 'lay', 'have,' etc., display an interesting asymmetry: they require an active construction when the subject is a man, and a passive one when the subject is a woman. This reveals that we conceive of male and female roles in sex in different ways: the male is active, the female passive. Some of these verbs—'fuck', 'screw', 'have'—are also used metaphorically to indicate deceiving, taking advantage of, harming someone. This shows that we conceive of the male sexual role as that of harming the person in the female role, and of a person who plays the female sexual role as someone who is being harmed.[40]

This is both interesting and revealing, but what is revealed is not enough to support Shrage's case. Why is 'the standard view of sexual intercourse'[41] revealed not in the standard, but in the vulgar, i.e. substandard way of talking about it? After all, everybody, at least occasionally, talks about it in the standard way, while only some use the vulgar language too. Baker justifies his focusing on the latter by pointing out that the verbs which belong to the former, and are not used in the sense of inflicting harm as well, 'can take both females and males as subjects (in active constructions) and thus *do not pick out the female role.* This demonstrates that we conceive of sexual roles in such a way that only females are thought to be taken advantage of in intercourse.'[42] It seems to me that the 'we' is quite problematic, and that all that these facts demonstrate is that some of us, namely those who speak of having sex with women as fucking or screwing them, also think of sex with them in these terms. Furthermore, the ways of talking about sex may be less fixed than Baker's analysis seems to suggest. According to Baker, sentences such as 'Jane fucked Dick', 'Jane screwed Dick' and 'Jane laid Dick', if taken in the literal sense, are not sentences in English. But the usage seems to have changed since his article was published; I have heard native speakers of English make such sentences without a single (linguistic) eyebrow being raised. The asymmetry seems to have lost ground. So the import of the facts analysed by Baker is much more limited than he and Shrage take it to be, and the facts themselves are less clear-cut and static too.

(iii) Shrage's third argument for the claim that our society thinks of sex with men as polluting and harmful to women is the weakest. Images of physical assault and imperialist domination are certainly not 'the metaphors we use for the act of sexual intercourse'; I do not know that anyone except Andrea Dworkin does. The most likely reason people do not is that it would be silly to do so.

What all this shows, I think, is that there is no good reason to believe that our society adheres to a single conception of heterosexual sex, the conception defined by the four cultural assumptions Shrage describes, claims to be epitomized in, and reinforced by, prostitution, and wants to ascribe to every single case of commercial sex in our society as its 'political and social meaning', whatever the beliefs and values of the individuals concerned. Some members of our society think of heterosexual sex in terms of Shrage's four assumptions and some do not. Accordingly, there are in our society two rather different conceptions of prostitution, which in this context are best termed (a) prostitution as commercial screwing, and (b) prostitution as commercial sex *simpliciter*. What is their relative influence on the practice of prostitution in our society is a question for empirical research. Shrage rightly objects to the former for being implicated in the oppression of women in our society, and one need not be a feminist in order to agree. But that objection is not an objection to prostitution in our society as such.

6. Conclusion

I have taken a critical look at a number of arguments advanced to support the claim that prostitution stands morally condemned. If what I have been saying is right, none of these arguments is convincing.[43] Therefore, until some new and better ones are put forward, the conclusion must be that there is nothing morally wrong with it.[44] Writing about pornography—another practice which has been condemned and suppressed by traditional morality and religion, and has recently come under attack from feminist authors as well—G. L. Simons said that in a society which values liberty, 'social phenomena are, like individuals, innocent until proven guilty.'[45] So is prostitution.[46]

Notes

1. I am concerned only with prostitution in its primary, narrow sense of 'commercial' or 'mercenary sex', 'sex for money', and not with prostitution in the derived sense of 'use of one's ability or talent in a base or unworthy way'. The question I am asking is whether prostitution in the former, original sense is a case of prostitution in the latter, secondary sense.

2. F. Engels, *The Origin of the Family, Private Property and the State*, trans. A. West (Harmondsworth: Penguin, 1985), 102.

The point was made as early as 1790; see M. Wollstonecraft, *Works*, J. Todd and M. Butler (eds.) (London: William Pickering, 1989), V, 22, 129.

3. Here I am drawing on K. Davis, 'The Sociology of Prostitution', *Deviance*, S. Dinitz, R. R. Dynes and A. C. Clare (eds.), 2nd ed. (New York: Oxford University Press, 1975).

4. Ibid., 328.

5. G. Dworkin, 'Paternalism', *The Monist* 56 (1972), 65.

6. L. Ericsson, 'Charges against Prostitution: An Attempt at a Philosophical Assessment', *Ethics* 90 (1979/80), 357.

7. D. A. J. Richards, *Sex, Drugs, Death, and the Law: An Essay on Human Rights and Overcriminalization* (Totowa, NJ: Rowman & Littlefield, 1982), 113.

8. Ibid., 146 n. 251. The study referred to is described in W. B. Pomeroy, 'Some Aspects of Prostitution', *Journal of Sex Research* 1 (1965).

9. L. Ericsson, loc. cit.

10. For an analysis of the two kinds of paternalism, see J. Feinberg, 'Legal Paternalism', *Canadian Journal of Philosophy* 1 (1971), 105–24.

11. Many authors who have written on prostitution as a 'social evil' have claimed that it is virtually never a freely chosen occupation, since various social conditions (lack of education, poverty, unemployment) force innumerable women into it. This argument makes it possible for Mrs Warren (and many others) to condemn prostitution, while absolving the prostitute. But even if the empirical claim were true, it would not amount to an argument against prostitution, but only against the lack of alternatives to it.

12. J. S. Mill, *On Liberty*, C. V. Shields (ed.) (Indianapolis: Bobbs-Merrill, 1956), 93.

It was clear to Mill that his rejection of paternalism applied in the case of prostitution just as in any other case, but the way he says that is somewhat demure; see ibid., 120–122.

13. M. Walzer, *The Spheres of Justice* (New York: Basic Books, 1983), 100–103.

14. Ibid., 103. (The parts of the quotation I have deleted refer to religious prostitution, which is not the subject of this paper.)

15. Augustine, *Concerning the City of God,* trans. H. Bettenson (Harmondsworth: Penguin, 1972), Bk. 14, Ch. 16, 577.

16. B. Mandeville, *The Fable of the Bees,* F. B. Kaye (ed.) (Oxford University Press, 1957), Remark (H.), I, 95–96, 100.

Mandeville discusses prostitution in detail in *A Modest Defence of Publick Stews: or, an Essay upon Whoring, As it is now practis'd in these Kingdoms* (London: A. Moore, 1724) (published anonymously). The argument I have quoted from the *Fable* is elaborated on pp. ii–iii, xi–xii, 39–52.

17. A. Schopenhauer, 'On Women', *Parerga and Paralipomena,* trans. E. F. J. Payne (Oxford: Oxford University Press, 1974), I, 623.

18. W. E. H. Lecky, *History of European Morals* (London: Longmans, Green & Co., 1869), II, 299–300.

19. B. Russell, *Marriage and Morals* (London: George Allen & Unwin, 1958), 116.

20. St. Augustine, *De ordine,* II, 4; St. Thomas Aquinas, *Summa theologiae,* 2a2ae, q. 10, art. 11.

21. H. Benjamin and R. E. L. Masters, *Prostitution and Morality* (London: Souvenir Press, 1965), 201.

22. See A. Goldman, 'Plain Sex', *Philosophy of Sex,* A. Soble (ed.) (Totowa, NJ: Littlefield, Adams & Co., 1980), in this volume, pp. 39–55; R. Vannoy, *Sex without Love: A Philosophical Exploration* (Buffalo: Prometheus Books, 1980).

23. Op. cit., 99–104.

24. Ibid., 103–104.

25. For examples of this kind of reasoning and a detailed discussion of its structure, see J. Wilson, *Logic and Sexual Morality* (Harmondsworth: Penguin, 1965), 59–74.

26. See J. R. Richards, *The Sceptical Feminist: A Philosophical Enquiry* (London: Routledge & Kegan Paul, 1980), 198–202.

27. B. Russell, op. cit., 121–122.

28. Here I find Russell's version of the principle of respect for human beings as such more helpful than the classic, Kantian one (H. J. Paton, *The Moral Law: Kant's Groundwork of the Metaphysic of Morals* [London: Hutchinson, 1969], 90–93); for Russell puts it forward as an independent principle, while in Kant it cannot function on its own, but only when accepted together with other tenets of Kant's ethical theory, which one may well find problematic (cf. H. E. Jones, *Kant's Principle of Personality* [Madison: The University of Wisconsin Press, 1971]).

29. L. Ericsson, op. cit., 342.

30. D. Archard, 'Sex for Sale: The Morality of Prostitution', *Cogito* 3 (1989), 49–50.

31. C. Pateman, 'Defending Prostitution: Charges against Ericsson', *Ethics* 93 (1982/3), 562.

32. But see A. Appiah, ' "But Would That Still Be Me?": Notes on Gender, "Race", Ethnicity, as Sources of "Identity" ', *The Journal of Philosophy* 87 (1990).

33. On the arguments pro and con see *Report of the Committee of Inquiry into Human Fertilisation and Embryology* (London: HMSO, 1984), Ch. VIII; M. Warnock, 'The Artificial Family', and M. Lockwood, 'The Warnock Report: A Philosophical Appraisal', *Moral Dilemmas in Modern Medicine*, M. Lockwood (ed.) (Oxford University Press, 1985).

34. *Report*, 45.

35. S. de Beauvoir, *The Second Sex*, trans. and ed. H. M. Parshley (London: Pan Books, 1988), 569.

36. By 'our society' Shrage most of the time seems to mean contemporary American society, but toward the end of the paper claims to have discussed 'the meaning of commercial sex in modern Western culture' (L. Shrage, 'Should Feminists Oppose Prostitution?', *Ethics* 99 (1989/90), 361). [This volume, pp. 323–338, at p. 335.]

37. Ibid., 354. [This volume, p. 330.]

38. Ibid., 355. [This volume, p. 331.]

39. M. G. Haft, 'Hustling for Rights', *The Civil Liberties Review* 1 (1973/4), 20, quoted in A. M. Jaggar, 'Prostitution', *Philosophy of Sex*, 1st edn., A. Soble (ed.), 350.

40. See R. Baker, ' "Pricks" and "Chicks": A Plea for "Persons" ', *Philosophy and Sex*, R. Baker and F. Elliston (eds.) (Buffalo: Prometheus Books, 1975).

41. Ibid. 50.

42. Ibid. 61.

43. I have not discussed those arguments against prostitution which I think have been effectively refuted by others. See L. Ericsson, op. cit., on the arguments that prostitution exemplifies and reinforces commercialization of society, that it is an extreme case of the general inequality between men and women, that sex is much too basic and elementary in human life to be sold, and on the Marxist critique of prostitution in general, and L. E. Lomasky, 'Gift Relations, Sexual Relations and Freedom', *The Philosophical Quarterly* 33 (1983), on the argument that commercial sex devalues sex given freely, as a gift.

44. That is, there is nothing morally wrong with it as long as the term 'morally wrong' is used in its robust sense, nicely captured e.g. by Mill: 'We do not call

anything wrong unless we mean to imply that a person ought to be punished in some way or other for doing it—if not by law, by the opinion of his fellow creatures; if not by opinion, by the reproaches of his own conscience' (*Utilitarianism,* G. Sher (ed.) [Indianapolis: Hackett, 1979], 47]. This is the sense the term usually has in everyday moral discourse. When we say, e.g., that stealing is wrong, we normally do not mean to say merely that stealing falls short of the ideal way of relating to other people's property, or is not part of the good life, the best use one can put one's fingers to, or something one would recommend as a career to one's teenage daughter; we rather express our condemnation of stealing and imply that it is appropriate to apply the pressure of the moral sanction on those who steal. Of course, those given to using the term in some wider, watered-down sense may well come to the conclusion that prostitution is wrong after all.

45. G. L. Simons, *Pornography without Prejudice: A Reply to Objectors* (London: Abelard-Schuman, 1972), 96.

46. I have benefited from conversations on the subject of this paper with Carla Freccero and Bernard Gert, and from critical responses from audiences at Hull, Liverpool, Newcastle, St. Andrews and York, where I read this paper in December 1990/January 1991.

My greatest debt is to Antony Duff, Sandra Marshall, and Walter Sinnott-Armstrong, who read an earlier version of the paper and made a number of critical comments and suggestions for clarification and revision.

The paper was written during my stay at the Morrell Studies in Toleration project, Department of Politics, University of York, in the Winter and Spring terms of 1990/91. I would like to acknowledge with gratitude a research grant from the British Academy, which made that possible.

SUGGESTED READINGS

General

Abramson, Paul R., and Steven D. Pinkerton, eds. *Sexual Nature, Sexual Culture* (Chicago: University of Chicago Press, 1995).

Davidson, Arnold. "Sex and the Emergence of Sexuality," *Critical Inquiry* 14:1 (1987): 16–48.

Davis, Murray. *Smut: Erotic Reality/Obscene Ideology* (Chicago: University of Chicago Press, 1983).

Gudorf, Christine E. *Body, Sex, and Pleasure: Reconstructing Christian Sexual Ethics* (Cleveland, Ohio: Pilgrim Press, 1994).

Laqueur, Thomas. *Making Sex: Body and Gender from the Greeks to Freud* (Cambridge, Mass.: Harvard University Press, 1990).

Leidholdt, Dorchen, and Janice C. Raymond, eds. *The Sexual Liberals and the Attack on Feminism* (New York: Teachers College Press, 1990).

Paglia, Camille. *Sex, Art, and American Culture* (New York: Vintage Books, 1992).

Posner, Richard A. *Sex and Reason* (Cambridge, Mass.: Harvard University Press, 1992).

Russell, Bertrand. *Marriage and Morals* (London, Eng.: George Allen and Unwin, 1929).

Scruton, Roger. *Sexual Desire: A Moral Philosophy of the Erotic* (New York: Free Press, 1986).

Soble, Alan. *Sexual Investigations* (New York: New York University Press, 1996).

———, ed. *Sex, Love, and Friendship* (Amsterdam: Editions Rodopi, 1997).

Stein, Edward, ed. *Forms of Desire* (New York: Routledge, 1992).

Whiteley, C. H., and Winifred N. Whiteley. *Sex and Morals* (New York: Basic Books, 1967).

Wojtyla, Karol [Pope John Paul II]. *Love and Responsibility* (New York: Farrar, Straus and Giroux, 1981).

Conceptual Analysis

Giles, James. "A Theory of Love and Sexual Desire," *Journal for the 1 Behavior* 24:4 (1994): 339–57.

Jacobsen, Rockney. "Arousal and the Ends of Desire," *Philosophy a logical Research* 53:3 (1993): 617–32.

Shaffer, Jerome A. "Sexual Desire," *Journal of Philosophy* 75:4 (1978): 175–89; reprinted in *Sex, Love, and Friendship*, ed. A. Soble (Amsterdam: Editions Rodopi, 1997), 1–12.

Taylor, Roger. "Sexual Experiences," *Proceedings of the Aristotelian Society* 68 (1967–68): 87–104.

Sexual Perversion

Kadish, Mortimer R. "The Possibility of Perversion," *Philosophical Forum* 19:1 (1987): 34–53.

Levy, Donald. "Perversion and the Unnatural As Moral Categories," *Ethics* 90:2 (1980): 191–202.

Vannoy, Russell. "The Structure of Sexual Perversity," in *Sex, Love, and Friendship*, ed. A. Soble (Amsterdam: Editions Rodopi, 1997), 358–71.

Homosexuality

Baird, Robert M., and M. Katherine Baird, eds. *Homosexuality: Debating the Issues* (Amherst, N.Y.: Prometheus, 1995).

Boswell, John. *Christianity, Social Tolerance, and Homosexuality* (Chicago: University of Chicago Press, 1980).

Finnis, John M. "Law, Morality, and 'Sexual Orientation,'" *Notre Dame Law Review* 69:5 (1994): 1049–76.

Hamer, Dean, and Peter Copeland. *The Science of Desire* (New York: Simon and Schuster, 1994).

Jung, Patricia, and Ralph Smith. *Heterosexism: An Ethical Challenge* (Albany, N.Y.: State University of New York Press, 1993).

LeVay, Simon. *Queer Science* (Cambridge, Mass.: M.I.T. Press, 1996).

———. *The Sexual Brain* (Cambridge, Mass.: M.I.T. Press, 1993).

Levin, Michael. "Homosexuality, Abnormality, and Civil Rights," *Public Affairs Quarterly* 10, no. 1 (January 1996): 31–48.

Mohr, Richard D. *Gay Ideas* (Boston, Mass.: Beacon Press, 1992).

———. *Gays/Justice* (New York: Columbia University Press, 1988).

———. *A More Perfect Union* (Boston, Mass.: Beacon Press, 1994).

Murphy, Timothy F. "Homosexuality and Nature: Happiness and the Law at Stake," *Journal of Applied Philosophy* 4:2 (1987): 195–204.

———, ed. *Gay Ethics: Controversies in Outing, Civil Rights, and Sexual Science* (Binghamton, N.Y.: Haworth, 1994).

Prager, Dennis. "Homosexuality, the Bible, and Us—A Jewish Perspective," *The Public Interest*, no. 112 (Summer 1993): 60–83.

Ruse, Michael. *Homosexuality: A Philosophical Inquiry* (New York: Blackwell, 1988).

Stein, Edward. "The Relevance of Scientific Research About Sexual Orientation to Lesbian and Gay Rights," *Journal of Homosexuality* 27:3–4 (1994): 269–308.

Sullivan, Andrew. *Virtually Normal: An Argument About Homosexuality* (New York: Knopf, 1995).

Sex and Love

Gregory, Paul. "Eroticism and Love," *American Philosophical Quarterly* 25:4 (1988): 339–44.

Lesser, A. H. "Love and Lust," *Journal of Value Inquiry* 14:1 (1980): 51–54.

Stafford, J. Martin. "Love and Lust Revisited: Intentionality, Homosexuality and Moral Education," *Journal of Applied Philosophy* 5:1 (1988): 87–100.

———. "On Distinguishing Between Love and Lust," *Journal of Value Inquiry* 11:4 (1977): 292–303.

Vannoy, Russell. *Sex Without Love* (Buffalo, N.Y.: Prometheus, 1980).

Abortion

Callahan, Joan C. "The Fetus and Fundamental Rights," *Commonweal* (11 April 1986): 203–7.

Paden, Roger. "Abortion and Sexual Morality," in *Sex, Love, and Friendship*, ed. A. Soble (Amsterdam: Editions Rodopi, 1997), 229–36.

Smith, Holly M. "Intercourse and Moral Responsibility for the Fetus," in *Abortion and the Status of the Fetus*, ed. W. B. Bondeson, H. T. Engelhardt, Jr., S. F. Spicker, and D. H. Winship (Dordrecht, Netherlands: Reidel, 1983), 229–45.

Soble, Alan. "More on Abortion and Sexual Morality," in *Sex, Love, and Friendship*, ed. A. Soble (Amsterdam: Editions Rodopi, 1997), 239–44.

Thomson, Judith Jarvis. "A Defense of Abortion," *Philosophy and Public Affairs* 1:1 (1971): 47–66.

Sadomasochism

Linden, Robin Ruth, Darlene R. Pagano, Diana E. H. Russell, and Susan Leigh Star, eds. *Against Sadomasochism: A Radical Feminist Analysis* (East Palo Alto, Calif.: Frog in the Well, 1982).

Samois, ed. *Coming to Power*, 1st ed. (Palo Alto, Calif.: Up Press, 1981); 2nd ed. (Boston: Alyson Publications, 1982).

Weinberg, Thomas S., ed. *S&M: Studies in Dominance & Submission* (Amherst, N.Y.: Prometheus, 1995).

Rape

Bogart, John H. "On the Nature of Rape," *Public Affairs Quarterly* 5 (1991): 117–36.

Parrot, Andrea, and Laurie Bechhofer, eds. *Acquaintance Rape: The Hidden Crime* (New York: John Wiley, 1991).

Pineau, Lois. "Date Rape: A Feminist Analysis," *Law and Philosophy* 8 (1989): 217–43.

Sexual Harassment

Dodds, Susan M., Lucy Frost, Robert Pargetter, and Elizabeth W.] Harassment," *Social Theory and Practice* 14:2 (1988): 111–30.

LeMoncheck, Linda, and Mane Hajdin. *Sexual Harassment: A Debate* (Lanham, Md.: Rowman & Littlefield, 1997).

Paludi, Michele A., ed. *Sexual Harassment on College Campuses: Abusing the Ivory Power,* rev. ed. (Albany: State University of New York Press, 1990).

Sanday, Peggy Reeves. *A Woman Scorned: Acquaintance Rape on Trial* (New York: Doubleday, 1996).

Superson, Anita M. "A Feminist Definition of Sexual Harassment," *Journal of Social Philosophy* 24:1 (1993): 46–64.

Wall, Edmund, ed. *Sexual Harassment: Confrontations and Decisions* (Buffalo, N.Y.: Prometheus, 1992).

Pornography

Assiter, Alison, and Carol Avedon, eds. *Bad Girls and Dirty Pictures* (London: Pluto Press, 1993).

Baird, Robert M., and Stuart E. Rosenbaum, eds. *Pornography: Private Right or Public Menace?* (Buffalo, N.Y.: Prometheus, 1991).

Dwyer, Susan, ed. *The Problem of Pornography* (Belmont, Calif.: Wadsworth, 1995).

Gubar, Susan, and Joan Hoff, eds. *For Adult Users Only: The Dilemma of Violent Pornography* (Bloomington, Ind.: Indiana University Press, 1989).

Itzin, Catherine, ed. *Pornography: Women, Violence and Civil Liberties* (Oxford, England: Oxford University Press, 1992).

Langton, Rae. "Speech Acts and Unspeakable Acts," *Philosophy and Public Affairs* 22:4 (1993): 293–330.

McCormack, Thelma. "If Pornography Is the Theory, Is Inequality the Practice?" *Philosophy of the Social Sciences* 23:3 (1993): 298–326.

MacKinnon, Catharine A. *Feminism Unmodified* (Cambridge, Mass.: Harvard University Press, 1987).

———. *Only Words* (Cambridge, Mass.: Harvard University Press, 1993).

Russell, Diana E. H., ed. *Making Violence Sexy: Feminist Views on Pornography* (New York: Teachers College Press, 1993).

Segal, Lynne, and Mary McIntosh, eds. *Sex Exposed: Sexuality and the Pornography Debate* (New Brunswick, N.J.: Rutgers University Press, 1993).

Strossen, Nadine. *Defending Pornography* (New York: Scribner, 1995).

Prostitution

Ericsson, Lars O. "Charges Against Prostitution: An Attempt at a Philosophical Assessment," *Ethics* 90:3 (1980): 335–66.

Green, Karen. "Prostitution, Exploitation and Taboo," *Philosophy* 64 (1989): 525–34.

Pateman, Carole. "Defending Prostitution: Charges Against Ericsson," *Ethics* 93 (1983): 561–65.

Shrage, Laurie. "Is Sexual Desire Raced? The Social Meaning of Interracial Prostitution," *Journal of Social Philosophy* 23:1 (1992): 42–51.

INDEX

abortion, xivn6, 10, 151–64, 165–69; and autonomy, 152–53, 157, 168; and sexual morality, xii

Acquired Immune Deficiency Syndrome (AIDS), 141, 142, 143, 287, 310

activity, sexual, 3–8, 27–28, 31, 34–35, 37, 40–42, 58, 69, 73–75; and pleasure, 6–7, 59–61

adultery, 4, 48, 57, 67, 91–92, 132, 339; as masturbation, 70; and sexual harassment, 229, 247n10

AIDS. *See* Acquired Immune Deficiency Syndrome

Allen, Woody: on masturbation, 55n6

American Psychiatric Association: on homosexuality, 111

American Psychological Association: on homosexuality, 147n9

Aquinas, Saint Thomas, 132; on prostitution, 347; sex and reproduction, 346

Archard, David: on prostitution, 352

Aristotle, 26, 40, 89, 90, 92, 93, 94, 294

arousal, sexual, 14–15, 25, 33, 46

Assiter, Alison, 320n57

Augustine, Saint (Bishop of Hippo), 15, 16; on prostitution, 347; on reproduction and sex, 346, 347

Austin, J. L., 25

autonomy, 112, 264–65; and abortion, 152–53, 157, 168; and sexual objectification, 289, 290, 291, 292, 294, 295, 296–97, 299, 300, 303, 307, 308, 313; and women's sexuality, 83, 168, 177

Baber, H. E., xiii

Bacon, Francis, xiiin1

Baker, Robert: on sex and harm, 331, 356–67

Barash, David, 99, 105, 116, 125n7

Bar On, Bat-Ami: on sadomasochism, 192, 201

Bartky, Sandra ("Feminine Masochism and the Politics of Personal Transformation"), 178–79, 181, 183, 185–87, 212n10

Baudrillard, Jean, 210n5

Beach, Frank, 116

behavior, sexual. *See* activity, sexual

Bell-Weinberg study, the, 110, 120–23, 125n8, 147n10

Bentham, Jeremy, 147n17; on homosexuality, 145

bestiality, 9, 28, 54, 69, 70, 91, 145–46

Booth, Wayne, 320n62

Butler, Joseph (Bishop), 40

Butler, Judith, 209; on consent and sadomasochism, 193

Califia, Pat (*Macho Sluts*), 280; on pornography, 195–96; on sadomasochism, 195–96, 208, 209, 211n6, 306

Callahan, Sidney, xii

Christina, Greta, xii, xiiin2

ABOUT THE CONTRIBUTORS

H. E. Baber received her Ph.D. from the Johns Hopkins University and is professor of philosophy at the University of San Diego. She has published in analytic metaphysics and theology as well as feminism.

Sidney Callahan is the author of *The Illusion of Eve* (1965) and *Parenting: Principles and Politics of Parenthood* (1973); she is also the editor, with Daniel Callahan, of *Abortion: Understanding Differences* (1984) and, with Brigitte Berger, of *Child Care and Mediating Structures* (1979).

Greta Christina is a writer. Her essays have appeared in *On Our Backs* and the *San Francisco Times*.

John Corvino is the editor of *Same Sex: Debating the Ethics, Science, and Culture of Homosexuality* (Rowman & Littlefield, 1997) and a popular lecturer on gay rights issues. He is completing a doctoral dissertation on Hume's moral theory at the University of Texas at Austin, where he has taught contemporary moral problems for several years.

John Finnis is professor of law at Oxford University. Among his writings are *Fundamentals of Ethics* (1983), *Moral Absolutes* (1991), and, with Joseph Boyle, Jr., and Germain Grisez, *Nuclear Deterrence, Morality, and Realism* (1987).

Alan Goldman is professor and chair of the philosophy department at University of Miami. He is the author of five books, including *Empirical Knowledge, Moral Knowledge,* and *Aesthetic Value.*

Robert Gray, originally an academic philosopher, switched to management information systems in 1979 and taught at Virginia Commonwealth University from 1981 to 1989 and in 1996. His current research is in genetic algorithms. He is a vice president with WIN Laboratories, a microcomputer manufacturer, and lives in Richmond, Virginia.

Jean Grimshaw teaches philosophy and women's studies at the University of the West of England, Bristol. She is the author of *Philosophy and Feminist Thinking* (1986) and of articles on feminism and philosophy and is a member of the editorial collective of *Radical Philosophy*.

Mane Hajdin has taught philosophy at McGill University, the University of Papua New Guinea, and the University of Waikato (in New Zealand) and has been a research associate at the University of California, Berkeley. He is the author of *The Boundaries of Moral Discourse* and coauthor, with Linda LeMoncheck, of *Sexual Harassment: A Debate* (Rowman & Littlefield, 1996).

Patrick D. Hopkins teaches philosophy at the University of Colorado at Boulder, specializing in ethical and social issues concerning technology. He is the editor of *Sex/Machine: A Reader in Gender, Culture, and Technology* and coeditor, with Larry May and Robert Strikwerda, of the second edition of *Rethinking Masculinity: Philosophical Explorations in Light of Feminism* (Rowman & Littlefield, 1996). He is writing a book on the influence of the nature/culture distinction on social and ethical issues.

Michael Levin is professor of philosophy at the City College and Graduate Center of the City University of New York. His book *Why Race Matters* appeared in 1997, and *Sexual Orientation and Human Rights* will appear in 1998. He has also written papers on epistemology and the foundations of mathematics.

Janice Moulton is professor of philosophy at Smith College. In philosophy she writes on language, ethics, feminism, and sports; in psychology, on perception and gender-bias; in linguistics, on syntax, modifier-marking, and the innate/learned controversy. Her publications include *The Guidebook for Publishing Philosophy* (1979, 1984, 1988), *The Organization of Language* (1981), *Ethical Problems in Higher Education* (1985), and articles on plagiarism and academic freedom in the *Encyclopedia of Ethics* (1992).

Thomas Nagel is professor of philosophy and law at New York University. Among his books are *The View from Nowhere, Equality and Partiality,* and *The Last Word.*

Martha C. Nussbaum is Ernst Freund Professor of Law and Ethics at the University of Chicago, appointed in the Law School, the Philosophy Department, and the Divinity School. She is the author of a number of books and articles on ancient Greek and Roman philosophy and on modern moral and political philosophy. Her most recent book is *Cultivating Humanity: A Classical Defense of Reform in Liberal Education* (1997).

Igor Primoratz is associate professor of philosophy at the Hebrew University, Jerusalem. He is the author of *Justifying Legal Punishment* (1989) and the editor of *Human Sexuality* (in press). He is working on a book on ethics and sex.

Natalie Shainess has been practicing psychiatry and psychoanalysis for over fifty years. She was on the faculty at the William Alanson White Psychoanalytic Institute and was a faculty member and training analyst at the Long Island Psychoanalytic Institute. She has also lectured in psychiatry at Columbia University Medical School.

Laurie Shrage is professor of philosophy at California State Polytechnic University, Pomona. She is the author of *Moral Dilemmas of Feminism: Prostitution, Adultery, and Abortion* (1994). She has also written about the comparable worth movement, feminist film theory, and Jewishness and identity politics.

Alan Soble is University Research Professor of Philosophy, University of New Orleans. Among his books are *Pornography: Marxism, Feminism, and the Future of Sexuality* (1986), *The Structure of Love* (1990), and *Sexual Investigations* (1996). He is working on a critique of feminist science studies, *The Limits of Feminist Scholarship* (Rowman & Littlefield, forthcoming).

Robert Solomon is Quincy Lee Centennial Professor, the University of Texas at Austin. He received his Ph.D. from the University of Michigan and has taught at Princeton University, the University of Pittsburgh, and the University of California. He is the author of over twenty books, including *The Passions, In the Spirit of Hegel, A Short History of Philosophy,* and *About Love* (Rowman & Littlefield, 1994).

Sallie Tisdale is the author of several books, including *Stepping Westward: A Long Search for Home in the Pacific Northwest* and *Talk Dirty to Me: An Intimate Philosophy of Sex*. She is working on a new book about the modern problem of food.

Edward Vacek, S.J., is professor of Christian ethics at the Weston Jesuit School of Theology in Cambridge, Massachusetts. He has taught courses in sexual ethics since 1979. He recently published *Love, Human and Divine: The Heart of Christian Ethics.*

Melinda Vadas is a disabled feminist philosopher who lives in Oak Ridge, North Carolina.

Robin Warshaw, a freelance writer from Elkins Park, Pennsylvania, is author of *I Never Called It Rape,* a book about acquaintance and date rape. Her work has appeared in many publications, including the *New York Times, The Nation, Woman's Day,* and *Ms.*

Robin West is professor of law at Georgetown University Law Center, where she teaches jurisprudence, feminist legal theory, and torts. She is the author of *Narrative, Authority, and Law* (1994), *Progressive Constitutionalism* (1995), and *Caring for Justice* (1997).

Ellen Willis, formerly a columnist for New York's *Village Voice,* is the author of *Beginning To See the Light* (1981) and *No More Nice Girls* (1992). She teaches journalism at New York University and is the director of that department's Cultural Reporting and Criticism Program.